The Rise of Israel

The state of Israel is one of the most controversial countries in the world. Yet its unique creation and rise to power in 1948 have not been adequately explained either by its friends (mainstream Zionists) or by its detractors (Arabists and post-Zionists).

Using a variety of comparative methodologies, from contrasting the Jewish state to other minorities in the Ottoman Turkish Empire, to the rise of the four Tigers in Asia, to newly independent countries and revolutionary socialist countries in Europe and Asia, Jonathan Adelman examines how Israel gained the strength to overcome great obstacles and become a serious regional power in the Middle East by 2007.

Themes addressed include:

- How the creation of Israel is strikingly different from that of most new states.
- How voluntarist forces, those of individual choice, will and strategy, played a major role in its creation and success.
- In-depth analysis of the creation of a revolutionary party, government, army and secret police as critical to the success of the socialist revolution (1881–1977).
- The enormous size of the forces aligned against the state, including major international and religious organizations representing billions of people, international reluctance to helping Israel in crisis, and internal Israeli and Jewish issues.
- The tremendous impact of revolutionary (socialist and semi-capitalist nationalist) factors in giving Israel the strength to survive and become a significant regional power over time.

Jonathan Adelman provides a fresh perspective on one of the most controversial states in the world and avoids the highly charged ideological descriptions that often plague such discussions. Understanding the rise of Israel, a key state in the region, helps to explain a great deal about the Middle East today.

Jonathan Adelman, who teaches at the Graduate School of International Studies at the University of Denver, has written 11 books on Russian and Chinese politics, revolutions and security studies. Having taught at Hebrew University and the University of Haifa, he applies his knowledge of revolutions and international affairs to explaining the creation and flourishing of Israel.

Israeli History, Politics and Society
Series Editor: Efraim Karsh
King's College London

This series provides a multidisciplinary examination of all aspects of Israeli history, politics and society, and serves as a means of communication between the various communities interested in Israel: academics, policy-makers, practitioners, journalists and the informed public.

The Rise of Israel

A history of a revolutionary state

Jonathan Adelman

 Routledge
Taylor & Francis Group

LONDON AND NEW YORK

First published 2008
by Routledge
2 Park Square, Milton Park, Abingdon, Oxon OX14 4RN

Simultaneously published in the USA and Canada
by Routledge
270 Madison Ave, New York, NY 10016

Routledge is an imprint of the Taylor & Francis Group, an informa business

© 2008 Jonathan Adelman

Typeset in Times New Roman by
RefineCatch Limited, Bungay, Suffolk
Printed and bound in Great Britain by
Antony Rowe Ltd, Chippenham, Wiltshire

British Library Cataloguing in Publication Data
A catalogue record for this book is available from the British Library

Library of Congress Cataloging in Publication Data
Adelman, Jonathan R.
   The rise of Israel : a history of a revolutionary state / Jonathan
Adelman.
      p. cm. – (Israeli history, society and politics; 49)
   Includes bibliographical references and index.
   1. Israel–History.   2. Israel–Foreign relations–20th century.
   3. Zionism–History.   I. Title.
   DS126.5.A64 2008
   956.9405–dc22

                                                    2007042980

ISBN10: 0–415–77509–4 (hbk)
ISBN10: 0–415–77510–8 (pbk)
ISBN10: 0–203–92829–6 (ebk)

ISBN13: 978–0–415–77509–0 (hbk)
ISBN13: 978–0–415–77510–6 (pbk)
ISBN13: 978–0–203–92829–5 (ebk)

For my loving Deborah

Contents

Tables

Preface

The idea for this book began 20 years ago, in Moscow, when I visited the Laboratory for the Study of Israel at the Soviet Academy of Science (the Soviet Union did not recognize Israel at that time). The Russians asked me to give an impromptu talk on Israel, where I had taught at Hebrew University two years earlier. An hour later I wound up my talk on how modern Israel actually was Russia incarnate. While giving that talk I came to realize how much revolutionary Russian movements had influenced Israel. Over time this idea developed into the theme of this book, on how Israel had been and remained a revolutionary state.

So many people in the fields of revolutions and Israeli studies have influenced me – Bernard Lewis, Michael Oren, Efraim Karsh, Shlomo Avineri, Jacob Talman, Gerry Steinberg, Jack Goldstone, Theda Skocpol, Crane Brinton, Seweryn Bialer, Orde Kittrie and many others. But I bear full responsibility for the ideas herein expressed and all errors that may have resulted.

On a personal note, I have been very fortunate to have found in Deborah Jordy the loving, intelligent and wonderful companion for the rest of my life. It is to Deborah that I gratefully dedicate this book.

Part I
The rise of Israel

1 Introduction

In the post-modern world we have lost our sense of wonder and awe at those once seemingly improbable events that have become our current prosaic reality. Who ever thought that small, ragtag, poorly armed bands of a few tens of thousands of men in the American colonies in 1775, in Russia in 1917 and in China in 1935 would amount to much? Yet they launched the American Revolution, the Russian Revolution and the Chinese Revolution that became world historical events that shook the world.[1] And who in 1900, when there were 50,000 largely religious and poor Jews in Ottoman Turkish Palestine, would have imagined that by 1948 a Jewish state would win the War of Independence and by 2007 become a regional First World power?

An analyst in 1900, asked about the likelihood of a Jewish state, would have replied: "Don't be absurd! Even Herzl admitted that the idea of a Jewish state, if proclaimed publicly, would be met with 'universal laughter.'[2] The Arabs derisively call the Jews 'the penniless of the weakest of people, whom all governments are expelling.'[3] The Jews, without a state in over 1,800 years, have no idea how to be soldiers, farmers or government officials. Lacking any international power, they think the idea is a mirage.[4] Over 99 percent of them don't live in Palestine or want to live in such a backwater. Those few who live there are dependent on *halukah* [foreign charity].[5] They are a drop in the sea of 600,000 Palestinian Arabs and 20 million Arabs."[6]

The analyst in 1916, when the expulsion of thousands of Palestinian Jews by Ottoman Turkey and war depredations left the community on the verge of destruction, would have exclaimed, "Don't be crazy! The Jews dream of settling the land but their two socialist parties have fewer than 2,000 agricultural workers and they own 2 percent of the land. Either the Germans will win the war and the Ottoman Turks will drive out the Jews (as they did the Armenians) or the British will win and create an empire. Over 300 million Muslims and 390 million Christians will never let tens of thousands of Jews control their Holy Places!"[7]

The analyst in 1942 would have exploded, "Nazi Germany is exterminating most of the Jews in the world at Auschwitz. The British Empire, enforcing the 1939 White Paper, is banning the survivors from Palestine and planning an independent Palestinian state in 1949. The Soviet Union supports the Arabs and persecutes the Zionists. The world is indifferent to their fate. The 500,000 Jews in Palestine will be destroyed, if not by the Nazi panzer divisions closing in on Palestine, then by tens of millions of Arabs, led by the Grand Mufti of Jerusalem, Haj Amin Al-Hussein."[8]

When the state of Israel was proclaimed in May 1948, the aged analyst would have proclaimed, "There are 650,000 Jews against 50 million Arabs. The Jews have no strategic depth, heavy weapons, American help or professional officers. They've done poorly so far and have an amateur underground army arrayed against five professional armies. Field Marshal Montgomery gives them three weeks, General George Marshall thinks they are doomed, British senior intelligence officers think the Arabs will win handily, the CIA gives them two years at the best and even Yigal Yadin gives them only a 50:50 chance of survival. Their situation is hopeless."[9]

This very elderly analyst would have been tasked with similar questions in 1967, when the ring of Arab enemies had tightened around Israel, and in 1973, when on the third day of the war Defense Minister Moshe Dayan said that "The Third Temple is falling."[10]

Perhaps Chaim Weizmann, Israel's first president, put it best when he declared that "To be a Zionist it is not perhaps absolutely necessary to be slightly mad but it helps."[11]

Weakness of the Jews

Given the often dismal history of the Jews in over 1,800 years in the Diaspora (forced conversions, massacres, pogroms, expulsions and the Holocaust), the analyst was reasonable. Two thousand years ago, 8 million Jews made up 20 percent of the population of the eastern Mediterranean and 10 percent of the Roman world. By the twenty-first century there should have been more than 100 million Jews in the world: there are but 13 million.[12]

Even many Zionists were dubious that a traumatized people could achieve nationhood. Leo Pinsker in *Autoemancipation* in 1882 derisively declared that "For the living, the Jew is a dead man; for the nations an alien and a vagrant; for property holders a beggar; for the poor an exploiter and a millionaire; for patriots a man without a country; for all classes, a hated rival."[13] In 1900 most Jews in the Russian Pale of Settlement were *luftmenschen* without a definite occupation, debarred from most government and professional positions. An 1892 American commission found their health and misery to be worse than those of the poorest Russian peasants and workers. Theodor Herzl confided in his diary that "We are a nation of *shnorrers* and beggars."[14]

In 1900 the small, largely religious Palestinian Jewish community seemed a weak reed for creating a Jewish state. Nor did the 10 million Jews in Europe, North America, the Middle East and North Africa seem more promising. For, as David Vital described their situation in 1900:

A pervading feature of the life of the Jews in their Exile has been their weakness; a permanent and notorious inability ever (and anywhere) to match strength for strength, pressure for pressure, or even benevolence for benevolence. Weakness was at the very foundation of their relations with the people among whom they lived and the alien rulers to whom they were subject . . . Nowhere were they masters, not even – in the final analysis – in their own homes . . . Herzl . . . sought . . . to reverse the course of Jewish history – in effect, to overcome the tremendous disparity between the splendid aims of Zionism and the pitiful means available to it.[15]

In November 1947 the new CIA in a report on "The Consequences of the Partition of Palestine" warned that, after initial successes the Jews, without strong and unlikely outside assistance, would probably be defeated within two years.[16]

Even after victory in 1948, Israel was still weak. Israel in the 1948 war lost East Jerusalem, the Etzion Bloc, Latrun, the Dead Sea potash works and 1 percent of its population. It had over 400 miles of narrow borders, with hostile neighbors and no natural barriers of protection. Syrian planes taking off from Damascus were 46 miles from the Galilee, and Saudi planes taking off from Guruet were 87 miles from Dimona. Israel had a Third World economy with $43 million in exports (led by Jaffa oranges). Israel was an educational backwater with some areas of excellence, only 700 university students and a weak health care system. Many Israelis and most new immigrants spoke poor Hebrew.[17]

The power and perseverance of their enemies

The Jews were well aware of their desperate situation. In two speeches in 1937 and 1939, David Ben Gurion analyzed the international balance of power:

> Great dangers await us on every front . . . Worldwide our strength is next to nothing alongside the mighty powers contending . . . What is our strength against gigantic powers . . . against the Arabs in their Arab countries . . . against the mightiest empire in history . . . the British Empire?[18] . . . [The Jewish people] stand powerless and defenseless. It has no navy, no army, no government, not even a tiny strip of land of its own. The world's rulers seem to believe that anything can be foisted on this helpless people.[19]

Their enemies then and later were numerous, powerful and often determined. These included great powers (the Tsarist Russian Empire, the Soviet Union, Nazi Germany, the British Empire 1937–49, the Ottoman Turkish Empire), regional powers (the Arab states), strong transnational religious movements (the Roman Catholic Church, the World Council of Churches, Islam), international organizations (the United Nations after 1951), most

Third World states after 1967 and global anti-Semitism. Walter Laqueur observed that "Zionism faced gigantic obstacles [and] had to fight for the realization of its aims in the most adverse conditions."[20]

Their enemies often acted with strength, power and persistence. Nazi Germany exterminated 6 million Jews (the reservoir of the future state), spread massive anti-Semitic propaganda and threatened to destroy the Palestinian Jewish homeland in 1941 and 1942. The Soviet Union, from 1924 to 1984 (save for 1948 and 1949), eliminated powerful Zionist organizations, destroyed the fabric of Jewish life, massively armed the Arabs against Israel and spread anti-Israel propaganda. Once supportive of Zionism (from 1917 to 1929), the British Empire barred hundreds of thousands or even millions of Jews looking to immigrate to Palestine in the late 1930s and in the 1940s and backed Arab nations in 1948. The Ottoman Turkish Empire limited Jewish immigration and investment in Palestine and threatened to annihilate the community during World War I.

Most of the Arab world, with its oil wealth, large populations and strong ties to both Western powers and the Soviet Union, opposed Israel in eight wars and two intifadas. Global religious movements, including Islam, the World Council of Churches and often the Roman Catholic Church, as well as various international organizations and the bulk of the new Third World states, also were hostile, especially after 1967. The correlation of forces was strongly negative for the Jews striving to create and develop a Jewish state.

The unlikely Israeli story

And yet, despite all this, Israel survived and did well. It won six wars and defeated the second intifada. It is one of the world's leading countries in ABM systems (Arrow), satellite systems, foreign intelligence services (Mossad), military power (Zahal), R&D (4.7 percent of GNP), high-tech (4,000) and biotech (1,500) startups, companies on the NASDAQ (80) and arms exports ($4 billion).[21] More Israeli patents (1,188) were granted in the United States in 2006 than Chinese (366), Indian (354) and Russian (268) combined.[22] Israel is a First World country with a $140 billion economy and $46.5 billion in exports (including $15 billion hi-tech). In 2005 Israel's foreign direct investment (FDI) was $5.6 billion and in 2006 $13.2 billion.[23]

Israel pioneered in new social forms such as the kibbutz, moshav, youth aliyah village, Nahal military settlements and mechina program for the disadvantaged. Hebrew University, Technion and Weizmann Institute are in the top ten universities in Asia, and there are over 150,000 students in higher education.[24] After immigration of 2.5 million Jews and rapid growth of its Arab population, Israel has 7 million people, a population equal to that of almost half the world's nations. Israeli Jewish males, with life expectancy of 76 years, had the world's third highest life expectancy, a year greater than American males. By 2007 the vast majority of Israelis spoke excellent Hebrew and created an authentic Hebrew culture.

Table 1.1 shows how the Israeli economy is competitive with that of leading First World countries.[25] Table 1.2 shows the strong scientific capabilities of Israel.

Difficult questions: How was Israel created and why did it flourish against all odds?

Only 5 percent of 4,000 peoples in the world have achieved statehood in the last several centuries. Most successful states had millions of people forming a demographic majority with a common culture, language, history, religion and power predominating in a single area for many centuries and controlling significant resources. Quebec, Scotland, Bavaria, Wales, the Basque land and Catalonia have shown that even possession of all or nearly all these attributes has been no guarantee of statehood. But the Jews in 1881 and even 1947, dispersed all over the world, lacked nearly all of the basic attributes of statehood.

In most Third World countries, nationalism was a mass reaction to alien European rule led by intellectuals. An early intellectual revolt led to a mass

Table 1.1 The economy of Israel, 2005, compared to that of more than 100 new nations created since 1945

Nation	GDP per capita (purchasing power parity) $
Singapore	28,100
Israel	24,600
South Korea	20,400
China	6,800
Jordan	4,700
India	3,300

Source: Central Intelligence Agency, *The World Factbook*, Washington, D.C.: CIA, 2006.

Table 1.2 Scientific capabilities of Israel and selected countries, 2005–06

Countries	Scientific papers citations (per million)
Israel	3,330
Singapore	3,075
Canada	2,890
Russia	299
Iran	142
Egypt	79
Syria	16
Saudi Arabia	1

Source: Scientific Citation Index, 2005–06.

revolt against the aliens. The intellectuals absorbed the frustration, resentment, impulses and experiences of the masses and expressed them in political form. As Ben Halpern has explained:

> But, for Diaspora Jews, not oppressed in their own country by a foreign garrison or administration or by landlords and nobles garnering the fruits of conquest, their mass response was not revolt but emigration. Their oppressors were not foreigners but the majority of the population or foreign rulers with majority support for oppressing Jews. The Jews lacked any control over the means of production for they were an exiled people without a strategic base. They needed a strategic base in a homeland to create Jewish workers or peasants. The Zionist task was to change the historic responses of emigration to better countries or passivity and to impose a new pattern. Nationalism, then, for the Jews, meant a revival of national culture and sovereignty, a reconstruction of a tradition that had faded away. The Zionists needed to change popular ideology.[26]

This leads to a series of difficult questions:

How could the Jews, who were expelled from their homeland over 1,800 years ago and lacked military experience or traditions, achieve statehood and flourish in a hostile environment? How could yeshiva students, ghetto denizens and middlemen from over 100 countries become farmers, soldiers and statesmen?[27] How could they overcome a harsh security environment that for 60 years had meant that a single Israeli defeat would mean the end of the state?[28]

How could the Jews, who merited no entries in the index of a 622-page book on the Ottoman Turkish Empire, create a state in the heart of the Muslim Middle East?[29] How could the Zionist movement, which was a failure in its first 20 years (1897–1916) and smaller than the Bundist movement in the 1920s, succeed when other national movements had floundered? How could a small state (with 5.4 million Jews in 2007) fight more wars than any other country in the last 60 years and not only survive but flourish and maintain a vibrant democracy?

Was the creation of the state of Israel in 1948 inevitable? Far from it. And were its flourishing and transformation into a strong First World state inevitable? Not at all. We need to understand much better why it succeeded and flourished.

Importance and neglect of the topic

Surprisingly, there is not a single work on Israel, by Arabists, post-Zionists or mainstream scholars, that raises and answers our questions. Only Efraim Karsh's edited volumes on Israel's first hundred years and his work on rethinking the Middle East devote any space to this question and this is confined to slightly more than a page. There Efraim Karsh, Mordechai Nisan, David Tal and Sasson Sofer separately speak of "the huge obstacles" that were overcome and the lacuna in the scholarship about how this came about.[30]

The Arabists, influenced by Edward Said's *Orientalism* and anti-Zionism, have not paid serious attention to the creation and rise of Israel.[31] Viewing Israel as a tool of colonialism, racism and imperialism, they see nothing positive in Israel, which is derided as a Western sub-agency. Since its power derives from the West, it is devoid of interest itself. Efraim Karsh has summarized the Arabist position:

> Nowhere has this "victimization culture" been more starkly manifest than in the historiography of the Arab–Israeli conflict. Dismissing out of hand the notion of Jewish nationalism and reluctant to acknowledge any wrongdoing on their part, the Arabs have invariably viewed Israel as an artificial neo-crusading entity created by Western imperialism in order to divide and weaken the Arab and Muslim nations. Israel's ability to surmount the sustained assault by the vastly larger and more affluent Arab World has thus been seen not as an indication of its intrinsic strength but as proof of the unwavering Western, particularly American, support; the collapse and dispersion of Palestinian society – as an exclusive result of Israel's imperialist grand designs.[32]

Given the Arabist belief in the power of anti-imperialist movements, this is a striking omission. The same is true of post-Zionism. Leading Israeli scholars (such as Avi Shlaim, Tom Segev, Benny Morris, Baruch Kimmerling and Ilan Pappe), influenced by the failures of Israel from 1973 to 1993 (the Yom Kippur War, Lebanon War and first intifada) and deconstructionism, have focused on Israel's failures, with minimal discussion of its successes.[33] Viewing Israel as morally dubious because it was born with the "original sin" of the expulsion of the Palestinians followed by numerous other failures, they see the Arabs as hapless victims of Zionist and Israeli aggression.[34] As revisionists and debunkers of what they deem to be Zionist "heroic myths," they are not interested in focusing on or understanding Israel's accomplishments.

But, while the scholars of the Arabist and post-Zionist camps refuse to confront this important reality, the mainstream scholars, who do recognize Israeli successes, have not seen them as problematic. There are a number of fine general works on Israeli history (Eban, Sacher, Gilbert, Stein, Bregman) but none see the rise of Israel as problematic.[35] Similarly, the rise of Zionism (Reinharz, Laqueur), the idea of the Jewish state (Halpern) and the Six Day War (Oren) are covered in a non-problematic fashion.[36]

Need for comparative historical studies

A useful way to understand the development of a state is to look at it in comparative perspective. Any state, no matter how exceptionalist, has much in common with the 200 states in the world. Israel has conformed to global trends by creating a socialist and then a semi-capitalist democratic First World society with a strong high-tech sector, extensive educational system and societal integration.

Apart from security studies, studies on nation building, state building, economic development, modernization and nationalism rarely include Israel, which is felt to not fit into accepted conceptual and experiential categories. Israel rarely appears in comparative political or Middle East studies.[37] Israel's rapid economic growth does not draw much scholarly attention.[38] Israel is seen as a country defining and playing by its own rules.[39]

There are comparative studies on Israel that look broadly (Barnett[40]), or show insights into its party system (Hazan and Maor,[41] Burk,[42] Kimmerling[43]), urban planning (Troen[44]) and military (Cohen,[45] Peled,[46] Horowitz,[47] and Maman, Ben-Ari and Rosenhek[48]). Jonathan Nitzan and Shimshon Bichler have shown that mainstream and revisionist studies overemphasize the role of the individual and often lack comparative historical perspective.[49]

A comparative historical approach to Zionism allows us to set the rise of the Jewish minority against other minorities (Lebanese Christians, Kurds and Armenians) in the Ottoman Turkish Empire who strove for statehood with very different results. The Lebanese Christians (the most promising of the group in 1920) achieved statehood in 1946 but lost dominance owing to the Taif Accords in 1989.[50] The more numerous Kurds (25 million) never achieved statehood despite the potential implied by the Treaty of Sèvres (1920). The Armenians, who suffered enormously from Turkish massacres (1894–95, 1915), failed to achieve statehood after the Paris Peace Conference and had to wait for statehood until the dissolution of the Soviet Union in 1991.

A comparative historical perspective is valuable in many areas. We can set the creation of Israel in the context of over 100 national liberation movements in the post-World War II era. With the extraordinary role of the military and security issues in Israeli society, we can conceptualize Israel by placing it in the context of comparative civil–military relations. New/old Israel can be profitably compared to other new societies (the United States, Canada, New Zealand and Australia) or to other rapidly growing Third World states (such as the Four Tigers of Asia).

The need for placing Israel in a revolutionary context

Most of all, we need to place Israel as the fruits of a revolutionary movement in the context of the literature on comparative revolutions. Yehezkel Dror has argued that, "despite pronounced differences, Israel's main features approximate the original visions of Zionism much more so than in the case of other revolutionary transformations."[51]

Zionism was both a national liberation movement and a social revolution. The socialist Zionist revolution (1881–1977) had profound goals that reached far beyond the re-creation of a Jewish state to a radically new democratic political, economic and social basis for the Jewish people. Israel can also be compared to bourgeois revolutions (such as the United States), with powerful similarities in wars of independence, immigrant societies, democracies and lack of externally imposed systems.[52]

Since 1977 Israel has been undergoing another revolution, this time globalizing and semi-capitalist, with a profound impact on the state. Samuel Huntington stated that:

> A revolution is a rapid, fundamental and violent domestic change in the dominant values and myths of a society, in its political institutions, social structure, leadership and government activity and policies ... Notable examples are the French, Chinese, Mexican, Russian and Chinese revolutions ... Revolution is the ultimate expression of the modernizing outlook, the belief that it is within the power of man to control and to change his environment and that he has not only the ability but the right to do so ... it is most likely to occur in societies which have experienced some social and economic development and where the processes of modernization and political development have lagged behind the processes of social and economic change.[53]

Numerous works on comparative revolution by Crane Brinton, Barrington Moore, Theda Skocpol, Jack Goldstone, Ted Gurr, Charles Tilly and Nikkie Keddie have advanced understanding of revolutions through comparative analysis of such revolutions as the English, French, American, Russian, Chinese and Iranian revolutions.[54] Works such as the volume by Aviel Roshwald, comparing the disintegration of the Tsarist Russian, Austro-Hungarian and Ottoman Turkish empires from 1914 to 1923, advance our understanding.[55]

To view Israel as a revolutionary country may surprise some readers. All the great revolutions (England, the United States, France, Russia, China, Iran) were directed against monarchical imperial authority. The first Israeli revolution, in a small dependent former colony rather than a great state, was not against a local, alien, oppressive regime but against those standing in the way of a social and national fulfillment in an ancient homeland. Commonly cited causes of revolution, such as large-scale peasant revolt against an oppressive ancient regime, demographic problems, significant fiscal crisis, division with the elite, desertion of the intellectuals, strong international pressures and failures in war, did not apply here,[56] and nor did the concept of a universalist ideology as an outcome, as Zionism (like Judaism) focused on a single people.

Yet the Jews were a different people. For almost 2,000 years the Jews lacked a state, peasantry, nobility, monarchy, army, elite or intellectual class. The task was to transform a relatively traditional, religious and passive people accustomed to hardships, repression and autonomy into one prepared to fight for and acquire a nation far away from their current state. The revolutionary impulse came not from a foreign oppressor but from the conditions under which European Jews lived from 1840 to 1945. Jonathan Frankel has commented that:

events such as the Damascus blood libel of 1840, the Mortara case of 1858, the recurring anti-Jewish excesses in Rumania during the 1870s, the pogroms of 1881–82, the expulsion from Moscow ten years later and the Dreyfus Affair involved the Jews, first and foremost, precisely as Jews, as a collective entity . . . these crises in Jewish life were the nearest equivalent to war and revolution in the history of a state, a sovereign society. At such a juncture, every assumption, however time-honored, may be called into question and ideas normally too utopian to voice, can enter the discourse of the everyday. This is the extraordinary moment in the outward flow of time.[57]

And if these were the equivalents of war and revolution in pushing the Jews towards a Zionist revolution in the nineteenth century, then how much more so were the pogroms of 1903 in Kishinev and 1905 across Russia, the expulsion of Jews in 1915 from the western border towns of Russia, the killing of upwards of 100,000 Ukrainian Jews in the Russian civil war, rising anti-Semitism in Eastern Europe in the interwar period and the Holocaust that massacred 6 million Jews?

The Zionist socialist revolution shared a series of features with other revolutions – a strong ideological fervor, the sense of a life-and-death struggle, a chiliastic sense of optimism about the creation of a new society and new man, a stress on justice and egalitarianism, the need to create a new party, government, army and secret police on a new more modern basis, and intense demographic pressures.

In the end, as in the other revolutions, state power would be centralized, enhanced and bureaucratized, a more egalitarian society would emerge in the short run and one party would dominate for a generation. The international environment would be a powerful factor, the revolution would be led by a small intellectual group who would build a version of a brave new world, and other countries would feel threatened. A strong modernization thrust would be evident and open, and the winning revolutionaries would emerge victorious but weak. Even the loss of life (22,000 dead, 70,000 injured) in Israel would be comparable to that suffered by the English in the 1640s civil war (100,000 fatalities), and less than the millions suffered in the Russian and Chinese civil wars.[58]

The second, semi-capitalist revolution would also promote a powerful role for Israel in the world as its economy boomed and its values aligned with the New World Order, and aspects of socialism would continue to be a part of the Israeli social and economic structure.

Israeli success: Palestinian failure

The success of the Jews, despite enormous obstacles, in creating and developing a strong state of Israel obviously raises a related question: why did the Palestinians, also (and often forgotten in the rhetorical battle) granted a state in United Nations Resolution 181 in November 1947, fail to create their own state and make it flourish? The numerically superior Palestinians with support from a number of other Arab states and foreign powers were as advanced as any of their neighbors in the Arab world and possessed a strong national identity by 1948.

Rashid Khalidi in *The Iron Cage* delineated their numerous failings, particularly "a striking lack of organization, cohesion and unanimity in the Palestinian polity" and the "frequent incapacity and weakness" of Palestinian leaders in dealing with outside forces before 1948. Khalidi depicts the "less than successful state building" of the PLO and Palestinian Authority, marred by poor leadership, autocracy, corruption, lack of foreign investment, failure to develop the rule of law, establishment of a patronage machine and rule by external Tunis returnees not relating to the local population. He also bemoans today "the almost criminal level of irresponsibility for Palestinian factions to fight one another in such circumstances."[59]

The numerous failures of the Palestinians highlight the importance of the factors present in Israeli success and absent in Palestinian failure: socialist and capitalist revolutions, alliance with the democratic West, building new societies, creation of strong modern organizations, a strong will to fight, and pragmatic and realistic leadership. The failure to mobilize voluntarist factors and international support doomed the Palestinians as it allowed the Israelis to overcome stronger obstacles and achieve a seemingly unlikely statehood and then regional power.

Structure of the book

Both hostile and friendly scholars rarely contemplate the unlikely nature of the rise and flourishing of Israel and how conditional its rise was on a series of forces that need to be delineated. The rise and the flourishing of Israel were both historically highly problematic. By looking at the obstacles and advantages possessed by the Zionist movement, by the view from 1900 and 1948, we gain a strong vantage point to understand this phenomenon.

The book is divided into three parts. Part I after this introduction looks at the literature on Israel and the value of seeing Israel through comparative eyes. Part II deals with the huge obstacles facing the creation and developing of the state of Israel. In addition to looking at internal obstacles in the Jewish and Israeli worlds, we examine such powerful external obstacles as the role of international and religious communities, the major powers and the unwillingness of the West to help in times of crisis. Part III seeks to understand the rise of Zionism through an examination of its historical roots and the nature of the two revolutions. Then it turns to understanding the power of revolutionary and international factors in the rise of Israel. The book provides in the conclusion an overview of the interaction of these factors in producing such a "unique" state.

The book has deliberately chosen to eschew the usual chronological and linear view that treats each topic in a clearly defined space and time. Rather it has chosen the thematic approach to avoid chopping up the book. At times, the reader needs to keep in mind the particular time and space under discussion. But, given that Israeli Jews, through the last 125 years (1882–2007), have faced a hostile international and regional environment (with shifting characters) with small numbers, limited resources, aid from the Diaspora and some help from the democratic West, this approach seems worthwhile. Despite all its successes, Israel's security dilemmas and threats today (a possible nuclear Iran, its Syrian ally and Islamic fundamentalist Hamas and Hezbollah on its borders) remain serious. Israeli leaders themselves draw such analogies. Only such a thematic approach can highlight the overall obstacles that have been overcome and revolutionary methods that have been employed to make this possible.

Limitations of the volume

This book has only a limited mission. It does not seek to provide a comprehensive history of Zionism or Israel. It does not provide a history of Zionist foreign policy, religion, Likud or the Labor Party; nor does it seek to provide an examination of Zionist or Israeli political theory. It does not focus, like so much other work, on the Israeli–Palestinian conflict, which has produced over 400 volumes.

The book is not based on original research but rather represents an attempt to better understand the rise of Israel through a synthetic, comparative political and revolutionary examination of Israel. There is an abundance, even plethora, of secondary material which is used for this purpose in the volume. The volume also does not mine any new ground in primary sources. Rather, like most volumes of its kind, it extensively utilizes secondary works in a comparative framework to bring up hopefully new and interesting ways to examine familiar subjects. The comparative method allows us to move away from philosophically charged views of Israel and to compare Israel with similar countries.

We address two interrelated questions: how, against all obstacles, was the state of the Jews created, and how and why did it flourish? We seek to understand the profound process of the creation and flourishing of the state of Israel. In that process we will learn much about the Jews and Israel, as well as the modern international political system.

Even many in the post-Zionist camp have conceded the "stunning . . . brilliant success" and "miracle" of Israel, truly in the words of Amos Oz "a dream come true."[60] From a Third World backwater in 1948, modern Israel has developed a First World economy, a progressive education and health system, a high-tech powerhouse and a home for Jews scattered and persecuted all over the world.[61] We need to understand how this "miracle" was created and sustained against enormous odds and at what cost. Let us begin.

2 Controversy over Israel

As its sixtieth anniversary nears, Israel remains one of the most controversial countries in the world. For every person pleased or thrilled by the seemingly miraculous rise of Israel, there have been far more people distressed, puzzled or angry at its success. Arab nationalist, Third World, Western leftist and even religious scholars and leaders have been particularly vexed by the success of Israel, which stands out against the failures of pan-Arabism, Arab nationalism, Third World socialism, Communism and Islamic fundamentalism and their foreign patrons (Nazi Germany, the Soviet Union).[1]

Israel's success in becoming a First World power has highlighted the failures of Middle Eastern authoritarian powers to catch up with the old European periphery (Greece, Spain, Portugal), the new European periphery (Central Europe) and the rising great powers of Asia (China, India) and Eurasia (Russia). As billions of people have adopted aspects of the New World Order values of democracy, export-led capitalism, the rule of law, the Internet, gender equality, tolerance for minorities, and free speech and press, the grave failures of most Middle Eastern regimes have led many to scapegoat Israel. While Israel is far from blameless, the explanations are often lacking in comparative or historical depth.[2]

Israel as a racist, colonialist state

Many scholars, such as Rashid Khalidi and Joel Kovel, have seen Israel as a foreign, colonial imperialist enterprise foisted on the region by Europe and the United States. They have spoken in terms of "ethnic cleansing," "South African-like apartheid," "subjugation and denial of rights," and "terrorization and subsequent flight of about 750,000 Palestinians from 1947 until 1949."[3] They have focused on the security barrier, settlements and numerous checkpoints as indicative of the colonial enterprise. Former President Jimmy Carter, in his book *Palestine: Peace Not Apartheid*, has asserted that Israeli total domination and suppression of violence have deprived the Palestinians of their basic human rights in a way not dissimilar to South African apartheid.[4]

Yet there are serious problems in seeing Israel as a rapacious colonial enterprise. Settlers usually went to colonies with which they had no emotional connection, while the Jews were returning to their ancestral homeland and rediscovering their past.[5] The Jews, with their religion, culture and history rooted in the land of Israel, were not alien to Jerusalem, Hebron, Safed or Tiberias, their four holy cities. They are integrally connected to the region. Half of all Israelis are Arabs or Sephardi Jews from North Africa and the Middle East and the majority of the rest (Ashkenazim) were born in the Middle East (Israel).

Many Palestinians, both today and before 1936, far from fighting the Jews, collaborated with them on grounds of personal or group benefit, opposition to Arab violence or belief that the Zionists were too strong to be opposed.[6] Even some scholars who are sympathetic to the notion of Israel having colonial aspects, like Gershon Shafir, acknowledge that Israel lacked many of the core aspects of European colonialism.[7]

Before 1918 the European powers, far from seeking to overthrow the Ottoman Turkish Empire and colonize the region, tried to prop it up. If the Ottoman Turks had stayed out of World War I, they would probably have survived. Even after the war, the British and French accepted mandates from the League of Nations that specifically envisioned their ultimate independence.[8] Hence, without the British and French trying to colonize the region after 1918, the Zionists could not have been colonial agents.

Colonies were usually run and directed by European great powers, while the Jews lacked a colonial Great Power or metropole to sponsor them or take them back if they wished to return. The Jews lacked a mother country to provide protection, investment and guidance. The Jews were largely at the beck and whim of two often hostile empires (the British and the Ottoman Turkish empires). The Ottoman Turkish Empire favored fellow Muslims (Arabs) from 1881 to 1918, and Great Britain favored the Arabs strongly from 1939 to 1948. Only from 1922 to 1929 was there mild and declining British support for their cause. A predominantly leftist Jewish Yishuv was not a natural ally for the British Empire, which eventually preferred the far more numerous Arabs.

Until 1948 the bulk of Jewish immigrants to Palestine came from Nazi Germany, Tsarist Russia (before 1917) and republican Poland (1920–40). None of these countries held the mandate for Palestine or were protectors of the Jews.[9] To the contrary, the Nazis were trying to exterminate all Jews, Tsarist Russia was trying to forcibly convert, repress or expel its Jews and Poland practiced extensive anti-Semitic discrimination against the Jews. When the Jews arrived in Turkish or British Palestine, they arrived with great difficulty, as local authorities tried to prevent their arrival, kept them from buying land and hindered them after they arrived.

From 1937 to 1948, the British Empire tried to prevent the creation of a state and severely restricted Jewish immigration. At a time when several million Jews might have tried to reach its shores, Palestine was largely closed to legal Jewish immigration.[10] The British repressed Jewish state-building activity. As the British withdrew from Palestine, they tried to turn positions over to the Arabs, actively sold weapons to Iraq and Jordan and refused to sell to the Jews.

Colonial powers generally provided safe passage for their citizens, a favored position in the colony, guaranteed trade and markets and protection from natives and rivals in the region. None of this existed for the Jews, who lacked imperial protection.

Settlers generally migrated to colonies for their economic potential. But Palestine was very poor and backward and the Jews came for ideological or religious, not economic, reasons. Economic prospects were far better in the United States or the West.

While most settlers built private estates and plantations for profit and gain, the Jews created hundreds of villages on a collective communal basis without exploitation. They bought the land from the Arabs at exorbitant prices rather than pushing them off the land. They did not use native Arab labor, preferring to use their own. They reclaimed the ancient language of Hebrew rather than using more familiar European languages.

Most settlers arriving in the colonies found predominantly nomadic or unsettled people, while the Jews found a largely settled population controlling and tilling the land. While settlers were lured to colonies by the prospects of free land, the Jews had to pay dearly for poor-quality semi-desert land. While most settlers relied heavily on local menial labor provided by native slaves and servants or imported indentured servants, the Jews relied on themselves or labor hired in the free market. Most settlers came to colonies with at least some means, while most Jewish refugees were poorer than the typical European settler.

The vast majority of colonies were abolished in the 1950s and 1960s. By contrast, Israel flourished and boomed only after the British colonial rulers, who favored the Arabs, left in 1948. And, while most settlers came to the colonies to settle the land, in Israel over 90 percent of the Jews settled in the new Jewish towns.

To the extent that Israel had colonial-like aspects as a settler colony of people coming to Israel from other lands, it mainly resembled the British settler colonies which gave birth to the United States, Canada, Australia and New Zealand.

There have been four major types of colonies: British pure settlement, Portuguese plantation, Spanish occupation and Spanish mixed colonies. The latter two, popular in Southeast Asia, coastal Africa and Latin America, were impossible for the Jews without the backing of a Great Power.[11]

From 1882 to 1900, under the tutelage of Baron Rothschild's French North African colonial experts and the failure of Jewish immigrants to strike roots in the soil, the rural model was that of a Portuguese plantation system. This system, with overseers, a small settler workforce and heavy use of local Palestinian labor, was tried and abandoned by 1900 as an economic failure that failed to attract Jewish labor.

But the British pure settlement model, which loosely seemed to fit the Israeli model after 1900, suffered not only from the numerous deficiencies listed above but one more critical difference: it rested on the removal and neutralizing or eliminating of the local native population. With the support of the British imperial power, the Indians in Canada and the United States and the Aborigines in Australia could be pushed aside. After independence, Americans forcibly removed the American Indians to reservations.[12]

The Jews, always an urban people, had under the Ottoman Turks and the British rule to pay large sums for poor native land. By 1947 they had acquired 260,000 acres (350 square miles), less than a good-sized ranch in Texas, in over 50 years of buying less than 5 percent of Arab land.[13]

There could be no exploitation of the local Palestinian population. Mostly rich absentee landlords prospered from the Jewish immigration. With largely remote and often alien Ottoman Turkish and British rule (1881–1948), the Jews had no enforcement power and after 1905 pushed for the "conquest of labor." This meant two economies, a Jewish self-contained economy and an Arab economy.[14] The Zionist socialist immigrants, opposing the use of cheap local labor which they saw as a moral threat, were interested in nation building, not exploitation.[15]

There has been no elimination of the local population on the British and American models. Indeed, there has been just the opposite. In 1910 there were 425,000 Palestinians from the Jordan River to the Mediterranean Sea.[16] Almost a century later the Palestinian population has soared to 4,200,000.[17] In Jerusalem, under Israeli rule since 1967, the Arab population has soared from 65,000 Arabs in 1967 to 235,000 Arabs by 2007.

Zionism, far from being an adjunct or servant of colonialism, successfully fought and overthrew British colonial rule in Palestine, which deployed close to 100,000 soldiers and paramilitary forces to maintain its rule in Palestine in the late 1940s. Zionism was diametrically opposed to traditional European colonialism. For, as Derek Penslar has observed:

> the Zionist movement sought to create a society *ex nihilo*, thereby allowing social reformist ideologies to cement themselves in the very foundations of the Yishuv. As to colonial models, there was a qualitative difference between the imperialist power's system of controlling and exploiting colonies for the benefit of the metropolitan government and the Zionist goal of using an international organization to create an autonomous homeland. There took place a wide-ranging transfer of technology from Europe to Palestine . . . This process was quite different from normal imperialist practice where a mere geographic relocation of technology was the rule and only the colonial rulers had access to sophisticated technical knowledge.[18]

Israel as an American/Western implant or offshoot

Arabists, leftist scholars and some neo-realist scholars often argue that the success of Israel has been due to massive Western and American support. John Mearsheimer and Steven Walt have asserted that the power of the Israel lobby has tilted American foreign policy towards Israel and allowed it to succeed.[19] John Kovel has argued that Israel is a "junior partner" of the United States and Great Britain and Israelis serve as "courtiers of the empire that is destroying the planet itself."[20]

Western sympathies for several decades were clearly on the side of the Jews, with their democracy and Western orientation, rather than the Arabs, with their autocracies and Islamic orientation. In 1947 Americans by two to one favored a Jewish state.[21] The United States has provided almost $100 billion in foreign aid to Israel since 1970, an impressive sum. It has given economic, military, political, diplomatic and technical support that has been invaluable to Israel. This has reflected, in Bernard Reich's words, "remarkable parallelism and congruence of broad policy goals," including preventing war, cooling down the Arab–Israeli dispute and supporting Israel's existence. There has never been a formal legal alliance, mutual security pacts, formal alliance or merging of armies.[22]

The impact of this aid was limited, less than the GNP of Israel in 2007 alone. The $2 billion to $3 billion in largely military aid given yearly by the United States to Israel pales in comparison to the several hundred billion dollars that the Arab oil states and Iran receive yearly for their export of oil and gas. The American aid is less than 1 percent of yearly American military spending and was minor compared to the $250 billion a year spent by the United States during the Cold War in Central Europe and Northeast Asia.[23]

Clearly, American help, while important, is only part of the story. Presidents, as Steven Spiegel and William Quandt have reminded us, play a critical role in Middle East decision making.[24] The United States under President Roosevelt refused to try to save millions of Jews during the Holocaust. While President Truman provided crucial recognition of Israel in May 1948, he imposed an arms embargo on Israel and in December 1948 forced Israel not to take the Gaza Strip and withdraw from El Arish in the Sinai.[25] As Bernard Reich has indicated, "At Israel's birth, the United States seemed to be a dispassionate, almost uninterested midwife – its role was essential but also unpredictable and hotly debated in U.S. policy circles."[26]

In 1957 President Eisenhower forced Israel to withdraw from the Sinai and Gaza without any compensation. In the 1967 war President Johnson, personally sympathetic to Israel, told Foreign Minister Eban that "Israel will not be alone unless it decides to go it alone," while Secretary of State Dean Rusk told him, "If Israel fires first, it'll have to forget the United States." President Gerald Ford in 1977 had his famous "reappraisal" that for more than six months froze new military supplies to Israel. In the 1973 Yom Kippur War the United States prevented an Israeli preemptive strike at the start of the war and delayed arms shipments to Israel as massive Soviet arms shipments were on their way to the Arabs. In 1979 at Camp David President Carter threatened to cut off American aid to Israel and in 1981 President Reagan sold AWACS to Saudi Arabia. In 1982 the United States distanced itself from Begin's war in Lebanon and in 1991 prevented Israeli retaliation against Iraq for Scud missile attacks. President Bush withheld loan guarantees to Prime Minister Shamir over settlement policy in the West Bank. In more recent years there were disagreements over Israeli reaction to the two intifadas and settlement activities.[27]

France, which helped Israel from 1955 to 1967, then sided with the Arabs. Germany, Italy and Britain provided almost no military or economic aid to Israel, save for Germany's one-time 1957 payment of $900 million for Holocaust restitution and the sale at reduced rates of five Dolphin class submarines in the early 1990s and 2007.

Overall, then, while benefiting greatly from Western help, Israel has been far from the favored stepchild of the West or the United States.

Israel as a stepchild of the Holocaust

Many scholars have argued that the main reason for the creation of Israel was the feeling of sympathy of Western powers for Jews after the Holocaust. Walter Laqueur declared that "the state owed its existence to the disaster."[28] Ben-Yehuda and Sandler felt that the Holocaust created "immense momentum" for the creation of the state of Israel.[29] Those hostile to Israel take the view of Iranian President Mahmoud Ahmadinejad, who in his September 2007 speech to the United Nations General Assembly asserted that "For more than 60 years Palestine, as compensation for the loss they occurred during the war in Europe, has been under occupation of the illegal Zionist regime."[30]

Especially in the United States and at the United Nations the Holocaust did build strong momentum for the creation of the state of Israel. Yet it was far from decisive. Anti-Semitism was quite strong in both the British and the American elites after the Holocaust. The Holocaust did not prevent the British Empire from openly siding with the Arabs during the Holocaust (1939–45) and afterwards (1945–48) arming the Arabs against the Jews. The Holocaust did not trump the European interest in oil or push the United States to revoke its ban on selling weapons to the Jews. Even the brief (1948–51) Soviet honeymoon with the Jews did not see open emigration to Israel and was caused not by the Holocaust but mainly by a desire to destroy British power in the Middle East.

In a deeper sense the Jewish state was created despite the Holocaust rather than because of it. The destruction of 6 million predominantly East European Jews destroyed the great reservoir of future immigrants to Israel from the main bastion of Zionism for the past three generations. Israel's population, as Efraim Karsh has pointed out, would likely be several times larger had there been no Holocaust.[31] Also, if the Holocaust was such a powerful force in the creation of a state, then why did the 1915 Armenian genocide, which killed 40 percent of all Armenians and created strong Western sympathy, not lead to an Armenian state in 1919 but only in 1991 after the dissolution of the Soviet Union?

Israel as a stepchild of the Diaspora

Many would stress the powerful role of a wealthy Jewish Diaspora. No doubt the Diaspora has played a significant part in the rise and flourishing of Israel, especially in the creation and early development of Israel after 1948. It has provided tens of billions of dollars of economic aid, worked diligently to obtain political support for Israel and shown a major interest in Israel. Yet, 99 percent of American Jews failed to immigrate to Israel, fight in the Israeli army or give major funds for economic development (a mere $2 billion of FDI from 1948 to 1988). In the last decade wealthy American Jews gave 94 percent of their mega-gifts to non-Jewish causes, and even then heavily to non-Israeli causes.[32] Seven times as many Israelis immigrated to the United States as American Jews immigrated to Israel. Diaspora pressure did not prevent a number of American presidents acting against Israeli interests.

Over time Diaspora aid has declined greatly as a percentage of the growing Israeli economy. Today, it accounts for no more than 1–2 percent of Israeli GNP. In the 1990s some leaders, such as Yossi Beilin, even thought Israelis should forgo it altogether. As the Israeli economy has been transformed from a Third World economy of a few billion dollars to a First World economy of $120 billion, the contribution of Diaspora Jews has inevitably declined. Diaspora Jewry (with a 50 percent intermarriage rate in the United States and 70 percent in Europe) has been shrinking in both absolute and relative size to an Israel that has grown from 650,000 Jews in 1948 to 5,200,000 Jews today. The American Jewish community, although wealthy, now devotes 80 percent of its charitable giving to non-Jewish causes (compared to 50 percent a generation ago) – and most of that does not go to Israel. Many American communities in the United Jewish Federation, facing an aging population, slow growth or demographic decline, Russian immigration and increasing need for social services, have substantially cut back their contributions to Israel. Israel typically receives less than one-third of all contributions made to Jewish federations across the country.

Finally, in the last 20 years, as Israel has gained broad international recognition and integrated into the global economy, it no longer needs to rely predominantly on its Diaspora Jewish base. The biggest investors in the Israeli economy are the decidedly non-Jewish "Oracle of Omaha" Warren Buffett, with his $4 billion investment in Iscar Metals, and Hewlett-Packard, with a $4 billion takeover of Mercury. The billions of dollars invested by such Silicon Valley titans as Intel and IBM have no ethnic base, and nor does the multibillion-dollar yearly trade with Russia, China and India.

Under these conditions the Diaspora, while still of value and rebounding somewhat during the second intifada, has faded significantly in importance, with fewer than 150,000 Western Jews in Israel constituting barely 3 percent of the local Jewish population and the Diaspora shrinking in size and Jewish identity.

Israel as a brutalizer of the Arabs

Many writers argue that Israel's success was caused by a willingness to use extreme brutality against local Arabs and the Arab world. John Kovel has spoken of the Israeli "python that is squeezing Palestine to death."[33] The post-Zionist Avi Shalim, echoing Ilan Pappe and others, has spoken of the "massive injustice" done to the Palestinians.[34] And, certainly, as seen in the imposition of military rule on Israeli Arabs from 1948 to 1965, discrimination against the local Arabs and at times harsh policies in the territories, there is some basis for this argument.

But international affairs have been remarkably brutal. For centuries, there was, in that famous phase, scarcely a year when there was not a war somewhere in Europe. Russian expansion to the east and American expansion to the west often entailed considerable brutality. Germany was created by Prussia after three wars from 1862 to 1870. The United States preserved its unity through a grinding civil war that took 600,000 lives and is remembered in the South for Sherman's march to the sea. Charles Tilly has coined a remarkable aphorism that "War makes the state and the state makes war."[35] The core of the neo-realist argument is that war (and its sub-agent brutality) has been a powerful and integral part of international affairs, showing no signs of disappearing in the new century.[36]

The creation and maintenance of Israel left the bulk of Palestinians (with the considerable majority having fled of their own accord) not only alive but living within the definition of historically mandated Palestine so defined in 1922.[37] In 1947 there were 1.2 million Arabs west of the Jordan River. Today, in 2007 there are 4.7 million Arabs west of the Jordan River (1.3 million in Israel and 3.4 million in the West Bank and Gaza Strip). The majority of the remaining Palestinians live adjacent to Palestine in Jordan (over 2 million), Lebanon (300,000) and Syria (200,000). Thus, the Palestinian population has grown almost sixfold since 1948, hardly a sign of excessive brutality. In the West Bank and Gaza Strip, the Arab population has soared from 1.0 million in 1950 to a projected 4.2 million in 2010 and will likely reach 6.0 million in 2025.[38]

The argument presupposes a peaceful growing over of national states that does not accord with the historical record. The Palestinians, resorting to violence in 1948 to try to throttle the state of Israel and two intifadas, and the

Arab involvement in six offensive wars with Israel (1948, 1967, 1969–70, 1973, 1991, 2006) show a strong record of Arab proclivity to violence.[39] As Walter Laqueur argued in his classic history of Zionism:

> Zionists are guilty of having behaved like other peoples – only with some delay due to historical circumstances. Throughout history nation-states have not come into existence as a result of peaceful developments and legal contracts. They developed from invasions, colonization, and violence and amid struggle.[40]

Although Israel has acted at times with great force to maintain peace and avoid terrorism in the West Bank and Gaza Strip, it has also shown an enlightened attitude towards the Arabs and Palestinians. If it were only a brutal repressive force, why would it voluntarily first occupy Gaza in the 1948, 1956 and 1967 wars and then leave it in 1949, 1957, 1994 and 2005? Israel withdrew from the territory on which 98 percent of Palestinians lived in 1994, and by 2000 60 percent of Palestinians lived under full Palestinian control. Israel offered at Camp David II in 2000 to leave 100 percent of the Gaza Strip, 95 percent of the West Bank, and East Jerusalem neighborhoods, and even territorial compensation for the annexed areas.[41] Even after the failure of Camp David II in July 2000 and the outbreak of the second intifada in September 2000, the Israeli Prime Minister Ehud Barak still went to Sharm el Sheikh (October 2000) and Taba (January 2001) to continue the negotiations, discuss a non-paper and make more concessions, even to the point of offering to absorb some refugees.[42] In August 2007 Israeli Prime Minister Ehud Olmert floated a withdrawal plan that was remarkably similar to that Ehud Barak offered in 2000.

From 1967 to 1991 Israel, while cracking down hard on terrorism, provided an unusually progressive occupation regime. From 1967 to 1987 Palestinians were given open access to Israel, and 140,000 of them worked in Israel. There were open bridges between Israel, Jordan and the West Bank. During the 1967–87 period the West Bank and Gaza Strip were among the fastest growing economies in the world. The Gaza Strip saw its income per capita soar from $80 in 1967 to $1,706 in 1987. The West Bank saw its GDP more than triple in the same period as one-third of its workforce worked in Israel in agriculture, building or services. By 1987, 120,000 workers a day were crossing into Israel. Israel allowed the creation of 6 universities and 14 vocational colleges where there were none before 1967. Infant mortality dropped from 86/1,000 in 1967 to 20/1,000 in 1989. In 1967, fewer than 20 villages were hooked up to communal water mains: in 1989, 200 villages were hooked up. In 1967 there were 113 clinics and hospitals in the territories: in 1989 there were over 378. Average life expectancy rose from 48 years in 1967 to 73 years in 1989. The Israeli economy, oil booms, capital inflows and Jordanian payments of Palestinian salaries fueled the boom.[43]

Finally, as a nation state Israel had a legitimate right to self-defense against terrorism directed at its citizens, especially within the Green Line.

Israel as a sub-agent of imperialism

Dependency theorists, such as Immanuel Wallerstein, L. S. Stavrianos and Andre Gunder Frank, argued that Zionism was an agent of imperialism in establishing a white settler state in Palestine, serving faithfully the interests of international capitalism and imperialism while oppressing the native Palestinian population.[44] Yet Zionism, far from being a reactionary movement, is, as Eyal Chowder has observed, a revolutionary ideology that mixes Marxist and Nietzschean themes. It is a "novel fusion of a creative notion of self with the quest for collective therapy, upon presenting normative metamorphosis as an individual achievement that also fosters grand collective action." The power of will and individuals is decisive with this modernist movement.[45]

Michael Barnett has shown that the anti-Zionist argument has logical and historical faults.[46] The Zionists were frequently at odds with the core imperialist powers, who often abandoned them because their cause did not serve the Great Power economic or strategic interest. This focus on capitalism is odd because Israel built up one of the few successful socialist movements in the Third World and did not fight on the side of the United States in either the Korean War or the Vietnam War.

If Israel was a sub-agent of imperialism, it seems odd that it did not receive strong backing from the United States during the first 20 years of the Cold War with the Soviet Union. It had to navigate this dangerous period replete with the help of a middling power (France), with the often open enmity of another middling power (Great Britain) and the at best benign neutrality of the United States. In its first 40 years it received a meager $2 billion of foreign direct investment from the international capitalist community, which was wary of socialist Israel and its precarious future.

It was also the socialist power (the Soviet Union) that saved it in 1948 with a supply of weapons from Czechoslovakia. Many American and British leaders (including President Truman) saw Labor Party Israel in its early days not as a sub-agent of imperialism but as a possible agent of Moscow, not Washington or London.

Can Israel, as Wallerstein implied, be located on the semi-periphery of global capitalism? Yet its high-tech industries are in the core of modern international capitalism. Was it, as Frank saw, a sub-imperialist country? Yet it has been often snubbed by major core powers. Israel until 1977 used its capital imports to build a socialist state and developed without substantial capital inflows from the core states.

Israeli intransigence

A common criticism has been that Israel is the enemy of peace, that it is Israeli intransigence, its "Holocaust mentality," its devotion to settlements, its repression in the territories and powerful military machine and secret police that have triumphed over the peace-loving attitude of the Arabs.[47] The flight of over 500,000 Palestinian refugees during the 1948 war (some of which was forced), its sometimes aggressive settlement policies, voluntary war in Lebanon in 1982, and the harder-line policies of Likud leaders (Begin, Shamir, Netanyahu, Sharon) have given some credence to these views.

But, while Israel has undoubtedly missed opportunities for peace, two facts need to be remembered. Middle Eastern leaders and Islamic fundamentalist groups, calling for the elimination of Israel, have launched or supported eight wars and two intifadas in the last 60 years. The 1948 calls for "driving the Jews into the sea" were echoed in 1964 by the Arab League summit in Cairo calling for the "final liquidation of Israel" and the 1967 calls by Nasser to put an end to the Zionist regime and liberate Palestine.[48] The massive terrorism of the Palestinians against civilian targets since 1967, the bloodbath of the second intifada, the nihilist rejection of Israel by Hamas and Hezbollah and their frequent rocket attacks on Israel and Iran's strident calls (as well as building of nuclear weapons) in 2005–07 for the liquidation of Israel have reinforced Israeli fears that the end could be in sight.

Yet Israel has been far from intransigent. The 1937 Peel plan, which envisioned a tiny Jewish state of 1,940 square miles (20 percent of Palestine) and no Jerusalem, was approved by David Ben Gurion and Chaim Weizmann and a vote of 299–160–6 in the 20th Zionist Congress. After the 1948 war Israel took back 30,000 refugees and offered to take back 70,000 more. In 1949 the three left-wing parties devoted to peace (Mapai, Mapam, Communists) gained 55 percent of the votes for the first Knesset compared to Herut with 12 percent. After the 1967 Six Day War, Levi Eshkol offered to return the Sinai to Egypt and a demilitarized Golan Heights to Syria for peace. Even the Likud leader Menachem Begin in 1978 returned the entire Sinai to Egypt, a position supported by 82 percent of the population and a Knesset vote of 84–19–17.[49] Labor Party Prime Minister Yitzhak Rabin (1992–95), backed by a popular majority, pushed through the Oslo I (1993) and Oslo II (1995) agreements withdrawing from the territories and signed a peace agreement with Jordan (1994). Likud Prime Minister Benjamin Netanyahu signed the Hebron Accord (1997) withdrawing from 80 percent of Hebron and initialed the Wye River Accord (1998). A weakened Labor Prime Minister Ehud Barak (1999–2001) made major concessions for peace at Camp David II (2000) and pursued negotiations at Sharm el Sheikh (2000) and Taba (2001). In 2007, after the second intifada (2000–05) and Lebanese War (2006), over 60 percent of the population continued to support peace talks.

As with all such criticisms, there is an element of truth in much of them. Israel has been far from perfect. But it has been much further from the racist, colonialist, repressive, brutal society, created only because of the Holocaust or the Diaspora, that its critics have depicted. In a virtual stage of siege, it has maintained a democratic, modern, progressive, high-technology society, with 30 political parties, free press and assembly, gender equality and the rule of law, elevating even its minority Arab population. In the coming chapters we will understand how this was accomplished through two revolutions that overcame massive obstacles and created the modern state of Israel.

3 The rise of Israel in comparative perspective

A comparative historical study of the rise and flourishing of the Jewish state can shed some significant light on Israel. Such comparative work has been uncommon. We could examine Israel in six comparative contexts:

- The rise of Israel can be compared to the fate of other minorities in the Ottoman Turkish empire. The question is why were the Jews the only minority to obtain a powerful state when other minorities (Lebanese Christians, Armenians and Kurds) seemed better situated in 1917?
- The rise of Israel can be compared to the fate of over 100 national liberation movements. The question here is why, despite their disabilities, were the Jews able to build one of the most powerful states and one of the few democracies among newly independent states after 1945 despite a virtual state of war?[1]
- The rise of Israel can also be compared to the efforts to build new societies, whether in remote colonies (the United States, Canada, Australia and New Zealand) or socialist utopias (Russia, China and Vietnam). The question here is why, despite their weakness, were the Jews more successful in creating a democratic socialism that endured and gradually gave way to globalized capital than the socialist countries, which yet bore some resemblance to the new settler colonies of the British model?
- The rise of Israel can be compared to the fate of other social revolutions. The question here is how did the Israeli revolution compare to those of other bigger nations?[2]
- The rise of Israel can be compared to that of the Four Tigers of Asia. The question here is why, despite a higher security burden and more threatening region, was Israel able to grow commensurately with the Four Tigers of Asia and exceed them in high technology?
- The rise of Israel can be compared to that of other countries with serious problems in civil–military relations. The question here is why, despite many prerequisites for an authoritarian, elitist, dominant military system (a state of constant siege, frequent wars and violence), is Israel not a militarist society?

Jews and other minorities in Ottoman Turkey

Let's start with the first question of how the least likely of the four significant minorities (Jews) in the Ottoman Turkish Empire achieved a strong nation state while one did and lost it in 1989 (the Lebanese Christians), one gained a weak state only in 1991 (the Armenians) and the one with the greatest numbers (the Kurds) is still waiting almost 90 years after the dissolution of the Ottoman Turkish Empire.

The four minorities were all ancient peoples with deep roots in the region. All suffered at the hands of the dominant Sunni Arab community. The Jews and the Christians spent centuries as second-class *dhimmis*, tolerated but persecuted for their heretical beliefs. The Kurds, as non-Arabs, non-Persians and non-Turks, suffered for their differences.[3]

All four minorities faced powerful enemies. Most of the Arab world and great powers (the Soviet Union, Nazi Germany, Ottoman Turkey and the British Empire 1937–49) strongly opposed a Jewish state. Turkey, Georgia, Azerbaijan and Russia opposed an Armenian state. The Kurds were opposed both by Arab states (Syria and Iraq) and by the non-Arab world (Turkey and Iran). The Arab Sunni world and Lebanese and Syrian Muslims opposed a Lebanese Christian state.

All suffered at the hands of the Ottoman Turks. In 1895–96 the Turks massacred 300,000 Armenians, and in 1915 500,000 to 1.5 million Armenian civilians died a brutal death. The Kurds suffered massacres at the hands of the Turks in the last century. The Jews in 1917 were on the verge of extinction. The Turkish authorities rounded up the 7,000 Jews of Jaffa and started them on a forced march to the north. In 1858, after a Maronite peasant uprising, Druze attacks killed 5,000–10,000 Christians and created upwards of 100,000 Maronite refugees. Only French intervention prevented further bloodshed.[4]

All four minority nationalities had Western patrons, including France (Lebanese Christians), Britain (Palestinian Jews), Britain (Kurds) and Russia and America (Armenian Christians), and anticipated some form of national independence. In 1920 the Lebanese Christians rejoiced at the creation of a Christian-dominated Lebanon under a French mandate. In 1920 the Kurds hailed the Treaty of Sèvres that offered them some autonomy and the ability to petition the League of Nations for a state in one year. In 1920 the Armenians still had an independent republic with international support. The 1917 Balfour Declaration, the 1921 appointment of Herbert Samuels as British High Commissioner in Palestine and the 1922 League of Nations mandate to Britain which spoke with favor on a Jewish national homeland in Palestine greatly encouraged the Jews.

The brightest future appeared to belong to the Lebanese Christians. Ever since 1861 the Mount Lebanon Maronites had enjoyed an autonomous status with special privileges and autonomy under an Ottoman Turkish-appointed Christian governor. They built a political, cultural and economic infrastructure for a Lebanese Christian state, which they created in 1920 under their

French patrons. They had the numbers (60 percent of the population or 1 million Christians), the wealth (highest among any minority in the Middle East) and the highest status (besides Greek Orthodox already expelled to Greece) among the minorities in the empire. In 1943 a Christian-dominated state was created in Lebanon.[5]

The next most likely candidate for statehood was the Armenians. They had world sympathy from the Turkish killings and support from the victorious Allies, who in the Treaty of Sèvres (1920) backed an independent Armenian state. Their numbers were adequate (3.5 million) and they were wealthier than the Kurds and the Jews. They had been the second highest ranking of the minorities in the Ottoman Turkish Empire. The 1920 Treaty of Sèvres promised them independence, which was supported by President Woodrow Wilson. The Armenians from 1918 to 1920 had an independent republic, their own Indo-European language and a unique Armenian Orthodox Church (Gregorian).[6]

The least likely candidate was the Jews. There were 65,000 Jews in Palestine in 1918. Jews lacked a compact territory they dominated (Jews were 10 percent of the population), a common language (few Jews spoke Hebrew), history (few Jews had lived in the region for 2,000 years) and psychology (frequent battles between religious and secular Jews, "bourgeois" and "socialist" Jews). In 1918, having narrowly avoided the fate of the Armenians, the Jewish community in the Ottoman Turkish Empire formed 0.2 percent of its 25 million people, 1 percent of the 5 million minority peoples, and 10 percent of the Palestinian population. There was often strong inter-sectarian rivalry in which the Jews were the low man on a long totem pole. Their fate seemed sealed.[7]

And the results of all those dreams? Armenian and Kurdish dreams of independence were soon crushed, and only the strong Lebanese Christians gained a proto-state. In September 1920, a month after the Treaty of Sèvres, Turkish forces invaded Armenian territory. By November the Armenian government had signed an armistice with Turkey leaving a tiny area under Armenian control. The Armenian prime minister, facing the advance of Russia and Turkey and the lack of Western support, opted in December 1920 for a Soviet republic without independence. By 1922 the Soviet Union had created an Armenian Soviet Socialist Republic, and the 1923 Treaty of Lausanne did not even mention Armenian independence.

Similarly, for the Kurds by March 1921 the Allies had reneged on their vague promises in the Treaty of Sèvres. With Ataturk having denounced the Treaty of Sèvres and occupied part of Kurdish territory:

> the Allies no longer had any interest in an independent Kurdish state. Only the British had ever been interested in the Kurds (and they even failed to list it as a possible mandate in January 1919) and they rapidly lost their interest as their forces dwindled in the region and the Turks advanced.[8]

By 1923 the Treaty of Lausanne, reflecting the triumph of Russian and Turkish power, did not mention an independent Kurdistan. The Kurds were left under alien governments (Ataturk's Turkey, Reza Shah's Persia and King Faisal's Iraq) without any mention of autonomy. Between 1923 and 1991 Kurdish was discouraged and then outlawed as a language.[9]

Things improved during and after World War II. Lebanon in 1943 became an independent state with Christian dominance enthroned in the constitution that guaranteed it 6:5 predominance in Parliament and the control of the presidency of the country. In November 1947 the United Nations voted for partition of the British Mandate in Palestine into an Arab state and a Jewish state. In May 1948 the Jews proclaimed their independence and won the Israeli War of Independence. But the Armenians remained a part of the Soviet Union and the Kurds, after the brief Mahabad Republic of 1945, also remained stateless.

By 2007 each minority had some political forms. The Armenians had a small state, the Kurds an autonomous region of Kurdistan in northern Iraq, the Maronites some authority (such as the presidency) in Lebanon and the Jews a strong, if beleaguered, state in Israel. But, except for the Jews, this fell far short of the hopes and dreams of 1920.

The 1989 Taif Accord after the civil war (1975–89) spelled a death blow to Christian dominance. Some 600,000 Maronites fled from Lebanon, and by 2007 Christians were less than one-third of the population. The 25 million to 30 million Kurds lacked a state, making them the largest minority in the world without a state. Even autonomous Iraqi Kurdistan, owing to strong opposition from Turkey, Syria, Iran and other Iraqis, was unlikely to become a state.[10] The Armenians had a small state (11,000 square miles and 3.3 million people), isolated by mostly hostile Muslim nations. The small Armenian economy had a GNP of only $12 billion.[11]

Decisive factors

Although the minorities issued many appeals for international support in 1918 and 1919, there were so many conflicts and such intermingling of ethno-national groups that such idealist appeals had a relatively small impact.

Neo-realism

Rather, national interest, power politics and the harsh realities of the international system would ultimately hold sway. After the 1895–96 killings of Armenians, an 1897 international conference called for reforms benefiting the Armenians. Russia opposed an independent Armenian state, the French supported Ottoman Turkey, the Germans wanted to become the protectors of Ottoman Turkey, the Austro-Hungarians were too involved in the Balkans and the Americans were absent. In 1915 during the massacres of the Armenians, the international community did nothing. As with European Jews during the Holocaust, morality meant little without the cold cash of international politics, without military and economic power.[12] Margaret Macmillan spoke of the Armenians, who had a powerful impact on the emotions of the British and Americans:

> Fine sentiments but they amounted to little in the end . . . Help was far away but Armenia's enemies were close at hand. Russians . . . would not tolerate Armenia or any other independent state in the Caucasus. On Armenia's other flank, Turks deeply resented the loss of Turkish territory and the further losses implied in the Armenian claims. In Paris Armenia's friends were lukewarm and hesitant.[13]

National cohesion

Given the strong forces opposing their projected new states, the minorities needed to mobilize all their resources for the struggle. Max Weber argued that the definition of a state is that institution which has the monopoly of the control of the instrument of violence in a given territory.[14] Given religious, ethnic, regional, tribal and clan tensions within the minorities, this could be a huge challenge.

Only the Jews, through their revolution, overcame the internal divisions that plagued other minorities. The Jews created a unified national leadership (the Jewish Agency) with a plethora of unifying institutions (Haganah Palmach, Histadrut, Mapai and even Herut). At the 1919 Paris Peace Conference there was one unified delegation and a modern concept of nation that was broadly accepted. In 1948 the government sank the *Altalena*, a ship bringing in French military supplies for Menachem Begin's separatist Irgun.

There were no modern parties or quasi-governments in the other three cases. The Kurds, unable to achieve national unity, were noted for their tribal warfare, religious differences (Sunnis, Shiites, Alawites, Sufis), secular/religious conflicts, urban/rural division, clan rivalries, and national and local influences. Often the Kurds fought each other as well as external authority.[15] As Margaret Macmillan reflected in *Paris 1919*:

> Unlike other emerging nations, Kurdistan had no powerful patrons in Paris and the Kurds were not yet able to speak effectively for themselves. Busy with their habitual cattle raids, abductions, clan wars and brigandage, with the enthusiastic slaughter of Armenians or simply with survival, they had not so far demonstrated much interest even in greater autonomy within the Ottoman Empire where the majority lived. Before the Great War, the nationalisms stirring among the other peoples of the Middle East had produced only faint echoes among the Kurds. Even the main center of Kurdish nationalism, consisting of a few small societies and a handful of intellectuals, was in Constantinople. The only Kurdish

spokesman in Paris in 1919, a rather charming man, had lived there so long that he was nicknamed Beau Sharif. He did his best.[16]

Divided among four major countries (Iran, Iraq, Syria and Turkey), they have not been able to unify their forces. The generations of "endless clashes" between the Barzanis and the Talabanis constituted a "dark chapter in the Kurdish history."[17] In 1945 and 1946 few Kurdish tribes, lacking national fervor and repelled by the Soviet Communist backing of the Kurdish republic, came to its aid. Iranian troops crushed the republic within a year and soon hanged its leader.[18] In 1945 Albert Hourani concluded that tribalism was a more powerful force among the Kurds than nationalism, which he found "limited" at the time.[19] Outside forces, including Saddam Hussein's Iraq, Iran, Syria and Turkey, have been able to mobilize some Kurdish forces against other Kurdish forces. The situation that Justin McCarthy depicted for the Kurds in 1918 had not totally changed even in succeeding decades:

> Nationalism was not an understood concept . . . Those Kurds, who were under the leadership of tribal chiefs, felt loyalty to those chiefs and to leaders of mystical religious sects . . . They had no wish to lose their authority to the government. This did not cause them to unite with other tribes in a common goal. Kurds in other tribes were occasional allies, occasional enemies, but no more. To speak of any sort of nationalism, or even ethnic identity, in such circumstances would be absurd. The other Kurds, those of the cities and those villages more or less independent of tribal control, were much like Turks in their relation to the state. Loyalties were to the sultan and religion.[20]

Kurds thus were divided by the five nations in which they lived, by their diverse tribes to which they owed significant loyalty, by their religion (mostly Sunnis but some Shiites or other sects), by a group of dialects that composed their language, by urban/rural origins, by geography and by social class and education.[21] Only since the American invasion of Iraq in 2003 and the rise of a Kurdish leader as president of Iraq (Talabani) have the Kurds at last achieved full regional autonomy, yet not nationhood.

The Lebanese Christians were handicapped by the divisions of religious differences, even within Christianity. Nearly half of Christians were not Maronites but Greek Orthodox, Greek Catholics, Syrian and Armenian Catholics, Chaldeans and other Christians. Greek Orthodox (nearly 40 percent of the size of the Maronites), fearing the fate of their large population in countries such as Syria and Jordan, were better integrated into Muslim society and some fought for the Muslims in the Lebanese civil war. They often resented their secondary role in the Maronite-led groups. Many Greek Orthodox and Greek Catholics, often poorer than the Maronites, were pan-Arabists rejecting the Maronite claim to Christian hegemony in Lebanon.

Some favored a Greater Lebanon, others a Lesser Lebanon focused on Mount Lebanon, the traditional Christian base.[22]

There were four major divergent Christian views on independence, dependence and their place in the Arab world in which they were located. A small but significant element, rejecting independence or a predominantly Christian Lebanon, thought this a futile endeavor given the size of the surrounding Arab Muslim world. A second larger group of older Arabs in the 1940s and 1950s saw Lebanon not as a future independent state or Christian-dominated state but rather as a place of refuge for persecuted minorities who needed mainly to preserve their autonomy at best. A third group, composed of Maronites and other Uniates (under the umbrella of the Roman Catholic Church), supported a pro-European Christian Lebanon oriented towards the Mediterranean and not the Arab world. The last group, composed of Christian nationalists, conceded that Lebanon would be an Arab country but the center of Arab Christians.

The clans, such as the Chamoun, Franjieh and Gemayel clans, often battled each other rather than forming a cohesive government under a single democratically elected leader. They also had a multitude of parties which sought to gain support from non-Christians. The Maronite church, which owned one-third of the fertile lands, had its own interest.

The Armenians, divided geographically (little Armenia proper and greater Armenia), were unable to mobilize a significant portion of their population. They were divided between supporters and opponents of the Soviet Union and Arab nationalism. At the 1919 Paris Peace Conference, the Armenians were so divided that they had two main rival delegations and 40 independent Armenian delegations.[23]

Will to fight

Smaller and less well-equipped militaries have destroyed bigger, even far bigger, opponents in large part because of their will to fight and die for a cause. The Jews, because of their predicament, history, modernism, revolution and socialism, have had a strong will to fight over the last 60 years. Without this stronger will to fight, the Jews would likely have been defeated by the Arab numerical preponderance.

There was a lower will to fight among the three other minorities. Some Greek Orthodox even fought against the Maronites in the Lebanese civil war. Many Lebanese Christians fled from the plains to the mountains to escape the fighting.[24] Many Kurds fought against other Kurds in repeated conflicts within Iraq. As for Armenians, they showed a greater will to fight than the Kurds or Maronites but still a lesser will than the Jews.

Immigration

Aliyah was a decisive element, with 400,000 Jewish immigrants before 1945 and almost 2.5 million more after independence in 1948. By contrast, there was virtually no immigration in the other three cases but often major emigration, especially from Armenia in 1918–22 and from Lebanon in the 1980s and 1990s. As for the Kurds, there was no migration from other Kurdish populations in the region to support a drive for national independence either after World War I or more recently.

Institution building and the economy

The Jews, lacking governmental or economic experience, created the base for a powerful government, military and secret police starting in the 1920s and accelerating before 1948. By 1948 this modest but significant government, military and economy were ready for statehood. By contrast, the Lebanese Christians never integrated their separate militias into a modern force and suffered accordingly. The Kurds often fought each other as much as the enemy. The Armenian army was modest but capable of achieving victories over Azerbaijan in Nagorno-Karabakh in the 1990s.

The Lebanese Christians failed to create a modern government. By including the vilarets of Beirut and Damascus in 1920 to the old Sanjak, the Maronites, who had a clear majority before then, reduced the Christian (and Maronite) portion of the future state and increased that of the Muslims.[25]

Even by the 1940s the Kurds had failed to create a modern or even semi-modern economy. There was just the beginning of the creation of a Kurdish bourgeoisie and intelligentsia. In the mountainous regions the majority of Kurds lived as nomads and semi-nomads, with farmers in the plains.[26] Starting in 1991 and accelerating after 2003 the Kurds began to build a good infrastructure for a state.

As for Armenia, the Soviet Union had during 70 years built up a skeletal republican government and socialist economy. It had educated the population and given tens of thousands of Armenians military and secret police experience, as well as even diplomatic and governmental experience. By 1991 Armenia had an excellent infrastructure for its new state.

Diaspora

The Diaspora was a major force in creating and sustaining the new state of Israel. By contrast, it played a minor role for the Kurds and only a modest role for the Armenians and the Lebanese Christians. The Lebanese Diaspora played a "weak role" in helping the Lebanese Maronites. Lebanese Greek Orthodox, Greek Catholics and Maronites lived in separate communities abroad and helped only their own community in Lebanon. There are 10 million to 13 million Lebanese living in the Diaspora (including 2 million in the

United States and 500,000 in Europe), many but not most of them Maronites. They sent money but were more occupied in settling and establishing their own communities abroad. The Maronites, though, were the most active of the Lebanese Diasporas.[27] The Kurds had a modest Diaspora, heavily in Germany and elsewhere. Predominantly nomads and peasants, they lacked religious, communal or cultural ties to the West.[28] Armenia had an active Diaspora that played a role, especially after 1991.

Level of modernization

Israel represented a powerful thrust towards modernization from a people that less than two generations earlier had largely been immured within the walls of the *shtetls* of Eastern Europe and the *mellahs* of North Africa. The Kurds were on the low end of modernization, and the Armenians and Lebanese Christians on the higher end. This did not translate into modern education, social forms, gender equality and the rule of law. In the 1940s, Maronites were primarily farmers and feudal landlords with a prosperous Beirut bourgeoisie. They were only 29 percent of the Lebanese population. Maronite and non-Maronite Christians formed 53 percent of the Lebanese population.[29]

International political support

Here the Lebanese Christians scored the highest. Their French patrons, who were predominant in Lebanon from 1920 to 1945, were willing to exert the full force of their power behind the creation and maintenance of a Lebanese state. By contrast, the Armenians (1919) and the Kurds (1920) received glowing words and promises of a state but in the end no power really helped them. President Woodrow Wilson, initially a great champion of the Armenians, saw his desire for League of Nations membership defeated by the United States Senate in 1919. Justin McCarthy has assessed that we:

> must judge the Allied treatment of the Armenians as craven. Idealistic support of the Armenian cause, no matter how wrong-headed, was proclaimed. Armenians were encouraged to resist their enemies, rather than try to come to accommodation with them, because the Europeans and Americans would soon give the Armenians all they wanted. Then it was, "Sorry, too expensive for us. You're on your own. All the best."[30]

Only the 1991 disintegration of the Soviet Union allowed Armenia to finally become a state, if one often embattled with the Muslims, especially Azerbaijan over Nagorno-Karabakh.

The Kurds, with frequent patrons, had none willing to fight for them and were repeatedly abandoned by Western and other powers. In 1946 the Russians abandoned them, in 1975 the Iranians abandoned them and in 1991 the

Americans and the British partially abandoned them but also created a no-fly zone that laid a base for an autonomous Kurdistan after the 2003 American invasion of Iraq.

The Jews had the most extensive ties to the West, both through their Diaspora and owing to their 2,000-year sojourn in the West. The Kurds, as peasants and nomads in the Middle East, were very weak in ties to the West. In between were the Armenians and the Lebanese Maronites, with significant ties but considerably less than the Jews.

The Jews and national liberation movements

The rise of Israel represented another of the national liberation movements that have swept to power in over 100 countries in the Third World since the end of World War II. There are some commonalities.[31] The Labor Party was a predominantly socialist political party that ruled for decades after independence and mobilized the population for modernization tasks. It led a struggle to oust a Western imperialist power ruling the colony. Israel used military force (Haganah/Palmach) and sporadic terror (Lehi) against a colonial power. It mobilized international support for its independence movement. It was an underdeveloped economy at the time of independence. It had young elites at the time of independence. The country had discrete collectivities divided by ethnic, communal, religious and linguistic differences. There was a strong post-colonial nationalism. Israel had strong socialist forms of governance and mobilization. It mobilized a Diaspora for support and legitimized its struggle through support at the United Nations (United Nations Resolution 181). Its moderate leadership stressed the role of nation over the role of class (David Ben Gurion's *mamlakhtiut*). Israel had chiliastic exuberant notions of achievements under an independent regime. There was considerable violence in the birth of the nation.

Several authors have suggested, despite the obvious differences in size and religion, that Israel be compared to India.[32] Both in 1948 were Third World countries with Muslim–non-Muslim civil wars that killed huge numbers of people. India and Israel emerged from British colonialism in a complex battle against both the British (largely peaceful) and the Muslims. Both divided the land of British rule in bloody warfare between themselves (Hindus and Jews) and the Muslims. India and Israel were Third World nations that immediately became democratic regimes under a dominant socialist party that ruled for 30 years (the Israeli Labor Party and the Indian Congress Party). Both later made a transition to global integration, free market capitalism and stronger alliance with the West and especially the United States in the 1980s and 1990s.

While Israel's rise to power reflected a number of aspects common to many other states, there were also some striking differences.[33] Israel had an urban semi-modern economy rather than an agricultural economy dominated by villages, peasants and low productivity. It had a well-educated, politically aware and mobilized populace rather than a narrow circle of modernizers and parochial, traditional, poorly educated masses heavily traditional in attitude. Its main struggle was not with an imperial power but war with a rival claimant to territory (the Palestinians) and external powers (Egypt, Syria, Lebanon, Saudi Arabia and Iraq). Israel suffered strong regional and international isolation after independence and was not allowed to join the newly independent bloc after 1948. It has had an ongoing violent and political struggle for existence in the last 60 years. Unlike most Third World countries, it has been a democratic regime from the onset of independence, with a decisive role for immigrants. There was no social revolution accompanying national independence.

The Jews and new societies

The Jews, as one of the oldest peoples in the world, ironically created one of the newest societies in the ancient land of Israel. Israel represented a revolution and transformation of traditional Jewish society. Starting over in its homeland with 24,000 Jews in 1880, the 5.4 million Jews in Israel by 2007 created a new society. If we adapt Louis Hartz's idea of European fragments being implanted in the Third World (the United States, Canada, Australia, South Africa and Latin America), Israel (which he does not discuss) could be considered a European fragment from the nineteenth-century Russian revolutionary movement.

From 1880 to 1977 Israel represented a cultural fragment of Russian revolutionary thought implanted in the Old/New Land.[34] This occurred despite the fact that half of its population of today did not originate in Europe but in the Islamic world, with 1.3 million Arabs and over 2 million Sephardim. It occurred despite the fact that the original Russian Revolution, consummated in the 1917 October Revolution, failed with the disintegration of the Soviet Union in 1991. Its inspiration was as much the populist narodnik tradition (ironically often anti-Semitic) as urban Menshevism and Bolshevism.

But the Israeli story fits the Hartz model in a number of ways. The transformation of European radicalism into a powerful nationalism was reflected in Ben Gurion's own slogan, "From class to nation." Socialism was reborn as a form of nationalism with socialist aspects such as "ideology becomes a moral absolute, a national essence." Israel lost its relationship to Russia and Europe, not only because of the ethnic dominance of non-Europeans and their distance from their European roots, but in Hartz's words because, "When a fragment of Europe becomes the whole of a new nation, it becomes unrecognizable in European terms." The lack of a native bourgeoisie against which to struggle, and the presence of national enemies reinforced this transformation of class to nation.[35]

Many aspects of Israeli society reflected its Russian revolutionary origins in authors ranging from Nikolai Chernyshevsky and Nikolai Nekrasov to Dmitri Pisarev and Vladimir Lenin. The Russian revolutionary heritage was brought by the numerous Russian pioneers of the first three aliyahs, especially the latter two. Walter Laqueur argued for the "powerful" impact of Russian socialism on Israel for "It is impossible to exaggerate the impact of Russian Socialism on the Zionist Labor Movement."[36] Most of the Jewish revolutionary leaders (Berl Katznelson, A. D. Gordon, David Ben Gurion, Chaim Weizmann, Yitzhak Ben-Zvi, Yosef Trumpeldor, Moshe Sharett, Eliezer Ben Yehuda and Golda Meir) came from Tsarist Russia, usually Belarus and northern Ukraine. Most Second Aliyah pioneers were young, single Russians hailing from eastern Poland, Lithuania and Belarus, who retained attachment to Russian rivers, fields and forests and believed in a Russian soul.[37]

The First Zionist Socialist Revolution reflected the Russian revolutionary stress on socialism (the Labor movement), ideology (a chiliastic utopia), highly ideological parties (Mapam, Mapai, Achdut Haavodah), high political self-consciousness, collectivism and communalism (kibbutzim, moshavim, Histadrut), doctrinal squabbling and the virtues of manual labor. Russian radicalism was also reflected in a strong group thrust to social life (with frowning on bourgeois individualism), the ideal of service and romantic notions about individual sacrifice for the group, and a Manichean view of the world. Russian realities also brought a heavy bureaucratic element to government activities (*bureaukratsiya*). The Israeli stress on high culture and education reflected its Russian origins as well.

It did this without civil war, save for the brief 1948 *Altalena* Affair. Israel reflected the power of a utopian vision (here New Socialist Jerusalem), modernity, modernization and struggle. But it had to be adapted to Israel, because neither Russian populism (with its stress on the peasant) nor Russian social democracy (with its stress on the working class) totally fit the Israeli reality. Israeli and Russian radicalism was bred in the reaction to the medieval and often retarding effect of massive Russian anti-Semitism (650 laws aimed at the Jews) and of Russian society itself. Michael Mann put the situation best:

> On representation, Russia was at the opposite extreme from the United States. By 1900 it remained the only autocratic monarchy in Europe, the only one without any pretense of party democracy, the one in which state elites and parties most interrelated as court factions. Its militarism was also distinctive in sustaining an empire surrounding the Russian "core" territories . . . Thus, militarism was unusually pronounced domestically as well as geopolitically. The Russian state crystallized as capitalist but also as highly monarchical, militarist and centralizing.[38]

The traditional Jewish class structure made a revolutionary utopia in Israel more practical. In Europe, the Middle East and North Africa the Jews had almost no elements of a traditional power structure: no nobility, aristocracy, landlords or guilds and a weak middle class. While in Poland, in 1931, 67.5 percent of Polish Christians worked in agriculture, only 4.4 percent of Jews did so. Even when Jews were concentrated in the trade and light industrial areas, many were *luftmenschen* and easily abandoned their pursuits.[39]

The power of migration and a new land opened the door to the achievement of a New Israel, much as the American migration created the New World in North America. Having fled persecution and oppression, the immigrants were ready to build a new classless world in a new land. They could start again in a new space without feudalism, capitalism, aristocracy, nobility, peasantry or officialdom. The Old World was far away geographically and soon mentally, even more so for the next generation for whom it was a distant shore. Also, the small, poor, dependent local traditional Jewish society was easily ignored and pushed aside in the search for the new utopia.[40]

Israel was far closer in the First Zionist Socialist Revolution to a remote Europe than to the modern United States. Few Western immigrants came to Israel or felt comfortable there. The goal of building the utopia, a New Jerusalem, with a heroic and glorious past, was a key to the Russian revolutionary myth. Yet Israel does bear some similarities to the equally new society of the United States, which also fought a war of liberation against British colonialism, conducted an internal war against enemies (Indians, the South) and conducted mass popular mobilization for war against superior external enemies. Like Israel too, the United States was a nation of immigrants with devotion to its new society (the New World), adoption of universal military service, and a militia-like structure against professional armies. Bound together also by common bonds of religiosity (here Protestantism) and history against its enemies, it showed a passionate commitment to democracy, civil society and the rule of law. It possessed a cohesive civil society more fluid than that of the home country.[41]

As in Australia, there would be little respect of wealth, no recalcitrant bourgeoisie, no capitalist credo and powerful yet moderate trade unions. Too, the nomadic and aboriginal natives were few in number and not a strong factor. The Labor Party was always very pragmatic, and the country was born modern, without a struggle against the non-existent past in a new space. Australia, like Israel, was born a radical nation without a past, only a future in a working-class paradise.[42]

The Jews and social revolutions

There is a strong literature on revolutions, spanning over 150 years from Karl Marx and Crane Brinton to Theda Skocpol and Barrington Moore and now Nikkie Keddie and Jack Goldstone. From this literature we can analyze several important points. First, we can look at Israel as a social revolutionary movement in a broader context. Then, we can look at the second stage of the Israeli revolution and its parallels with other socialist movements that have moved on towards global capitalist integration.

There are numerous causes of social revolutions that transform the economic and political structures. They include alienation of the intellectuals and bankruptcy of the treasury (Brinton[43]), growing tensions between means and forms of production (Marx[44]), rise of the bourgeoisie and peasant revolts (Moore[45]). Revolutions are caused by world time and international pressures from military defeats (Skocpol[46]), demographic pressures on brittle economic and state structures (Goldstone[47]) and relative deprivation (Gurr[48]).

For the Jews these factors do not work since the Jews never had their own state and sought it in their original homeland that most had left 2,000 years earlier. For them, thereafter, the equivalents of these factors were the oppression and repression that they suffered on the margins of European and Middle Eastern societies and states.

Israel and the Four Tigers of Asia (1950–2007)

Israel can also be viewed as a rapidly growing Third World country like the Four Tigers of Asia (South Korea, Singapore, Taiwan and Hong Kong). It shares a number of attributes with these countries (and colony).[49] It has close political and economic ties with the West, which provided substantial foreign aid for strategic and symbolic reasons and had a strong impact.[50] Israel has powerful nearby enemies that require sustained military effort, similar to the Four Tigers (China for Hong Kong, North Korea for South Korea, Malaysia for Singapore, and China for Taiwan). The Jewish state has powerful state elites, motivated by foreign threat and patriotism, and used autonomous and state resources for the development of a diverse industrial base and not for its own aggrandizement. Israel has experienced rapid economic export-led growth that transformed a Third World backwater in 1950 into a First World economic powerhouse by 2007. It has had weak foreign investment, fearful of political and economic instability, and weak ties to the original colonial metropole. Israel is a former colony, like the Four Tigers.

With weak natural resources, Israel too has a smallish population, a modest to weak agricultural endowment, a weak landed class and no frontier. Blessed with a strong educational and technological thrust, it has experienced massive immigration (like Hong Kong and Singapore) and a positive international environment. As a small trading country, Israel is vulnerable to external economic and political shocks.

Until the 1980s, Israel, as a democratic regime of largely Jewish origin, lacked the highly authoritarian politics, the powerful neo-Confucian ideology and the strong Chinese ethnic element (save South Korea) of the Four Tigers. It has strong, not weak, universities, a stress on technology rather than consumer goods and no relation to the prevalent Japanese cartel model in East Asia. Its savings rate is much lower than in Asia, its consumption level is much higher and it is quite innovative in the social sector. Israel has had socialism and strong trade unions, neither of which has been found in the Four Tigers.

From 1950 to 1970 Israel resembled East Asia. But it lacked the above-mentioned aspects of the Asian model and could be compared to both Latin

America and the United States. Its low savings rate and high rate of consumption resembled the United States. Its temporary hyperinflation, high debt ratio, heterodoxy, difficulties with governability, high inflation and negative balance of payments resembled Latin America.[51]

Israel is a vulnerable state with security concerns driving foreign policy in a hostile regional environment that have fostered seven wars and two intifadas in the last 59 years. It has multiple and superior opponents, limited resources and a hostile environment. Uniquely, it has raised the importance of the military to a very high level and fulfilled the desires of Jewish identity for a Jewish majority and reliance on a Jewish Diaspora. Shibley Telhami found that, while neo-realism can explain much of Israeli foreign and defense policy, the ideological element is relevant as well.[52]

Israel and a militarist society

Israel on the surface would seem a prime candidate for an authoritarian, militarist society like imperial Germany or Sparta. Besieged by powerful and significant enemies for 60 years (as well as before statehood) and forced to mobilize its citizens to be soldiers or reservists ready to serve, it would seem a likely candidate for militarism. Indeed, Yitzhak Rabin's famous quip "Who is an Israeli? He is a soldier who spends 11 months a year on leave as a civilian" would seem to show this tendency. So too would the predominance of famous generals and military men as prime ministers (Yitzhak Rabin, Ehud Barak, Arik Sharon) and as leaders of various companies.

How can we understand that Israel has avoided becoming a militarist state? Moshe Lissak has shown that Israel has mild militarism, a multi-party system, frequent criticism of the military, civilian control of the military, a high degree of professionalism in the military and a limited role of the military in the economy and politics.[53] Many features of classic militarism – a highly offensive security doctrine, emphasis on territorial expansion, glorification of war and chauvinism, lack of a powerful civilian counter-culture, and regulatory power of the military – do not exist in Israel.[54] Rather Israelis, in the 1990s (heyday of "Peace Now") and even today, still have a strong, even passionate, desire for peace, not war.

Other factors – the power of revolutions, the ideals of new societies, the universality of military service, the reserve system civilizing the military, and the early retirement program – have played a key role in preventing a militarist system. So too may have the very small size of the country and some Jewish atavistic tendencies that historically have debunked military leaders, secrecy and harsh authority and yearned for peace.

This chapter has shown that Israel, while certainly exceptional in many ways, can be fruitfully compared to other new states, new societies, revolutionary states, the Four Tigers of Asia and states avoiding militarism. It has shown how Israel overcame great obstacles to be the only one of the four significant minorities in the Ottoman Turkish Empire to achieve a highly successful First World state 90 years after the dissolution of the Empire. Such comparisons also move us away from the highly ideologically charged discussions of Israel in Chapter 2 to using traditional political science and sociological categories for understanding Israel. For, at the end of the day, Israel needs to be analyzed as a state, however exceptional, in comparison with the 200 other states in the world. These comparisons have shown dramatically how successfully Israel has done, with the greatest similarities to highly successful other states such as the United States and the Four Tigers of Asia.

Part II

Obstacles to the rise of Israel

In Part II we turn to a detailed look at the great obstacles; obstacles faced by very few national liberation movements, in the path of the creation and flourishing of the state of Israel. These included internal obstacles (Jewish issues), territorial obstacles (Israeli issues), the hostility of major powers (Ottoman Turkey, Tsarist Russia, the Soviet Union, the British Empire 1937–49, Nazi Germany), regional powers (many Arab powers and Iran 1980–2007) and international religious and political groups (the Roman Catholic Church, liberal Protestants, Muslims, Third World nations and the United Nations), and the unwillingness of friendly Western powers to help in times of crises.

To overcome such huge obstacles, Israel needed to do more than mobilize the talents and resources of the 13 million Jews in the world, millions of whom before 1989 had lived immured in a Communist world hostile to Israel. It needed to find a multiplier that would unleash massive new capabilities and allow the Jews to create and propel their new state forward in the international arena. These new revolutions (socialist, then capitalist) did precisely this, as they have done for other states and peoples lagging behind in the international arena.

Amos Elon has observed that "Arab enmity has helped the Zionists to maintain what too often disappears in other revolutionary regimes – the atmosphere of 'permanent revolution.' "[1] Israel's permanent revolution has endured for several generations and allowed the lengthy socialist revolution in the late 1970s to merge into a semi-capitalist revolution (under the Labor Party as well as the Likud Party).[2] The costs of the revolution would not be low – frequent semi-hysteria in Israeli public discussion, popular obliviousness to significant flaws in Israeli realities, poor treatment of minorities and immigrants, a growing social gap, significant pollution issues and the downplaying of other social issues.[3]

But the power that revolutions unleashed, together with other significant factors, helped create the state and make it a leading regional power within a few decades. In a terrible security environment this has made most Israelis supportive of the revolutions that have saved them from the huge obstacles they faced, even at a significant cost.

Let us now turn to examining the plethora of great and medium-sized obstacles with which Israel has had to contend over the last 125 years and especially the last 60 years, and even now to a significant degree.

4 Jewish issues

The Zionist movement had to accomplish far more than the usual national liberation movement for, as Jacob Talmon delineated its tasks, it had to:

1 focus the passions and will of diverse Jewish communities all over the world;
2 create on a voluntary base a government, parliament, bureaucracy and army long before the Jews had even settled in the land of Israel in any number;
3 win over the support of a significant portion of the non-Jewish world and utilize that to gain aid and recognition from the top international bodies;
4 build, without compulsion, a nation state from immigrants from extremely diverse climatic, cultural and economic backgrounds;
5 establish self-governing towns, villages, agriculture, industry and self-defense bodies;
6 create a new basis for a civilization with a new language and social experimentation;
7 organize civil disobedience, underground acts and guerrilla movements and then fight five professional armies in 1948 and several more in succeeding decades;
8 maintain a democracy and strong education and culture while surrounded by hostile Arab states;
9 win every battle and war against Arab nations who possessed quantitative superiority in manpower and military equipment;[4]
10 take the relatively dead ancient language of Hebrew (spoken by 20,000 Jews in 1905) and make it a vibrant language of 5 million Jews by 2004.[5]

How could it happen in the face of so many obstacles?

Finding the Jews to populate the land of Israel

Some of the greatest problems were issues on the Jewish street. The Jews historically loved Zion but had not gone to Zion. In 586 BCE the Babylonians destroyed Judea and scattered the Jews in exile. When the Persian King Cyrus the Great 50 years later allowed the Jews to return to their land, the majority of them decided to stay in the Diasporas of Egypt and Mesopotamia. Even with the aid of Ezra and Nehemiah the return was a slow and painful process. By the time of the flourishing of the Jews in the Second Temple during the middle Roman period, perhaps 60 percent of Jews remained in the Diaspora.[6] How could this fate be avoided this time and the wandering Jews find a home in Israel?

By 1900 half of the 10 million Jews in the world lived poor and embittered lives in the vast Pale of Settlement of Tsarist Russia while the rest were scattered in the United States and Canada, Western and Central Europe, the Middle East and North Africa. The Jews lacked a common territory, language, economic life or culture. The Eastern European Jewish communities were divided into a number of states with their own autonomous institutions, intense jealousies and suspicions and desire for positions and status.[7]

Why would the tradition-bound Jews of Europe as well as North Africa and the Middle East come to Palestine/Israel when Zionism represented a radical assault on tradition? For, as David Vital put it well:

> Besides, to rebel against the Jewish condition, as against any long-established status quo, was to incur resistance. The more radical the intent and the more effective the means to implement it, the greater was the resistance. This within Jewry; thus without. Change required a mobilization of human and material resources, defined purposes, organization . . . But every settled thing in Jewry militated against a radical approach to its ills; habit of mind, precedent, the Tradition itself in its most explicit forms, the invertebrate, powerless and partly voluntary structure of the nation, and the private views and purposes of a majority – if indeed a diminishing majority – of the Jews themselves.[8]

Jews had many options besides Zion, including emigration to the West, Communism, Bundism, Orthodox Judaism, Reform Judaism, assimilation and conversion. The ultimate other Zion would be the United States, and especially New York, which by 1900 had the largest Jewish population in the world. Most Jews considered the United States the "Land of Promise" ("goldene medine") as opposed to the "Promised Land." By 1914 over 1 million Jews lived in New York, where they enjoyed political and religious freedom, economic opportunities and a strong Jewish life so lovingly described by Irving Howe in *The World of Our Fathers*. Over 2.5 million Jews went to the United States.[9] The lure of America was so strong that, when 4,500 Jewish legionaries from Britain and the United States found themselves in Palestine at the end of World War I, less than 6 percent chose to stay there rather than return to Anglo-America.[10]

There was also the lure of other Zions. Baron Hirsch resettled 45,000 Jews in Argentina by 1914 while the Soviet Union resettled 30,000 Jews in the 1930s in the less hospitable realm of Birobidzhan.[11]

Founded by Karl Marx (a converted Jew) and with many Jewish leaders (such as Bernstein, Lassalle, Luxemburg and Trotsky), revolutionary socialism's "messianic appeal" was "irresistible."[12] While its atheism, historical determinism, centralization and impersonal forces alienated traditional Jews and denigrated Jewish nationalism as a reactionary bourgeois phenomenon, it appealed strongly to marginalized Jews.

Many Jews were attracted to leftist Bundism (founded also in 1897), which called for a Jewish autonomous socialist entity. In the 1905 Russian Revolution the Bundists played a major role and over 4,000 Bundists languished in jail.[13] Bundism, extolling Yiddish culturalism and denouncing Zionism as a bourgeois, utopian romantic dream, dominated Poland, the largest Jewish center in the world, from 1920 to 1940.[14]

Many remained adherents of traditional Orthodox Judaism, which was hostile to Zionism until after the Holocaust. Orthodox Judaism, dominant in Eastern Europe until 1914, often depicted Zionism as a heretical, false messianic delusion of the premature return to Zion. Most rabbis, notables and communal leaders opposed Zionism and moving to Palestine. Most German, Hungarian and Eastern European Orthodox movements before the Holocaust fought Zionism and excommunicated those who went to Palestine.[15]

Many other Jews in the United States, Germany and Hungary were attracted to Reform Judaism, which from 1840 to 1940 was staunchly opposed to Zionism. Reform Jews saw Judaism as a religion, not a nation.[16]

After the French Revolution, assimilation, conversion and intermarriage were powerful forces, especially in Central and Western Europe and more recently in North America. While Eastern European Jews lived as recognized national minorities with linguistic, cultural, social and religious institutions in a state of persecution by the authorities, Western and Central European Jews enjoyed full citizenship and access to the fruits of the Emancipation. As Barry Rubin put it well:

> At that time, Jews began to be offered choices and opportunities in place of a way of life hitherto taken for granted. That era saw a transition from a traditional Jewish society wrapped in religion, though a period of demoralization, division and uncertainty, to a more complex solution of adverse religious interpretations and general acceptance that Jews are a people. Christians expected Jews to convert; leftists expected them to dissolve themselves in socialism and liberals expected them to become equal but identical citizens. Each such solution occurred in hundreds of thousands of cases. There also arose a distinctive assimilating Jewish subculture and massive participation in a wide range of intellectual and political movements, reflecting the dilemmas that Jews were facing.[17]

As early as 1492 only 50 percent of Spanish Jews expelled from Spain left the country: the remainder assimilated and converted, with only a small minority remaining secretly Jewish. In the 1830s Heinrich Heine argued that conversion was "the admission ticket to European culture." By the 1890s Theodor Herzl foresaw assimilation as the main enemy, declaring that "Whole branches of Jewry may wither and fall away." All leading Berlin Jewish hostesses of literary salons in the early nineteenth century eventually converted to Christianity, as did all but one of the children of Moses Mendelssohn.

From 1871 to 1933 assimilation (and a low birth rate) in Germany was so strong that the number of Jewish children plummeted 50 percent. In Hungary by 1940 there were as many as 100,000 former Jews professing Christianity. In 1914 one-third of Jews were intermarrying in Berlin and Hamburg. In the 1920s the rate in Hungary was 33 percent and in liberal Amsterdam 70 percent. Famous converts from Judaism included Karl Marx, Heinrich Heine, Felix Mendelssohn, Benjamin Disraeli, Gustav Mahler, Bernard Berenson, Ludwig Wittgenstein and Boris Pasternak. In Tsarist Russia in 1839 there were 40,000 Jewish converts to Orthodox Christianity living in Moscow and Saint Petersburg. Barry Rubin seems to guess that 10–15 percent of world Jews today (perhaps as many as 2 million Jews) are no longer Jews, owing to conversion and descendants of conversion. In the United States today there are 200,000 formal converts to Christianity and other religions and 1.4 million children of some Jewish aspect no longer considering themselves Jews.[18]

However, the impact of assimilation before 1917 was limited. Conversions among 7 million Russian Jews between 1904 and 1914 averaged only 1,000 to 1,500 a year, and some of them returned to Judaism.[19] Only under the Soviet Union would assimilation increase, to the point where the intermarriage rate by the late 1980s was closing in on 60 percent, a rate roughly comparable to the United States.

There were enemies for Zionism even within the non-radical, non-assimilationist, non-Orthodox camp. Most Jews, even in the Ottoman Turkish Empire, initially rejected the premise that their home was in Palestine, rather than in the countries in which they resided. In 1909 none of the four Jews elected to the new parliament were Zionists.[20]

Why Palestine?

And why would they go to Palestine? Before 1940 most Jewish theologians, as well as most American and European Reform and Orthodox Jews, were opposed to Zionism.[21] A. J. Sherman depicted the legacy by 1917 of 400 years of Ottoman Turkish rule:

> a poor and backward territory ... For centuries under the Turks Palestine had lain neglected and forlorn, without roads, without water supplies, without a railway and almost without schools and hospitals ... even [without] a water supply. The Church of the Holy Sepulchre stood in danger of collapse. There were no telephones. The life of the fellahin

pursued its slow round of dust, disease and debt. So had it been since the days of the Old Testament.[22]

Palestine in 1918 suffered from extensive deforestation, plagues of locusts, repeated crop failures, a collapsing agricultural economy and "almost universal poverty, malnourishment and disease among both Arabs and Jews."[23] In 1920, 97 percent of Jewish workers in Tiberias came down with malaria.[24] The land was often infertile, the climate harsh and unhealthy and the work rough and unfamiliar.[25]

In the early twentieth century, Jerusalem suffered from malaria, trachoma, cholera, typhus, typhoid, ringworm, malnutrition and pox. It lacked a modern plumbing system and in the winter its unpaved streets turned into quagmires. In the summer its air was "polluted by clouds of gagging dust." In 1919 bubonic plague and relapsing fever broke out in Jaffa. In the early 1920s, 14 percent of Jewish children died before their first birthday. Trachoma afflicted the eyes of 40 percent of Jewish school children.[26] In the early 1920s Jerusalem had no radio, no cinema and no libraries but significant filth.[27] In the 1920s and 1930s malaria killed hundreds of workers who drained the swamps of the Galilee and laid stones by hand for the streets of Tel Aviv.

For Arabs the average life expectancy in Palestine in the 1880s was 27 years – a level not seen in the West for several hundreds of years. In 1931, 86 percent of Palestinian Arabs were illiterate and most were peasants. Some Arab villages had no electricity, sanitation or roads; people used camels for transport, rode donkeys and used wooden ploughs in the fields. As late as 1948 Arab life expectancy was 48 years, over a decade below that of the West.[28] Even during British rule over Palestine (1918–48), Palestine lagged behind the West. There were kibbutzim like Shefayim in the 1930s:

Shefayim was wretchedly poor. Its treasury was always empty, the food was inadequate, and the "public buildings" were one barracks, pretentiously called the "refectory" and one barn used for work during the day and for recreation at night. The area was infested with scorpions and poisonous snakes and, by a special dispensation of the Almighty, enjoyed stifling heat in summer and violent storms in winter.[29]

In 1948, Israel had a Third World economy, minimal exports, almost no industrial exports and relatively low health standards. It was the only major state in the world (outside Taiwan) whose legitimacy remained disputed by many states in the world.[30] Mass immigration led to a sharp decline in the standard of living, rationing, black markets and the erection of wooden shacks (*ma'abaroth*) bereft of electricity or running water for hundreds of thousands of immigrants. Why would they come to a state with perpetual physical threat, heavy military service, a low standard of living and an onerous tax burden?[31]

In 1914 the 35,000 Zionists in the New Yishuv were less than the 50,000 religious members of the Old Yishuv, and only 1 percent of world Jewry belonged to the Zionist movement.[32] The Conjoint Foreign Committee, representing British Jewry in external affairs, placed an anti-Zionist statement in *The Times*. In 1917 the majority of British notables were anti-Zionist.[33] From 1880 to 1914 over 1.5 million Russian Jews immigrated to the United States, 200,000 to Britain and 65,000 to Palestine.[34]

Emigration was also a major problem. Probably 60–70 percent of the Bilu group in the early 1880s left the country.[35] Perhaps 70 percent (David Ben Gurion claimed 90 percent) of the famed Second Aliyah (1904–14) of 40,000 immigrants that founded the modern state left the country.[36] During the recession in 1927, 30 percent of the 80,000 largely Polish immigrants of the Fourth Aliyah emigrated from Palestine. The next year as many Jews left the country as arrived.[37] Since 1948 over 2.5 million Jews have come to Israel while perhaps 750,000 Israelis have left the country, mainly for the United States.[38] The passage of restrictive immigration laws in the United States in 1925 lessened the flow of Jews by 90 percent by the late 1920s and 95 percent by the early 1930s.[39]

Overcoming numerous barriers to integrating the immigrants into a new society

Unlike the history of most new states, Jewish history played out for over 1,800 years in over 100 countries. With no unified Jewish state since 70 CE, Diaspora customs, reflecting sharp differences in culture, history and social structure, were often disruptive. Edwin Montagu, British Colonial Secretary for India in World War I, only mildly exaggerated the problems when he wrote in a 1915 memorandum to Prime Minister Herbert Asquith:

> There is no Jewish race now as a homogeneous whole. It is quite obvious that the Jews in Great Britain are as remote from the Jews in Morocco or the black Jews in Cochin as the Christian Englishman is from the Moors or the Hindoo . . . I cannot see any Jews I know tending olive trees or herding sheep . . . Hebrew to the vast majority of the Jews is a language in which to pray but not a language in which to speak or write . . . [It would be forming a state out of] a polyglot, many-colored, heterogeneous collection of people of different civilizations and different ordinances and different traditions.[40]

Until 1948 the Yishuv (pre-1948 Jewish community) was 85 percent Ashkenazi. The immigration in the 1950s of 650,000 Sephardi Jews from North Africa and the Middle East created an acute conflict between the Ashkenazim and Sephardim.[41]

The gap today between 2 million Sephardim (1950s immigrants) and 1 million Russians (mostly 1990s immigrants) and 2 million veteran Ashkenazim is substantial and significant, though diminished over time. In the first two decades of the state the Ashkenazim dominated every facet of society, from the institutions to businesses, universities, schools and clubs. This created a sharp conflict when the rising Sephardim and later the new Russians would demand their place in society and the state. As late as 1967, families from Asia and Africa earned less than 50 percent of the amount earned by those of European origin. Only after 1967, with the rise of a new Israel-educated population and the availability of cheap Palestinian labor from the territories would the Sephardim rise into the white-collar and middle class.[42]

Israel faced serious problems in "absorbing" the immigrants.[43] It had to transform them into Hebrew-speaking members of an economy with a very different occupational profile than in the Diaspora. Almost 39 percent of Diaspora Jews were in commerce but only 14 percent of Palestinian Jews were in commerce. A revolution in the profile and psychology of immigrants would be necessary after they arrived in the Promised Land.[44] For as Stephen Schecter wrote in a review of a novel by A. B. Yehoshua:

> I find myself nodding at the Ishmaelite's words, as would anyone who knows anything of the workings of a Jewish organization. What Jew ever listens to another Jew? What Jew is ever persuaded by another Jew of anything? What Jewish organization ever sticks to a decision when someone always has a better idea after the decision was taken? And yet, Jewish organizations thrive, a Jewish country exists.[45]

Certain Diaspora Jewish traits needed to be changed. Jews, with their notion of "three Jews, four opinions," were not ready for discipline and organization. Jews, used to being minorities, tended not to push an active political agenda in public but rather deferred to authority. In 1932 Chaim Arlosoroff wrote to Weizmann of the failure of Zionist aims due, in Laqueur's summary, to "a return to the time-honored Jewish fatalism, to Micawberish expectations that something would turn up."[46]

In the 1890s Jewish leaders doubted the capacity of impoverished Eastern European Jews to lead the movement against significant Jewish and non-Jewish opposition. In 1896 Baron Edmund de Rothschild called Eastern European Jews an "army of *shnorrers*" (beggars).[47] The establishment of authority was the life task of David Ben Gurion, for:

> He undertook a task that could justifiably be called a mission impossible. After all, the problem of imposing a single authority on the Jewish people – to close their ranks and guide them along a single national course – has been the leitmotiv of Jewish history. The Bible is full of narratives indicating that prophets or kings – or even higher authority – were not always equal to the task . . . For some two thousand years, the Jewish people had a dubious distinction; lacking their own land, they recognized no central authority . . . In their dispersion the Jews obeyed,

in matters temporal, the political authority that happened to govern their host country; in matters spiritual they heeded their local rabbi . . . there developed a genuine distinction between Eastern and Western Jewry.[48]

Unlike the case in common international practice, Israel took nearly all Jewish immigrants under the Law of Return. From 1948 to 1952 the Jewish population of Israel more than doubled, and doubled again from 1952 to 1972. The vast majority of the new immigrants were impoverished refugees needing food, clothing, housing, jobs, education and a language (Hebrew) to function in a new and strange society. David Ben Gurion outlined the immensity of the task facing the new country:

> There are fifty-five nations of origins represented in the army and you have no concept of how great are the distances and how considerable the differences between these national groups. The great majority of our nation is not yet Jewish, but human dust, bereft of a single language, without tradition, without roots, without a bond to national life, without the customs of an independent society. We must mend the rifts of the Diaspora and form a united nation.[49]

While the earlier immigrants were more ready for the challenge, many of the 2.5 million immigrants after 1948 lacked the mental orientation, the positive and euphoric notions about heroism, sacrifice and conquest in a modern society. The Jews, save for German Jews in the 1930s, brought almost no capital and few skills. Except for Soviet Jews, most came with no real livelihood – and among them entrepreneurship was rare. An element had never even seen an electrical appliance in their lives and brought significant Third World health problems with them to Israel.[50]

The biggest issue was a cultural and mental one. The 1930s had shown, to use Jacob Talmon's felicitous phrase, that, for the European immigrants, "the world was now divided into countries which wanted to get rid of the Jews and countries which did not want to let them in." As Talmon continued:

> Wooed at one time as a community of vast influence and accepted then as an ally, the Jews had shrunk to the status of hunted animals and unwanted refugees . . . And as their needs grew more desperate, the power of the Jews continued to decline . . . Humiliated, betrayed, forsaken, the Jews were left almost entirely defenseless before Hitler's genocidal campaign . . . A whole people was surrendered to an assassin with the sole stipulation that every member of it, every man, woman and child, healthy or sick, normal or paralyzed, should be put to death, individually or collectively, by the bullet of a thug or in specially built human abattoirs, after being starved, tortured, flushed out from every hiding place and brought to the factories of death from the remotest corner of Hitler's empire . . . The Allies were far away . . . There was no judge to

appeal to for redress, no government to turn to for protection, no neighbor from whom to ask for succor, no God to pray for mercy.[51]

The 350,000 Holocaust survivors who came to Israel after the war were mentally and physically exhausted and beaten. They had been expelled from their homes, lost most or all of their families, been robbed of their assets and been battered physically and mentally.[52] Always before them would be the horrors of the hiding places, the hatred of their neighbors, the roundups, the trains, the dogs, the camps and the extermination chambers, and the fates of their families. A common "survivors' syndrome" entailed perpetual anxiety, symptoms of isolation and withdrawal, psychosomatic incidents and frequent signs of trauma. Most Holocaust victims, often in poor physical and mental condition, showed signs of a desire to be left alone, a survivor's guilt for being alive when so many close relatives and friends had died, a feeling of total abandonment, helplessness, uprooted adolescence, shame, and destruction of security and self-identity. All this complicated the task of making use of their talents and energies in the new Israel.[53]

The 650,000 largely poorly educated Sephardi immigrants from North Africa and the Middle East were not well prepared for life in Israel. As second-class *dhimmis* (Peoples of the Book), their lives with limited rights in Arab lands and Iran left them fearful, passive and apolitical. The *dhimmis* had lived in ghettos (*mellahs*), where they paid higher taxes than Muslims, wore special distinctive clothes, owned smaller houses and had no ability to own horses.[54]

The Sephardim resented their treatment by the Ashkenazim.[55] When they arrived, they were sprayed with insecticide and sent to live in primitive huts and tents. They were disproportionately sent to do menial labor in villages and remote and inaccessible areas that created a double marginality, both socio-economic and geographic.[56] Their ancient culture was often derided as obsolete by Ashkenazi Labor-dominated government emissaries.[57] Most immigrants wound up in *ma'abaroth* (tent cities with many wooden shacks). Once given apartments, they typically received tiny apartments of 8–35 square meters with 1.5–2 rooms.

Israelis cheered as 49,000 Yemenites, who had been in Arabia for 1,500 years, came on Operation Magic Carpet in 1949 and 1950. Most of the poorly educated, largely rural Yemenite Jews were in poor physical shape, with the average adult male weighing but 80 pounds. Tuberculosis, venereal diseases and bilharzia were common, while many children suffered from malnutrition.[58]

Israelis also cheered as the Ethiopians arrived against great odds (4,000 of them died crossing the desert into Sudan). But absorbing 70,000 Ethiopians, with 20,000 more Falash Mura waiting in Ethiopia, has proved a daunting task. The great majority of them lived in rural areas raising cattle in extended patriarchal families. With poor education and health, they faced further traumas in the camps in Addis Ababa and on the long journey to Israel. Today, 70 percent of the adults are unemployed in modern Israel.[59]

Few Jewish immigrants had democratic experience and many no industrial experience. Most were poor and many were in poor health. Most did not speak Hebrew or relate to Zionist ideas. How could they overcome the ingrained habits of centuries and effectively enter the modern world? As Israel Zangwill put it in *Children of the Ghetto*:

> People who have been living in a ghetto for a couple of centuries are not able to step outside merely because the gates are thrown down, nor to efface the brands on their souls by putting off the yellow badges. The isolation imposed from without will have to come to seem the law of their being.[60]

Given the threats from their neighbors, Israel had to create a strong military with a citizen army. Before emancipation in the nineteenth century, Jews had been barred from citizenship and participation in warfare. In World War I, 1.5 million Jews served in the armies and 140,000 were killed. But few served as officers or general staff officers.[61]

Israel's first prime minister, David Ben Gurion, was concerned about Jewish ability to adapt to statehood, for "Exile has planted into us a distrust of all governments. We were a people perpetually in opposition to all government, because we were not in control of our own fate." He saw the Jews before and after 1948 as akin to the Jews wandering for 40 years in the wilderness after the exodus from Egypt but before arriving in the Promised Land. They brought slave features with them even as they escaped from slavery, for:

> The people of Israel has not yet been sufficiently imbued with political state-like consciousness and responsibility as befits a self-governing nation . . . a people used to Exile, oppressed, lacking independence for thousands of years, does not change overnight by fiat or by a declaration of independence . . . Most of our public knows how to demand from the state more than a hundred percent of what it owes the state . . . In our country even personal manners are deficient.[62]

There was one saving element – the violent and turbulent experiences of explosive anti-Semitism, war, revolution and migration showed most Jewish immigrants that their old strategies for survival were now unbearable and often irrelevant. Their experiences of flight and persecution prepared them for a brave new world that Israel, with a Jewish majority, promised to build for them.[63]

Divisions within the Jewish people

Although there were numerous rivals to Zionism from outside the movement (Communism, Socialism, Bundism, assimilation, religiosity), there were many divisions within Zionism as well. There were profound differences between religious Zionists (Mizrahi), socialist Zionists (Mapai), revisionist Jews (Herut) and liberal Zionists (General Zionists). Even within these categories there were sharp differences between ultra-orthodox and orthodox Jews and between Communist and socialist Jews (who also came in several varieties). Secular squared off versus religious, Ashkenazim versus Sephardim, socialists versus bourgeoisie, assimilation versus deeply Jewish commitment, and culturalists (Ahad Haam) versus practical (Chaim Weizmann).

There were deep arguments over what Zionism meant. Was it the creation of a utopia or simply another nation state? Should the state be a deeply Jewish state or simply a state of the Jews? Was the goal political rejuvenation after 1,800 years or a cultural revival? Could the Jewish state be discarded if it didn't work? Did this mean the beginning of the End of History since it meant a manmade solution to the lengthy Exile? The divisions within Zionism reflected the fact that "many of the weaknesses of the Zionist movement were so many reflections of the internal weaknesses, the fissiparity and heterogeneity of the Jewish people."[64]

Creating a Jewish state with an impoverished Zionist movement

The financial resources at the disposal of both the immigrants and the international Zionist movement were weak. Joseph Chaim Brenner's denunciation of the Diaspora Zionist movement as nothing more than "verbal Zionism" seemed apt.[65] Theodor Herzl dreamed of tapping the wealth of a small class of rich Jews to buy a charter for the Jews from Ottoman Turkey and to support the development of Jewish communities in Palestine. Yet, with few exceptions, the wealthy Jews were neither Zionists nor willing to give. In 1907 the budget of the Zionist Organization was $20,000, equal to the yearly spending of a single wealthy German or British family. The Jewish National Fund in 1907 had only $250,000 to spend, an "extremely limited" amount.[66] In 1920 Keren Hayesod pledged to raise over $125 million for development in the next five years: instead it barely raised $15 million in six years. The budget of the 1933 World Zionist Congress was less than $1 million, which allowed them to buy only 11,000 acres in the next 20 months.[67]

In the mid-1930s, at the height of the Great Depression, the budget of the World Zionist Organization was significantly smaller that that of any major Diaspora community. The Zionist Organization of America in 1932 had 8,400 members and, even by 1939, 43,000 members with minimal donations. In 1935 less than 10 percent of world Jews belonged to the Zionist movement. The numbers ranged from 33 percent in Palestine, 20–30 percent in Lithuania and Latvia, 10 percent in Poland to only 3 percent in the United States.[68] Only after the Holocaust did the number reach 200,000 in 1945. Walter Laqueur has noted:

> The freedom of action of the Zionist movement was severely circumscribed by its extreme poverty; land could not be bought, sufficient

support could not be given to immigrants and funds for political work in Palestine and in the Diaspora were altogether inadequate.[69]

The prospects for Zionism, financially strapped with small numbers and smaller funds, seemed hopeless before World War II and the Holocaust. The weakness of the Zionist movement before 1940, the backwardness of Palestine, the divisions within the Jewish people, their poverty and trad-itionalism, the traumas and the attractions of other parties or countries all boded ill for the success of the enterprise. And yet, despite the massive losses suffered during the Holocaust, the tentative shoots of Zionist socialism would blossom in the post-war world, providing the impetus for the success of the First Socialist Revolution in the first 30 years of statehood.

5 Hostility of the major powers

A major problem for new states is the implacable hostility of other states. For the Armenians the hatred of the Turks and dislike of the Russians were a major hindrance in creating a state for generations. For the Kurds the hostility of four major Middle Eastern states (Iran, Iraq, Turkey and Syria) helped prevent the emergence of an independent Kurdistan. For Lebanese Christians, the hostility of the Muslim world ultimately destroyed their state. For Israel, the hostility of the Ottoman Turkish Empire, Tsarist Russia, the British Empire (1937–49), the Soviet Union, Nazi Germany and the bulk of the Arab world was a massive problem for the creation and flourishing of Israel. While it can have some positive effects (promoting internal cohesion and immigration to Israel), its negative effects are serious. Michael Oren has observed that, after generations of powerlessness, the Jews had to confront "immense forces" arrayed against Israel that posed "existential challenges" to its very creation and existence.[1] Joel Migdal, who was more sanguine about the impact of foreign threats on Israel, has written:

> Outside enemies, of course, can have the most devastating impact on the ability of leaders to achieve their goals of state predominance within a given territory. In the worst of circumstances, they can militarily defeat the state and its leaders and demand the most drastic sorts of changes. Even in less severe circumstances, they can cripple the state's domestic control through war economic sanctions and more. They can also aid directly those internal groups that are struggling with the state for social control.[2]

The hostility of the Ottoman Turkish Empire (1881–1917)

While the popular image of the Ottoman Turkish Empire in its last decades was as "the sick man of Europe" cutting a slightly ridiculous figure, it possessed enough power to destroy the Zionist enterprise. Even on its last legs during World War I, the Ottoman Turks massacred 600,000 to 1.5 million Armenians, defeated Britain and France at Gallipoli and Iraq and stopped a Russian invasion force.

Under Ottoman Turkish rule, the population of Palestine, during a time of rapid growth elsewhere, remained 300,000 in 1517 and 1817. There were 6,000 Jews in 1517 and 1838. Political instability, economic decline and hostility to Jews threatened the Palestinian Jewish community with bankruptcy or expulsion. It was a traditional, artificial community, dependent on foreign subsidies and "constant vigilance" to ward off greedy threats from Ottoman Turkish officials or hostile neighbors. This kept the pre-Zionist community small, dependent, pious and frightened.[3]

The Ottoman Turkish Empire, especially Sultan Abdul Hamid II (1876–1908) and his Young Turk successors (1908–18) opposed the Jewish desire to create their own state.

Having lost Balkan territory (1878) and Muslim territory (Egypt and Tunisia in 1882 and 1883) to European imperialism, Sultan Abdul Hamid feared the Jewish nationalists seeking to wrench away Palestine. He resented the Jews, who came largely from Russia, which wanted to destroy Ottoman Turkey. He feared Europeans who imposed the Capitulations (foreign concessions and extra-territoriality). The Sultan opposed working with the Jews, who seemed to lack the money to make such a deal worthwhile.[4]

From 1882 to 1918 Ottoman Turkey repeatedly restricted Jewish immigration and purchase of land. In 1881 the Porte announced that Jews could immigrate to the empire anywhere except Palestine. They could not come in groups or receive privileges and must become Ottoman Turkish citizens. In 1882 Jews were banned from the four holy cities (Jerusalem, Safed, Tiberias and Hebron). Only in 1888 did Ottoman Turkey officially allow some Jewish immigration. In 1891 the Porte tried again to close the empire to all Russian Jews. In 1892 and from 1897 to 1902 the Mutasarrif of Jerusalem banned land sales to Jews. In 1893 it tried to get Russia to not allow Jews passage on ships bound to Ottoman Turkey. In 1899 the Mufti of Jerusalem called for the expulsion of Jewish newcomers to the land. In 1900 the government announced that only Muslims could settle in Jerusalem. In 1901 there were new restrictions on immigration and land sales. In 1906 the Ottoman Turkish authorities levied heavy taxes on Jewish settlements and stopped construction of some plants. In 1908 the Young Turks renewed a ban on land sales to Jews.[5]

The Jews, who bribed Turkish officials and gained protection from European consuls, achieved some success. The 24,000 Jews in 1882 rose to 70,000–80,000 Jews in 1908. By 1910 the Jews, who owned less than 2 percent of the land, were 10 percent of the local population.[6]

In 1914, with the revoking of Capitulations to European powers and Turkey's entering the war, this protection was gone. As most Palestinian Jews held foreign (mostly Russian) passports, Jews were seen as alien elements. Already harmed by the siege of Turkey and the decline of the Ottoman Turkish Empire, the Yishuv was cut off from overseas markets and its supportive Diaspora. By the middle of 1916 the exigencies of war would leave 75 percent of Palestinian Jews on social welfare.[7]

In December 1914 the aging Turkish governor of Jaffa, Beha-a-Din, ordered the expulsion of the 6,000 Jews living in the city. That month 12,000 Jews were expelled to Alexandria and 500 recent immigrants were expelled from Palestine.[8] In 1915 many Jews were sent to punitive and even dangerous labor service. After the disastrous Turkish campaign against the British in early 1915, its commander, Djemal Pasha, appointed Beha-a-Din as his "secretary for Jewish affairs." He closed the Anglo-Palestine Bank, Zionist newspapers, schools and political offices, banned Zionist public activities and encouraged Arabs to attack Jewish villages. Zionist leaders, such as David Ben Gurion and Yizhak Ben-Zvi, were sent into exile. Hundreds of Jewish youths in "labor battalions" were marched off in chains to prisons or forced labor in Damascus; others were exiled to Brusa, Constantinople and the pits of Tarsus. By March 1915, 10,000 Palestinian Jews were exiled to Egypt, half of them in refugee camps.

Only the intervention of the German Foreign Minister, Arthur von Zimmerman, and the United States Ambassador to Ottoman Turkey, Henry Morgenthau, prevented disaster in 1915. But, with the British invasion of Palestine in early 1917 and the discovery of the pro-Allied Aaronsohn spy ring, the situation of the Jews again turned dire. In 1917 the 7,000 Jews of Jaffa and Tel Aviv were expelled and marched towards the north to an uncertain fate.[9] Only the intervention of the German foreign ministry, German diplomats in Istanbul and General von Falkenhayn prevented the Turks from expelling the Jews of Jerusalem in 1917. Suffering from starvation and disease, only one-third of Jerusalem Jews remained in Jerusalem by the end of 1917.[10]

Hunger and disease decimated the Old Yishuv of Jerusalem, Safed and Hebron. Only the rapid British military advance into Palestine, taking Jaffa (November 1917) and Jerusalem (December 1917), saved the Yishuv from total disaster. As Sachar related:

> The rejoicing [in Jerusalem and Tel Aviv] was premature. With the winter rains, Allenby's campaign stalled and Jews in northern Palestine remained hostages under Turkish military rule. Their last remnants of security were gone by then, for Ottoman troops began indiscriminately confiscating Jewish farms, and arms deserters by the thousands ran amok, terrorizing Jewish settlements, looting property, even killing. It was during the final phase of Turkish occupation in Palestine that the Yishuv endured its worst torment. By the time the British resumed their offensive in the spring, and ultimately overran the last of the enemy's forces in September 1918, the Jewish population had been reduced from its pre-war figure of 85,000 to less than 55,000. Of those lost, between 8,000 and 10,000 had perished of hunger, illness and exposure.[11]

The hostility of Tsarist Russia

Tsarist anti-Semitism, reflected in 650 anti-Jewish laws, repeated pogroms, expulsions, massive social, economic and administrative discrimination, creation of the Pale of Settlement, Black Hundreds, blood libels and popular slogans ("Beat the Jews and Save Russia"), left the Jews powerless without national communal organizations to defend themselves.[12] Anti-Semitism was deep and pervasive. As Pyotr Stolypin, chairman of the Russian Council of Ministers, declaimed:

> We can observe them [the Jews] the way we observe and study animals, we can feel disgust for them or hostility, the way we do for the hyena, the jackal or the spider, but to speak of hatred for them would raise them to our level ... Only by disseminating in the popular consciousness the concept that the creature of the Jewish race is not the same as other people but an imitation of a human with whom there can be no dealings, only that can gradually heal the natural organism and weaken the Jewish nation so it will no longer be able to do harm or will completely die out. History knows of many extinct tribes. Science must put not the Jewish race but the character of Jewry into such conditions as will make it perish.[13]

The authorities banned formal Zionist organizations, and in 1907 the Zionist Organization was declared illegal. In 1908 there were numerous arrests of Zionists and the stopping of their fundraising. In 1910, in an empire of 5–6 million Jews, there were only 70,000–100,000 members of Zionist organizations. By 1913 there were 150 trials of Zionists.[14] During World War I hundreds of thousands of Russian Jews were expelled from border areas into the interior. Hundreds of Russian Jews were executed on charges of treason; others were taken as hostages or subjected to pogroms.[15]

The growing hostility of the British Empire (1920–49)

The British embrace of the Jews during the Balfour Declaration and early period of British rule of Palestine didn't last and ultimately proved nearly fatal. Throughout the interwar period, there were conflicts between pro-Jewish forces (early British leaders, the Colonial Office, led in the 1930s by W. G. A. Ormsby-Gore) and anti-Jewish forces (military leaders, the Foreign Office, led in the 1930s by Anthony Eden). There were also conflicts between those who wanted to rule as cheaply as possible and those who had a broader strategic view. Many forces pushed in an anti-Jewish direction: British anti-Semitism, the ouster of Lloyd George in October 1922, the British imperial need to control the Middle East to protect the vital oil routes, Iraq, the emirates and the Suez Canal, the need to gain support from the predominantly Arab Middle East and Muslims worldwide, the strategic importance of Palestine, the need to propitiate the Arab majority in Palestine and the improbability that the Jews would ever have a state.[16]

Enthralled by the romance of the Arab East (Lawrence of Arabia), many in the British elite found Arabs physically attractive, hospitable, courteous and friendly to an extent that the Western Jews were not. By contrast, they often detested the "bad and tiresome tribe deniers of Christ and eternal wanderers, often obnoxious."[17] During World War I the "London [government] believed in powerful, mysterious Jewish societies."[18]

The British military administration (1918–20) refused to publish the Balfour Declaration in Palestine.[19] By April 1920, when Arab riots inside the Old City of Jerusalem killed some Jews and injured several hundreds, the rioters shouted "The government is with us!," while Arabs in the British police joined the Arab rioters and British police stayed outside the walls of the Old City. British army units prevented Jewish forces from patrolling the Old City and sentenced their leader Vladimir Jabotinsky to 15 years at hard labor in the Acre prison. British officials were often more comfortable with the Arabs than the more Europeanized Jews.[20]

In May 1921, when Arab rioters killed 42 Jews and attacked Jewish farm colonies, they received light sentences.[21] The British inquiry blamed the Jews and their immigration for causing the riots.[22] The British civilian government (created July 1920) created a largely Arab police force and government bureaucracy.[23] When British authorities restricted Jewish land purchases in the 1920s and 1930s, this forced the Jews to pay high prices to Arab landowners. Even by 1939 the Jews owned only 5 percent of Palestine.[24]

In 1922 the Churchill White Paper proposed limited Jewish immigration, created Transjordan and rejected the idea of Jewish statehood. In 1922 the House of Lords voted to revoke the Balfour Declaration but the House of Commons restored it.[25] The British civilian administration, by appointing the radical nationalist Haj Amin Al-Hussein as Grand Mufti of Jerusalem, discouraged moderate Arab elements.[26]

The growing Arab struggle against the Jews, the rising European threat from Nazi Germany and Fascist Italy, the British involvement in the Arab Middle East and the fear that their days were numbered turned the British against their former allies. The Arab riots of 1929 led to the 1930 Passfield White Paper, which urged restrictions on Jewish immigration and land sales and retracted the promise that the Jews could develop Palestine.[27]

The Arab Revolt (1936–39) pushed the British against the Jews. In 1936 the British did little to stop the Jaffa riots or over 2,000 attacks on the Jews. As the attacks grew increasingly anti-British, they began to react in kind. By 1937 the Peel Commission called for an Arab state, with 80 percent of Palestinian territory, and a small Jewish state. The Arab Revolt, as in 1921 and 1929, led to further concessions to Arab radicalism and terror. While in the mid–1930s 45,000 Jews arrived yearly, in the late 1930s the British, despite the looming Holocaust, cut immigration to 13,000 Jews a year.[28]

The 1939 British White Paper abolished the Mandate and Balfour Declaration, calling for the creation of an Arab Palestine in 1949 and the limiting of Jewish immigration to 15,000 a year for five years and then zero if the Arabs opposed it. Land purchases by Jews would be banned in some areas and restricted by others. The House of Commons approved the White Paper by 268 to 179.[29] As Prime Minister Neville Chamberlain asserted in April 1939:

> We were now compelled to consider the Palestine problem mainly from the point of view of its effects on the international situation. It was of immense importance, as Lord Chatfield had pointed out, to have the Moslem world with us. If we must offend one side, let us offend the Jews rather than the Arabs.[30]

Strategic geography (guarding the route to India and the Far East), oil (for war) and numbers guided the British decision to close the doors to Palestine for the Jews.[31] At the March 1939 St. James Conference in London the British assured the Arabs of their support after the war for a bi-national unitary state with a permanent Arab majority.[32] The 1939 White Paper and conference doomed hopes of creating a small Jewish state which could absorb hundreds of thousands or even millions of Jews anxious to flee Europe.[33] While in 1936 Chaim Weizmann thought 700,000–1,000,000 Jews could be brought to Palestine, David Ben Gurion estimated there were 2–5 million Jews who could be saved.[34] The British turned back ships bearing tens of thousands of Jewish refugees, arrested Haganah members, confiscated arms and stopped new settlements.[35]

In 1940 new land regulations prevented Jews from buying land in 95 percent of Palestine. In November 1940, 250 Jews on the SS *Patria* drowned in Haifa Bay, and in February 1942 over 750 Jews were lost in the Black Sea on the SS *Struma*. Although during the war Palestinian Jews sided with the British and 120,000 Jews volunteered to fight for the British Empire, the British mounted raids on kibbutzim. Jews caught trying to immigrate to Palestine were sent to camps in places like Mauritius where conditions were harsh.[36]

When Jews volunteered for the British army in 1940, they were initially made laborers at low pay. Even when they volunteered for dangerous commando missions to Syria, Iraq and East Africa (with casualty rates exceeding 50 percent), the British treated them with contempt. Only in January 1944 did the British allow the creation of a Jewish Brigade of 24,000 Jews to serve in various police and paramilitary units at home and in Italy.[37] In June 1941, British troops, camped outside of Baghdad after the demise of pro-fascist Prime Minister Rashid Ali, did little to stop the riot that killed 150 Jews, wounded 450 others and inflicted £800,000 of damage on Jewish property.[38] In 1943 and 1944 the British helped sponsor the new Arab League, which called for an Arab Palestine.[39]

Motivated by anger at the Jewish desire to expel them from Palestine, anti-Semitism, Jewish terrorism and fear of a Communist Israel, Britain after the war opposed the creation of Israel.[40] The new British Labor foreign secretary, Ernest Bevin, in 1945 characterized the American view as "let there be an Israel and to hell with the consequences."[41] Richard Crossman remembered that Bevin "added that he would not be surprised if the Germans had learned their worst atrocities from Jews."[42]

In 1945 the British government rejected allowing 100,000 European Jewish refugees into Palestine. In June 1946 tens of thousands of British soldiers arrested hundreds of members of the Jewish Agency and Haganah officers and over 3,000 other Jews but uncovered only one arms cache, at Kibbutz Yagur. By 1947 the British maintained 80,000 troops and 16,000 British and local police units in a country of fewer than 2 million people. Enormous army and police structures were erected at a cost of £2 million. Massive arrests, curfews, deportation and fences were aimed at destroying the nascent Jewish army and will to fight.

While many Jews were eager to come to Palestine (700,000 would arrive from 1948 to 1951), the British kept them away at a critical juncture in 1947 and 1948. The British kept 40,000 Jews in Cyprus camps and many of 250,000 Jews in European detention camps and 600,000 Sephardim in the Middle East from coming to Palestine. They did little to stop 5,000 Arab irregulars from infiltrating Palestine by January 1948.[43] After the United Nations voted 33–13 to create Arab and Jewish states in Palestine in November 1947, the British refused to cooperate with the Jewish Agency. The British:

> wished to see a far smaller and weaker Jewish state than that envisaged by the UN Partition Resolution and did its utmost to bring about such an eventuality . . . to cut Israel "down to size" and to stunt its future population growth through the prevention of future Jewish immigration . . . British policy-makers sought to forestall an Israeli–Tran Jordanian peace agreement unless it detached the Negev from the Israeli State.[44]

The British maintained a strict embargo on Jewish immigration and weapons acquisition until their departure in May 1948. While the British released Arabs caught with weapons, Jews caught with illegal weapons were sentenced to jail. While the British did little about local Arab armies, they carried out customs inspections against Jewish imports and raided kibbutzim looking for weapons.[45] They turned a blind eye to the Arab blockade of Jerusalem (which left civilians eating 1,000 calories a day), and Arab movement into the Galilee and Jaffa threatening Tel Aviv. In March 1948 they disarmed surviving Jewish soldiers after the loss of the Etzion bloc. The British removed Palestine from the sterling bloc and abrogated arrangements for the supply of vital commodities.[46] In February 1948 they approved £300,000 for the Supreme Muslim Council.

In April 1948, soon after the Deir Yassin massacre of over 100 Arabs, Jerusalem Arabs killed 78 Jewish doctors and nurses on the road to Mount Scopus. British forces, five minutes away, refused to intervene for seven hours despite pleas from the Jewish Agency, Haganah, Hebrew University and Hadassah Hospital. British convoys passed the vehicles with the medical personnel and did nothing.[47]

The invading Jordanian Arab Legion had 7,400 Arab soldiers led by many British officers, 24 cannons and 45 armored cars. British weapons and ammunition were sold to pro-British allies such as Egypt, Jordan and Iraq. While a few strategic points were handed to the Jews, the army camps at

Sarafand, Tel Litwinsky, Lydda Airport and Latrun and cities such as Safed were handed over to the Arabs.[48]

The British pressured the United States to maintain its arms embargo against Israel. Its naval blockade prevented arms from reaching Israel and Jewish youth from reaching Israel until May 1948. The British fought to detach the Negev from Israel, to prevent a Jewish land corridor from the coast to Jerusalem, to maintain control of the port of Haifa and to push the transfer of the Eastern Galilee to Syria. Britain did not recognize Israel until nine months after May 1948 and fought Israel's admission to the United Nations.[49]

In 1948 Great Britain imposed an oil embargo on Israel. In November 1948, the British drafted a United Nations resolution negating Israeli gains and proposing to hand over southern Palestine to the Arabs. In December 1948 Great Britain abstained on a United Nations vote recognizing the state of Israel. In January 1949 near El Arish, the two sides nearly came to blows. The Israelis shot down five British planes in the Sinai, and Britain threatened to invoke its treaties with Egypt and Jordan. After the Israelis withdrew from the Sinai, the British recognized Israel.[50]

After 1948 the British maintained their treaties with Iraq and Jordan, which were hostile to Israel, and Sir John Glubb Pasha ran the Jordanian Arab Legion until 1956. In 1955, when negotiating the withdrawal from the Suez Canal, the British did not negotiate freedom of passage for Israel through the canal.[51] In 1955, with their mutual defense treaty with Jordan, British commanders drew up plans for bombing major Israeli cities and Israeli airfields. In the run-up to the 1956 Sinai Campaign the British had operational plans (Operation Cordage) to come to Jordan's aid by bombing Israeli airfields, laying a naval siege and attacking Israeli naval bases from the sea.[52] While the British alliance with Israel during the 1956 Sinai Campaign changed the tone of the relationship, it lasted only a brief time. Overall, the British Empire, then a great power and even a superpower, posed grave obstacles to the creation of Israel.

Dangerous enmity of Nazi Germany (1933–45)

The rise of Adolf Hitler to power in Germany in 1933 created a massive threat to Zionist plans. Germany was the greatest military, economic, scientific and technological power in Europe. The Nazi desire to destroy the "Judeo-Bolshevik conspiracy" had to be taken seriously by 400,000 Palestinian Jews who lacked even a state. Hitler tried and nearly succeeded in killing all 10 million European Jews, destroying the Palestinian Jewish Yishuv and mobilizing European and Arab support against Palestinian Jewry.

Even as Hitler was going down to defeat in 1944 and 1945 he continued to destroy European Jewry. This was seen in the killing of 500,000 Hungarian Jews in 1944 and the continuation of the concentration camps when their transport and personnel were needed for the war effort. In Prague the Nazis constructed a Museum of the Extinct People to show their victory over the now defunct Jews.[53]

The Afrika Korps under Field Marshal Erwin Rommel in North Africa from 1940 to 1943 nearly destroyed the British Empire and Jewish homeland in Palestine. As David Ben Gurion warned Felix Frankfurter in a memorandum in 1942:

> The invasion [of Palestine] by Hitler, even temporarily, may result in the complete annihilation of the Jewish community there – men, women and children – and the total destruction of their workers by the Nazis with the help of the Mufti. To the Jewish people throughout the world, this will mean more than the massacre of some 600,000 Jews; it will be the ruin of their Third Temple; the destruction of their Holy of Holies.[54]

The impact of fascist anti-Semitism was enduring. Many European Jews, even after liberation in May 1945, were afraid to return to their homes. In the Middle East the impact was powerful, for as Bernard Lewis observed:

> But the poison continued to spread and from 1933 Nazi Germany and its various agencies made a concerted and on the whole remarkably successful effort to promote and disseminate European style anti-Semitism in the Arab world. The struggle for Palestine greatly facilitated the acceptance of the anti-Semitic interpretation of history, and led some to blame all evil in the Middle East and indeed in the world on secret Jewish plots. This interpretation has pervaded much of the public discourse in the region, including education, the media and even entertainment.[55]

The Nazis killed almost 80 percent of the 7.8 million Jews living between the Atlantic sea ports and the borders of the furthest German advance into the Soviet Union. In Auschwitz, Treblinka, Dachau, Bergen-Belsen, Majdanek and dozens of other concentration camps created for the "final solution" of the "Jewish question," Jews were murdered through being worked to death, starvation, diseases, beatings, shootings or gassing.[56] By 1945 the 500,000 survivors typically weighed 60–80 pounds and faced severe mental torture. Those who had fled to the Soviet Union and the West or gone into hiding were also scarred for life. During the war only 90,000 European Jews reached Palestine.

The Holocaust largely eliminated the Jewish reservoirs of future immigrants to Israel. Poland, which had 3,300,000 Jews in 1938, had fewer than 300,000 Jews by 1945. Hungary, which had 650,000 Jews in 1940, had fewer than 150,000 Jews in 1945. Germany, which had 520,000 Jews in 1938, had fewer than 30,000 Jews in 1945. The 16 million Jews in the world in 1940 were now barely 10 million Jews by 1945. Nearly half were in the affluent United States. With a low Jewish birth rate, the number of Jews would never regain its pre-war high, topping off at 13 million in 2007.

Given the Arab population, which grew from 50 million Arabs in 1950 to 285 million Arabs in 2007, and Palestinian population, which grew from 1.2 million Palestinians in 1950 to almost 8 million Palestinians in 2007, this was a huge loss, not only morally and ethically but strategically as well.[57]

Today we can hardly capture the feelings of the survivors. Perhaps only poetry and literature can come close. Paul Celan (1920–70), a Rumanian Jew whose parents were killed in the Holocaust, who spent time in a labor camp and later committed suicide, came closest in his poem "Death Fugue":

> Black milk of dawn we drink it at dusk
> We drink it at noon and at daybreak we drink it at night
> We drink it and drink it
> We are digging a grave in the air there's room for all
> A man lives in the house he plays with the serpents he writes
> He writes when it darkens to Germany your golden hair Margarete
> He writes it and steps outside and the stars all glisten he whistles for his
>   hounds
> He whistles for the Jews he then digs a grave in the earth
> He commands us to play for the dance
>
> Black milk at dawn we drink you at night
> We drink you at daybreak and noon we drink you at dusk
> We drink and we drink
> A man lives in the house he plays with the serpents he writes
> He writes when it darkens to Germany your golden hair Margarete
> Your ashen hair Shulamite we are digging a grave in the air there's room
>   for us all
>
> He shouts cut deeper in the earth to some the rest of you sing and play
> He reaches for the iron in his belt he heaves it his eyes are blue
> Make your spades cut deeper the rest of you play for the dance . . .
>
> Black milk of dawn we drink you at night
> We drink you at noon death is a master from Germany
> We drink you at dusk and at daybreak we drink and we drink you
> Death is a master from Germany his eye is blue
> He shoots you with bullets of lead his aim is true
> A man lives in the house your golden hair Margarete
> He sets his hounds on us he gives us a grave in the air
> He plays with the serpents and dreams death is a master from Germany
>
> Your golden hair Margarete
> Your ashen hair Shulamite[58]

Would there be a need for a Jewish state after the Holocaust? Jewish Agency representative Arthur Lichtheim wrote to Nahum Goldmann, President of the World Jewish Congress, in September 1942:

The most optimistic forecast today is that 1½ million [Jews] may survive
. . . the basis of Zionism, as it was preached during the last 50 years, has
gone . . . The main argument was that 4 or 5 or 6 million in Eastern
Europe need and want a home in Palestine . . . After the victory of the
Allied Nations there can be no problem in resettling this small number of
surviving Jews in that "freed" and "Democratic" (or Communist?)
Europe of tomorrow where they will be given equality of rights.[59]

In 1948 David Ben Gurion lamented, "For thousands of years we were a
nation without a state. Now there is a danger that Israel will be a state
without a nation."[60] After World War I, several great powers had seen the
Jews as allies. With the destruction of the important European Jewish community, the victorious Allies of World War II had little interest in the Jews. In
1945 the Jews were not invited to attend the opening San Francisco meeting
of the new United Nations. The Allies, as seen by Roosevelt's 1945 meeting
with Saudi King Ibn Saud, courted the more powerful Arabs.[61]

The hostility of the Soviet Union

The hostility of superpowers like the Soviet Union posed huge problems for
Israel. Such powers, with their nuclear, massive conventional and technical
capacity, predominance in the world order, permanent membership in the
United Nations Security Council and far-flung influence throughout the
world, left small states such as Israel with minimal margins of error to avoid
catastrophe. The Soviet Union destroyed the Zionist movement at home,
exported tens of billions of dollars' worth of arms to anti-Israeli Arab states,
and prevented over a million Jews from immigrating to Israel before and
after 1948. Only 103,000 Soviet Jews went to Israel from 1917 to 1972, less
than 5 percent of all immigrants.[62] After the 1955 Czech arms deal, Soviet
involvement in the Middle East grew until by 1980 it supplied and trained
most major Arab armies, including the Egyptian, Syrian, Iraqi, Libyan,
Algerian and Yemenite armies. It pushed the Arab cause at the United
Nations, provided economic aid and put military pressure on Israel.[63]

Marxism, anti-Semitism, oil and a desire to gain a foothold in the Arab
Middle East contributed to the Soviet hostility towards Israel. Marxist ideology was notably hostile to Zionism and Israel. As Robert Wistrich has
observed:

Marxists have frequently argued that the survival of the Jewish collectivity
– whether in a purely religious, a national or a state form – is politically
reactionary. They have followed . . . the young Marx who dismissed
Judaism as a wholly negative phenomenon . . . anti-Semitism was a temporary and secondary phenomenon; with its dissipation the last factor
encouraging the "illusory" national cohesion of the Jews would also
fade.[64]

Lenin, condemning anti-Semitism and pogroms, called for Jewish assimilation and attacked Jewish nationalism and Zionism. Stalin in 1913 stressed that Jews, lacking a common territory or culture, were not a nation worthy of national self-determination.[65]

In 1917 a powerful Russian Zionist movement, with 1,200 branches with 300,000 members, became "the dominant political force among the Jews," with Zionists outnumbering Bolsheviks on the Jewish street by more than 50 to 1.[66] In Odessa on the occasion of the issuance of the Balfour Declaration, a two-mile-long march of 150,000 Odessa Jews passed the British consulate singing the British and Jewish anthems.[67] A Ukrainian Jew in Kiev remembered that:

> From early morning thousands of Jews, dressed in their holiday clothes and Zionist emblems, streamed to the university campus on Vladimir Street. All balconies of Jewish homes were decorated in blue and white. Three military bands marched at the head of the parades and Zionist flags flew above . . . The British consul . . . received a bouquet of flowers and expressed his gratitude in an emotional voice.[68]

In January 1918 the Zionists won 60 percent of the vote to the Jewish Congress. In some centers, such as Minsk, the Zionists (65,000 votes) trounced the socialists (11,000).[69] At the time that several million Russian Jews were turning towards Palestine, the Bolsheviks came to power determined to destroy such movements. Although they initially moved slowly, they liquidated the movement within seven to ten years. Hebrew language classes, newspapers and libraries, Zionist organizations and farms preparing Russian youth to immigrate to Israel were banned by 1924, and Jewish religious institutions were severely under attack. By 1924 several thousand Zionists were in exile, special prisons or camps, and the next year several thousand Zionists were under arrest.[70]

Almost echoing the old Bundist proposals for autonomy, the Soviet regime recognized Jews as a nationality, created a Jewish Section of the Communist Party of the Soviet Union (Evsektsiia), and allowed a flowering of Yiddish schools, institutes, publishing houses, newspapers and theaters. By the late 1920s the Zionist movement lay in ruins.[71]

In the 1930s Joseph Stalin, Georgii Chicherin and Maxim Litvinov created the Siberian Palestine (Birobidzhan), which attracted tens of thousands of Jews to the Far East. The near Arctic climate, wilderness and swamps, geographic isolation from Europe and lack of Jewish roots doomed it. During the Great Purges, Stalin liquidated the remaining Zionist leaders, the leaders of the Evsektsiia and the organizers of Birobidzhan.

After the relatively liberal World War II interlude (including the creation of the Jewish Anti-Fascist Committee), Stalin unleashed anti-Semitic purges in Eastern Europe including Czechoslovakia (Stansky trial) and Rumania (Ana Pauker trial). The final years of his life (1948–53) were the "black years of

Soviet Jewry" which saw the disbanding of the Jewish Anti-Fascist Committee, the closing of all Yiddish schools, the shooting of 30 Jewish poets and thousands of Jewish intellectuals, the murder of the famous theater director Solomon Mikhoels (head of the Jewish Anti-Fascist Committee) and the massive firing of Jews. The 1953 Doctors Plot involved nine doctors (six of them Jews) accused of trying to poison Stalin and other party leaders. Stalin ordered the preparation of labor camps in Siberia for the deportation of Jews of Moscow and Leningrad, but he died before this could occur.[72]

In September 1948 Israel's first Ambassador to the Soviet Union, Golda Meir, arrived in Moscow in time for High Holiday services:

> The street in front of the synagogue . . . was filled with people, packed together like sardines . . . Instead of the 2,000 odd Jews who usually came to synagogue on High Holidays, a crowd of close to 50,000 people was waiting for us . . . Within seconds, they had surrounded me, almost lifting me bodily, almost crushing me, saying my name over and over again . . . the crowd still surged around me, stretching out its hands and saying, "Nasha Golda" (our Golda) and "Shalom, shalom" and crying."[73]

As Arkady Vaksberg recounted Stalin's reaction:

> Stalin was frightened by the flood of letters that the Lubyanka comrades reported to him (probably with some exaggeration). Heroes of the war, awarded so many medals and ribbons, were pleading to be sent to Palestine to repel "Arab aggressors and British fascists." He was particularly incensed by the information from Abakumov and Suslov that some Jews were already collecting money to build a Jewish Soviet squadron, the Josif Stalin, for Israel.[74]

After some critical help in 1948 in recognizing Israel and shipping arms to it through Czechoslovakia, the Soviet Union quickly returned to its traditional hostility. By December 1952 the Soviet Union vetoed its first pro-Israel resolution at the United Nations. In 1955 the Soviet Union, through Czechoslovakia, signed a major arms deal sending 100 T-34 tanks and over 100 MIG 15 fighter planes to Egypt. After initial temporizing, Prime Minister Nikolai Bulganin threatened a rocket attack on France and Britain if they did not cease their advance. As he cabled David Ben Gurion:

> The Soviet Government has already expressed its definite condemnation of the armed aggression by Israel . . . the Government of Israel, acting as a tool of foreign imperialist Powers, continues the foolhardy adventure challenging all the peoples of the East who are waging a struggle against colonialism . . . The Government of Israel is playing with the fate of peace, with the fate of its own people, in a criminal and irresponsible

manner. It is sowing hatred for the State of Israel among the peoples of the east, which cannot but affect the future of Israel and which will place a question upon the very existence of Israel as a State.[75]

After the ceasefire, the Soviet Union threatened to intervene with volunteers if the advancing armies did not withdraw. A new arms deal with Egypt was announced after the war ended.[76] In the next several years the Soviet Union made a series of arms deals worth $700 million to $1 billion. By 1967 Moscow had sold 2,300 sophisticated first-line tanks (including T-54/T-55s) and self-propelled artillery pieces and 800 combat planes (including MIG 21s) to Egypt, Syria and Iraq. The Arabs had a 2:1 superiority in first-line fighter interceptors and tanks over the Israelis.

In the early 1960s, 85 percent of synagogues were closed and Jews were handed 65 percent of the 110 death sentences imposed for "economic crimes." Trofim Krychenko published his anti-Semitic tract *Judaism without Embellishment*.[77] Only in the 1970s would Brezhnev allow 250,000 Jews to emigrate, but it took the end of the Soviet Union to allow over 1 million Jews to go to Israel. From 1968 to 1985 over 200 Soviet Jews (led by Anatoly Sharansky) were imprisoned after applying for emigration to Israel.[78]

In 1966 and 1967 Moscow was especially belligerent against Israel. By 1967 the Soviet Union had shipped $2 billion of military aid to the region, including 1,700 tanks, 2,400 artillery pieces, 500 jets and 1,400 advisers. In mid-1966 a joint Syrian–Soviet communiqué issued in Moscow described Israel as "a military arsenal and base for aggression and blackmail against ... the Arab people" and pledged full Soviet support for the Arabs "in their just cause against colonialist Zionism."[79]

The Soviets erroneously told Syria in April 1967 that Israel was massing troops on the Syrian border. By May Egyptian President Gamal Abdel Nasser moved 100,000 troops and 1,000 tanks into the Sinai, obtained the quick withdrawal of the United Nations Emergency Force by Secretary General U Thant, closed the Straits of Tiran to Israeli shipping and pushed the Israelis to a full mobilization for war. The Soviet Union seemed to be prodding the Arabs towards war.[80]

Near the end of the war, the Soviet Union cut off diplomatic relations with Israel, sent 70 warships into the Mediterranean and threatened "independent action." But, as before, it did not intervene directly itself nor re-supply the Arab side until after the war was over.[81] After the war it sent nearly 50,000 tons of weapons to Egypt.

After the second failure of Soviet allies and arms, Moscow began to escalate its commitment to the Arab cause. With the United States tied down in the Vietnam War and the Russians seeing an opportunity in fighting for their Arab allies against "Israeli occupation," a new strategy emerged. In the 1969–70 Attrition War, the Soviet Union escalated its role in the anti-Israel coalition. By the end of 1970 the Soviet Union had over 200 active pilots flying 150 MIGs at six exclusive airfields for Egypt, 12,000–15,000 men in missile crews manning 80 missile sites (with advanced SAM 3s) and another 4,000 advisers for the Egyptian army.

In July 1970, the Russians, contravening the terms of the ceasefire agreement, installed 40 missile sites with 500–600 launchers near the Suez Canal. The next year Moscow sent a large number of MIG 21s to Egypt and doubled the number of SAM missile batteries. But, in July 1972, after the Soviet Union refused to send more offensive and advanced weapons (such as modern bombers and guided surface-to-surface missiles) to Egypt, Anwar Sadat ousted nearly all the 15,000 Soviet advisers and closed down their bases. The Soviet Union then signed a $700 million arms deal with Syria and provided it with 3,000 military advisers. In 1973, after a mild rapprochement between Moscow and Cairo, the Soviet Union provided 30 Scud missiles, a few MIG 25s and more ammunition to Egypt. It also returned 1,500–2,000 advisers to Egypt in time for the war. By October 1973 Egypt had over 400 MIGs and a small number of modern bombers, almost 800 surface-to-air missile launchers, 1,700 artillery pieces, almost 2,000 tanks and numerous anti-tank weapons, all of Soviet origin.[82]

Buoyed by the early success of the Arabs in the Yom Kippur War, the Soviet Union urged Arab nations to support Egypt and Syria, threatened Israel, delayed a ceasefire and massively re-supplied the Arab armies from the fourth day of the war with 100,000 tons of equipment (twice that sent by the United States), including 700 modern T-62 tanks. By the sixteenth day of the war when the tide had turned against the Arab armies, a note from Soviet President Leonid Brezhnev to American President Richard Nixon threatened "unilateral actions" if the Israelis continued to advance against the Syrians. The placing of Soviet airborne divisions on alert and the arrival of more Soviet ships in the Mediterranean led the United States to place its troops on a DEFCON 3 alert status. But the Soviet Union did not send its troops or pilots into combat, restrained the supply of the most advanced weapons and supported the ceasefire.[83]

In the three wars the Soviet Union threatened military intervention against Israel at the end of each war. Although there were limitations on Soviet actions against Israel in these wars, from 1954 to 1970 over 50 percent of Soviet global military aid went to the Arab cause. This placed a great burden on Israel. It went on a continual war footing, created a virtual garrison state and required its typical male to spend seven years in the military from 18 to 54 years of age (combat units until 40 years old).[84] In the 1982 war in Lebanon, the Soviet Union only made verbal threats and sent a few ships into the Mediterranean.[85]

After the rise of Gorbachev in 1985, pressures on Israel stopped and relations improved. By the time of the dissolution of the Soviet Union in 1991, diplomatic relations were already restored. If the million Russian Jews who came to Israel after 1991 had been allowed to go by 1948, the difference would have been critical for Israel.

Overall, the challenges from Ottoman Turkey, the British Empire (1937–49),

Nazi Germany, Tsarist Russia and the Soviet Union were great and nearly destroyed the state before it began and after it was formed. Dealing with such great external challenges helped force the Zionists, both before and after statehood, to support revolutionary and radical measures in order to withstand such great pressures on a yet relatively weak structure. But it also meant that, even today, with the new challenge from Iran, Israel has remained a virtual garrison state with all attendant costs therein.

6 Enmity of the Arab world and Iran

Israel has also faced massive threats from some of the 22 Arab states and the Palestinians over the last 60 years of statehood and the decades before statehood. As some of the old threat waned after 1979 (Camp David) and 1994 (the Israel–Jordan Peace Treaty) there was added the new threat from Iran after 1979 and Islamic fundamentalism in the 1990s and 2000s. In 1947, 650,000 Israeli Jews faced five Arab states with 27 million people and 1.2 million Palestinians nearby. In 2007, 5.3 million Israeli Jews faced 20 hostile Arab states with 215 million people, two Palestinian entities with 3.5 million people and Iran with 70 million people.[1]

Zeev Maoz found that from 1948 to 2004 Israel was the most "conflict-prone" state in modern history and led the world for the most intense international rivalries in the last 200 years. It faced six inter-state wars, two civil wars and 144 dyadic militarized inter-state disputes, threats and displays or use of force against another state. He concluded that "Israel still lives by the sword."[2]

For over 80 years there has been an "all consuming conflict" that is "endemic and intractable" between the Jews and the Arabs. In 1937 the Peel Commission wrote of the "cavernous gulf between Arabs and Jews, between a highly organized democratic modernity and an old fashioned world." In 2006 Rotberg wrote that "Anti-Israeli sentiment has been strong and widespread in the Arab world during the last few years."[3]

After eight wars and two intifadas, only two of the 22 Arab states (Egypt and Jordan) recognize Israel's right to exist, and a handful of states (Morocco, Tunisia and some emirates) maintain *sub rosa* relations. Hamas-led Gaza, the Islamic Republic of Iran, Hezbollah in Lebanon and parts of Fatah in the West Bank are virulent in denying Israel's right to exist. For almost 60 years some of the Arab states and now Islamic fundamentalist movements have waged a multi-faceted war to destroy Israel. The Middle East with 60 percent of the world's oil reserves and two of the three major gas reserves, has the wealth and power to mount a significant threat to resource-poor Israel.

Over the last 60 years the nature of the conflict has changed from an inter-state one with the Arabs to an inter-ethnic one with the Palestinians with little Arab state involvement. From 1948 to 1973 there were five wars with Arab states, sometimes one state at a time (1956, 1969–70) and other times several states (1948, 1967, 1973). With the declarations of Arab leaders (1948, 1967) that they would wipe Israel off the map, there was "intense instability." As Ben-Yehuda and Sandler found, "Given the hostile nature of the Arab–Israeli milieu, nonaccommodative outcomes seem the most reasonable way to conclude a confrontation, leading to a perpetual cycle of violence that begets violence with short intervals of non-crises periods between escalation.[4]

After 1973 the cold peace with Egypt (and the warmer one with Jordan in 1994) stabilized the Arab–Israeli conflict and prevented any new major wars since 1973 save with Syria in Lebanon in 1982. The first Palestinian intifada (1987–91) was relatively peaceful with notable exceptions. However, the cold peace has involved a low degree of cooperation, hostile Egyptian elites and media and no extensive security, political, economic or cultural interactions.[5]

After the end of the Cold War, with the 1991 Madrid Conference, the 1993 and 1995 Oslo Accords, the 1997 Hebron Accord, the 1998 Wye River Accord and the 2000 Camp David II negotiations, the confrontation seemed to be "winding down," for as Ben-Yehuda and Sandler observed in 2002:

> The gravity of the crises was reduced, the number of crises was reduced, the number of crisis actors was smaller and the level of both military and political involvement by the superpowers in the conflict was decreasing. The trend has been matched albeit to a more limited extent by a decline in the severity of violence in crises and a move to more peaceful modes of crisis management. Similar symptoms were detected in the form and content of crisis outcomes.[6]

Countries such as Morocco, Tunisia, Qatar and Oman developed some relations with Israel in the 1990s and met with Israel at international meetings.

But the failure of the peace process led to a recrudescence of violence with the second more violent Palestinian intifada (2000–05), the rise of Hamas and Islamic fundamentalism among the Palestinians and the Arabs, the summer 2006 war in Lebanon with Hezbollah and the threat of Iran to obtain and use nuclear weapons against Israel. The refusal of Iran and its Islamic fundamentalist allies (Hamas and Hezbollah) to accept the existence of Israel has revived the existential threat to Israel that seemed to have vanished two decades ago. The breadth and depth of the resistance to Israel mark it as a unique case. After 60 years of Israel's statehood, books still debate "Will Israel survive?"[7]

One thing has helped Israel: that its regional enemies have overwhelmingly been Third World autocratic dictatorships known for their "abysmal" military performance, with poor tactics, inept generals, weak information management, limited use of weapons and maintenance and weak morale and training. There has not been an effective, coordinated inter-state alliance to eliminate Israel, or a real coalition. This has given Israel a breathing space but not eliminated the real challenges to the state's existence.[8] For the

Arab world, hating Israel has become almost a way of life. As Barry Rubin observed:

> the manipulation of the Arab–Israeli conflict is one of the most powerful weapons in the arsenal of antireform regimes, hard-line ideologues and radical Islamic opposition. They argue that there can be no internal change, no softening of autocracy and no cooperation with the United States unless the issue is first resolved in a way that satisfies their stringent demands. Nothing can be done until Israel is defeated or destroyed and since this does not happen, nothing can be done.[9]

Whatever modest decline in Arab virulence against Israel was observable by 2007, it was more than matched by the rise of Iranian virulence against Israel from 1988 (after the end of the war with Iraq) to 2007. Actively supporting the two intifadas, building nuclear weapons to threaten Israel's existence and extending massive funding, arms and training to terrorist organizations, Iran has repeatedly been named by the Department of State as "the most active sponsor of terrorism" and a member of the Axis of Evil.[10]

This veritable multi-generational war against Israel has been fought in four dimensions: conventional (and nuclear) warfare, unconventional (guerrilla or terrorist) warfare, economic warfare (boycott and embargo) and political (diplomatic and propaganda) warfare. The players have changed: Egypt dropped out after Camp David and the Israeli withdrawal from the Sinai in 1981, and Jordan limited its involvement after its defeat in 1967 and dropped out after the 1994 Peace Treaty with Israel. Iran, Hamas and Hezbollah replaced them. Oil-rich Saudi Arabia and the Gulf states have historically been hostile but limited in their actions to economic and political warfare.

Conventional warfare

In the 1948 war, so uncertain were Israeli leaders of their fate that David Ben Gurion secured only a 6–5 vote to declare the state of Israel, whose existence was in doubt for its first few months. In the 1956 war Prime Minister David Ben Gurion said that, in the face of Egypt's massive arms supply from Russia, the war was a "matter of life or death."[11] In 1967 the Israelis feared that the Egyptian–Syrian–Jordanian alliance would achieve its goal of "driving the Jews into the sea." In 1973 the sudden Egyptian–Syrian attack on Yom Kippur achieved such early success that Moshe Dayan feared that the Third Temple was coming to an end. In 1991 the Iraqi missile attack with 39 Scuds provoked considerable anguish in Israel, which lacked the weapons to shoot them down.

In 1948 the Jews faced multiple threats. The 650,000 Palestinian Jews were outnumbered almost 2:1 by 1.2 million Palestinian Arabs and outnumbered 40:1 by the 27 million Arabs in the region. With 70 percent of the Jewish population located in the Tel Aviv, West Jerusalem and Haifa areas, the Arabs controlled most of the land. There were long lines of communications between the three cities. Most Jewish settlements in the Negev and Galilee were isolated not only from the big cities but also from each other. Jerusalem, the Etzion bloc near Jerusalem and the western Galilee were surrounded by Arab areas, while Tel Aviv and Haifa were near large Arab towns and settlements.

Five professional Arab armies invaded the country on May 15, 1948. By contrast, the Haganah had been an illegal organization that had never operated above the company level. While not a single Haganah officer had ever commanded a battalion, most of its soldiers had never seen significant combat.[12] As Ben Gurion said, "Our men in the Army are good Zionists but they have yet to become soldiers."[13]

The Jews could mobilize from diverse sources. At the beginning of the war, the Jews counted on 18,000 soldiers. During the war they added 32,000 more men from the Haganah and 9,500 youth (15 to 18 years old) from the Gadna youth battalions. Most Haganah men were middle-aged men or untrained adolescents. Several thousand foreign volunteers (Mahal), mostly with military experience, fought for Israel.[14]

The army was outgunned at the beginning of the war, which started at the end of November 1947. Initially it had no tanks, fighter planes, bombers and heavy artillery. Most of its weapons were unreliable, antiquated World War I rifles and homemade submachine guns and mortars. In November 1947 it had nine light airplanes, 10,000 rifles, 3,500 submachine guns and 1,050 medium and mainly light machine guns. The army had only 40 Jewish pilots, 20 of whom had been in the RAF.[15] In May 1948 the balance of weapons favored the Arabs (Table 6.1).

Even later in 1948 Israel had only 13 tanks and a single modern post-war tank. Most of its fighting power consisted of half-tracks, jeeps and hand-made armored cars.[16]

The Jews possessed a relatively unified military and political command, while the Arabs lacked a unified command and had five separate armies. Almost the entire Jewish population supported the state, which strictly organized its resources. The Arabs were split in loyalties to different states and to different Palestinian leaders, often of low caliber. Save for the small

Table 6.1 Weapons balance, May 1948

	Arabs	*Jews*
Field guns	152	0
Armored cars	140–159	0
Tanks	20–40	0
Fighter planes	55–59	0

Source: E. Luttwak and D. Horowitz, *The Israeli Army 1948–1973*, Cambridge: Abt Books, 1983, p. 30.

Transjordanian Arab Legion, all the Arab armies were essentially derived from traditional colonial armies, with near obsolete weapons, geared more for internal security than external defense. Riots in Egypt in 1946 and Iraq in 1948 prevented the British from enhancing Arab military capability. The relatively low economic, social and educational attainments of most Arab states were reflected in their limited military capabilities.[17]

The Jewish soldiers were highly motivated and there were some excellent younger officers (Yitzhak Sadeh, Yigal Allon, Moshe Dayan, Yigal Yadin, Arik Sharon, Yitzhak Rabin), while the Arabs had few talented officers. The Jews had a stronger will to fight and learned better over time. By contrast, Arab soldiers and officers were divided between urban and rural, tribes and families, and split over the role of the Mufti. The Arab states refused to give the Grand Mufti a leadership role as they created in December 1947 their own Arab League Military Committee.[18]

In January 1948 the Haganah had units of 100 men, a consultative headquarters and no artillery, armored cars or airplanes. By December 1948 the Israeli army had a series of brigades, a semi-professional core, headquarters, 250 guns, armored cars and a nascent air force. Despite serious problems (chaotic administration, inexperienced officers, open debates and decentralization), it was more professionalized than the Arab armies. Unlike the Arab armies, it was operating on internal lines of communications.[19] With help from the Diaspora, the Israelis in 1948 bought $12 million in arms, including 25 Messerschmitt 109 aircraft, 5,000 light machine guns and 24,500 rifles.[20]

The war developed in five stages. The first stage (December 1947 to March 1948) saw the Arabs on the offensive as the Jews tried to protect their cities and 300 Jewish settlements. Maintaining communication, supplies and weapons by armored trucks and bus convoys with isolated settlements was difficult and expensive. Jewish units were small, never greater than a company. Jerusalem was besieged by Arabs, especially in February and March 1948, while the Jews lost 1,200 lives, half of them civilians.[21]

The second stage (April 1948 to May 14, 1948) saw the Jews go over to the offensive. In Operation Nachshon nine companies opened the road to Jerusalem. In April shipments from Czechoslovakia brought 4,200 rifles and 240 machine guns. The battle for Deir Yassin, a village overlooking the road to Jerusalem, saw the Irgun seize the village, killing over 100 civilians and accelerating the Arab flight from Palestine. In May 1,200 Jews in Safed overcame 12,000 Arabs and took the town. The Jews seized vital parts of the Upper and Lower Galilee. At Yad Mordechai the resistance of 140 soldiers held up the 2,300 Egyptian soldiers with modern weapons for almost a week. At the same time, in May the Arabs seized the four settlements of the Etzion bloc.[22]

The third stage (May 15, 1948 to June 10, 1948), with the declaration of independence and import of heavier weapons from Czechoslovakia, saw the creation of a nascent modern Jewish army. Five modern Arab armies invaded from three directions, but lacked an overall plan, failed to use their weapons well and refrained from helping each other. The Israeli army managed to stop all five armies but lost East Jerusalem, Latrun (on the road to Jerusalem) and the Gush Etzion bloc.

The fourth stage (July 9 to July 18, 1948) came after a truce that allowed the Israeli forces to import arms and consolidate their positions. Despite the loss of Kfar Darom in Gaza, they seized Nazareth and much of the Lower Galilee, took Lod and Ramle near Tel Aviv and shelled Tyre in Lebanon.

The final stage (after October 10, 1948) saw Israeli forces on the offensive everywhere. With an army of 120,000 men, 60,000 rifles, 220 artillery pieces and 7,000 vehicles, the Israelis created a regular army with ranks and a command structure. In four major operations the Israel Defense Forces (IDF) seized the Upper Galilee, marched into Lebanon, defeated the Egyptian army in the Negev and took the bulk of the Negev and Beersheba and part of the Gaza Strip as well as part of the Sinai. At the end of the war the new Israeli air force shot down five RAF planes and lost none.[23]

Like other revolutionary armies, the Israeli army was hardly a professional army in 1949. It was a hodgepodge of soldiers, without military tradition, and an agglomeration of makeshift units, with officers largely lacking military knowledge, no firm unified command structure and highly diverse tables of weapons and organization. Owing to the refusal of most countries to sell arms to Israel, weapons had been bought all over the world as needed without any regard for standardization.[24]

Prime Minister David Ben Gurion dealt with these problems after the end of the war. Arguing that a new war would not occur for six to eight years, he reduced the army to 27,000 men. He dissolved the Irgun (by force in the *Altalena* Affair in June 1948), Lehi (after the assassination of Count Bernadotte in September 1948) and the Palmach (at the end of the war). Ben Gurion created a unified army with a small professional core, a larger conscripted army and a large reserve element (on the Swiss model). Israel kept a reservoir of trained soldiers available on short notice while allowing most people to pursue their normal civic routines.

The reserves, providing 65 percent of the men in combat units, were based on informal and familiar bonds between officers and men. Rank was little observed or emphasized. All men, soldiers and officers, were called on a first-name basis and served under the same conditions. A number of close groups formed over the years and decades of reserve service. Coupled with yearly memorials of comrades who had died in the service, the men came to know each other intimately and fight well together.[25]

The Israeli military had a hard time in the early 1950s dealing with the thousands of fedayeen guerrilla raids from Jordan, the West Bank and Gaza Strip that killed or wounded over 1,200 Israelis and disrupted the Israeli economic infrastructure. Early responses were poorly conducted and relatively ineffective. In 1953 the army turned to Arik Sharon, a reserve major studying at Hebrew University. With the help of Moshe Dayan, Sharon created Unit 101 with 40 soldiers, many of them Sharon's friends, including the redoubtable Meir Har-Zion. They carried out commando raids deep into enemy territory. But even by 1956 they had failed to stop the fedayeen raids.[26]

The 1955 Czech arms deal with Egypt changed the balance of power in the region and emboldened Egypt against Israel. Israeli leaders, led by Prime Minister David Ben Gurion and Chief of State Moshe Dayan, wanted to stop Egypt, achieve peace on their borders, open the Straits of Tiran, gain Western allies and improve precarious borders.[27]

With help from France (angry over Algeria) and Britain (angry over the nationalization of the Suez Canal), which deployed 80,000 soldiers, 13 warships and hundreds of bombers and fighters, the Israeli army matched up well with the Egyptian army in the Sinai. The Israeli Southern Command had almost as many men as the Egyptian Eastern Front (5:6 brigades), more tanks (250:58) and a modest inferiority in airplanes (81:109).[28]

The Israeli army started the war with a deception move, the dropping of 360 Israeli paratroopers under Rafael Eitan 125 miles deep into the Sinai. Within four days the Israeli army, led by 250 tanks, seized almost the entire Sinai Peninsula and the Gaza Strip, at a cost of 177 men. Despite problems, the Sinai Campaign led to free navigation through the Straits of Tiran, the end of fedayeen raids and new international respect.[29]

By 1967, feeling that their 1948 and 1956 defeats were caused by long-gone regimes and by British and French intervention, the Arabs were dragged into another round of warfare. Russian misinformation about Israeli massing of troops on the Syrian border, Nasser's aspirations to lead the Arab world, miscalculations and emotionalism on the Arab street led to war. In May and early June 1967 Nasser moved 100,000 troops and 1,000 tanks into the Sinai, blockaded the Straits of Tiran, took over the control of the Jordanian army, pushed the Iraqi army to begin to move its troops into Jordan and demanded that the Israelis evacuate Eilat and Nitzana.

The odds seemed stacked against Israel in the Six Day War. In 1967 the surrounding Arab states had a strong superiority in manpower (456,000 to 275,000 men), tanks (2,755 to 1,093), artillery pieces (2,084 to 681) and fighter bombers (682 to 286).[30] The initial Israeli air strikes destroyed the aerial capabilities of Egypt, Jordan and Syria. Within four days Israeli forces had reached the canal and in little over a day scaled the Golan Heights. Casualty rates were 25 to 1 in Israel's favor, while the POW rates were almost 400 to 1. No fewer than 10,000–15,000 Egyptian soldiers died and 12,000 were taken prisoner, while the Israelis on all three fronts lost 700 soldiers killed.[31] Over $2 billion worth of Egyptian military equipment was destroyed. Years of planning, practice, intelligence, tight operational control, imagination and discipline paid off.[32] After six days Israel had taken East Jerusalem, the West Bank, Gaza Strip, Sinai Peninsula and Golan Heights, territory with 42,000 square miles, five times the size of Israel.

During the War of Attrition (1969–70) along the Suez Canal, the army was on the defensive and forced to dig in. The Bar Lev Line, with its 30 fortifications and armored reconnaissance units between the forts, represented a radical change for the army. Massive Egyptian artillery shelling and a large Soviet presence (15,000 advisers, SAM 3 missile bases, MIG 21 jet fighters and hundreds of Russian pilots) posed a real challenge to Israel. Israeli deep-penetration raids, shooting down five Russian-piloted MIGs over the canal without losses, armored expeditions on the western bank of the canal and offensive operations led to a truce at the cost of 720 Israelis.[33]

The 1973 Yom Kippur War, which began as an intelligence and military failure, saw Israel again outgunned and outmanned. The Arab states had a significant advantage over Israel in manpower (505,000 to 310,000 men), tanks (4,841 to 2,000), artillery pieces (2,055 to 570) and airplanes (1,254 to 476). While the Arab goals may have been more limited than in 1948 and 1967, they posed a serious threat to Israel.[34]

Arab surprise and planning gave them an edge in the first days of the war. The Egyptians (with a 40:1 manpower advantage) and massive anti-tank and anti-air weaponry achieved their initial goals on the Suez Canal, as did the Syrians (with a 4.5:1 tank advantage on the Golan Heights).

The tide turned as the advantages of surprise wore off, Israeli reserves were mobilized and the Israeli army developed counter-measures to the large-scale Arab anti-tank missiles and SAM anti-air networks. Together with extensive air power (Israel lost over 100 planes in the war), the Israeli tank forces pushed the Syrians off the Golan Heights and moved towards Damascus on October 12. In the west, a massive Egyptian offensive in the Sinai was repelled. A crossing of the canal by Arik Sharon and his unit led the Israeli army to move rapidly up and down the canal and then to strike towards Cairo. The Israelis encircled the Egyptian Third Army in the Sinai. The war ended with the Israeli army 60 miles from Cairo and 30 miles from Damascus. Over 2,500 Israeli soldiers and 16,000 Syrian and Egyptian soldiers were killed.[35]

The war in Lebanon (1982–85) was a war of choice. In June 1982, Sharon evidently did not tell the Cabinet of his true plans. Israeli forces in three days overran the 25-mile Palestinian zone with a loss of 25 killed. Within a week the Israeli army was on the outskirts of Beirut. The siege of Beirut led to the withdrawal of Palestinian forces to Tunis and Syrian forces to Syria. In September the murder of Bashir Gemayel and massacres in the Palestinian camps of Sabra and Shatilla (for which the Kahane Commission pinned indirect responsibility on Arik Sharon) turned the tide. The Israelis withdrew from Lebanon, save for a six-mile-wide security strip on the border. The Israeli army performed well (82:1 kill ratio in the air, 10:1 kill ratio in tanks) but the results depressed many Israelis.[36]

Since 1985 the army has been involved, often peripherally, in several more wars. In 1991 Iraq fired 39 Scud missiles with conventional warheads at Israel, killing one Israeli and damaging 4,000 apartments. Under American pressure, Israel did not respond. In 2003 Israel did not participate in the Allied coalition war in Iraq. In July 2006, after the kidnapping of Israeli soldiers, Israel launched a 34-day ground assault against Hezbollah in Lebanon.

Hezbollah launched over 4,000 missiles, killing over 100 Israeli soldiers and 50 Israeli civilians and damaging 2,000 buildings. The highly limited Israeli ground offensive was largely confined to the area south of the Litani River. Almost 10,000 Israeli air force sorties damaged Hezbollah's strategic infrastructure and its headquarters in the Dahiya district of Beirut. But Hezbollah, by surviving, claimed victory.

The army currently faces a multitude of threats in a rapidly changing strategic arena. It increasingly has to deal with remote missile threats from nearby (Syria) and faraway countries (Iran) that may develop biological, chemical or nuclear weapons.[37]

Unconventional warfare (terrorism)

Israel also has faced massive unconventional war (terrorism) which is "violence directed to political end by non-state actors."[38] Seeing Israel as innately evil, "almost all Arabs" have endorsed anti-Israeli terrorism.[39] This terrorism escalated after Arab defeats in 1948, 1956, 1967, 1969–70 and 1982.

Carried out mainly by Palestinians, terrorism has roots in the 1920s and recurrent failures in its inter-ethnic struggle with the Jews, Arab states and the British Empire. The political, economic, societal and military weakness of the 600,000 Arabs in 1900, 1.2 million Arabs in 1948 and 4.7 million Arabs in 2007 in historical Palestine and the strength of its enemies have produced a sense of shame, frustration and humiliation that has provided a strong base for terrorism, rejectionism, radicalism and now Islamic fundamentalism.[40]

The key has been repeated Palestinian failure to achieve statehood and the elimination of Israel. This started well before the two "naqbas" (catastrophes) of 1948 and 1967. The first important failure was that of the Arab Revolt (1936–39) primarily against the British colonial rulers and secondarily against the Jews. The British, using ruthless tactics and working at times with the Jews, exhausted the Palestinians, who were internally divided, lacked adequate arms or trained soldiers and failed to coordinate their attacks. The British destroyed most of their political capabilities (trade unions, associations and parties) and drove out and crushed their elite. With fewer than 25,000 British troops and 15,000 Jewish auxiliaries by late 1938, the British imposed military rule over 1 million Palestinians. Five thousand Palestinians died (one-fourth killed by fellow Arabs), 15,000 were wounded and 5,600 were arrested. The demise of the urban elite led to a failed revolt by the rural elite and the fragmentation of the Palestinian elite. The moderate Nashashibis were pitted against the radicals led by the Grand Mufti of Jerusalem, Haj Amin Al-Hussein, who was driven into exile in Iraq and Nazi Germany. Although the 1939 White Paper met most Palestinian demands (a state in 1949, a ban on aliyah and land sales after 1944), it was rejected by the Mufti while the "Palestinian Arabs were exhausted and fractured."[41]

Despite their defeat, the Palestinians adamantly opposed both the 1937 Peel Commission giving them an Arab state with 80 percent of Palestine or the 1938 Woodhead Commission giving them even more territory. In 1939 at the St. James Conference in London they refused to sit in the same room as the Jews or shake hands with them.[42]

The first and searing "naqba" was the defeat and flight of the Palestinians in 1948. The early successes of the forces of the 1.2 million Palestinian Arabs in late 1947 and early 1948 turned into disaster. By April 1948 the Israelis had taken Jaffa and in May Haifa. Mustering only 2,000–3,000 fighters, together with fewer than 4,000 for the Arab League and 5,000 for Abdal Qadir al Husseini (killed in April 1948), the Palestinians "were ill prepared to fight." They lacked internal coordination, and Palestinian factions often detested each other. The numerically inferior Jews, "organized for total war," quickly routed the Palestinians and destroyed 350 villages. Most of the 520,000–760,000 Palestinians refugees, encouraged by the Arab League and Arab leaders, fled voluntarily, but some were forced from their homes. The defeat shocked the Palestinians, who expected a quick victory and return to their homes.[43]

From 1948 to 1967 Egyptian rule in the Gaza Strip and Jordanian rule in the West Bank limited any development of Palestinian aspirations. Hundreds of fedayeen raids from 1951 to 1955, often with Egyptian and Jordanian support, killed 905 Israelis.[44] After the Israeli victory in the 1956 Sinai Campaign, these attacks were largely limited. The second "naqba" in the 1967 Six Day War was a devastating defeat for the Palestinians, who believed that Egypt would "drive the Jews into the sea" and hand Israeli territory over to them. After the 1967 Six Day War reunited the Palestinians under Israeli rule, there developed a growing Palestinian drive for independence.

Inspired by successful revolutionary movements in Algeria, Kenya, Cuba, Vietnam and China, Yasir Arafat, after the massive defeat of the Arab states in the Six Day War, tried to establish a permanent revolutionary base in the newly occupied territories. In a "dramatic failure" he and his entourage fled the West Bank in less than two months in August 1967. Palestinian terrorism greatly escalated. By December 1967 Israel, arresting almost 1,000 guerrillas and implementing collective punishment, established order in the territories.[45]

Energized by the Khartoum summit which rejected any negotiations, peace or recognition of Israel, Arafat transferred his base from the West Bank to Jordan. Together with the Gaza Strip, Lebanon (1968–73) with 5,000 guerrillas and Jordan (1968–70) with 20,000 guerrillas, Arafat in August 1970 proclaimed his intention to "liberate the land from the Mediterranean Sea to the Jordan River" by "uprooting the Zionist entity from our land and liberating it." From June 1967 to March 1971 terror raids into Israel killed 120 civilians. There were nine hijackings of airplanes from 1969 to 1972, including spectacular events at Athens, Munich and other airports.[46]

After George Habash's Popular Front for the Liberation of Palestine hijacked three planes and blew them up in Zarqa, the Jordanian army using tanks, artillery and airplanes inflicted a "shattering defeat" on the Palestinians.

Killing 3,000 Palestinians in September 1970, Jordan closed Palestinian institutions and arrested and expelled their leaders.

In 1971 the Palestinian guerrillas tried to re-establish themselves in the Gaza Strip. Arik Sharon's "iron fist" policy, killing 100 guerrillas, arresting 750 Palestinian guerrillas and resettling 160,000 refugees, crushed them as Palestinian attacks were "almost absent."[47]

Arafat, forced out of Jordan, established a military base with 15,000 guerrillas in southern Lebanon and a political base among the 235,000 Palestinian refugees in Lebanon. Palestinian terrorism provoked both the local population led by the Maronite Christians and Israel. In 1970 the Lebanese army and guerrillas clashed, and in the 1975–89 Lebanese civil war over 150,000 civilians and combatants were killed. Syrian intervention in 1976 dealt the Palestinian forces supporting the leftists and Muslims a devastating defeat. The Israeli invasion of southern Lebanon in 1978 in Operation Litani defeated local Palestinian forces. The 1982 Israeli invasion of Lebanon routed the Palestinian forces in several days and two months later in August 1982 forced the evacuation of the Palestinians from Beirut to Tunis. While many did return to Lebanon within two years, the elite remained in Tunis for ten years. Syrian and Libyan support for Fatah Colonel Abu Musa killed hundreds of Palestinians, while Arafat was deported from Damascus to Tunis.[48]

The first intifada (1987–92), which started spontaneously, was relatively peaceful. Rocks rather than guns and suicide bombers prevailed, with Arabs killing 528 Arabs while killing 12 Israeli civilians and wounding 1,268 other civilians. But it did not end the occupation or achieve national independence. By June 1991 the Israelis had exiled 69 of its leaders, killed 600 Palestinians and arrested over 40,000 Palestinians. This Israeli success in containing the revolt, the loss of support from the Soviet Union (which dissolved in 1991) and alienation of the Arabs by their support for Iraq's invasion of Kuwait (1990–91) led to the expulsion of over 200,000 Palestinians from Kuwait and the end of most Arab aid. The guns turned inwards as almost half of the Palestinians killed in the first intifada were killed by other Palestinians. The only success was when King Hussein in July 1988 disclaimed interest in reclaiming the West Bank.[49]

Iraq, Syria and Libya actively supported Palestinian terrorism, as did Egypt before 1973. From 1968 to 1975 only three of 204 terrorists caught in Europe remained in jail. In 1972 at the Munich Olympics, Black September terrorists killed 11 Israeli athletes, an act that led to the end of leniency by the mid- and late 1970s. The 1973 Algiers summit recognizing the PLO as the sole legitimate representative of the Palestinians and the 1974 address of Yasir Arafat to the United Nations General Assembly, which recognized the PLO as the representative of the Palestinians, brought a sharp decline in Palestinian terrorism. From 1968 to 1984, 15 Palestinian terrorist organizations carried out 131 attacks on Israeli targets. The most well-known included the 1974 killing of 26 children and adults at Maalot and 16 civilians in Kiryat Shemona.[50]

After the creation of the peace process in the 1990s, the Palestinian leadership returned in 1994 and ruled the territories as autonomous units for the rest of the decade. After Oslo I and II, the Israelis gave sole control of Palestinian cities (save Hebron) and the large refugee camps to the Palestinians.[51] By 1997 the Israelis had left most of Hebron and the Palestinians held open elections. Their record, as seen in the rise of Hamas, was poor. Their massive bloated bureaucracies (Israel had ruled Gaza with 5,000 bureaucrats, and the PA needed 40,000), large-scale corruption and ineptitude left 40 percent of the Gaza workforce on the public payroll. Instead of the 9,000 security personnel proposed by Oslo, the Palestinians had 45,000. There was minimal promotion of education, social services, infrastructure development and the economy. Yet it seemed likely there would be a Palestinian state.[52]

The failure in the 1980s in the territories and the hardships suffered by the refugees opened the door for Hamas to build a social system independent of the secular PLO. From February 1989 to March 2000 it launched 27 attacks that killed 185 Israelis. By 1991 Hamas was the leading terrorist group and the second leading political group in the territories. In 1992 Israel deported 415 Hamas and Palestinian Islamic Jihad activists to Lebanon. In 1993 Hamas launched its first suicide bomb attack. In 1996 the PLO arrested hundreds of Hamas activists. In the 1990s it had somewhere between 750 and 1,250 fighters.

In the second intifada (2000–05) Hamas took the leading role, with 52 suicide bombings and 425 terrorist attacks killing 377 Israelis from September 2000 to March 2004. While the suicide bombings (which involved only 3–20 kilograms of explosives) were less than 1 percent of attacks, they killed over 50 percent of Israelis who died in that period. They caused grave damage to property and people and created broad media coverage. The shahid (Muslim martyr in a holy war) was promised heaven as a reward. The suicide bombings involved recruitment of the attacker, physical and emotional training in isolation, intelligence, the operational plan, preparation of combat means and collaborators, a farewell ceremony on videotape, perpetration of the attack and tapping media potential. They were cheap, simple and hard to stop, inflicted heavy casualties, left no one behind to be taken captive and had a strong impact on enemy public opinion.[53]

Suicide bombers killed 20 mostly Russian teenagers at the Dolphinarium disco in Tel Aviv (June 2001), blew up 14 patrons at the Sbarro restaurant in Jerusalem (August 2001) and massacred 20 mostly elderly patrons at a Passover seder in the Park Hotel in Netanya (March 2002). The second intifada killed over 1,000 Israelis (70 percent civilians) and wounded over 5,000 people.

The second intifada, feeding the illusion that the Israelis would fade away, was a protest against Israeli power and Palestinian corruption and inefficiency. It helped destroy the fragile political institutions, physical structures, economy and educational structures of the territories. It led to the return of Israeli forces to the territories and the coming to power of Arik Sharon

(2001–05) in Israel. The intifada, far from ending the occupation or gaining a state, promoted the rise to power of Hamas by January 2006 in Palestinian legislative elections.[54]

Israeli counter-actions and Palestinian terrorism led to economic catastrophe and the more than doubling of unemployment. The GDP per capita plummeted 40 percent from $1,490 (1999) to a meager $934 (2004), while the poverty rate more than doubled to 48 percent. Together with the 9/11 attacks in the United States and suicide attacks in Europe, it turned public opinion in the United States, France and Britain against the Palestinian cause.[55]

After the defeat of the second intifada in 2005, Hamas turned to hundreds of mortar attacks and allowed over 4,000 Qassam rockets to be fired into the Negev. After winning the January 2006 legislative elections, Hamas in June 2007 physically took over the Gaza Strip. By late 2007 it had as many as 13,000 men under arms.[56]

Hamas (Islamic Resistance Movement), the leading terrorist group in the territories, was founded in 1988 by Sheikh Ahmed Yassin. Its charter called for the destruction of Israel, a Palestinian state, the integration of Islam and Palestinian nationalism, opposition to the peace process and the declaration of Hamas as the sole representative of the Palestinians. Its roots are in the Egyptian Muslim Brotherhood, founded in Ismailiya in 1928 by Hassan al Banah, who integrated pan-nationalism and religious fundamentalism. By 1947 the Palestinian Muslim Brotherhood had 25 branches with 12,000–25,000 members. After the 1967 war Hamas gained strength in the Gaza Strip and after 1976 in the West Bank.[57]

Hamas has raised large sums of money for its social and military activities from the territories, the Arab world (especially Saudi Arabia and the Gulf states), Iran and the West. It received millions of dollars from Iran and until 2003 $25,000 for the families of each suicide bomber from Iraq. Hamas has received as much as $30 million a year in foreign funding out of an overall budget of $30–$90 million.[58]

Headquartered in Gaza City, Hamas has run a series of profitable economic ventures, a network of charities and extensive Islamic fundraising. It runs medical clinics, educational institutions, nursing homes, sports clubs, religious institutions, women's institutes, media forums, technology schools and early childcare centers, which built strong support from needy Palestinians not served by the PA.[59] Its mosques, hospitals, clinics and schools provide meeting places for terrorists, sites for the burial of arms caches and explosives, cars and homes for ferrying and hiding fugitives and tens of thousands of people willing to assist Hamas in return for its social services.[60]

Hamas is not a unified organization. Rather it has divisions, between the internal leadership (Gaza Strip) and the external (Syria), the moderates and the extremists, the Palestinian-first and the Islamist-first factions, and the Gazans and the Kuwaitis/Syrians.[61]

Palestinian Islamic Jihad has operated on a smaller but still lethal scale. It does not provide social welfare as does Hamas. It works extensively with Iran.

The assassination of its leader, Fathi Shiqaqi, in Malta in 1995 dealt it a severe blow from which it never has fully recovered. Yet it has significant capacity to do harm as a terrorist organization.[62]

A major non-Palestinian Shiite terrorist group has been Hezbollah (Party of God), which began in 1982 after the Israeli invasion of Lebanon. For 18 years it fought to oust Israel from the Security Zone (three to six miles wide in southern Lebanon) and succeeded in May 2000. In October 2000 its leader, Sheik Hassan Nasrallah, incited "holy war" against Israel, called for suicide bombing and rendered material aid to Palestinian guerrillas. Syria provides financial and military aid to Hezbollah. In July and August 2006 Hezbollah rained 4,000 katyusha rockets down on Israel, killing 150 Israelis and forcing over 1 million Israelis to flee the north of the country.[63] By the summer of 2007 it had rebuilt its weaponry, redeployed despite the presence of UNIFIL and Lebanese army troops in the south, and posed a significant threat to Israel's north and perhaps even its center.

Israel faced threats from terrorist groups associated with Fatah. The Al Aqsa Martyrs Brigades, founded in September 2000, was a secular, national and violent offshoot of Fatah. An armed militia operating somewhat independently of Fatah, it carried out many suicide bombings in Israel after January 2002. The Tanzim, a youth paramilitary wing derived from the Fatah Hawks in 1995, had 3,500 activists in 2000. It carried out a series of shootings and car and roadside bombings within the West Bank and Gaza Strip. In April 2002 the arrest of its leader, Marwan Barghouti, weakened the movement.[64]

Economic warfare

The Arab boycott of Israel differed from most boycotts which were aimed at containment of a threat (China and Cuba) or change in a political system (South Africa and Rhodesia). The Arab states adopted a war footing in peacetime against a targeted state with primary economic sanctions to foreign businesses dealing with Israel while blacklisting third parties refusing to comply with the boycott. The boycott was of indefinite duration, evaded international law and reflected a willingness to incur losses to achieve its goal.[65]

The Arab and Muslim world after the defeat in the 1948 war launched a large-scale economic boycott of Israel. Their oil production, huge capital equipment, infrastructure needs and lingering global anti-Semitism enhanced the effectiveness of a boycott against an originally weak Third World state. Most Third World countries after 1948 and the Communist world after 1967 with varying degrees of enthusiasm maintained the boycott until the late 1980s. Some states, such as Iran (until 1979), Turkey, Romania and Kenya, refused to abide by the boycott.[66]

The boycott had a long history even before 1948. From 1922 to 1937 there were numerous calls among Palestinians and Arabs to boycott Jewish businessmen in the region. The new Arab League in March 1945 called for the Arab world to ban the import of Jewish goods from Palestine. In 1946 a

Permanent Committee implemented the boycott, which was formalized in a May 1948 ban on all commercial and financial transactions with the new Israel. The Arab League imposed an air, sea and land blockade on Israel and eliminated postal, radio and telegraphic communications with the new state. By 1951 a Council resolution established a Central Boycott Office in Damascus with branches in all Arab states. By 1956 Egyptian seizure of ships bound to Israel halted tanker traffic to Haifa and forced Israel to build its own merchant fleet. Major shipping companies refused to call at Israeli ports. Only after the 1956 Sinai Campaign was the Gulf of Aqaba open and only in 1975 did the blockade of the Suez Canal (begun in 1950) come to an end. In the 1970s the Boycott Office had 18 branches with 200 people.[67]

The major macro instruments of the boycott were a blacklist, maritime blockade, diplomatic, trade and financial threats against those trading with Israel, and oil, weapon and trade isolation. The micro instruments included customs legislation, ship regulations, boycott questionnaires, contracts, letters of credit and ship documents. There was not only a primary boycott but also a secondary boycott against all foreign firms that dealt with Israeli affiliates, subsidiaries or provision of credit. In Lebanon, second offenders of the boycott garnered life sentences, while in Syria there was a prison sentence with hard labor. Goods shipped through Alexandria, Port Said and Suez bound from or to Israel were confiscated and ships searched for Israeli materials.[68]

The European reaction was mixed. Even after the 1975 European Economic Committee/Israel Free Trade Agreement, the European group showed a widespread pattern of Arab boycott compliance and discrimination. France, which had been aligned with Israel from 1955 to 1967, had over 350 firms on the boycott list and maintained a limited anti-boycott law, still showed a widespread pattern of compliance with the boycott. After de Gaulle in 1967 ended the special relationship, France by 1973 was excluded from the oil embargo and until 1981 accommodated the boycott.[69]

Great Britain formally opposed the boycott and by 1973 had 1,200 firms on the boycott list. But for four decades it strongly complied with the boycott and in 1973 was exempted from the oil embargo and production cuts. Only by 1995, when Great Britain ended its arms embargo on Israel, did British companies work extensively with Israel.[70] Japan was the largest country obeying the boycott for decades. Almost totally dependent on oil imports, anxious not to offend the Arab world, removed from the conflict and with no special ties to the small Jewish state, Japan for four decades maintained the boycott against Israel. Only in the 1990s, as the Israeli market grew, Jordan and the Palestinians negotiated with Israel and Arab oil power declined, did Japan move away from the boycott. But until then Japan provided no investment, state credits or development aid to Israel and little trade. In 1984 Japanese exports to the Arab world were $12.9 billion, to Israel $200 million. Japan's imports from the Arab world were $30 billion, as it received 40 percent of its oil imports from the Arab world. While 150 Japanese companies (including Sony, Hitachi and Olympus) were on the blacklist, perhaps 90 percent of

Japanese companies (including Mitsubishi, Toyota, Honda, Suzuki, Japan Air Lines and Yamaha) would not deal with Israel. All this changed markedly in the 1990s, but the lack of Japanese investment, technology transfer, imports and aid in Israel's first four decades was a major impediment to development.[71]

The United States often complied with the boycott from 1950 to 1980. While Congress and the public often opposed the boycott, much of the bureaucracy (especially the State, Commerce and Transportation departments), motivated by a desire for political and economic relations with the Arabs, preventing the rise of Soviet influence in the Middle East and residual anti-Semitism, were opposed to anti-boycott actions. From October 1975 to September 1976, 92 percent of 169,700 boycott requests were honored by American firms. In 1976 and 1978 Congressional legislation and ensuing Commerce Department action tightened anti-boycott regulations against the desire of the Arab lobby and oil companies. President Reagan also vigorously tackled the boycott. By 1983 less than 4 percent of companies complied with the boycott requests.[72]

The 1973 oil embargo, levied on the United States and the Netherlands after the Yom Kippur War, reinforced the power of the Arab world. The price of oil skyrocketed fourfold in 1973 and had nearly tripled again by 1980. Arab oil exports soared from $4 billion in 1972 to $60 billion in 1980 and the embargo reinvigorated the power of the boycott aimed at Israel.

In 1980 Egypt, after signing a peace treaty with Israel in 1979, cancelled the boycott – yet continued for many years to ask American companies for boycott compliance. The 1982 Israeli invasion of Lebanon increased the power of the boycott, which extended to 26 other non-Muslim countries. In the 1990s the Oslo peace process and growing peace process limited the impact of the boycott. By 1994 the Gulf states had ended their indirect boycott of Israel. The 1994 Peace Treaty with Jordan ended Jordan's boycott the next year. By 1997 Qatar and 14 Arab states had some economic relations with Israel. Four Middle East and North Africa economic conferences in the mid-1990s broke down Israel's isolation. But the Netanyahu era (1996–99), failure of that process after Camp David in 2000, and the launching of the second intifada (2000–05) reignited the boycott activists. Most non-Muslims did not reinstate the boycott. FDI into Israel more than quintupled from 1991 to 1995. From 1990 to 1997 Israeli exports to India quintupled and doubled to Japan.[73] This pace even accelerated in the following decade.

Many companies evaded the boycott by operating through third parties and other deceptive means. The Arab world could push hard only if companies had a significant interest in the Arab market. Before 1969 Cyprus and Iran were easy markets for third parties to promote Israeli trade with forbidden countries. The Arab world lacked control of most third-party companies, and Israeli goods were often high-quality and less expensive than those available in the open market place. Israeli origins were often concealed, while Israeli companies worked through brokers and often falsified certificates. After 1977 Israeli companies often bought European companies, further concealing their identity. Many major companies (such as Ford, Coca-Cola, RCA and Sheraton) were powerful enough to ignore Arab pressure.[74]

The boycott's direct impact on exports may have been limited (an Israeli Ministry of Finance study found that from 1972 to 1983 exports would have been 1 percent greater without the boycott), but it had an impact on investment and people. From 1955 to 1985 Israel received only $2 billion in FDI, as companies were loath to lose the larger Arab market. Israel had a hard time finding foreign partners for production and research. The boycott harmed technology transfer to chemical, pharmaceutical, metals and electrical industries and use of cheaper Israeli labor. Not being able to send ships through the Suez Canal until the late 1970s imposed a transportation cost on Israeli exports. There was the loss (except through secret means) of the nearby Arab market (which in the late 1930s had taken 12 percent of Jewish Palestine's exports). Oil cost more without access to nearby Arab sources. An Israeli Chamber of Commerce study found that from 1951 to 1991 the boycott cost Israel $45 billion, as few of the Fortune 500 companies invested in Israel. Foreign tourism was impacted significantly. Israel paid more for more distant imports, phantom trade operations were costly, and expensive import substitutes and self-sufficient capital equipment and technology misallocated resources to high-cost and inefficient operation.[75]

Political warfare

There was a brief period of time after World War I when it seemed that the Arabs and the Jews might work together. In 1919 Emir Faisal and Chaim Weizmann during the Versailles Peace Conference negotiated their difference. But the developing nationalism of the Arabs and the anti-Semitism and high political ambitions of the Grand Mufti of Jerusalem placed the Arabs and Jews on a collision course. After the failure of the Arab Revolt (1936–39), the Palestinians, under the Grand Mufti, increasingly turned towards Nazi Germany, where he lived during the war.

During the 1950s and 1960s the Arab states sought to politically isolate Israel. Much of the world responded by not recognizing the new Jewish state. The acme of this effort came in 1975 with the passage of the "Zionism is Racism" resolution at the United Nations, with support from the Communist bloc, Muslim bloc and many Third World states. Israel, recognized by only 80 countries, became "virtually a pariah state, internationally condemned and isolated."[76] Only the end of the Cold War, the decline in oil prices and the 1990s peace process transformed the situation, and in 1991 the resolution was repealed. By 2000 Israel was recognized by more than 150 states, and had peace treaties with Egypt and Jordan, peace negotiations with the Palestinians and attendance at a series of international meetings with the Arabs. But the failure of the peace process at Camp David II (July 2000), the outbreak of the second intifada (2000–05), rising international criticism of Israeli actions in the territories, the sharp increase in oil prices and the ascent of Iran and the Islamic fundamentalist movements promoted anti-Israelism globally.

The four kinds of warfare – conventional war, unconventional war, economic boycott and diplomatic isolation – forced Israel to expend significant energy to maintain its existence. Israel extensively resorted to secret diplomacy.[77] Israel became for decades a pariah state, a garrison state, swimming upstream until the 1990s against the currents of international politics, economic and military. Then, with the rise of Islamic fundamentalism and a potentially nuclear Iran towards the end of the first decade of the twenty-first century, Israel again faces significant threats to its existence. It faces a form of possible, evolving "fundamentalist encirclement" from Iran and its allies (Syria, Gaza, southern Lebanon, and possibly southern Iraq after the departure of American forces) and the distant missile and nuclear threat of the Islamic Republic of Iran. In the future there remains the danger that the West Bank might come under the dominance of Hamas, thereby beginning to close the circle on Israel, especially if either of the moderate regimes in Egypt and Jordan were to be overthrown. The serious enemies are no longer states thrown on the trash heap of history (Tsarist Russia, the Soviet Union, Nazi Germany, Ottoman Turkey), to use Trotsky's term, but new threats that also endanger the state.

7 Major international and religious organizations

The Jews faced major obstacles from organizations representing over 3 billion people, including Catholics, mainline Protestants and Muslims, who opposed the state of Israel for decades. Overcoming significant religious opposition was a major hurdle, as was the opposition of the United Nations and Third World through much of this period.

The opposition of the Roman Catholic Church

For many centuries the supersessionist philosophy of Catholicism argued that the Jews were replaced by the Christians as the new Israel and the Holy Land belonged to Christians. In the 1960s and 1970s, two new ideas battled for theological supremacy. Neo-Marcionism, which emphasized accommodation to Muslims, Eastern Christians and secular liberals, gained support from most liberal Protestant denominations and many Roman Catholics. Christian Zionism, which stressed good relations with the Jews and the state of Israel, found support among fundamentalist and evangelical Protestants. As Paul Merkley has written:

> The real contest within Christianity – on which the survival of the Jews may well depend – is over one of the oldest theological issues in the Church: How the destiny of the Jews is related to the destiny of the Church.[1]

For the 10 million Jews in 1900 and the 13 million Jews in 2007, the opposition of a church representing over 1 billion Roman Catholics was a serious problem. For many centuries the hostility of the Roman Catholic Church was seen in support for laws directed against the Jews, the Crusades that devastated Jewish communities in the Rhineland and Palestine, the Inquisition that expelled the Jews from Spain and burned them at the stake, and the ghettos established in the sixteenth century. The quasi-silence of the Church during the Holocaust reinforced this image.[2]

The Roman Catholic Church, as a transnational institution, has significant ideological and moral authority going back 2,000 years. It has over 2,000 dioceses and 540 archdioceses all over the world and is recognized by over 120 countries, including the United States and countries in Western Europe and much of the Third World. Its 1 billion adherents constitute 16 percent of the world's population, a majority of all peoples in Latin America, close to half of Europe's population and hundreds of millions in Africa and Asia. Its strongly hierarchical organization and ties with European and Latin American countries provide it with a global reach. The position of the Roman Catholic Church was likely to have global resonance through its role in the Holy Land, which gave birth to Christianity.[3]

For over 100 years the Roman Catholic Church has been openly or covertly hostile to the creation and flourishing of the state of Israel.[4] Only in the last decade, with the rise of Islamic fundamentalism and the growing power of the state of Israel, has the relationship between Israel and the Vatican become friendlier. Concerns about its relationship with the Islamic world and non-Catholic Third World, identifying with European thought, protecting Arab Catholics, safeguarding its churches, monasteries, convents and educational institutions in the Holy Land, fearing an intolerant Jewish government, and its historical anti-Jewish theology have played a significant role. Its global ideological power pushed it to conceive of its relationship with the Zionists and Israel in a context that was often profoundly anti-Israeli.[5]

In 1899 American Ambassador to Ottoman Turkey Oscar Straus told Theodor Herzl that he "considered Palestine impossible to attain . . . The Greek and Roman Catholic Churches would not let the Jews have it." Herzl told Straus that the Church "is the rich brother who hates the poor brother."[6] That year the Jesuit daily *Civilta Cattolica* called the Jews "A race of murderers of God, even if supported by all the anti-Christian sects."[7] As early as 1904 Pope Pius X told Theodor Herzl that:

> We cannot encourage this movement. We cannot prevent the Jews from going to Jerusalem – but we could never sanction it. The ground of Jerusalem, even if it were not always sacred, has been sanctified by the life of Jesus Christ. As the head of the Church, I cannot tell you otherwise. The Jews have not recognized our Lord, therefore we cannot recognize the Jewish people . . . The Jewish religion was the foundation of our own; but it was superseded by the teachings of Christ and we cannot concede it any further validity . . . If you come to Palestine and settle your people there, we shall have churches and priests ready to baptize all of you.[8]

In 1917 the Vatican opposed the Balfour Declaration. In March 1919 Pope Benedict, finding that "truly harrowing indeed is the thought that souls should be losing their faith and hastening to damnation on that very spot where Jesus Christ Our Lord gained for them life eternal at the cost of His Blood," called Jews "infidels" whose coming to power would cause "terrible grief for us and for all the Christian faithful."[9] In September 1921 the Cardinal

Secretary of State declared that Jewish mass immigration to Palestine would be "immoral, illegal and . . . quite contrary to Christian sentiment and tradition." A 1922 Roman Catholic Church memorandum opposing key aspects of the Balfour Declaration was presented to the League of Nations.[10] Chaim Weizmann declared that "the Vatican is moving Heaven and Earth against us, and the old fight between Judaism and paganism has been renewed with vigor."[11]

Vatican opposition to Zionism continued throughout the interwar years. In 1929 the Vatican, while deploring the Arab riots, blamed the Zionists as the root cause. In October 1938 Vatican Under Secretary of State Domenico Tardini told British representatives that "there was no real reason why [the Jews] should be back in Palestine . . . Why should not a nice place be found for them, for instance, South America?" In 1939 the Vatican endorsed the anti-Zionist British White Paper.[12]

During the Holocaust, although there were some pro-Jewish acts, most Vatican leaders maintained their silence, for "the extermination of European Jews had no substantial impact on the set pattern of Vatican hostility toward political Zionism." In the fall of 1944, a memorandum prepared by the Vatican's Secretariat of State for Pope Pius XII before his meeting with Winston Churchill stated that "the Holy See has always been opposed to Jewish domination in Palestine . . . to give [Palestine] to the Jews would offend all Christians and infringe upon their rights." In 1945 Moshe Shertok met Pope Pius XIII but the visit "went nowhere." Even after 1945, the refusal of the Church to return Jewish children handed over to their care during the war and its role in helping Nazi war criminals escape to Latin America showed no change in an anti-Jewish direction.[13]

In 1947, given world sympathy to the Jews after the Holocaust, the Vatican kept a studied neutrality to the struggle at the United Nations over creating Israel. This allowed the United States and Jewish forces to convince many Catholic Latin American nations (almost half of the General Assembly) to back partition and a Jewish state. Yet, in 1948 the Vatican opposed the partition plan, calling the creation of Israel on May 14:

> another tragic milestone in the Via Crucia of Palestine . . . [for Israel was] not the heir to Biblical Israel. The Holy Land and its sacred sites belong only to Christians; the true Israel. Catholics simply are not in a position to understand the centrality of the state of Israel for modern Judaism.[14]

After 1948, a shaken Vatican supported non-recognition of Israel, internationalization of the holy sites and Jerusalem, repatriation of Palestinian refugees and retreat of Israel to the 1947 United Nations Resolution 181 frontier lines. Cardinal Spellman, who urged President Truman not to admit Israel to the United Nations until it internationalized Jerusalem, opposed Israel making West Jerusalem its capital.[15]

In the 1950s much Vatican work went to charity for the Palestinian refugees, both Muslim and Christian. By the early 1960s the Vatican, seeing the staying power of Israel, increasingly pro-Israel American policies and the growing power of Jewish Diaspora communities, moved towards equidistance between the two parties. Pope John XXIII's Second Vatican Council (1962–65) promoted Catholic–Jewish reconciliation, eliminated the use of the words "perfidious Jews" and made a historic call that the Jews were a "people most dear to God," for Jesus was born "of the living tradition of the Jewish people." In 1964 Pope Paul VI, a strongly pro-Palestinian pope, visited both Jordan and Israel and talked with King Hussein and Israeli President Zalman Shazar on a visit to the Holy Land. But his 11-hour stay in Israel was brief and unproductive.[16]

The Six Day War pushed the Vatican towards a more positive view of Israel. However, the Church condemned the Israeli annexation of the Old City of Jerusalem. The growing number of Third World Catholics, European pro-Palestinian policies and resentment of Israeli domination of the Holy Land and treatment of the territories prevented Vatican diplomatic recognition of Israel. In 1974 and 1975 the Vatican recognized Palestinian national rights. In 1973 in a letter to the president of the Pontifical Mission for Palestine, Monsignor John Nolan, Pope Paul VI declared, "The Palestinians . . . are particularly dear to us because they are people of the Holy Land, because they include followers of Christ and because they have been and are still being so tragically tried."[17]

Despite his personal warmth towards the Jews going back to his childhood in Poland, Pope John Paul II was far from an uncritical admirer of Israel. Despite the support for the 1979 Israeli–Egyptian Peace Treaty and meetings with Shimon Peres and Yitzhak Shamir, the Vatican continued to be strongly pro-Palestinian.[18] Pope John Paul II met with Yasir Arafat in 1982, 1988 and 2000 and expressed his support for a Palestinian state. In 1995 the Vatican created an Office for the Representative of the PLO to the Holy See, clearly a forerunner of formal recognition of the PLO. In the 1990s, the pope repeatedly appointed Palestinians inside Israel who were hostile to the Oslo peace process. In 1994, the Church recognized Israel.[19] In 1998 the Vatican issued "We Remember: A Reflection on the Shoah," which represented progress in Jewish–Catholic relations.

In March 2000, during the jubilee year, Pope John Paul II made an historic four-day trip to Israel. The pope visited Yad Vashem and prayed alone at the Western Wall. Here, echoing his 1986 comment on a visit to a Roman synagogue that Jews are "the older brothers of the church," he left a famous note at the Western Wall that read:

> God of our fathers, you chose Abraham and his descendants to bring your name to the nations. We are deeply saddened by the behavior of those who in the course of history have caused those children of yours to suffer, and asking your forgiveness, we wish to commit ourselves to genuine brotherhood with the people of the covenant.[20]

By 2007 the Vatican balancing act between Israel and the Arabs was continuing. However, several issues were not resolved after over ten years of negotiations – the legal and tax status of the Church, access to Catholic holy places, the upkeep and sanctity of the areas around the holy places and the decline of the Christian population in the West Bank.[21]

Overcoming the opposition of world Protestant churches

Despite early British and American Protestant sympathy with Zionism, the mainline American Protestant churches had serious problems with Israel. Like the Roman Catholic Church, they shared a theology that saw the destruction of the Second Temple in Jerusalem in 70 AD and Jewish exile and persecution as a divine punishment for the death of Jesus and refusal to accept him as their savior. Christians believed that they would replace the Jews, who would wither away and die. They saw the New Israel (Christian Church) replacing the Old Israel (the Jewish people). The Jews had lost not only their identity as Israel but their divine right to the Holy Land. Christian theology considered Palestine to belong to them and not the Jews, who had forfeited their rights. They wished to keep Palestine as an historical museum to their past.

Zionism threatened Christian beliefs that the Jews were a doomed, powerless people without rights. Jewish nationalism was unwelcome to Christians who saw Jews as Christ killers and a repetition of the fatal error in rejecting Jesus. As a leading Protestant theologian put it in 1948, "His own people, the Jews, want to set up again a narrow Jewish political nationalism, against which he protested at the cost of his life." Protestant liberals, basing themselves on the Gospels, supported the Palestinians out of concerns for social justice, peace and Third World national liberation.[22] Many Protestant theologians from 1917 into the middle 1960s, influenced by the strong missionary movement in the Middle East, wanted to convert the Jews, rather than recognize an increasingly powerful and disconcerting Jewish state.[23] Many preferred rising Arab nationalism to Jewish nationalism and manifested a disdain for Jews, American, European or Israeli.[24]

The mainline, liberal Protestant churches were indifferent or hostile to Zionism from the beginning. They were particularly influenced by Protestant missionaries who had been active in the Middle East since 1819 and who in 1866 had created the Syrian Protestant College (now American University of Beirut). At the 1919 Paris Peace Conference the president of the American University of Beirut, Howard Bliss, opposed the Balfour Declaration and called for Palestine to be wrapped into a Greater Syria under an American protectorate. The August 1919 report of the presidential King–Crane Commission opposing a Jewish homeland in Palestine and supporting an Arab kingdom for the region was led by Henry King, the president of Presbyterian Oberlin College.[25]

Focused on reconstructing and strengthening their own denominations in the interwar period and strongly isolationist, most mainline Protestant churches did not support Zionism. As the *Christian Century*, an independent Protestant weekly, put it in August 1927 deriding "aggressive Jews" who wanted to claim the country as a "homeland":

> Historically the Jew has never been in possession of Palestine. It is the conviction of most modern Biblical scholars that the Old Testament contains no anticipation of a restoration of the Jew to its ancient homeland which can apply to the Jewish people and the present age.

The weekly, deriding Jewish nationalism, immigration to Palestine and Jewish land purchases in Palestine, called the 1917 Balfour Declaration "a mischievous and ambiguous promise" which "could not be realized consistently with justice to other elements of the population."[26]

In the 1930s, with the rise of fascism, persecution of the Jews and some Arab sympathy for the fascists, the National Council of Churches became less hostile to the Jews. Yet, until 1939 no major organized body of American Protestantism supported a Jewish state or Zionism. In 1933 the *Christian Century* denounced Zionism as a "chimerical scheme" that would entail "the slaughter of hordes of Arabs." The weekly also asserted that Jewish nationalists had crucified Jesus Christ. In 1937 the weekly opposed the Peel Commission and its call for partitioning Palestine. It asserted that the "separatist" Jewish religion, which was an "alien element in American democracy," needed to encounter the "universalist" Christian Church. In 1939, endorsing the anti-Zionist British White Paper, the *Christian Century* declared that "The ambition to make Palestine a Jewish state must be dropped" but Palestine could be "a cultural and spiritual center for world Jewry."[27]

By 1948, the pressure from Arab Protestants and local missionaries, supersessionist theology, oil ties, dislike of Jews and the emphasis on peace and justice issues led the new World Council of Churches to be ambivalent or even hostile to the new state. In May 1948 a bitter *Christian Century* blamed the creation of Israel on New York Jewish voters. In 1948 such renowned anti-Zionist Protestant leaders as Virginia Gildersleeve (dean of Barnard College), Henry Sloane Coffin (former president of Union Theological Seminary), Bayard Dodge (president of American University of Beirut), Harry Fosdick (minister of Riverside Church) and Paul Hutchinson (editor, *Christian Century*) formed the Committee for Justice and Peace in Washington, D.C. to oppose United Nations Resolution 181 that had called for a Jewish state in Palestine. The American Friends of the Middle East, the first overtly pro-Arab organization formed in the United States after 1948, numbered 18 leading Protestant clergymen on its 65-member national council.[28]

After 1948 the *Christian Century* and leading American Protestant churches supported the internationalization of Jerusalem. The plight of the Palestinian refugees from the 1948 war helped turn the churches further against Israel. The *Christian Century*, bemoaning the "catastrophe" and "deep injustice" suffered by the Palestinians, called for the return of the refugees to their home and property in Israel. Either they would be politically repatriated or nothing would be accomplished. In 1951 and 1956 the World Council of Churches held refugee conferences in Beirut that became increasingly politicized and anti-Israel. In 1949 Henry Sloane Coffin, in an influential article in the *Christian Century* entitled "Perils to America in the New Jewish State," derided Israel as parasitic, aggressive and fanatical."[29] By 1954 the Second Assembly of the World Council of Churches meeting in Evanston, Illinois dropped any reference to Israel in its resolutions. In 1956 Princeton Theological Seminary professor O. T. Ellis queried, "Does the Israeli cause deserve to succeed? . . . We believe the verdict of history will be, No!" In 1957 the *Christian Century* warned of a "darkest tragedy" and the need "to rescue Judaism, a religious faith from Zionism, a nationalistic creed."[30]

During the 1967 Six Day War the World Council of Churches and its leading Protestant denominations were silent. Official Protestant bodies provided no support for Israel's right to exist and did not show concern that Israel might be destroyed. They seemed to link Israel's right to exist to the resolution of the Arab refugee problem. Many clergymen and theologians (including the National Council of Churches) refused to sign a statement of conscience in support of Israel, while only a minority (many more fundamentalist) supported Israel's right to exist.[31]

The 1967 Six Day War transformed a moderate preference for the Arabs into a passionate support of their cause. Israel, no longer David, had become Goliath and a Western power occupying Arab lands. The cause of the weak and victimized Palestinians seemed irresistible. Leading Protestant theologians and professors "with deep horror" attacked Israeli "crimes" for, in the words of Presbyterian minister and Yale professor William Oxtoly, "Israel deserves no support from the religious men because it inflicted suffering through acts of premeditated brutality." The National Council of Churches, while opposing Israeli annexation of Jerusalem, did call on the international community to recognize Israel. The American Jewish Committee found there was no clear moral commitment of most churches to the survival of Israel or its population.[32]

The Israeli victory in the war ruined a spiritual Judaism. In August 1967 the Central Committee of the World Council of Churches deplored Israeli annexation of the territories and demanded their withdrawal. In August 1969 the Central Committee of the World Council of Churches declared that the establishment of Israel in 1948 had done injustice to the Palestinians and called for Palestinian self-determination and political independence. In 1980 the council condemned the Israeli annexation of Jerusalem. At the 1983 Vancouver meeting, the World Council of Churches called for a Palestinian state. The 1987 Palestinian first intifada drew strong support from the liberal Protestant churches. In 1989 the World Council of Churches presented the United Nations Commission on Human Rights with a document supporting Yasir Arafat and a Palestinian state, while denouncing the Israeli occupation as unlawful. In the 1990s problems with the Oslo peace process were blamed on the Israelis. In 2000 the Commission of Churches on International Affairs submitted a document to the United Nations detailing a long series of unjust Israeli actions.[33]

In 1974 Arab influence in the World Council of Churches was enhanced by the creation of the Middle East Council of Churches (MECC), representing Arab clergy in 17 Christian denominations with 14 million Christians (including Eastern Orthodox, Oriental Orthodox, Catholic and Protestant) in the region. In 1979 the MECC held a conference on the Palestinian refugees and in 1983 opened a travel agency to promote Palestinian and Arab causes to Westerners. In 1986 it denounced the Christian Zionist International Congress. In 1988 the council stated that "we stand with the refugees and the deported, with the distressed and the victims of injustice." A 1990 ecumenical assembly in Cyprus supported the Palestinian cause.[34]

With the second intifada (2000–05), the mainline Protestant churches intensified their hostility towards Israel. Presbyterians, Episcopalians and Lutherans supported Palestinian self-determination and condemned Israeli occupation of the territories while the Methodists remained neutral. A 2004 study of the four largest mainline Protestant churches (United Methodist, Evangelical Lutheran, Episcopal and Presbyterian) and their two leading councils (the National Council of Churches and the World Council of Churches) found that from 2000 to 2003 Israel was condemned 37 percent of the time and the United States 32 percent of the time. As Erik Nelson and Alan Wisdom observed:

> It also demonstrated what can only be considered a fixation on the Israel–Palestinian conflict in which churches have clearly taken sides against Israel. The most difficult questions this study cannot answer – but which these data clearly raise – are: Why do mainline churches exhibit this focus on the Israeli–Palestinian conflict? . . . Why do they devote so little attention and insensitivity, by comparison, to human rights abuses elsewhere in the world?[35]

The authors suggest many reasons, including solidarity with leftist European elites, identification with Arab Christian churches, multiculturalism and ethical relativism, holding the United States responsible for global conflicts and anti-American imperialism. For Israel it meant that the churches of the hundreds of millions of mainline Protestants often condemned Israel and even questioned its existence.[36]

A similar position was taken by the Church of England. Gerhard Falk found that, under the influence of the same forces as liberal American Protestantism, British establishment Protestantism demonstrated "almost universal hostility towards Israel."[37]

Despite Israel's withdrawal from southern Lebanon (2000) and Gaza (2005) and Hezbollah's massive katyusha assault on Israel from Lebanon (2006), many mainline Protestant churches remained overtly hostile to Israel.

In 2004 the Presbyterian General Assembly voted overwhelmingly for a "phased selective divestment" from MNCs operating in Israel. Although it modified this resolution in 2006, the assembly called for the 1967 borders, ending the occupation, criticizing the security barrier beyond the 1967 line and "constructive engagement" replacing divestment.[38] In 2005 the United Church of Christ voted for "economic leverage" against Israel, while the World Council of Churches urged its constituent members to "seriously consider" divestment.

Overcoming the opposition of Islam

In 2007, 1.3 billion Muslims make up 20 percent of the world's population and account for one-fourth of the nations in the world (57 countries). Their dislike and hatred of Zionism, especially among Middle Eastern Muslims (Arabs and Persians), is legendary. In a poll in 2003, 59 percent said that the person they hated most in the world was Arik Sharon, the Israeli prime minister. Only two of the 23 Arab and Persian Muslim countries (Jordan and Egypt) have diplomatic relations with Israel.[39]

When Zionism developed at the end of the nineteenth century, the great majority of Muslims were strongly opposed to a non-Muslim state in the heart of the Middle East. When Israel won five wars from 1948 to 1973 against numerically superior Muslim forces, the outrage in the region was palpable.[40]

The causes of Islamic dislike and hatred for Israel run deep. Jews (like Christians and Zoroastrians) were treated as second-class People of the Book in the Moslem world. The Iranian Revolution (1979), seizure of the Grand Mosque in Mecca (1980), assassination of the peacemaker Anwar Sadat (1981) and the Israeli invasion of Lebanon promoted the backlash. So did the intifadas and Islamic fundamentalist terrorism from New York and London to Madrid and Ankara and the American invasions of Iraq and Afghanistan, as did the lengthy occupation of the Gaza Strip and West Bank after 1967.

The Islamicization of the Arab–Israeli conflict brought Muslim nations to the side of radical anti-Israeli Palestinians. State-run Arab media (as well as private media) denied that Israel was a nation and hence a state and was stunned that a *dhimmi* people dared to fight against the Muslims in the center of the Arab world and repeatedly win. They denied Jewish claims to the Holy Land, spoke in anti-Semitic terms, and denigrated Zionism as an agent of global imperialism bent on expansion and confiscating Palestinian land. They saw Israel waging a war of genocide against the Palestinians.[41]

Overcoming the opposition of the United Nations and the Third World

The United Nations, dominated by Western and Latin American countries, from 1945 to 1952 was friendly towards the creation of Israel. From 1952 to 1991 it was quite hostile. The change in the role of the Communist bloc and the rise of independent Third World countries transformed the United Nations. After the 1973 oil embargo, the Arab world garnered increased support for almost 20 years. While there were no national agencies for over 60 million refugees worldwide, it created UNRWA (United Nations Relief and Work Agency) with 17,000 employees solely for the Palestinian refugees. It did not restrain the guerrillas operating in UN supervised areas. In United Nations Resolution 3236 (passed 89–8–27), the United Nations supported the inalienable right of the Palestinians to self-determination, independence and sovereignty. In 1974 Yasir Arafat attacked Zionism from the podium of the United Nations General Assembly with a gun in his holster, saying:

> An old world order is crumbling before our eyes, as imperialism, colonialism, neo-colonialism and racism, the chief form of which is Zionism, ineluctably perish. We are privileged to be able to witness a great wave of history bearing peoples forward into a new world which they have created. In that world just causes triumph.[42]

In September 1975 Ugandan President Idi Amin received a standing ovation for declaring from the podium of the General Assembly that "I call for the expulsion of Israel from the United Nations and the extinction of Israel as a state, so that the territorial integrity of Palestine may be ensured and upheld." While expulsion of Israel was avoided by American and Western action, the cheering showed the sentiment on the floor.[43]

In December 1975 the United Nations passed General Assembly Resolution 3379 (72–35–32) denouncing Zionism as racism. Although passed with fewer than 75 votes, it remained United Nations policy until repeal in 1991. This resolution was matched by other resolutions that established the United Nations Committee for the Exercise of the Inalienable Rights of the Palestinian People and recognition of the PLO as the official representatives of the Palestinians. From 1969 to 1972 there were four anti-Zionist resolutions a year, from 1973 to 1978 16 per year and in 1982 44 resolutions.

The United Nations Secretary General Kurt Waldheim in his September 1979 annual report to the General Assembly on peace and security failed to mention the Camp David Peace Accords. The United Nations tried for decades to undermine the moral and legal basis of the state of Israel. Its platform for the PLO served as a "valuable entrée to public opinion in Europe, which was largely supportive of the concept of the United Nations as a world forum." Only American threats to withdraw funds and membership in the General Assembly and any United Nations body supporting an expulsion resolution kept Israel in the United Nations against repeated Arab pressure in the early 1980s.[44]

In the late 1980s and early 1990s the United Nations moved towards a more nuanced stance on Israel. The decline of the PLO, the waning power of OPEC, an increasingly anti-United Nations American policy, the end of the Cold War and victory of the United States led to the number of nations recognizing Israel soaring from 70 in 1988 to over 160 by 2007. These included Russia, India, China and all of Eastern Europe.[45]

But the second intifada (2000–05) again pushed the United Nations against Israel. In September 2001 the UN Durban World Conference against Racism repeatedly attacked Israel as a racist state. The NGO Forum adopted a document equating Zionism with racism. All references to anti-Semitism and the Holocaust were deleted. Only the United States and Israel walked out of the conference. In August 2004 John Dugard, the United Nations special rapporteur on human rights in the territories, said Israeli rule in the West Bank and Gaza "was worse than South Africa" and constituted apartheid. In May he called for an arms embargo against Israel for its raids in Rafah to stop attacks on Israel.

The opposition of the Roman Catholic Church, mainline Protestant churches and organized Islam, as well as the United Nations (1952–91), was and often remains a major obstacle to Israel. While the degree of threat has waxed and waned since the 1920s and 1948, for Israel dealing with this diffuse and multi-faceted opposition has provoked a deep sense of isolation and loneliness in the region. International conferences and United Nations forums have often been scenes of serious criticism of Israel, with rarely a word said in its defense, except at times from the United States. Overall, then, despite all the progress made by Israel in escaping international pariah status, this deep-seated enmity remains a major concern for Israel.

8 Western unwillingness to help Israel in crises

But Israel's problems did not end with its enemies and detractors. The West, despite often being friendly to Israel, was reluctant to intervene in crises and wars involving Israel.

Overcoming Western unwillingness to support Israel in major wars and crises

While the Soviet Union inevitably supported the Arab side before 1988, the Israelis could not in wartime count equally on the West. Except for the French before 1967, Israel never received major support in wartime from Europe after 1967, while the United States refused to sell major arms to Israel from 1948 to 1962.

Israel has received strong support from the United States over the last 60 years. But it also had to battle presidents (like Eisenhower, Nixon, Ford and Carter) who often were hostile or had other agendas. Given the power of the attitudes, style and advisers of the president, who could be somewhat independent, if limited by a number of factors (Congress, interest groups, bureaucracy, the international system and the media), this was hardly surprising.[1]

Israel faced strong ambivalence and even antipathy in certain arenas (the State Department and the Defense Department) in the United States. In 1917 the State Department "vehemently" opposed the Balfour Declaration and felt that "a Jewish state should never be tolerated." Secretary of State Robert Lansing opposed the Balfour Declaration.[2] Franklin Roosevelt repeatedly waffled on his support for the creation of the state of Israel. In a letter to Congress in March 1945 about his meeting with Saudi King ibn Saud, he wrote that, "of all the problems of Arabia, I learned more about the whole problem, the Muslim problem, the Jewish problem, by talking with Ibn-Saud for five minutes than I could have learned in exchange of two or three dozen letters."[3] Monty Penkower depicted Roosevelt as "actually veer[ing] toward State's anti-Zionist standard." Public pledges in late 1944 and early 1945 to support Zionism were balanced with confidential promises through the State Department to Moslem rulers opposing Zionism.[4]

A sympathetic Harry Truman, while supporting the creation of Israel, waffled as well. After supporting Israel in November 1947, the United States seemingly backed away from the partition plan and pushed a trusteeship for Palestine until May 1948.[5] In May 1948 future Secretary of State Dean Rusk wrote: "We have told them [the Jews] that if they get in trouble, don't come to us for help in a military sense."[6] Secretary of State George Marshall, supported by the CIA, Defense Secretary James Forrestal and leading State Department diplomats (Dean Rusk and Leroy Henderson), warned President Truman that he would vote against him if he supported the creation of Israel.[7]

In 1948 the Americans seemed to collaborate with the British in supporting the mediator Count Bernadotte's plans that focused on replacement of Israel by a bi-national state. These plans, ended by his assassination in September 1948 and Israeli victories, included demilitarization or international control of Haifa, surrender of large areas of southern Palestine to the Arabs in return for the western Galilee, the incorporation of the Negev into Transjordan, the internationalization of Jerusalem and the joint control of Jewish immigration by Jews and Arabs through the union of the two territories in a dual state.[8] In 1949 at the Lausanne Conference the United States called for Israeli withdrawal from the southern Negev, repatriation of 200,000–250,000 refugees and no direct contacts between Israel and the Arabs.[9] The Truman administration tried to placate the Arabs and win their support through concessions.[10] But, at the same time, American support for the partition plan and early recognition of the state of Israel were critical to the creation and early success of the state of Israel.

Dwight Eisenhower often used American Jewish funding of Israel as a club to wrest concessions. In 1954 Assistant Secretary of State Henry Byroade:

> maintained . . . that the Zionist ideology of Israel and its free admission of Jews were a legitimate matter of concern both to the Arabs and to the Western countries . . . America also took drastic steps to enforce Israeli submission to restrictions of its sovereignty in the civilian development of the demilitarized zones and it maintained a stiff avoidance of Israeli Jerusalem after it became the effective and proclaimed capital of the country. In addition, America from time to time expressed a vague sympathy, if not support, for plans to cut back Israel's territory in vital areas.[11]

In the middle 1950s the United States and Great Britain, which was closely allied with the Arab world, floated two secret peace initiatives code-named Alpha and Gamma. In Alpha Israel would concede large parts of the southern Negev in return for an Arab pledge of non-belligerency. Egypt would have received huge quantities of American arms and a land bridge across the Negev to Jordan. In December 1955 Secretary of State John Foster Dulles called for reparations and repatriation for refugees and cession of the southern Negev so that Jordan and Egypt would be able to touch each other. In 1956 the Gamma plan proposed trading Egyptian non-belligerency for more Israeli land.[12] That year too President Eisenhower rejected an Israeli request for an American–Israeli alliance in face of the threat to its existence posed by the Czechoslovak arms sales to Egypt.[13]

The United States refused to sell Israel weapons from 1948 to 1962. Yet even here the record was mixed. In 1948 Israel faced five better-armed Arab armies, but the United States would not budge. However, this embargo (December 1947) also allowed Great Britain, which probably would have sold more weapons to the Arabs than the United States to the Jews, to drastically cut back its military aid two months later to all Arab states, save Transjordan.[14]

In 1950 the United States, Great Britain and France issued the Tripartite Declaration calling for keeping the peace by preventing arms imbalance in the region. Declassified documents have revealed that, from 1950 to the mid-1950s, the United States and Britain had detailed military plans for operations to be launched against Israel if it committed any aggression against its neighbors.[15] While talking about arming Iraq in the mid–1950s, the United States refused an Israeli request for arms. Even when the Russians through Czechoslovakia sold Egypt 250 MIG jets in 1955, the United States refused an Israeli request for 48 F-86 jet fighters and 60 Patton tanks.[16]

In the 1956 Sinai Campaign, President Dwight Eisenhower criticized the Sinai Campaign and forced an Israeli withdrawal. Ambassador to the United Nations Henry Cabot Lodge called for United Nations members to provide no economic, military or financial aid to Israel until it withdrew to the 1949 armistice lines.[17] In 1957 Secretary of State John Foster Dulles threatened "serious consideration" of economic sanctions and the possible lifting of the tax-exempt status of the United Jewish Appeal if Israel did not withdraw totally.[18] In 1960 the United States sold radar equipment to Israel. In 1962 President Kennedy broke the boycott by selling Israel Hawk anti-aircraft missiles. Not until 1968, 20 years after the creation of Israel, would the United States in the wake of the Six Day War become the major weapons supplier to Israel.[19]

In 1967 the United States, preoccupied with Vietnam, did not help Israel as it faced the Egyptian army moving into the Sinai and Gaza. It was dilatory even on its 1957 guarantee for Israel's right to pass through the Straits of Tiran. In May 1967 the State Department implied that the United States had no commitment to Israel and that the Sixth Fleet would likely remain neutral if there were fighting.[20]

The United States in 1967 delayed any response to an Israeli request for such arms as 100 Hawk missiles, 140 Patton tanks and 24 Skyhawk jets and refused to appoint a liaison with the Israelis. As Israeli Ambassador Avraham Harmon told Eugene Rostow, "If war breaks out, we would have no telephone number to call, no code for plane recognition and no way to get in touch with the Sixth Fleet." The day before the war started, President Lyndon Johnson sent a letter to the Israeli government stating that, "I must emphasize the

necessity for Israel not to make itself responsible for the initiation of hos-
tilities. Israel will not be alone unless it decides to go alone. We cannot
imagine that it will make this decision." While President Johnson was pro-
Israeli, he was unable or unwilling to take a determined stand on Israel's side
unless Israel seemed threatened by extermination. Secretary of State Dean
Rusk was less than friendly towards Israel.[21]

President Nixon was often confrontational towards the Israelis. In 1973 the
United States refused to warn Israel of the upcoming war and spare Israel
much devastation and trauma. It also cautioned that Israel not fire the first
shot, thereby ensuring some Arab successes.[22] The Soviet Union re-supplied
Egypt and Syria on the fourth day of the war, while the Americans waited
until the tenth day of the war. In the middle 1970s President Ford carried
out a famous "reassessment" of American support for Israel until forced to
change his position. President Carter, supportive of a Palestinian homeland,
was often critical of Israel and sold 62 F–15s to Saudi Arabia.[23] In 1982
the United States, which the year before had sold AWACS planes to Saudi
Arabia, did nothing to aid the Israelis in the war in Lebanon and was often
critical of it.

In 1991 the United States prevented Israel from retaliation after being hit
by a barrage of 39 Iraqi Scud missiles that killed one Israeli and damaged
4,000 apartments. In 2002 the Bush administration frequently admonished
Israel not to retaliate after major terrorist attacks, a position that changed
only after June 2002. Only after the *Karine A* affair, 9/11 and protracted
Palestinian terrorism did the Bush administration become more sympathetic
to the Israeli position. This was seen again in the green light given to Israel
in July 2006 in its campaign against Hezbollah and a $30 billion ten-year
military aid package proposed in the summer of 2007.

Israeli leaders often spent a lengthy amount of time in negotiations and
consultation with Washington before taking action. When they failed to
adequately consult (as in the Phalcon sale to China), they were reprimanded.
Israel was still dependent on the United States in a way that significantly
limited its freedom of action.

The situation was more problematic (save for France from 1956 to 1967)
with regard to other Western powers. The congruence in values (democracy,
free market economies, the rule of law, free speech and the Internet) and major
trade between Israel and Europe did not translate into European support for
Israel during crises.

Global anti-Semitism and anti-Israelism

The Jewish desire to create and maintain the state of Israel ran into extensive
anti-Israelism that stemmed from anti-Semitism, oil dependency, Third World
romanticism of the Palestinian victims and post-modernism. Anti-Semitism
had deep roots in both the Christian and the Muslim worlds. It is true that
Jewish history also had significant periods of hospitable Jewish existence

from the Babylonian Diaspora in Talmudic times, Ptolemaic Egypt and much of the Roman Empire to Muslim and pre-Christian Spain, the pre-partition Polish–Lithuanian Commonwealth, the Austro-Hungarian Empire, pre-Nazi Germany and the United States today.[24] But, as Cecil Roth has written, for 1,400 years in Europe until the French Revolution the Jew was:

> subject to a systemic degradation, an exclusion from opportunity, a warping of his natural bent and a distortion of his normal position . . . They were compelled to live together in a separate quarter of the town, known as the Ghetto, which was generally unhealthy and rarely large enough to accommodate them without the most appalling overcrowding. The Ghetto gates were closed every night and, until they were opened again in the morning, no Jew might show his face outside and no Gentile might venture within . . . In the streets, sometimes in the Ghetto too, the Jew had to be distinguished by an ugly badge of shame, a yellow circle worn on the outer garment above the heart in Germany, a yellow or crimson hat or kerchief in Italy . . . Each Sabbath the Jews were forced to attend conversionist sermons, where they were compelled to hear long tirades against Judaism. Their children might be seized and forcibly baptized . . . Jews were not allowed to ride in coaches or to be addressed with the customary courteous prefixes . . . On Good Friday, in many places, they were stoned by the rabble and buffeted by the authorities, sometimes with fatal results . . . They were harried with absurd accusations . . . So many restrictions, in fact, were placed upon the Jew that life would have been impossible for him had he obeyed them all. Evasion was necessary, if he were to exist.[25]

In Europe blood libels, accusing Jews of killing Christians for use of their blood, were widespread from 1144 to 1407 in such towns as Paris, Munich, Prague, Krakow and London.[26] During the Crusades tens of thousands of Jews were killed in over a dozen German towns, from Cologne to Worms to Prague in 1096. Forcible conversions of Jews occurred for over a thousand years in Marseilles (591), Paris (629), Spain (1146, 1391, 1411, 1492), Krakow (1407), Toulouse (1431), Portugal (1497), Rome (1543, 1783) and Ukraine (1648–56). Tsar Nicholas I introduced 25-year military service for Jews (1827, 1874) and 12-year-old Jewish children were often forcibly converted to Orthodoxy.

To the east and south, matters were not much better. After 644 AD, when Jews were not willing to accept Islam they were expelled from the Hijaz by Muslim rulers. In Persia as late as 1848 the Jewish community of Meshed was forcibly converted to Islam. In the Byzantium Empire there were four major campaigns (640, 721, 873 and 930 AD) when popes ordered forcible conversion and baptism and forbade the practice of Judaism.[27]

Jews were expelled from England (1290), France (1306, 1322, 1394), Germany (1096–1192), Hungary (1349–60), Lithuania (1445, 1495), Spain and Portugal (1492, 1496). During the Black Plagues of the 1340s, Jews were blamed for poisoning the wells, and over 300 Jewish communities were attacked. The Spanish Inquisition (1492–1820), which claimed 341,000 victims, burnt Jews at the stake in auto-da-fés for heresy, persecuted former Jews (merinos) and relentlessly focused its power on the Jews.[28]

The rise of Protestantism (1517) did not immediately change matters. In 1543 Martin Luther in "On the Jews and Their Lies" called for setting fire to synagogues, destroying their prayer books, forbidding rabbis to preach, smashing and destroying Jewish homes, seizing Jewish property, expelling the Jews and even making them do forced labor.[29]

The Chmielnicki massacres (1648–56), led by the Cossack leader Bogdan Chmielnicki, killed over 100,000 Jews in Poland and Ukraine and tortured or abused tens of thousands of other Jews.[30] In Russia, Tsar Ivan IV declared in 1550 that "It is not convenient to allow Jews to come with their goods into Russia since many evils result from them. For they import poisonous herbs and lead astray Russians from Christianity."[31]

Anti-Semitism, with the entry of the masses into politics after the French Revolution, resurfaced with a vengeance in the modern world. Many leaders of the French Enlightenment were anti-Semitic.[32] In Europe the leading anti-liberal movements (Communism, fascism and nationalism) displayed varying degrees of anti-Semitism, despite (or perhaps because of) the emancipation of the Jews west of the Elbe. Napoleon freed the ghettos of Europe but they were restored after his demise in 1815. The failed 1848 Revolution led to emancipation in Italy (1848–70), Britain (1858), the Austro-Hungarian Empire (1867) and Germany (1871).[33]

Despite its numerous leaders of Jewish origins, Communism often had leaders who reviled the Jews. This started with its founder Karl Marx (himself of Jewish origins), who wrote *On the Jewish Question* in 1844:

> The real God of the Jews is money. Their God is only an illusory bill of exchange ... What the Jewish religion contains in the abstract – the contempt of science, of art, of history, of man as an end purpose in himself; all this is the conscious view, the virtue of the money man ... The chimerical nationality of the Jew is the nationality of the merchant ... The Jewish law, of a people without a land, is the religious caricature of morality and law ... Judaism ... is by nature narrow minded and soon exhausted ... The social emancipation of the Jew is the emancipation of society from Judaism.[34]

The Dreyfus Affair from 1894 to 1906 reflected strong anti-Semitism in the center of Europe. When Alsatian Jewish Colonel Alfred Dreyfus was charged and convicted falsely with treason in the case of missing documents, the mob in Paris shouted "Death to the Jews," thus inspiring Theodor Herzl's promotion of modern Zionism. It took over a decade before he was exonerated and brought back from exile in Devil's Island. In Vienna, an anti-Semitic mayor

(Karl Lueger) won election three times starting in 1895 on the platform of anti-Semitism and the need for anti-Semitic legislation.

In France and Germany anti-Semitic racialist doctrine, based on a crude version of social Darwinism, became popular. In 1853 the French Comte Joseph de Gobineau proclaimed the superiority of Aryan virtue over the degenerate Semitic and Latin types. In 1863 Ernst Renan in his *Vie de Jesus* declared that "the Semitic race, compared to the Indo-European race, represents an inferior level of human race." By the late 1880s Édouard Drumont had founded the Anti-Semitic League and its daily paper, *La Libre Parole*.[35]

Anti-Semitism was particularly pervasive and even deadly east of the Oder in Russia, Poland and Rumania. After the Rumanian government in the late 1860s and 1870s made clear that it wanted to expel its Jews, the majority had immigrated to the United States by 1914. In Russia, plagued by pogroms, discrimination, resident restrictions in the restricted Pale of Settlement and dire poverty, over 2 million Jews had immigrated to the United States by 1914. In 1903 the Tsarist secret police (Okhrana) in the fraudulent *Protocols of the Elders of Zion* claimed that Jews secretly ran the world. During the 1918–20 civil war in Russia over 30,000 Jews were killed in over 2,000 Ukrainian pogroms, and 150,000 Jews may have died from wounds and illness.[36]

Anti-Semitism reached its height during the Holocaust when the Nazis killed 6 million Jews during World War II. At the Evian conference (1938) none of more than 30 states (save the Dominican Republic, which later reneged on its pledge) were willing to take in any Jewish refugees. In Vichy France (1940–44) Marshal Henri Pétain resurrected anti-Semitic restrictions on Jews and allowed the deportation of 82,000 French Jews to Auschwitz. The Romanian government of Marshal Antonescu killed over 200,000 Romanian Jews in its own camps.[37] In the Soviet Union anti-Semitism led to the removal of most Jewish leaders in the Great Purges, Stalin's refusal to appoint almost any Jews to the new elite and discrimination against Jews entering into universities.

Anti-Semitism was strong in the United States, where an overwhelming majority in 1938 said the United States should keep out political refugees.[38] President Franklin Roosevelt, a friend of the King of Saudi Arabia, told General Nogues in Casablanca in January 1943 that he understood "the specific and understandable complaints which the Germans bore towards the Jews in Germany" and would keep in place discriminatory quotas against Jewish professionals in North Africa.[39]

Even after the Holocaust, anti-Semitism and resultant anti-Israeli attitudes remained strong. Anti-Semitism remained strong even after the liberation of the camps and demise of Nazi Germany by May 1945. Stalin unleashed the "dark years of Soviet Jewry," highlighted by the Doctors' Plot (1952), the shooting of 30 leading Jewish poets and preparations for deporting Soviet Jews to labor camps in Kazakhstan. Anti-Semitic political trials were widespread in Eastern Europe in the late 1940s. In the United States, President

Truman repeatedly expressed himself in an anti-Semitic manner, and key advisers, such as George Marshall, Dean Rusk and Robert Lovett, were strongly opposed to the creation of the state of Israel.[40] The British in 1948 favored the Arabs as they left Palestine and offered to sell upwards of 50,000 machine guns to Jordan and Iraq.

In the first decade of the twenty-first century, there has been a resurgence of global anti-Semitism. Thinly veiled anti-Semitism is now common in much of the Third World and at the United Nations. In 2002 the outgoing Malaysian prime minister at the Office of the Islamic Conference declared that "The Jews rule the world by proxy" and received a standing ovation from the representatives of 57 Islamic countries. United Nations resolutions condemning anti-Semitism are regularly omitted from resolutions condemning racism, discrimination and prejudice, while the Jewish state has been attacked in several hundred United Nations resolutions. In Europe almost one-third of the population remains anti-Semitic, and Israel, until recently, received scant support. Thousands of anti-Semitic incidents have occurred since 2000 in Europe, especially in France. The United States Congress in 2004 passed a Global Anti-Semitism Act requiring the State Department to form an office to issue an annual report on anti-Semitism around the world. Massive Arab, Nazi and Soviet anti-Semitism have fed global anti-Semitism, which continues to pose a threat to the Jewish state in 2007.

Western unwillingness to help Israel in crisis has been a serious problem for Israel. It has accentuated the sense of international isolation when even its friends are reluctant to get involved on behalf of a small state. Given its thin margin for survival and the regional and international forces opposing it, this issue can achieve cardinal importance for Israeli leaders and push them at times towards preemptive strikes. It leaves Israel feeling alone in a largely hostile Arab–Iranian sea (especially when the bulk of the Egyptian and Jordanian populations are hostile towards Israel) and even questioning whether Israel will be able to survive in the years and decades ahead.

9 Israeli issues

Not all the problems facing Israel have been external. There have been a series of specifically Israeli issues that have further complicated the rise and flourishing of Israel.

The centrality and visibility of the land of Israel

A key problem for Israel has been the centrality of the Middle East in the geography, history, culture and mythology of the world. The 600 billion barrels of oil reserves (60 percent of the world's reserves) of the Middle East are critical to the global economy. The Middle East stands at the crossroads of three powerful regions (Europe, Africa and Asia), with great powers contesting it for thousands of years. Cartographers in the Middle Ages placed Jerusalem at the center of world maps. James Parks wrote that "Spiritually, geographically and economically it [the land of Israel] lies at the heart of humanity."[1]

Three factors made the Arab–Israeli dispute a central issue in world affairs. The Arab–Jewish contest over Israel occurred in modern times. It happened in the center of the Middle East and Arab world and developed at the religious crossroads of Western civilization, in areas and places (such as Jerusalem) that arouse great sentiment in hundreds of millions of people.

Jerusalem is the holiest city to Jews, the second holiest city to Christians and the third holiest city to Muslims. This is the city which King David walked, where Jesus trod the Stations of the Cross and died on the cross, where Muhammad ascended to heaven. This is the land that Egyptians, Greeks, Persians, Romans, Arabs, Turks, Mamelukes and Jews fought over and died for. This is the land key to three great Western monotheistic religions.

Disadvantages in size, numbers, weapons and borders in major wars with the Arabs

Joel Migdal has stressed the impact that recognized borders have on the development of a state.[2] Israel has probably had more borders than any other state in the world:

1 Ottoman Turkey (1900–18) – no borders but part of three sanjaks (Jerusalem, Nablus and Damascus) of empire;
2 British Occupation (1918–22) – historical Palestine including Trans-jordan;
3 British Mandate (1922–48) – Palestine west of the Jordan River;
4 Israel (1948–67) – smaller Israel of 7,800 square miles;
5 Israel (1967–81) – larger Israel with East Jerusalem, Sinai, the Golan Heights, the West Bank and the Gaza Strip;
6 Israel (1981–94) – medium Israel without the Sinai Peninsula but still with the Golan Heights, the West Bank and the Gaza Strip;
7 Israel (1994–2004) – medium Israel with self-rule in Gaza and the West Bank;
8 Israel (2005–07) – medium/smaller Israel without Gaza and four former settlements on the West Bank and occupation of much of the West Bank, and also the Golan Heights.

Here is an incomplete list of plans that have been floated for the final borders of the state of Israel and their relative portion of historical Palestine west of the Jordan River:

1 Peel Commission (1937) – 20 percent of Palestine;
2 Woodhead Commission (1938) – 5 percent of Palestine;
3 British White Paper (1939) – no Israel but an Arab independent state (1949);
4 United Nations Partition Plan (1947) – 45 percent of Palestine and no Jerusalem;
5 International Peace Plans (1967 onward) – pre-1967 borders with small modifications;
6 Rogers Plan (1969) – pre-1967 borders with minor modifications;
7 Begin Plan (1977 onward) – Israel without the Sinai Peninsula but with East Jerusalem, the West Bank and the Golan Heights;
8 Baker Plan (1981) – pre-1967 borders with small modifications;
9 Clinton Plan (2000) – pre-1967 borders with annexation of major settlement blocs;
10 Saudi Plan (2002) – pre-1967 borders;
11 Geneva Plan (2003) – largely pre-1967 borders;
12 Sharon Plan (2005) – pre-1967 borders plus annexation of major settlement blocs (15 percent of the West Bank).

From 1948 to 1967 Israel operated with one of the most vulnerable borders in the world. With no strategic depth (a waist 9 miles wide), small Israel (7,800 square miles) had 615 miles of borders – 350 miles with Jordan, 130 miles with Egypt, 68 miles with Lebanon, 50 miles with Syria and 37 miles with Gaza.[3] The long, ill-defined, ill-protected borders with Jordan had hundreds of thousands of refugees on the other side, as did the smaller borders with Gaza, packed with refugees from 1948. This geographic vulnerability was compounded by the lack of natural barriers to protect Israel.[4]

Israel has been one of the few countries without fixed and internationally recognized borders. During the pre-1949 period, its potential size careened from 10,000 square miles (Mandatory Palestine) to 1,870 square miles (1937 Peel Commission Plan) to 5,630 square miles (1947 Partition Plan) to 7,800 square miles (1949 armistice lines).[5] From 1948 to 1982 its borders were armistice lines from the war. Only in 1982 did it gain a fixed recognized border with Egypt and in 1994 with Jordan. Even in 2007 its borders with Syria, Lebanon and the Palestinians are neither recognized nor finalized.

These borders, beyond being strategic defensive lines, served as cultural markers, legal and achieved dividing lines and ideological statements of the identity of a country. They provide cognitive and mental maps with sacred spaces (graveyards, battlefields) to which people become attached.[6] For Israel the natural borders of the state of Israel were issues of contention even within the Jewish community. Were these the borders promised to Abraham in the Torah (very expansive borders from Egypt to the Euphrates) or those concomitant with the land of Canaan, the narrower borders of the Return from Babylon and the two kingdoms or the wider borders attained by King David? In 1918 the Zionists prepared a brief for the Versailles Peace Conference with broad borders, but political realities led by 1922 to dropping claims over southern Lebanon, Transjordan and the Golan Heights.[7]

Surrounded by five largely hostile Arab neighbors (save for Jordan), Israel was geographically isolated from friendlier Western countries, which were not bound by treaty to come to its aid in time of war.[8] Things were even worse with Jerusalem, the capital. The Jordanians occupied East Jerusalem (including the Old City) from 1948 to 1967. As a volume on Hadassah in Jerusalem depicted the situation:

> Jerusalem offered no easy locations. Fashioned by nature in the shape of an outstretched hand – of ridges and valleys – the city was further limited for reasons of security. Jewish Jerusalem was the end of a salient that began in the Judean foothills to the west and stuck out like a thumb, in the gut of the heavily populated sections of Arab Palestine that had recently been annexed by Jordan. Arab military positions dominated the city from high points to the south and north. On the eastern border, which cut through the middle of Jerusalem's commercial section, Jordanian sentries sat perched on rooftops. Few sites anywhere were at that time beyond the effective range of Arab guns.[9]

The separation of Jordan from Palestine in 1921 left the future state of Israel exposed to danger. For, as Howard Sachar has observed:

> The accord represented a painful setback for the Jews. To the north and northeast the country was deprived of its most important potential water

resources, including the Litani River, a key fount of the Jordan, the spring arising from Mount Hermon and the greater part of the Yarmuk . . . Moreover by failing to approximate any natural geographic frontiers, the borders left the country perennially exposed to armed invasion. This heritage of economic and military vulnerability was to curse the Palestine mandate and later the entire Middle East, for decades to come.[10]

Israel's tiny size and vulnerable frontiers represent a serious liability that cannot be overcome by modernization and development. Israel lacks the strategic depth of the United States (shielded by the Pacific and Atlantic Oceans), Great Britain (protected by the English Channel), Russia (with 6.5 million square miles) or France (enclosed by the Atlantic Ocean and Pyrenees). The nuclearization of the Middle East threatens Israel as the majority of its Jewish population lives in three metropolitan areas (Jerusalem, Tel Aviv and Haifa).

Large countries provide regional insurance, redistributive schemes, larger markets, economies of scale, better defense and lower cost of public goods per capita. Larger states are able to afford such public goods as defense, finance, judiciary, monetary institutions and infrastructure such as embassies, health facilities, police, parks, community services and crime fighting. With no economies of scale, small states such as Israel are forced to provide a higher relative level of government spending. Without homogeneity, Israel lacks a major benefit of many smaller states.[11]

Numbers were also a major problem. In 1948 Israel had 650,000 Jews, while the surrounding Arab states had 27 million Arabs. By 2007 Israel had 5.4 million Jews, and the 22 Arab states had 285 million Arabs.

Israel's small size and awareness of the explicit Arab threat to throw Israel into the sea led Israel to undertake preemptive actions in its first three wars (1948, 1956 and 1967). In its major wars Israel faced an imbalance in numbers and weapons. The Arab states fielded bigger armies with a strong quantitative preponderance.[12] As Yaacov Lifshitz summed up the permanent security dilemma facing Israel:

> There is a great different in human and material resources between Israel and the Arab states. This absolute fact, and its far-reaching economic implications, have been and remain of first importance in formulating Israel's national security . . . As Ben Gurion noted in the 1950s, "Our trouble is that we cannot afford defeat, because then we are finished . . . they can be defeated once, twice, if we defeat Egypt ten times it means nothing" . . . in victory, however great, Israel could not anticipate that the security problem would be solved . . . even after victory it was necessary to prepare for another round of war.[13]

This also dictated an approach focused on human resources, high technology and offensive doctrine. Sophisticated manpower was needed to maintain sophisticated military weapons systems. It promoted an Israeli military with a small permanent career service nucleus, mass conscription of both men and women and a large reserve corps.

From 1964 to 1997 Israel's Arab and Persian antagonists imported roughly $300 billion and Israel $45 billion of weapons from the United States and Russia, a 7:1 edge for Israel's foes. At its height the Middle East from 1974 to 1989 imported $15 billion in weapons every year, of which Israel imported $2 billion.[14]

Economic backwardness of Palestine

There were serious obstacles to the creation of a viable economy. The Jewish homeland, as we have seen in an earlier chapter, had to be built "under exceptionally difficult circumstances." Palestine for 400 years was ruled by the Ottoman Turkish Empire through an authority in Damascus that ruled three sanjaks in Jerusalem, Acre and Nablus. Palestine before 1920 was so dangerous that towns were walled and closed at night. In 1900, when there were no wheeled vehicles or metallic roads, it took nine hours to travel 40 miles by train from Jaffa to Hadera. The train after 1892 took four to six hours to travel less than 60 miles from Jaffa to Jerusalem. In 1914 there were no paved roads, telephones or electricity and a lone motor car in Ottoman Turkish Palestine. Only 17 percent of the industries used any kind of engines. Apart from a couple of workshops and mills and basic agricultural industries such as soap making, tanning and shoe making there was no modern industry. A 1928 British study found that machinery "was almost unknown" in Palestine, 150 years after the start of the Industrial Revolution in Britain.[15]

Israel is located in one of the least modern areas of the world. Apart from oil and natural gas, the level of development, apart from sub-Saharan Africa, is the lowest of the major regions of the world. Entrepreneurial capitalism, high technology and commercial capitalism are very weak. Local regional markets were unavailable due to the Arab boycott, which limited Israeli ability to trade and import technology from abroad.

Zionism, as Baruch Kimmerling has shown, was not economically profitable. Much that the Zionists needed to do for political purposes was economically irrational.[16] The period from 1881 to 1950, despite enormous Zionist efforts, saw "extremely slow" economic progress that left the validity of the Zionist economic experiment "in doubt."[17]

The development of the land of Israel was an expensive proposition. Centuries of Ottoman Turkish neglect had led to massive soil erosion, made worse by the marauding habits of large numbers of goats and frequent raiding and village wars between fellahin and the Bedouin. From 1881 to 1948 the price of land in Palestine under Ottoman Turkey and the British Empire was very high. In 1936 poor land in Palestine sold for $128 per acre when better land was selling for $31 per acre in the United States. By 1944 poor land in Palestine sold for $1,050 per acre in Palestine but richer land was selling for

$35 per acre in the United States. The land needed another 50 percent of the purchase price for draining and irrigation before it was ready for use.[18] Even then the land was often unprofitable.

By 1937 the Jews owned 5 percent and, in 1947, 7 percent of the land of Palestine.[19] Only after the flight of 500,000–700,000 Palestinian Arabs during and after the War of Independence did the Jewish state gain control of the great majority of the land.

Labor, like land, which historically is cheap in the Third World, was rather expensive. Given the conflict between the Arabs and the Jews, Arab labor became expensive and hard to find. Jews preferred to use more expensive but reliable Jewish labor. In 1936, 15 percent of the employees of the Jewish economy were Arabs: the number dropped precipitously after the Arab Revolt.[20]

Terrible health and sanitary conditions made the cost of preparing the stony and poor land for modern production a long and arduous process. In 1878 the settlement at Petach Tikvah was started, and four years later it was abandoned after recurrent bouts of malaria had devastated the workers and harvests were poor. That year the settlement at Rosh Pinah was started, only to be abandoned two years later for the same reasons plus active Arab hostility. In 1890 a settlement was started in Hadera: by 1910 the majority of the workers had died from malaria. Only an idealistic commitment to overcome these objective conditions could make Zionism work.[21]

Another key factor of production missing was natural resources. In a region famous for vast natural resources, the state of Israel has almost no oil or gas, minimal minerals, a shortage of water and a vast desert that needed huge economic investment.

Another factor was education. While the Jews were better educated than the Arabs, they still lagged well behind the West. With the stress on farming, pioneering and socialism and wars, there was little emphasis on universities. A backward economy could not attract well-educated immigrants, who (except for the German Jews in the 1930s) had more attractive opportunities in the West. While the American Jewish community in the 1950s numbered hundreds of thousands of college students and graduates, there were 700 Jewish university students in Palestine in 1948 – and one-third of them were killed in the 1948 War of Independence.[22]

Then there was the lack of modern transportation and infrastructure. There were few modern roads even by the 1920s. In the 1920s Bedouin raids across the Jordan were "still a constant trouble."[23] In 1917 when David Ben Gurion proposed to his future wife, Paula, he declared, "You will have to leave America and journey with me to a small, impoverished country without electricity, gas or motorized transport."[24]

Yet another problem was the military burden. After the declaration of the state of Israel in May 1948, this burden fell on the Jewish sector. By the 1970s Israelis spent 5.5 times more per capita on military expenses than comparable states. Men were taken for three years of service from 18 to 21 and remained eligible for combat duty until 40 and military service until 53. Women were taken for two years of service from 18 to 20. This removed prime manpower from the labor force 5 to 8.5 times more than in other states.[25]

Capital imports were another problem for economic development. Arab hostility, a weak economic base, the Great Depression of the 1930s, World War II and then the massacre of European Jews during the Holocaust contributed to weak capital inputs before 1948. Total capital investment was less than $300 million. Agriculture, industry and transportation received less than 50 percent of investment.[26]

Foreign capital, until the 1990s, was largely absent in Israel's development. Lack of natural resources, thin population, poor agricultural endowment, high wages, a small domestic market, frequent wars and intifadas, the Arab boycott, isolation from the region and the lack of a strong domestic capitalist class slowed FDI to a trickle until recently. The Zionists found some capital from wealthy Diaspora Jews, initially Baron Edmond de Rothschild and more recently a group of Western businessmen. While foreign capital was largely absent from Palestine before 1948, from 1948 to 1988 foreign capital invested a paltry $2 billion in Israel. Only after the end of the Cold War in 1991 did billions of dollars of foreign capital begin to flow into Israel. The threat to the Zionist enterprise was palpable. As Michael Barnett has commented:

> The lack of capitalist interest in Palestine presented . . . [a] threat to the very viability of a Jewish homeland; the Zionist mission was premised on attracting other Jews to Palestine, which was dependent on having a dynamic economy, and economic and political conditions were so severe that some years saw more Jewish immigration from, than to, Palestine.[27]

Owing to the security situation, World War II and resultant 1948 war, tourism was virtually non-existent before the 1950s. In 1952 only 32,000 tourists came to Israel. The victory in the Sinai Campaign, a more peaceful home front, Western prosperity, and the advent of jet planes boosted this number to 100,000 by 1959 and several million by the 1990s, before the second intifada derailed it, a situation reversed only with its end.[28]

Security for the economic system, usually a near free product, was expensive for the Zionist effort. Although it shared expenses with the Ottoman Turks or the British Empire, security before 1947 required outlays for guards, arms and defense organizations. After the formation of the state, Israel became a virtual garrison state with huge expenditures on defense. Ilan Troen showed how security and ideological considerations trumped economic rationality in building up the state. Jerusalem, the holy city, had to be built up and defended against all costs, although surrounded by the Jordanians, for:

> Israel's Jerusalem is not typical of how contemporary cities have been planned. The city was intended to serve religious and political purposes, as it did when it was first established by King David 3,000 years ago. With

the city's function so defined, the economic irrationality of developing a modern metropolis in the Judean Mountains was a problem that had to be overcome. In the ancient world, as in the modern world, the Mediterranean coast is where great cities developed far more naturally. Centers of ritual and political capitals were removed from the coast and thereby from the dangers of attack from the sea . . . if a political compromise were reached, there would be little justification for maintaining Jerusalem as a modern metropolis.[29]

For security, it was necessary to build large numbers of villages on the country's borders at great expense and far removed from the center of the country and international trade routes. To cover the 400-mile border, the Zionists had to build 650 new villages from 1881 to 1967 without regard to economic rationality. With socio-political ideological concerns and security concerns replacing economic concerns, a core of professional planners, architects and organizational officials displaced normal market forces. Dozens of development towns were established with great cost and little economic basis. For Kiryat Shemona over 75,000 immigrants have gone there and left.[30]

Even successful new towns and villages came at great cost. Beersheva, the capital of the Negev, in 1900 was an oasis for nomad Bedouins and in 1948 it was a ghost town 84 miles from Tel Aviv after the local Arabs fled. Only massive government aid helped to build a modern city.[31]

In 1949, when Golda Meir went to the new Knesset for approval to build 35,000 new apartments for new immigrants pouring into the country she emphasized that the apartments would have one large room per family and that the state had no money to build them. Many immigrants in the 1950s wound up in tents and shacks that provided an abominable lifestyle. The arrival of hundreds of thousands of poorly educated impoverished immigrants doubling the population of the country in three years left the economy on "on the verge of collapse."[32] In 1949 exports were $43 million while imports were $263 million. In 1950 exports edged up to $46 million while imports were $328 million. GNP was a tiny $1.3 billion.[33]

The security primacy led to the building of over 200 kibbutzim, with strong strategic and military functions. Israel was the only non-Communist state to support collective farming. In the 1948 war it was kibbutzim that slowed the Egyptian advance in the south (as at Yad Mordechai and Kfar Darom) and on the Lebanese, Jordanian and Syrian borders.[34] For, as Ilan Troen has shown:

> The socialist villages (kibbutzim and moshavim) were a unique village ideal, comparable to American family homesteading and European estates and plantations in distant colonies. Built on the model of medieval Europe, they stressed self-sufficiency and opposition to all modern economic nostrums: mechanization, large farms and use of cheap Arab labor. In a romantic vision, they were to turn the most urbanized people

in the world into rural farmers on remote pieces of land far from urban centers.[35]

The arrival of massive waves of new immigrants, poorly educated and largely destitute, caused huge short-term economic difficulty. Many of these urbanites were transformed into farmers with great difficulty. In the early 1950s Dov Joseph imposed austerity which prevented the purchase of new appliances and sharply decreased the standard of living. Total exports brought in only 11 percent of the cost of imports, while the annual foreign exchange deficit was $200 per capita.[36]

By 1936, with the immigration of wealthier German Jews, the Jewish economy produced 64 percent of needed goods and was worth £37 million.[37] From 1936 to 1944 the Arab economy barely grew 20 percent while the Jewish economy doubled in size, largely from immigration and British war contracts.[38] From 1950 to 1974 almost $20 billion of capital investment flowed into Israel. Fully 63 percent represented transfer payments to individuals and institutions, mainly from German reparations and the United Jewish Appeal. Another 30 percent came in the form of medium- and long-term loans, mainly Israel Bonds. Only 7 percent ($1.3 billion) came in the form of private FDI. Two-thirds of all investment flowed to the government, only one-third to private individuals.[39] Only in the 1990s did major FDI begin to pour into Israel. But by 2005 the defeat of the second intifada, the death of Arafat and global recovery saw the Israeli economy beginning to pick up. In 2006 the Israeli economy grew over 5 percent and received $14 billion of FDI.

Problems specific to Israel – Arab semi-encirclement, lack of factors of production (expensive labor, weak natural resources, minimal foreign capital until the 1990s), long and often unrecognized vulnerable borders, limited tourism, cities and villages built for security and not economic reasons, millions of poorly educated immigrants, the historical economic backwardness of Palestine, and the virtual garrison state (eight wars and two intifadas) – have posed serious economic, political and social issues for the development of the state of Israel. While many states, especially in the Third World, have some of these issues (often worse than Israel), few states have faced such a large and deep number of enduring problems in their development. The unavailability of a strong regional market (save for secret and limited trade with the Arabs) further has intensified these problems. These specifically Israeli issues then are also a significant obstacle to the development of Israel, facing the serious regional and international obstacles elucidated in earlier chapters.

Part III

Revolutions and the rise of Israel

In Part III we will examine how, especially with the help of two revolutions, Israel overcame so many and such large- and medium-sized obstacles to its existence and development. A number of factors, including the rise of a friendly democratic West, the demise of Arab international allies, historical accidents and strange bedfellows, also aided success. But, without the great power unleashed by first the socialist and then the ongoing capitalist revolution, Israel would likely never have been created or sustained itself.

We begin by looking at the historical roots of these two revolutions and their foundations. Then we look at a series of revolutionary military-security factors (the will to fight, the revolutionary army and the secret police) and revolutionary civilian factors (aliyah, education and the revolutionary government and party) that helped transform Israeli power and capabilities. We conclude Part III by looking at the broader international factors that helped overall to sustain Israel. These revolutionary factors, often ignored in the case of Israel, not only made great powers out of other previously lagging countries, such as Russia, China and Vietnam, but also have the capability to transform the ability of medium to small powers as well. Yet Israel also largely (but not totally) avoided the very high costs borne by many otherwise "successful" revolutions. This part will show the workings of the revolutions in Israel in detail.

10 Historical roots of the revolutions

The Jews for almost 2,000 years were a dispersed, powerless and passive people. Ignited by the failure of the nineteenth-century Emancipation and European nationalism, the Zionists offered a revolutionary national and socialist solution to the Jewish masses. The first Israeli revolution was a social/economic/cultural revolution that re-created the Jews as a nation, and the second Israeli revolution integrated Israel into the global, capitalist revolution sweeping the world in the last several decades. Arthur Hertzberg wrote that Zionism is:

> indeed the heir to the messianic impulse and emotions of the Jewish tradition ... it is the most radical attempt in Jewish history to break out of the parochial molds of Jewish life in order to become part of the general history of man in the modern world.[1]

Religious roots

Although the First Zionist Socialist Revolution revolved around socialist and national themes, it had deep religious roots. This seems paradoxical on first sight, as the socialist Zionist stress on collective secular nationalism, stinging critique of the Diaspora, notions of national autonomy, and worldly goals of physical survival and cultural regeneration without divine will or intervention separated them from the Orthodox believers.[2] The ultra-Orthodox, seeing Zionism as a sharp break with Jewish tradition, the Talmud, Oral Law and God, often fought Zionism in Palestine and Israel.[3]

Most immigrants before the 1980s came from traditional religious homes against which they rebelled but from which they were not cut off. The socialists substituted the Torah for the Talmud, infused religious holidays with socialist meaning and created a "holy community" with hidden layers of religious meaning and charisma. Socialist Zionism, with its stress on the Bible, Israel, the Homeland, the Return to Zion from Exile, the Jewish National Fund and the Hebrew language, had sanctified and binding roots in Jewish religion. It extensively used traditional symbols to speak to the non-socialist masses. Too, socialist Zionism was more congenial for the Jewish masses than

Bundism or Communism. The socialists preserved an age-old separate identity that many were willing to jettison. As Irish and Polish nationalism were linked with Catholicism, Russian nationalism to Orthodoxy and Arab nationalism to Islam, so too was Jewish nationalism tied to Judaism in fostering a Jewish national and social identity.[4] As Emanuele Ottolenghi argued, the role of religion fit in as "Zionism was born in the midst of a prolonged struggle for the reinterpretation of Jewish identity" produced by the Enlightenment, Emancipation and the rise of modern anti-Semitism.[5] In the early days of Zionism (Mizrahi) a small religious Zionist movement arose to bridge the gap.[6]

Much of Judaism revolves around the land of Israel, Jerusalem and the Temple. The 24 holy books of the Tanakh (Torah, Prophets, Writings) contain over 700 references to Jerusalem. The Jewish calendar and the major holidays (Passover, Chanukah, Sukkoth, Shavuoth) revolve around the land of Israel. The Passover seders end every year with the final words, "Next year in Jerusalem." Jewish prayers focus heavily on Jerusalem and the land of Israel. Jews prayed facing Jerusalem five times a day in antiquity, three times a day more recently. In the morning service Jews pray, "Bring us in peace from the four corners of the earth and lead us upright to our land."

Jewish ritual events focus heavily on Jerusalem and Zion. During the circumcision of a boy at eight days old, the reader recites Psalm 137, "If I forget thee, O Jerusalem, may my right hand wither." Even during weddings, a glass is broken to remember the sadness of losing Jerusalem and the Promised Land. The groom seeks to "elevate Jerusalem to the forefront of our joy." On Tisha B'Av, religious Jews fast for the day and lament the destruction of Jewish sovereignty in the Promised Land. The grace after meals ends with a prayer for the rebuilding of "Jerusalem, the Holy City, speedily and in our days." In times of mourning, the mourners are comforted with the prayer, "Blessed are You, O Lord, Consoler of Zion and Builder of Jerusalem." Prose and poetry reinforced this message in Hebrew, Yiddish and Ladino.[7]

The dreaming of Zion is focused on Jerusalem, the Western Wall and the Temple Mount. The coming of the Messiah is to be preceded by the return of the Jews to the Promised Land from the four corners of the earth. The final redemption of the Messiah is expected to take place in the Old City of Jerusalem. Harvard scholar Ruth Wisse declared at Bar Ilan University that "No hero of chivalry or romance was ever truer to his beloved than the Jewish people to the Land of Israel" for over 2,500 years.[8]

Non-religious roots

As Howard Sachar observed, throughout the period of Exile the land of Israel:

> functioned as a binding integument of the Jewish religious and social experience. Rabbinic and midrashic literature, the prayer book, medieval

literary treatises, all displayed a uniform preoccupation with the Holy Land. Poets, philosophers, mystics, liturgists . . . traditionally vied with one another in expressing the yearning of the People of Israel for the ravished cradle of its nationhood . . . for Russian Jews . . . the Holy Land was no mere featureless idol, to be embellished in lullabies and fireside tales. The recollection of its loss was a visceral wound . . . Russian Jews continued to nourish the vision of a future apocalypse, the redemption of sacred soil.[9]

Abraham, the first Jew, is told by God to leave Ur and "Go forth from your native land and from your father's house to a land that I will show you." Abraham journeyed to the Promised Land, where he lived in Beersheva and is buried, with his son Isaac and grandson Jacob, in Hebron at the Cave of the Machpela. Under Moses the Jews left Egypt and wandered for 40 years in the Sinai desert before entering the Promised Land.[10] About 1000 BCE King David made Jerusalem his capital. His son King Solomon built the First Temple, making Jerusalem the political and religious center of the nation. About 400 years of independence under David's descendants followed before the Babylonians in 586 BCE destroyed the Temple and sent the Jews into exile. Psalm 137 expressed their acute sense of loss:

> By the rivers of Babylon, there we sat and wept
> As we thought of Zion . . .
> If I do not keep Jerusalem in memory even at my happiest hour
> May my right hand wither[11]

Within 50 years the Persian King Cyrus had restored the Jews to their land, later under Ezra and Nehemiah. They built the Second Temple and enjoyed some self-rule under the Persians (528–333 BCE) and Hellenistic rulers (322–142 BC). Independence came through the Maccabee revolt (Hanukkah), which led to the Hasmonean dynasty (142–63 BCE). Then Roman repression beginning in 63 BCE led to Jewish revolts. After four years of fighting, in 70 CE Rome crushed the Jewish Revolt, destroyed the Temple in Jerusalem, killed 300,000–600,000 Jews and sent 300,000 Jews into slavery and exile. After crushing the Second Jewish Revolt under Simon Bar Kochba in 135 CE the Romans evicted Jews from Jerusalem and renamed the country Palestine.[12]

The remaining Jewish community recovered and replaced the Temple services and high priests with rabbis and synagogues. Arab rule (636–1096) seriously reduced the size of the community. The Crusader period (1099–1187) further reduced the Jewish presence in the land. There was a revival with trickles of immigration fleeing persecution from North Africa (1191–98), Spain (1492 onward) and the Ukraine (1648 onward). Followers of the false messiah Shabbtai Zvi (1666 onward) and then hundreds of Hasidic families came in the seventeenth century. By 1800 there were only 6,000 Jews eking out a living in the four holy cities (Jerusalem, Hebron, Safed and Tiberias).[13]

In the twelfth century, Judah Halevi during the Golden Age of Spain wrote of the Holy Land. In his *Kuzari*, Halevi demonstrated how the Exile had eliminated the critical ties between Jewish Law, the People of Israel and the land of Israel. Only with the coming of the messiah could these critical links be re-established, for:

> My heart is in the east
> And I am in the far off west
> How can I find an appetite for food?
> How shall it be pleasing to me?
> How shall I render my vows and my bonds?
> While Zion lies beneath the fetters of Edom?
> And I in Arab chains?
> It would seem to me to be easy to leave all the
> Ground of Spain as the dust and destruction of the sanctuary
> Has become precious to my eyes.[14]

Before the Emancipation brought about by the French Revolution and the 1830 and 1848 revolutions west of the Elbe, European Jewry had a strong religious culture and communal organization with an intense attachment to Judaism, intellectual freedom and various communal organizations. The Jews suffered in Exile until Redemption to Zion.[15]

Modern Zionism begins with the failure of the Emancipation of European Jews from the ghetto and second-class status. West of the Oder Emancipation and Enlightenment were carried through in the nineteenth century, but east of the Oder (especially in Russia, Poland and Rumania) there was no Emancipation. The French Revolution of 1789, confirmed through the meeting of the Sanhedrin (rabbis and Jewish notables) with Napoleon in 1806, gave Jews as individuals equal rights and citizenship, but the Jewish community lost its traditional, national autonomous rights. The hope for the Return to Zion had to be discarded for the new loyalty to the French state. The Emancipation of Jews accelerated with the dissolution of the ghetto after the 1848 Revolution, as many Jews were attracted to liberalism, socialism and nationalism. Full equality came in the 1850s and 1860s in Britain, Germany, Hungary and Italy. Even in Russia under Tsar Alexander II there were symbols of liberalization. Assimilation and Reform Jewry were the main intellectual currents of the mid-century. In Russia the Haskalah (Enlightenment) movement was the Eastern image of Western Reform Judaism.[16]

Given the hopes of the emancipated masses for entry into European society, proto-Zionism was a weak movement. Emancipation seemed to triumph everywhere. Lord Rothschild was the leader of European finance, Benjamin Disraeli (a convert) was the British prime minister, Adolphe Crémieux was influential in France, and Ferdinand Lassalle was emerging as a leader of German socialism. Anti-Semitism would seemingly fade away as modern society would jettison feudal religious fanaticism.

Proto-Zionism never died out. Heinrich Graetz (1817–91) focused on the geographical, political and national aspects of Judaism, the Jewish people and the land of Israel.[17] His history starts with the entry of the Israelites into the land of Canaan. Shlomo Avineri argued that "the pragmatic significance of Graetz's position is enormous and revolutionary; the Jews are a people, a nation, not just a community of faith ... the messianic dimension of Judaism has clear political connotations inextricably connected with Palestine."[18]

Moses Hess (1812–75), a colleague of Karl Marx, penned *Rome and Jerusalem* (1862).[19] Hess, stressing the land of Israel as the birthplace of Israel and the Diaspora as Exile, wrote, "Two periods of time shaped the development of Jewish civilization: the first, after the liberation from Egypt, and the second the return from Babylon. The third shall come with the redemption from the third exile."[20] Viewing Jews as a people in terms of national liberation movements and upset by anti-Semitic European nationalism, Hess argued for a Jewish socialist commonwealth in Palestine.

While most Orthodox rabbis opposed Zionism in the nineteenth century, a few promoted the return to Jerusalem. Both Rabbi Yehuda Hai Alkalai (1798–1878) and Rabbi Zvi Hirsch Kalischer (1795–1874) spoke of the need for the land of Israel to be built up before the Messiah would come to Jerusalem. Rabbi Alkalai, who emphasized speaking Hebrew, buying land in Palestine and electing a Jewish assembly, immigrated to Palestine in his old age. Rabbi Kalischer, arguing for a slow Return to Zion, purchasing land and redefining the idea of redemption, opened the door for religious Zionism.[21] For, as he wrote in *Seeking Zion* (1862):

> Why do the people of Italy and of other countries sacrifice their lives for the land of their fathers while we, like men bereft of strength and courage, do nothing? All the other peoples have striven only for the sake of their own national honor; how much more should we exert ourselves, for our duty is to labor not only for the glory of our ancestors but for the glory of God who chose Zion![22]

The Dreyfus Affair in Paris, the Lueger election in Vienna, and Russian pogroms in the 1880s and 1890s showed the limitation of hopes for Emancipation. In Russia, Tolstoy and Ivan Turgenev, many college students and newspapers and the leftist Narodnaya Volya did not condemn pogroms. In France much of the elite either did not condemn the attack on Dreyfus or even supported it. The same was true in Vienna. In Eastern Europe the masses began to look to America and Palestine for hope of redemption.[23]

After the shock of the 1881 Russian pogroms, Peretz Smolenskin (1842–85) foresaw the need for Jewish immigrants to Palestine to change occupations. The 1897 Russian census showed that 74 percent of Russian Jews were in trade or manufacture while less than 4 percent of Jews were in agriculture.[24] Moshe Lilienbaum (1843–1910) saw the rise of European nationalism creating a new and virulent anti-Semitism. He saw the redemption and liberation of the Jewish people coming through the impoverished masses.[25]

Leo Pinsker (1821–91), in his *Autoemancipation* (1882), attacked both the liberals who looked to Emancipation and the religious who maintained their passivity in the face of oppression. Pinsker called for political activism, building national institutions and stress on the fate of the nation over the individual. Though uncertain as to where the Jewish home should be, "we may give up our endless life of wandering and rehabilitate our nation in our own eyes and in the eyes of the world."[26] Pinsker headed the first proto-Zionist group, the Hovevei Zion (Lovers of Zion), which had 8,000–15,000 members in the 1880s. It raised $25,000, not enough to settle 20 families a year in Palestine.[27]

The eccentric Eliezer Ben Yehuda (1858–1922) transformed Hebrew into a modern language for Israel. For, as he understood:

> The Hebrew language can only live if we revive the nation and return to its fatherland . . . The nation cannot live except on its own soil: only on this soil can it revive and bear magnificent fruit as in the days of old.[28]

In 1897, Theodor Herzl (1860–1904), the flamboyant Hungarian journalist, turned these intellectual musings into the calling of the First Zionist Congress in Basel. Although an assimilated Central European Jew, his principal followers were the more traditional and oppressed Jews of Russia, Poland and Rumania. In *The Jewish State* (1896) and *Alteneuland* (Old-New Land) (1902), Herzl envisioned a populist and quasi-socialist Jewish state in Palestine, with public ownership of land, cooperative rural settlements, advanced technology, universal and free schooling, radical transformation of Jewish social structure, public housing for workers and a seven-hour day. Herzl foresaw a tolerant and universally humanitarian Zionism. The Emancipation of the Jews could be effectuated only in Palestine.[29] Meeting with world leaders (sultan, kaiser and pope) to no avail, Herzl, without money or political muscle, made Zionism an international political actor. As Herzl said at the First Zionist Congress:

> We are here to lay the foundation state of the house which is to shelter the Jewish nation . . . Anti-Semitism has given us our strength again. We have returned home . . . Zionism is the return of the Jews to Judaism even before their return to the Jewish land.[30]

Eastern European Jews, after Herzl's death, emphasized socialism, revolt against the ghetto, and land development in Palestine.[31] Max Nordau (1849–1923) argued that there was a tension in Western European society between the Emancipation of the Jews and public attitudes towards them. The Emancipation, by liquidating the ghetto, put an end to Jewish national identity. While Eastern European Jewry faced economic misery, Western European

Jewry faced moral poverty. The revolutionary phase of Zionism in Palestine would entail a mammoth project. As Nordau wrote in 1902:

> The Zionists know that they have taken upon themselves a task of unprecedented difficulty. Never has it been attempted to uproot, peacefully and in a short time, millions of people from different countries and integrate them in a new country; never has it been attempted to transform millions of feeble, unskilled proletarians into peasants and shepherds, to link to the plow and Mother Earth shopkeepers and peddlers, brokers and seminarians, all of them city-dwellers alienated from nature. It will be necessary to acquaint Jews from different countries with each other, to educate them in practice towards national unity and to overcome the enormous drawbacks stemming from the difference in language, culture, modes of thinking, prejudices and deviations grafted from alien nations, which all of [the immigrants] will bring from their old homeland.[32]

Nachum Syrkin (1867–1924) produced the first systematic formulation of socialist Zionism, arguing that it:

> has its roots in the economic and social position of the Jews, in their moral protest, in the idealistic strivings to give a better content to their miserable life. It is borne by the active, creative forces of Jewish life.[33]

Only socialism could unify the Palestinian Jewish community, for "what is utopian in other contexts is a necessity for the Jews. The Jews were historically the nation which caused division and strife; it will now become the most revolutionary of nations."[34]

A. D. Gordon (1856–1922), who immigrated to Palestine at 47 to be an agricultural laborer, became the ideological seer of the Labor Zionist Party. His stress on the centrality of manual labor to personal and national salvation and rejection of decadent urban culture meant a radical rejection of the urban petty-bourgeois Jewish Diaspora. Only revolution could end the Exile period and create a new Jewish existence.[35]

Zionism was more than a political revolution but rather a socio-economic, cultural and psychological revolution as well. The center of world Jewry would change from the Diaspora to Palestine and, within Palestine, from the middle-class Diaspora Zionist leaders to the Palestinian Jewish Labor movement.

Religious Zionism emerged under Rabbi Abraham Kook (1865–1935), the first Ashkenazi chief rabbi of the British Mandate. The traditional religious view that Zionist socialism was a false messianic movement began to change in reaction to new circumstances. Rabbi Kook stressed the religious centrality of the terrestrial and not merely the heavenly land of Israel, dialectic between Judaism and secular Zionism and universal meaning in the Jewish renaissance.

Living in the Diaspora meant a life of unholiness that could be remedied by returning to the land of Israel. He saw the People of Israel, the Torah and the land of Israel as one, for "The hope for the return to the Holy Land is the continuing source of the distinctive nature of Judaism." Rabbi Kook argued that secular Zionists were doing Godly work by reviving the land of Israel. The rebirth of Israel and ingathering of exiles would have not only Jewish significance but universal significance.[36] These thinkers laid the intellectual groundwork for the first socialist revolution (1881–1977), which established Israel and transformed Jewish society.

Jews and socialist revolution

The First Zionist Socialist Revolution was embedded in the attraction of many Jews from 1880 to 1940 towards socialism.[37] In 1896 the Russian Marxist leader Georgi Plekhanov told a conference of the Socialist International that "the Jewish workers may be considered the vanguard of the labor army in Russia."[38] Lenin told Maxim Gorkii that "An intelligent Russian is almost always a Jew or a man of Jewish blood."[39]

The early Marxist socialists included many of Jewish origin (Karl Marx, Ferdinand Lassalle, Edward Bernstein). By 1904 Jews, only 3 percent of the Russian population, were 40 percent of Russian radicals.[40] Many Bolsheviks (Leon Trotsky, Grigorii Zinoviev, Lev Kamenev, Karl Radek), Mensheviks (Jules Martov, Theodore Dan, Pavel Axelrod, Martynov) and Socialist Revolutionaries (Isaac Sternberg, Marc Nathanson) were of Jewish origins. In August 1917, 47 percent of the members of the Menshevik Central Committee were of Jewish origins, while 30 percent of the members of the Bolshevik Central Committee were Jews.[41] Many Polish (Rosa Luxemburg) and Austrian (Otto Bauer) leaders were also Jews. As Kaul Kautsky wrote in 1914, "the Jews have become an eminently revolutionary factor."[42]

In the 1919 Hungarian Revolution Bela Kun and over 60 percent of 48 people's commissars and 79 percent of 203 top state officials were of Jewish origin.[43] The 1919 Bavarian Revolution was led by Kurt Eisner, Eugene Levine, Gustav Landauer and Ernest Toller. The 1919 Vienna Uprising was led by Egon Kisch.[44] After World War II, despite Stalin's anti-Semitism, Jews were major leaders in Communist parties in Poland (Jacob Berman, Hilary Minc, Roman Zambrowski), Romania (Ana Pauker, Vasile Luca), Hungary (Matyas Rakosi, Ernst Gero, Mihaly Farkas, Joszek Revai) and Czechoslovakia (Rudolf Slansky, Bedrich Geminder).[45]

These leaders represented a small element of alienated Jewish intellectuals assimilated into the Russian or European revolutionary parties and heavily internationalist. They were doubly alienated people, shunning the Jewish community and being shunned by the Gentile community.[46] Most European Jews refused to follow these alienated (and often converted) Jewish intellectuals into radical utopias thought to be dangerous by most Jews and non-Jews. As Jacob Talmon has depicted their fate:

At the end of a Shakespearian tragedy, the stage is strewn with corpses. Leon Trotsky has his skull split by the axe of a Stalinist agent; Rosa Luxemburg's battered body is dragged out of a river; Kurt Eisner and George Landauer fall victims to assassin's bullets; Zinoviev, Kamenev and so many others are hanged in the small hours in some cellar; Slansky perishes as a traitor; the Paukers, the Bermans, are dying in oblivion and obloquy. The survivors live not only to be dismissed from their posts and abused but to be told . . . that no self-respecting movement could allow a disproportionate number of the members of an alien race to have an undue influence on its national policies.[47]

The continuity between Labor Zionism and mainstream Russian socialism was striking. These themes echoed Lenin's 1902 volume *What Is to Be Done*, which called for a small intellectual party elite to bring socialist consciousness to the workers who were incapable of more than working-class consciousness.[48] They echoed the Russian Mensheviks and the German Social Democrats in stressing sacrifice and democracy. The call to go to the land represented an echo of the rural populist socialist narodniki movement of the 1870s. Finally, they echoed the 1860s earlier work by Chernyshevsky that called for self-sacrifice of a self-conscious elite to radically transform Russian society.

The Zionists were a powerful force on the Jewish and Russian streets. During and after the 1905 Revolution, the two Zionist socialist parties (Poalei Zion and Zionist Socialist Workers Party) had 42,000 members (Table 10.1), almost as many as the entire Bolshevik Party (46,000) and more than the Menshevik Party (33,000 members) and Bundists (33,000). In 1917 there were 300,000 Russian Zionists, compared to 23,500 Bolsheviks in February 1917 and 400,000 in October 1917.[49]

Unlike the doubly alienated Jewish radicals, they had strong roots in their

Table 10.1 Jewish members of Russian radical parties, 1905–07

Parties	*Jewish members*
Zionist socialists*	42,000
Jewish Bund	33,000
Jewish Socialist Workers Party	13,000
Mensheviks**	8,000
Bolsheviks**	5,000
	101,000

Source: R. Brym, *The Jewish Intelligentsia and Russian Marxism: A Sociological Study of Intellectual Radicalism and Ideological Diversity*, New York: Schocken Books, 1978, p. 79.

* The Zionist socialist parties were the Poalei Zion and the Zionist Socialist Workers Party. The Jewish Socialist Workers Party (not counted in the bloc) was supportive of a territorial solution to the Jewish problem in Russia.
** Estimates.

own community. They borrowed revolutionary forms and adapted them to a nationalist program of building a socialist society in Palestine that could attract the support or sympathy of most Jews. For, as the anti-Zionist Isaac Deutscher conceded, while Eastern European Zionism in general was "implicitly anti-revolutionary," in fact:

> It breathed the air of the Russian revolution . . . On Zionism that movement of ideas left an indelible mark. The young Jew who in Kiev, Odessa and Warsaw distrusted the Russo-Polish revolutionary ideologies and longed to pioneer for the Jewish State in Palestine was as a rule hypnotized by the ideologies from which he fled: and he found this out after he landed in Palestine. He came to Palestine with the crumbs from the table of the Russian revolution; and he used those crumbs as the seed with which to sow the sacred desert of Galilee, Samaria and Judea.[50]

The Zionist power on the Jewish street represented its attachment to Jewish values. The least popular party (the Bolsheviks) was the most Russian party that rejected religion and tradition, including Jewish religion and tradition. The most popular were the Zionists and Bundists, who incorporated aspects of Jewish tradition with a modernizing socialist blend. On a 1–4 scale of being embedded in the Jewish community, those Jews with minimal attachment (3.5) were Bolsheviks, with modest attachment (3.0) were Mensheviks, with significant attachment (2.0) were Bundists and with strongest attachment (1.4) were socialist Zionists.[51] The socialist Zionists were neither internationalists nor alienated from their Jewish roots. Their social democracy was close to Bundism and Menshevism.

The Jews were stronger in Menshevism, where they played an "enormous role," than in Bolshevism. Socialist Zionism grew out of democratic Russian socialism before it was destroyed by the Bolsheviks after the 1917 October Revolution. The democratic socialist emphasis on internationalism, industrialization, modernization, the working class and egalitarianism appealed to Jews who suffered from pogroms, reaction, obscurantism and chauvinism.[52] Thus, the socialist Zionists had a strong base among Russian and Eastern European Jews to carry forth their revolution in Palestine.

The Zionist revolution had a strong historical and political base among the Jewish masses in Europe. It had both religious and non-religious roots, fusing the two initially in a modern version of the Return to Zion (religion), creation of a new/old state (nationalism) and social transformation of the Jews (socialism). The power of the Zionist revolution was a response to the political realities of the failure of the Emancipation of the Jews east of the Elbe (Poland, Rumania and Russia), growing anti-Semitism inspired by the entry of the masses into politics and attendant growth of European exclusivist nationalism. All this laid the basis for a Zionist revolution, in its first form a socialist revolution, in Palestine.

11 Two modern Zionist revolutions

Israel carried out two nationalist revolutions, a socialist Zionist revolution (1882–1997) and a second, incomplete, semi-capitalist, globalizing revolution (1977–2007).

The great revolutions in history created powerful armies, states, economic systems and social identities, which defeated more powerful enemies.[1] The English Revolution of the 1640s laid the basis for Oliver Cromwell's New Model Army and the later rise of Britain to superpower status. The American Revolution (1776–81) led to independence from Great Britain and created a future superpower.[2] The French Revolution (1789–99) saw Napoleonic armies dominate Europe before 1814 and its ideas become the salient values of Europe. The Russian revolutions (1917 February and October revolutions) transformed a weak Russia into a superpower Soviet Union that defeated Nazi Germany. The Chinese revolutions (1911 Nationalist Revolution and 1949 Communist Revolution) transformed a weak and often defeated China during a century of "shame and humiliation" (1838–1945) into a powerful China by 2025.

The Zionists carried out two revolutions in a once dependent colony that brought victories over a larger Arab world, a First World economy and regional military predominance.

First Zionist Socialist Revolution (1882–1977)

The First Zionist Socialist Revolution (1882–1977) was a successful, democratic socialist revolution that, under the Labor Party (in all its forms), created the state, won five wars, absorbed millions of immigrants, fostered egalitarianism and new social forms and created a vibrant economy. Given the unprofitability of the settlements, urgency of the tasks and necessity against major obstacles, socialist collective methods were ideologically and politically sound. As Jacob Talmon has trenchantly observed:

> This idealistic social endeavor is sure to remain the most distinctive, most original and most precious aspect of the Zionist effort in Palestine . . . That ferment of social ideas, that intensity of feeling, that sustained

dedication to a chosen way of life, that wealth of experience (the kibbutz, the moshav, the Histadrut) in the field of social organization – all this is probably without precedent, especially when we consider the exiguous number of men and the paucity of assets with which everything had to work itself out. An egalitarian puritanical society emerged, combining in a fine blend the virtues of individual self-reliance and an enthusiastic readiness to join in cooperative endeavor. This has been the main secret of every success scored by the Yishuv – in agriculture, in the struggle for survival and growth and finally in armed victories.[3]

The revolution was based on Russian socialism brought over by its Russian-born leaders. The schools, military, ceremonies, myths, monuments and parades of the Yishuv and the state reflected the revolutionary ethos. Moshe Shamir declared that the nation was "born from the sea," without tradition, freed from the yoke of Exile which was left at sea.[4]

As Shlomo Avineri has written of the revolutionary nature of Socialist Zionism:

> Zionism was the most fundamental revolution in Jewish life. It substituted a secular self-identity of the Jews as a nation for the traditional and Orthodox self-identity in religious terms. It changed a passive, quietist and pious hope of the Return to Zion into an effective social force, moving millions of people to Israel. It transformed a language relegated to mere religious usage into a modern, secular mode of intercourse of a nation-state . . . It is the quest for self-determination and liberation under the modern conditions of secularization and liberalism. For the Zionist revolution is very basically a permanent revolution against those powerful forces in Jewish history, existing at least partially within the Jewish people, which have turned the Jews from a self-reliant community living at the margin of and sometimes living off of alien communities . . . Zionism is a revolution against those trends in the Jewish people, which enabled the Jews to accommodate as individuals even to the harshest realities of Exile in situations of almost total powerlessness, yet perpetuated Exile as a way of life for the Jewish people as a whole. Zionism is an attempt to bring back into Jewish life the supremacy of the public, communitarian and social aspects at the expense of personal ease, bourgeois comfort and good life of the individual.[5]

The models were the apparatchiki running the socialist movement – Mapai, Mapam, Achdut Haavodah parties, kibbutzim, moshavim, Histadrut, Haganah and Palmach. The revolutionary transformation promoted socialist avant-garde figures to replace scholars and rabbis as authority figures and leaders. The old bourgeoisie, large and petty, were demoted as hostile to the new socialist vision. The "strong, reformist, utopian qualities" of Zionism "contained within it a revolutionary ethos that sought to make radical changes in the social, economic and cultural structures of European Jewry."[6]

The modern Zionist Socialist Revolution did not merely copy models from earlier revolutions. Socialist Zionism represented a revolt against the nineteenth-century European bourgeois establishment that would restore nationhood to the Jews and liberate them from perceived religious-based passivity.

The revolution proclaimed by Theodor Herzl at the First Zionist Congress in 1897 meant that the political, diplomatic and concrete tasks of obtaining and building a state were now at hand. There would be a number of distinctive features to the revolution:

Unlike earlier national and social revolutions, the First Zionist Socialist Revolution involved no transfer of the state machinery from one elite to another, no civil war and almost no internal violence. Much of the important action occurred outside of the territory in which the revolution occurred. Yet the re-creation of a Jewish state, and a socialist one at that, represented a radical transformation of Jewish life.[7]

Unlike most national liberation movements, where social, cultural and economic aims were subordinated to the national struggle, Zionism, starting from outside the land it sought to liberate, had to operate in a different manner. As Jehuda Reinharz has observed:

> Owing to the anomalies of the Jewish position, all Jewish ideologies since the eighteenth century Enlightenment had to define cultural, social and economic, as well as purely political aims and adopt humanitarian reform or revolutionary rather than purely civil, political methods. This necessity caused not only Zionism but all modern Jewish ideologies to assume a character distinctly different from comparable movements among other peoples.[8]

The Zionist revolution was unique in a number of ways: it focused on rural revolution rather than urban revolution. Most earlier revolutions (the 1640s English Revolution, the 1789 French Revolution, the 1848 European Revolution, the 1917 Russian revolutions) were heavily urban in nature. The First Zionist Socialist Revolution, with its agrarian populist romanticism, rooted the urban Jews in the land and created a new productive class. This would be radical, for Jews in much of the world were barred from owning land or being farmers. The new rural commune replaced the small-town urban *shtetl* as the ideal mode of life for the Jewish masses.

While other nations had their land, religion, culture and history, the Zionist revolution called on a people who had been expelled from the land 1,800 years ago to return and build a new nation in a country they had imagined in their dreams. Jewish nationalism in Palestine was radical, since it replaced the Jewish alienation from oppressive anti-Semitic states (Eastern Europe, the Middle East and North Africa). It transformed Jews from a traditional religious community to a national community and Jewish holidays from religious celebrations into national celebration.

It focused on physical labor rather than mental labor. The new radical ideal was the kibbutznik or moshavnik who worked the land and the industrial worker who worked with his hands. Traditional Eastern European Jewish society deprecated manual labor and praised scholarly activities, epitomized by rabbis and yeshiva *bokhers*, who held the highest-status positions in the traditional Jewish community.

There was a romantic glorification of the land of Israel. The socialist Zionists saw the Bible as the literary record of Jewish national glory in Palestine during the first and second Jewish commonwealths. The first Israeli prime minister, David Ben Gurion, frequently studied with Biblical scholars and interpreted contemporary events in a Biblical mode. Israeli culture has stressed an intimate association with the land through extensive hiking and physical contests.[9]

There was a physical transformation of the landscape by eliminating the old, traditional, pre-modern structures and building a revolutionary, modern new country. The kibbutzim and moshavim were to be the new, socialist, egalitarian rural forms of the future. Deganya (founded in 1909) was to be the model socialist kibbutz, Haifa the gleaming new international port city and Tel Aviv (founded in 1909) the Vienna on the Mediterranean, the symbol of urban Zionism.[10]

There was the need for sacrifice and heroism. Historically, immigrants moved from more economically and politically retarded countries to more modern ones. Here the reverse would be true: Palestine was more backward than Russia or Eastern Europe.

It was explicitly socialist in form rather than capitalist. Since there was not yet a socialist state in the world (the Soviet Union was not created until the 1917 October Revolution), this would require new communal forms. These would be the communal kibbutz (created at Deganya in the Galilee in 1909) and the partly communal moshav (first created before World War I in Palestine). In cities this would be the role of Histadrut (trade union), which would operate many companies, provide a social welfare state and guarantee the workers owned the means of production. There would also be various socialist parties, including Mapai, Mapam and Achdut Haavodah and youth groups such as Hashomer Hazair. This would be a radical change for Jews, who were historically seen as a capitalist stratum and passive political force in society. Socialism was built around the concept of social justice and a simple lifestyle as key to a new Jewish personality.

There were popular, universal, voluntary, decentralized military organizations. Rather than the standing armies, seen as repressive agents of the state, there would be new revolutionary, egalitarian military forms. Formed around the Hashomer watchmen before World War I, this would morph into the Palmach and Haganah. This would be radical, since Jews had been largely barred from military service for centuries or, more recently, from serving as officers in national armies.

There were communal forms of child rearing rather than parent-oriented child rearing. This was pioneered in the kibbutzim where children were raised in children's homes by communal teachers rather than by parents. This would be continued by Youth Aliyah, which brought more than 100,000 orphans and semi-orphans to Palestine and Israel for communal boarding school education. In the 1970s and afterwards the principle would be extended to include youths with parents who were living in Israel in disadvantaged circumstances largely from the Middle East and North Africa.

There was a strong emphasis and even "veneration" for secularism and modern technology achieved through social engineering rather than romanticism. Technical expertise would direct the social restructuring of the immigrants to Palestine and represented the secular knowledge that would create a new Jewish nation.[11] This was a radical change from the religiously oriented traditional society that venerated traditional learning, not modern secular learning and technology.

Ideal types of collective farmers, literary figures, political organizers, warriors and technicians transformed reality rather than passively accepting their fate. These ideal types represented the pragmatic needs of settling the land, organizing the settlement of the land, inspiring those who settled the land, making the economy grow and defending it. They represented a radical change from the traditional ideal types of rabbis, yeshiva scholars, pious individuals, *luftmenschen* and charitable individuals in Eastern Europe, none of whom either worked the land or did physical labor.

There was a new type of counter-cultural lifestyle featuring equality, women's rights, physical activity, simple attire, forthright honesty, community orientation and plain speaking. Rituals were nationalistic and communal and focused on the land, the Bible and Hebrew.[12] This new lifestyle was a radical change from Eastern Europe with its emphasis on *pilpul* interpretations of the Talmud (discussions on fine intellectual points), a strong religious hierarchy of status, special dress (for rabbis and Hassidim), male predominance, religious holidays and family and synagogue centrality.

It stressed a secular society with nationalism, action, merit and secular ideas. This was a radical change from a religious, traditional society with stress on the supernatural, religious belief and passivity. The messianic belief in the end of days and Return to Zion now in the secular world would be accomplished through rational acts of man rather than through supernatural intervention.[13]

It revived an ancient language (Hebrew) that had been used mainly in synagogues and not in daily life for nearly 2,000 years. Hebrew was vital because it was the language of Jewish sovereignty back to the First Temple and could unify immigrants from over 100 countries. In 1900 the vast majority of world Jews spoke Yiddish, Arabic, Ladino or other languages. Almost none could speak Hebrew. Eliezer Ben Yehuda created thousands of words for the modern world.[14]

Vital institutions to carry out the revolution were created, including the Anglo-Palestine Bank, the Jewish National Fund, the World Zionist Organization and local institutions such as kibbutzim, moshavim, Histadrut, Youth Aliyah, Hebrew University (1925), Technion (1924), Weizmann Institute (1934) and other organizations key to creating the state. The universities were important in creating the trained manpower needed for the creation and maintaining of the state and in producing those cultural artifacts important in the language of imagination to the creation of the mythic claims at the core of nationalism.[15]

There was a lack of economic integration into the region. The Arab–Persian rejection of Israel, even when peace treaties were signed, meant that Israel would forgo the natural benefits of comparative advantage enjoyed by European states (the EU), the United States (NAFTA) and Asian states (ASEAN).

The lack of a pre-state territorial base for Zionism was unusual and important. Anthony Smith has stressed the importance of territory not just as borders dividing nations but in the territorialization of memory for emotional physical identification (battlefields, temples, heroes, saints, rivers, mountains) and for the sanctification of territory (holy deeds of ancestors, quest for liberation, "holy people").[16] All of this would be important in the development of Israel.

The socialist revolution stressed collective action, self-sacrifice, secularism, asceticism, the sabra man and state ownership of the means of production. Large state-owned and -run companies, subsidies of basic commodities, extensive state intervention in the economy, limitations on the private economy, state planning and high taxation of income, inheritance and luxury goods defined the economy. The ideal types were the pioneer (*halutz*), kibbutznik, military officer, trade union organizer and party apparatchiki.

The Zionist Socialist Revolution occurred despite a paucity of socialists. Most immigrants after the Second Aliyah (1904–14) were not socialists. The 1920s Polish immigrants and 1930s German immigrants were largely middle-class refugees. The Sephardim after 1948 came from nationalist and religious motives. The European refugees after 1945 had little socialist motivation, and Soviet immigrants in the 1970s disliked socialism.[17]

The Labor Zionists built an infrastructure to absorb and re-socialize the immigrants. Many, after their terrible experiences, were open to the notions of a socialist utopia. The lack of a strong indigenous structure allowed building a new society from a clean slate. The socialists, accepting some capitalism, foreign aid from the bourgeois West and alliances with Great Britain and the United States, were practical. They changed from socialism to revolutionary constructivism, from class to state, in the battle for survival.[18]

From 1882 to 1948 the Israeli economy was a pre-emergent market economy with a small, dispersed and weak private sector. Power resided after the 1920s mainly in the Histadrut, Mapai Party, kibbutzim and other collective organizations. Nearly all the main power institutions were founded from 1901 to 1925 – the Jewish National Fund (1901), Bank Leumi (as Anglo-Palestine Company, 1902), the first kibbutz, Deganya (1909), Histadrut (1920), Bank Hapoalim (1921), Solel Boneh (1923) and Hasneh (1924). After 1948 the Histadrut controlled Bank Hapoalim and Koor, the Jewish Agency controlled Bank Leumi, and private interests controlled the Israel Discount Bank. Mapai and Histadrut controlled jobs, social services, culture and ideology. During the interwar period the future class of wealthy capitalists – the Hacohen, Ruppin, Shertok and Elyashar dynasties – established themselves.[19]

During the first three decades after 1948, the Labor movement dominated the state while politicians and parties dominated public life, which had only weak autonomous social groups. The party ran a powerful government with a large public sector. The prime ministers (David Ben Gurion, Moshe Sharett, Golda Meir, Yitzhak Rabin) were from the Labor Party, which dominated the Histadrut (leading trade union and employer of workers), the Jewish Agency (director of Jewish immigration and absorption), kibbutzim and moshavim. In the eight Knessets from 1949 to 1976 the Labor camp received 53–75 of the 120 seats. The Labor Party ran all the key ministries, set the political agenda, passed 93 percent of all laws, directed the Histadrut, the Jewish Agency and many municipal and local governments, and formed what Medding called "government by party" until 1967.[20]

The Labor movement developed a powerful statism throughout the socialist period. The state played a major role in running the economy and society, kept inflation low, maintained a high growth rate and established a manageable balance of payments deficit in the 1950s. The state developed a generous universal welfare network in an expanding economy. Its austerity program in the 1950s laid the base for a new economy and polity.[21] In the 1950s the state dominated capital formation, credit allocation, setting prices, establishing exchange rates, regulating foreign trade and directing industrial and agricultural development. The state, controlling Diaspora donations and investments, German Holocaust payments, American loans, government concessions, abandoned Arab land and the domestic budget, ran the economy.

The state owned over 90 percent of the land. The land, property, businesses and fields of the 600,000 Arabs who fled Israel during the 1948 War of Independence amounted to 30 percent of its territory and increased state land by one-third. The abandoned land was worth $300 million, or 50 percent of the Israeli GNP. The state allocated 1–2 million acres to kibbutzim, Jewish organizations and industries.[22]

The state controlled most of the capital. As in East Asia, with foreign investors scared away by political and economic instability, MNCs accounted for 5 percent of FDI in the early decades. No less than 70 percent of Israel investment came from foreign capital, much of it funneled directly or indirectly through the state.[23] Most Diaspora capital, cash flows and German reparations went through the public sector. Fully 75 percent of capital imports were directed to the public sector, which financed 65 percent of investment. Foreign capital inflow was modest, ranging from 0.5 percent to 1.7 percent of GDP, while capital outflow was minimal.[24]

The state controlled labor, with half of the workers being employed outside of the private sector. The tripling of the population in the first decade gave the government control over the labor force. The state promoted egalitarianism, with the top 20 percent earning 3.3 times more income than the bottom 20 percent, compared to 9.5 times in the United States.[25]

The state controlled much of the economy. In 1948 the Histadrut, which owned most of the key industrial, manufacturing and banking companies, was the leading source of scarce capital.[26] In 1960 Histadrut enterprises accounted for 35 percent of the GNP.[27] From 1950 to 1976 the government budget was 50 percent of GNP.[28]

The identification of the Labor Party with the state, the deference of new immigrants, the awareness of the benefits provided by the party, the recruiting of new members and the imperatives of survival allowed the Labor Party to maintain its dominance despite major immigration and social and economic change. So too did the small size of autonomous groups outside the powerful party system. The Labor Party provided security through a strong military, self-reliance and current borders, a powerful government and social welfare network, a significant role for the private sector, the status quo on religion and a pro-Western foreign policy which were widely popular. In the Eastern European tradition, the party was powerful and oligarchic.[29]

Numerous family-owned enterprises run by Eastern European shopkeepers promoted a capitalist sector that produced 60 percent of domestic GNP in 1948.[30] Israel had a mixed economy, especially since two forces (small local businesses and foreign Jews) supported a more Western, capitalist economy. In the 1950s and 1960s foreign investors were given tax exemptions, specific privileges, exclusive business rights and access to the privatizations of state assets.[31]

The base was laid for the future transition to capitalism. By the 1970s statism was in decline, as the five dominant capital groups (Bank Leumi, Bank Hapoalim, Israel Discount Bank, Koor and Clal) ran 46 of the top 100 companies and 14 of the 20 top companies. The power of wealthy Jewish foreign investors (Armand Hammer, Nissim Gaon, Meshulam Riklis, Robert Maxwell, Edgar Bronfman, Isaac Wolfson, Shaul Eisenberg and the Rothschilds) produced a web of friends, retainers and managers, drawn from government, the military and security. Many foreign companies, such as IBM, Hewlett-Packard, TRW and Intel, opened in Israel. The government sold such companies as Paz, Arkia Airlines, Shekem Oil and Jerusalem Economic Corporation. The 1967 war reintroduced a significant free Palestinian labor market which eroded the Histadrut monopoly. By 1977 a strong new middle class and Jewish labor aristocracy emerged.[32] Yet capitalism, hampered by the Arab boycott, the priority to security, the absorption of huge numbers of immigrants, the strength of the socialist sector, the constant wars, terrorism and the weak level of Israeli technology, remained limited.[33]

The socialist economy registered impressive gains of 11 percent a year in the 1950s and 8 percent a year in the 1960s. This was aided by rapid population growth (4.7 percent a year in the 1950s, 3.5 percent a year in the 1960s) and by major foreign capital inflow, German Holocaust payments, American grants, Diaspora donations and the distribution of Arab property. The 1967 Six Day War brought 900,000 Palestinians under Israeli control, while 140,000 Palestinians worked in Israel, accounting for 14 percent of the labor force. By 1973 significant American loans had been brought into the mix. Large-scale arms production boosted the economy. By 1977 primary exports dropped to 14.7 percent of exports, while manufacturing and heavy industry rose to 32.7 percent. This promoted a form of state capitalism.[34]

Second partial capitalist revolution (1977–2007)

Israel, beginning with the Likud victory in 1977, entered into a partial capitalist revolution. Dozens of countries, from China and India to Hungary, Poland and Mexico, abandoned Communist or autonomous, autarkical, often socialist, economies for global capitalist integration. Many factors promoted the new revolution. The demise of Communism in the Soviet Union and Eastern Europe, the defeat of Saddam Hussein in Kuwait and massive immigration from the former Soviet Union played key roles. The success of the First Zionist Socialist Revolution promoted the rise of Sephardim in society, lessening their allegiance to the Labor Party. By 1981 almost 70 percent of the Sephardim were voting for Likud.

Success in the 1967 Six Day War and economic integration into GATT and then the EU freed Israel from its isolation before the war. The end of military government over the Arabs promoted their partial integration into Israeli society. The inclusion of the Herut Party in the government and the role of Labor Party defector Moshe Dayan as defense minister on the eve of the Six Day War foreshadowed the end of Labor dominance. The failures in the early days of the 1973 Yom Kippur War played a role. In 1977, when Menachem Begin became the first non-Labor Party prime minister, he took Dayan, elected by the Labor Party to the Knesset, as the foreign minister.[35]

Internal changes within the Labor Party also led to its downfall. The retirement of David Ben Gurion in 1963 and the failure to find an adequate successor was a major failing. The Lavon Affair in the 1960s and battling between Shimon Peres and Yitzhak Rabin in the 1970s weakened the party. The rise of apparatchiki signified the end of ideology. The rise of nationalism after the Six Day War and the issues of the territories moved the central issue away from class and nation towards tradition and religion, the stronghold of the Likud Party of Menachem Begin. The provision of government services outside the party lessened its role and importance. So did the lack of new Eastern European immigrants in the 1960s and 1970s, and the arrival of anti-Communist immigrants from the former Soviet Union in the 1980s and 1990s dried up the pond for a revival.

The base for the second revolution was created in the 1960s. Universities taught the power of the market to a new generation of future bureaucrats. The state began dismantling economic protectionism in 1962 with increasing trade liberalization and the elimination of import controls. After 1967, planners began to replace import substitution with stress on an East Asian-style sophisticated export economy. The role of the private sector rose as the statist direction of the economy faded. The state supported a growing military industrial sector, first state run and then increasingly private and independent.[36]

By 1977 a new class of elite bureaucrats, trained in neo-classical economics and the Chicago school of economics (Milton Friedman), was ready to support capitalism and trust the market to allocate resources. Despite the great success of socialism, they felt that global and local conditions needed economic liberalism, more decentralization and competition in place of government statism. The 1965–67 recession also promoted the transition to supporting the private sector.[37]

There has not been a dominant Likud revolution but a change from a dominant Labor Party model to a competitive party system.[38] After the Likud domination from 1977 to 1992 under Menachem Begin and Yitzhak Shamir (with an interlude of a national unity government), the Labor Party ruled for six years (1992–96, 1999–2001) and the Likud for six years (1996–99, 2001–05) and then Kadima (2005–07), a spinoff of Likud with admixtures of both parties under Arik Sharon and Ehud Olmert. Strong military and demographic pressures have enhanced the role of traditional state institutions, the army and the government. External forces, particularly the peacemaking process, threats of terrorism and the emergence of a potentially nuclear Iran, have overwhelmed the more "normal" forces at work here.

The transition period from 1977 to 1990 was difficult. By 1984, with high military expenditures, inflation hit 400 percent. During the 1976–89 period, economic growth slowed from 10 percent per year to 3.2 percent per year, hit by a slowdown in immigration and high fuel prices. Government spending rose from 50 percent of GDP in the 1950s to 75 percent by 1982. Net external debt rose from $.5 billion in 1964 to $17.7 billion in 1983. A national unity government in 1985 slashed domestic spending, imposing price and wage controls and devaluing the currency. By 1992 inflation was barely 9.2 percent and in 2006 zero.[39]

During the 1990s the economy, aided by mass immigration from the former Soviet Union, saw a 42 percent rise in GNP from 1990 to 1995. By 1995 Israel had a GNP of $86 billion with a strong First World economy of $15,500 per capita. The government budget declined to 49 percent of GDP, defense to less than 10 percent of GDP and unemployment to only 6 percent.[40]

The second partial capitalist revolution (1978–2007) has created a more nationalist, globally integrated First World capitalist economy, integrated 2 million Sephardim and 1 million Russians into the new society, and allied itself with the United States. The revolution (*mahapakah* or reversal) has stressed traditional and religious cultural values, capitalism, nationalism, free markets, the rise of the ethnic underclass (Sephardim and Russians), individualism, gratification, emotionalism and business. The government has lessened government intervention in the economy, hailed the free market, decreased subsidies of consumer and producer goods, sold off governmental enterprises, eliminated limitations on foreign currency holdings, floated the shekel and lifted the stock market. The Histadrut has disintegrated as a major power, several hundred thousand guest workers have come from abroad, labor has lost most of its power, the role of government has shrunk, and solid fiscal and monetary policy is on the rise. The 1975 agreement to create a free trade zone with the European Economic Community was a forerunner of these changes, as was the free trade zone with the United States.[41]

The new era witnessed a sharp decline in ideological and party fervor, the rise of the importance of the personality of the leaders and a strong pragmatism. The decline in the role of traditional ideological blocs and traditional elites, and of party power over individuals, led to a rise in new capitalist actors (industrialists, bankers, lawyers, doctors, professors) as well as mayors and the rise of new interest groups. Wealth replaced egalitarianism as a factor in public discourse. Electoral fluidity and diffusion of power within and between parties led to political surprises, such as the rise of Benjamin Netanyahu in 1996 and Arik Sharon in 2001. By 1992 the party bosses had lost their grip with party primaries in both the Labor and the Likud parties. The media, courts and interest groups became important in the political process. The rule of law and administration saw a diffusion of political power and increasingly decentralization of power. A new liberal corporatism replaced the old socialist monism, with consensus on the needs of society and the economy. Parties, lacking direct control of resources, lost their role in political socialization, interest articulation and interest aggregation.[42]

And yet, even in the 1990s, 60 percent of the population favored socialism.[43] The government controlled 50 percent of the economy, with the state budget equaling 40 percent of the GNP. Fully 33 percent of Israelis were employed under government direction, including the IDF, the Jewish Agency, Kupat Holim, municipalities, national government, and government corporations, not including Histadrut companies.[44]

The kibbutzim and moshavim survived financial crises, and the Histadrut and welfare state were still significant forces. The Labor movement came to power under Shimon Peres, Yitzhak Rabin and Ehud Barak. But it dropped socialism, opposed large-scale state intervention in the economy and promoted liberalization, individualism, pluralism and privatization. Labor movement leaders too had close ties to wealthy Israeli and Diaspora businessmen and Israeli economic, commercial and financial elites.[45]

The level of trade rose sharply during the 1990s globalization. In the 1970s imports equaled 37 percent of the GDP, while in the 1990s imports rose to greater than 50 percent of the GDP. While FDI remained quite modest in the 1980s and 1990 (0.5 percent of GDP in 1980), it accelerated in the 1990s to 2.0 percent of GDP by 2000.[46]

Israel entered on the path of globalization and export-led economies in the 1970s, accelerating this process in the 1980s and especially in the 1990s. By the 1990s it had created a centralized transnational ruling elite that was part of the transnational capitalist class. Massive capital inflow in the 1990s, attracted by the peace dividend, high technology and capital flight elsewhere, promoted the conversion of the Israeli economy to globalism and trans-nationalism.[47] The older ideal types have been replaced by new ideal types of entrepreneur, high technologist and lawyer. Egalitarianism has given way to a highly differentiated socio-economic structure where the top 10 percent of the population make almost $7,000 a month and the bottom 10 percent a mere $323 a month. Admiration of socialist sacrifice has been replaced by an open admiration for wealth and the United States.

There has been a growing concentration of power and wealth in a new ruling class. The high-technology boom and massive foreign investment of the 1990s promoted the predominance of a small number of firms in the economy. A few giant conglomerates, a few focused companies and large, self-liquidating government firms in the process of being privatized dominated the economy.[48] Five private groups (Israel Discount Bank, Ofer Group, Koor, Dankner Group and Arison Holdings) owned companies worth 41 percent of the capitalization of the Tel Aviv Stock Exchange (TASE). By the late 1990s foreigners owned 14 percent of the value of the TASE companies.[49]

The non-socialist alternative (the Irgun)

The triumph of the semi-capitalist, national second revolution after 1977 did not come in a void or solely from external globalizing forces and the rise of a new high-tech elite and Sephardim in Israel. Its seeds lay in the significant role of the relatively small capitalist nationalist forces embodied in the Jewish underground (the Irgun) from 1943 to 1948 in the fight against British coloni-alism. They were the followers of the Polish revisionist leader Vladimir Jabotinsky, who favored a non-socialist, capitalist revolution in Palestine. The Irgun commander Menachem Begin (1943–48), a recent arrival from Poland with no significant military background, in 1944 declared a revolt against Great Britain.

The small size of the Irgun (200–3,000 fighters) compared to the Haganah (40,000 fighters in 1947) dictated urban guerrilla warfare against the British. The Irgun tried to kill the British high commissioner, Sir Harold MacMichael, and did kill the British resident in Cairo, Lord Moyne, in 1944. In July 1945 the Irgun destroyed the main link of the Cairo–Haifa railroad. In October 1945, 700 Irgun fighters (and 150 Lehi Stern Gang fighters) together with the Haganah mounted 250 attacks across Palestine. By the winter of 1946 the British had evacuated all dependants and non-essential civilians, moved the rest into Bevingrads and built up their forces to over 90,000 men. From October 1946 to April 1947 Irgun actions killed 80 British soldiers and civil-ians, making Palestine ungovernable for the British. The blowing up of the

King David Hotel in 1946 (91 British, Arab and Jewish dead) and the death of 100–200 Arab civilians in the battle of Deir Yassin in April 1948 at the expense of 38 Irgun dead and wounded remain quite controversial. So too does the *Altalena* Affair in May 1948, when the Palmach shelled a ship bringing in weapons for the Irgun. Although the Irgun was dissolved in September 1948, there is little doubt that it was a significant factor in driving out the British from 1945 to 1947 and terrifying the Arabs in the War of Independence. Amos Perlmutter calls its achievements "considerable and complex . . . but not crucial," while Martin van Creveld spoke of "the considerable roles that Etsel [Irgun] and Lehi [Stern Gang] played in ejecting the British [but] both were strictly underground organizations with extremely limited capacities for overt military action." It also lay the basis for the second semi-capitalist globalizing revolution under Prime Ministers Begin and Shamir after 1977.[50]

In the end, the combined efforts of the Irgun and Stern Gang (together at times with the Haganah) inflicted limited losses on the British. They suffered 125 dead and 259 wounded in a force of 100,000 men from the summer of 1945 to the summer of 1947.[51]

The modern Zionist revolutions thus provided enormous change to the Jewish world. The first socialist revolution was distinctive in many ways: its urban orientation, the focus on return to a land not seen by many for almost two millennia, the romanticism of physical labor, the land and modern technology, communalism, voluntary military service, socialist forms (kibbutz, moshav, Histadrut) and sacrifice. Political changes, military setbacks, the university education of the bureaucrats, global trends and the incessant need to maintain a qualitative edge over the Arabs all pushed towards a second, semi-capitalist globalizing revolution. In this, the hitherto peripheral role of the Irgun, with its nationalist and capitalist emphasis, emerged as more salient and provided a leadership role for its leaders, such as Begin, Shamir, Netanyahu and Sharon, in the last 30 years.

12 Revolutionary military-security factors

There are few explanations how Israel overcame so many obstacles to independence and creating a First World state. With the correlation of forces strongly favoring their enemies, the Jews had to make a conscious political effort on a scale unknown in other national independence struggles. For, as Nathan Rotenstreich has written:

> The creation of the State of Israel . . . [was] accompanied by catastrophes, difficulties and stresses, by demographic and international problems . . . The State of Israel, as such, is first of all the culmination of conscious decisions taken by Jews. It is not a reality created by force of circumstances but a reality which we wanted to create and establish from the outset . . . The asserted element of artificial construction should, I suggest, be seen as an essential element. Essential is surely the opposite of artificial.[1]

The twin revolutions in radically transforming Israeli society and infusing it with a powerful will to fight created a more powerful state, army, secret police, government institutions and economy that led them to victory over more powerful enemies.

Given the Hobbesian state of war that continues to exist in the international arena, revolutionary military-security factors are critical to survival in the world. There are a number of key military-security factors. First among them is a strong will to fight.

Revolutionary will to fight

The willingness to fight and die, to sacrifice for a cause, has often been vital in changing history. Napoleon Bonaparte remarked that in war the mental is to the physical as 3:1.[2] George Patton demurred that the mental to the physical is closer to 5:1. In many revolutions (English, American, Russian, Chinese, Vietnamese and Iranian), the side weaker in weapons and numbers but superior in will to fight triumphed. This will to power, as Friedrich Nietzsche has asserted, was critical to success.[3] Alon Peled observed that, in modern armies, the most important factors for success are internal cohesion and the dedication of its soldiers.[4] Mossad chief Meir Amit asserted that "The human factor is the biggest and most crucial for our society and our security services."[5]

A weak will to fight has repeatedly led to disaster.[6] In 1940, the French, despite equal numbers of tanks and manpower to the Germans, lacked a will to fight and were defeated in a six-week campaign. In 1975 the South Vietnamese army, despite massive qualitative and quantitative advantage, was rapidly routed by an inferior North Vietnamese army which lacked airplanes, tanks or sophisticated equipment – but had a greater will to fight. In Afghanistan in the 1980s the Soviet Union had tremendous qualitative superiority but lost to the Islamic radicals who had a much stronger will to fight.

After millennia of persecution, the Holocaust and Arab terrorism, the Jews had a very strong will to fight. They were well aware that they had nowhere to go. They saw the struggle as a life-and-death one determining the fate of the Jewish people. David Ben Gurion told his commanders that "We will not win by military might alone. Even if we could field a larger army, we could not stand. The most important thing is moral and intellectual strength."[7] Yigal Yadin, Israel's first chief of staff, assessed the will to victory as the most important factor in the victory in 1948, for:

> If we are to condense all the various factors, and there are many, which brought about victory, I would not hesitate to credit the extraordinary qualities of Israel's youth, during the War of Independence with that victory. It appears as if that youth has absorbed into itself the full measure of Israel's yearning, during thousands of years of exile, to return to its soil and to live in liberty and independence, and like a giant spring which had been compressed and held down for a long time to the utmost measure of its compressibility, when suddenly released – it liberated.[8]

During the 1945–48 period they fought against the British Mandatory government and then the Arabs. The British had almost 100,000 soldiers and police, first-class equipment, international legitimacy, Arab support and the halo of their great successes in World War II. The far fewer Jews, unable to mobilize openly, with little military experience, without uniforms or heavy equipment, fought off first the British and then the numerically superior Arabs to achieve independence in May 1948. They showed a strong will to fight.

In May 1948 at Yad Mordechai near the Gaza Strip, the Egyptians deployed 2,000 trained soldiers, 32 cannons, airplanes, tanks, armored cars, a battery of mortars and 18 smaller mortars and 12 machine guns. On the first day they fired several thousand shells at 115 Israeli defenders with no heavy weapons and 37 rifles, 6 machine guns, 2 mortars, 1 anti-tank gun, 400 hand grenades and 2,000 rounds of ammunition. Only 24 had been trained in the Haganah and British army and a few others in the Polish and Russian armies. One-third of their force were young boys as young as 14 to 16 years old. Lacking fortified positions or even helmets, they fought behind barbed wire, a pill box, some mines and cover in trenches amidst inflammable wooden buildings.

The contest over the kibbutz, which was named for the commander of the Warsaw Ghetto Uprising, Mordechai Anilewicz, should have been over in a day or even hours. The Israelis repelled over a dozen infantry attacks as they held out for six days and inflicted 300 Egyptian casualties. The Israelis came with "exceedingly high morale" and willingness to fight and die. Before retreating after losing 26 dead, they delayed the Egyptian advance long enough to move the Givati Brigade into the region.[9]

The Egyptians, fighting on foreign soil with low morale and no stake in the outcome, were reluctant to press their advantage.[10] At Deganya in the Galilee, the kibbutzniks, lacking any heavy weapons, allowed the Syrian tanks to enter the compound and then set them afire with Molotov cocktails thrown at close range.[11]

In eight wars the Israelis have shown a strong will to fight and won six of the wars against superior foes. In 1948 the Israeli army mobilized 16 percent of the population (100,000 soldiers) in a country of 650,000 Jews. Israel suffered 6,000 killed and 30,000 wounded. Since 1947 Israel has suffered 22,000 killed and over 60,000 wounded in war.[12]

The revolutionary army

For thousands of years, international wars, civil wars, genocide, terrorism and violence have driven international politics. In the last century over 100 million people died violently in conflicts which have transformed the map of the world, for "the history of international relations has not been much more than the history of war."[13] Charles Tilly has stressed that in Europe states made war and wars made the state, with war making for centuries often accounting for the majority of state budgets.[14] John Mearsheimer's statement about the pressure felt by great powers in international politics could be applied to Israel in a more hostile environment than that faced by great powers:

> The sad fact is that international politics has always been a ruthless and dangerous business and is likely to remain that way . . . the structure of the international system forces states which seek only to be secure nonetheless to act aggressively toward each other.[15]

Facing a ring of hostile Arab states led policy-makers for decades to stress the doctrinal idea that "the central aim of Arab countries is to destroy the state of Israel whenever they feel able to do so."[16] Israel's first prime minister, David Ben Gurion, emphasized the importance of the revolutionary Israeli army, "The State of Israel exists only thanks to the Jewish people and first and foremost thanks to the Israel Defense Forces."[17] For Israeli Jews, remembering their history as well as their current predicament, the need for a powerful army was obvious. Jews from 1800 to 2000 lost 50 percent of their population, mainly to massacres and the Holocaust.[18] Henry Kissinger put it best: "Israel's margin of survival is so narrow that its leaders distrust the great gesture or the stunning diplomatic departure; they identify survival with precise calculation."[19]

There would be no savior, no deus ex machina, to protect the Jewish state from being driven into the sea. The Jews had been alone for almost 2,000 years and still were – and they knew it. The Western arms embargo of the late 1940s, after the limited British protection was gone, made this an urgent matter. Before 1967, when Jordan controlled East Jerusalem, the main highways between Tel Aviv and Jerusalem were a few miles from the border. Even in 2007 Israel is in places less than 10 miles wide and Tel Aviv is less than 40 miles from the Gaza Strip. Hezbollah rained down 4,000 katyushas on the Israeli north in the summer of 2006. Hamas since 2001 has fired or allowed to be fired more than 4,000 Qassam rockets at Sderoth, one kilometer from the Gaza Strip, and now is beginning to fire longer-range katyusha rockets at Israel.[20]

Revolutions have historically created modern armies with tremendous capabilities.[21] The English Revolution created Oliver Cromwell's New Model Army, which in the 1650s was the most powerful English land army in history. The French Revolution created the Napoleonic army that conquered most of Europe and was defeated only by four coalitions of superior enemies after more than ten years of warfare. The 1917 Russian Revolution created a Red Army that won the Russian Civil War (1918–20) against much better-officered White armies. In World War II the Russian Red Army, despite massive early reverses, went on to defeat the elite German army and occupy Berlin, Budapest, Bucharest and Prague. The Chinese revolutions (1911, 1946–49) helped create a strong Chinese Red Army that swept to victory in 1949, pushed the American army out of North Korea in the fall of 1950 and then stalemated the American army in Korea for three years until the armistice.[22]

Founded on Leninist organizational principles, extensive politicization and party hegemony, the revolutionary Israeli army was quite removed from more conventional Western armies.[23] As in the Russian, Chinese, Vietnamese and Yugoslav revolutions, so too in Israel did the army create the state and bring the revolutionaries to power.[24] The revolutionary army became an integral part of Israeli society, a nation in arms, and remains so to this day. As Sara Helman has written:

> The construction of the Israeli army as a popular army and of Israel as a "nation in arms" have been instrumental in the pursuit of the logic of the Israeli state ... Military service and war management became the main integrative mechanism in a state and society made up of

settler-immigrants. Jewishness was redefined in light of war and conflict and the army became the utter expression of the nation. The construction of the military service in terms of a community that both embodies and shapes Israeliness and that mediates between the individual and [national] society is one of the utmost expressions of the capacity of the Israeli state to shape society ... Ongoing participation in the reserves, and especially in combat roles, is experienced as a token of commitment and willingness to live a full and meaningful life in Israel ... a world suffused by military service.[25]

David Ben Gurion in 1938 indicated the importance of building a military, for:

The time we are living in is one of power politics. Moral values no longer have any force. The ears of the leaders are closed and all they can hear is the sound of cannons. And the Jews of the Diaspora have no cannons.[26]

In 1946 Ben Gurion began preparations for a life-and-death struggle with the Arabs as to when independence would be declared. In 1948 he was both prime minister and defense minister.[27]

The Jews needed a revolutionary army that would harass the British after World War II, survive the War of Independence against superior Arab forces, win six wars and establish predominance in the Middle East against larger and better-equipped armies. The Israeli army had numerous revolutionary features:

1   universal conscription, with predominance to civilian reservists (providing 65 percent of all elite combat units), men serving in combat to 40 and in the military to 55;[28]
2   extensive reserve service, able to mobilize the bulk of the army engaging enemies within 72 hours, providing the majority of all combat soldiers;
3   extensive use of women (including instructors, pilots, bureaucrats, operations and intelligence and technical operators) and minorities (Druze, Bedouins, Circassians);[29]
4   universal conscription for paramilitary Gadna (youth battalion) training from 14 to 18;[30]
5   careers open to talent (promotion from below and without admission to elite academies), with soldiers and NCOs playing a role in the selection of officers;
6   with early retirement, the bulk of the officer corps remaining strikingly youthful (in 1967 most brigade commanders were in their late 30s and in 1948 in their 20s);
7   egalitarianism, group orientation, socialism and kibbutznik officers;
8   informality, without real saluting, parade ground discipline, drill, resplendent uniforms, dress uniforms and martial posturing;[31]

9   stress on volunteerism, leadership and self-sacrifice;

10 strategic doctrine stressing the role of the few against the many, speed, short and offensive war, war of survival, a strategy of attrition, geographic pressure and the time factor, preemptive attack, offensive, fighting at night and in darkness, blitzkrieg, and the preeminent role of the air force, armored forces and intelligence;

11 extensive combat experience, improvisation and combat flexibility, with a strong role for junior officers;

12 officers expected to lead from the front by example ("After me") rather than the rear;

13 Nahal (pioneering farming youth corps);[32]

14 predominantly civilian ethos and culture despite the powerful role of security threats and the military.[33]

Creating a strong military was a difficult task for the Jews. Often excluded from serving in armies in European Christendom and in the Islamic Middle East in the preceding 1,800 years, Diaspora Jews were almost defenseless against pogroms and massacres. In 1900 Jews were barred from most officer positions in Central and Eastern European and Ottoman Turkish armies. They were stereotyped as weak, effete scholars and merchants unwilling to fight. The Jews were not found on the list of "martial nations." Reviving the fighting spirit of the Maccabees (Hanukkah), Masada, Simeon Bar Kokhba (leader of the Second Jewish Revolt in AD 135) and the first and second Jewish commonwealths, when Jews were prized as fighters and soldiers, was central to the Zionist enterprise.

In 1909 the secret association of watchmen known as Bar-Giora (after the famous Jewish leader in the revolt against the Romans in 70 CE), created a loose public organization known as the Hashomer (watchmen), whose Jewish guards provided defense against Arab marauders. An elitist secret society of fewer than 100 watchmen, the Hashomer was a response to robberies, lawlessness, village land wars, blood feuds and frequent Bedouin raids. They wore no uniforms, affected Circassian and Arab dress, and provided guard services, escorts and recovery of stolen property.[34]

During World War I the Ottoman Turks outlawed the Hashomer. In March 1915, 500 Palestinian Jews were expelled to Egypt, under the leadership of Vladimir Jabotinsky and Joseph Trumpeldor, formed the Zion Mule Corps, which carried food and supplies for the Allies at Gallipoli in April 1915. Their badge was that of the Star of David. The unit was disbanded after it refused to suppress the Irish rebellion.[35] In 1917 the British created a 5,000-man Jewish Legion (including David Ben Gurion and Yitzhak Ben-Zvi), which was disbanded only in 1920. Constituting one-sixth of the British army under General Allenby, it helped drive the Turks out of Palestine.[36]

But after 1920 the British banned the bearing of arms. Vladimir Jabotinsky initiated the Jewish legion, a self-defense effort, during the 1920 riots, but his efforts were suppressed by the British government and he was arrested and deported from the country. Hashomer was disbanded after it failed to cope with the Arab riots. Joseph Trumpeldor, with six fighters, died defending the isolated outpost of Tel Hai in the Galilee. While three other settlements had to be abandoned, Trumpeldor became a model for the future Jewish fighter, and his alleged last words – "No matter, it is good to die for our country" – became famous for generations to come.[37]

In the wake of the 1920 Arab riots a new, secret, underground, mainstream broad defense effort (Haganah) was started by the Achdut Haavodah Party and later taken over by the Histadrut. In 1921, when Jaffa Arabs attacked Tel Aviv, there were 300 Haganah men armed with sticks out of a population of 10,000 Jews in Tel Aviv. Training courses were held for officers and secret armories established to make light weapons. The stress was on "self-restraint" and "purity of arms." On a Marxist model a permanent military structure was created with the Trumpeldor Battalion, which performed agricultural, construction and mining work and military functions.

The 1929 Arab riots, which included the killing of 59 yeshiva students in Hebron and over 90 Jews across the country, forced the abandonment of old Jewish communities.[38] Haganah members were subject to long jail sentences if found with forbidden weapons. By 1929 the Haganah had grown to several tens of thousands of men, who drilled and trained and hiked twice a week. Weapons were stored in underground chambers, commanders were appointed for every town and settlement and each community had its own defense unit. Yet nationwide there were only 12–24 full-time soldiers and most Haganah members had no military experience.[39]

After the 1929 riots, the Haganah planned a nationwide defense. The British military and Haganah's limited capabilities forced the creation of defense blocs and buying weapons abroad from Austrian socialists. A small underground arms industry was created in 1929 and formalized in 1933. The Haganah in 1929 had a budget of less than $10,000 for defense.[40] The Arab Revolt (1936–39), led by the Grand Mufti of Jerusalem, Haj Amin al-Husseini, killed 520 Jews and wounded 2,500 Jews. The British, also under Arab attack, distributed weapons to 3,000 *ghaffirs*, who were uniformed Jewish auxiliary troops but actually Haganah members, to crush the revolt. By 1939 the Supernumerary Police included 22,000 Jews and 8,000 rifles, a basis for the later army.

In 1938 British Captain Orde Wingate, commander of the *ghaffirs*, created special night squads to guard the oil pipeline and other vital objects. He carried out audacious raids, fast patrols, long marches, short sharp attacks at night, decoys and feints marked by surprise, tricks and good reconnaissance and intelligence. Although he was shipped back to England, Captain Wingate left behind a strong legacy that would transform the Jewish forces into a successful and creative offensive force. Future commanders such as Moshe Dayan and Yigal Allon developed their professional expertise under Wingate, while Yitzhak Sadeh developed the Plugot Sadeh that same year.[41]

By 1939 Haganah had become an increasingly professionalized and enlarged paramilitary force directed by the Jewish Agency. Its general staff and centralized command had a chief of staff (Professor Yohanan Rathner), talented officers (Moshe Dayan, Yigal Allon and Yitzhak Sadeh) and operational plans. With 15,000 members (200–300 full time), 6,000 rifles, 24,000 hand grenades and 1 million rounds of ammunition, the Haganah often mounted ambushes and spoiling attacks. In 1937 it developed Plan Avner in case the British should leave the country. This foresaw reorganizing Haganah into divisions with an army of 50,000 men and garrison forces of 17,000 men. Fifty-two settlements were built, and many kibbutzim, which provided the majority of top commanders, became paramilitary bases. By 1939 the skeleton of a national army was in place.[42]

During World War II the Jewish Brigade (3,500 men), established by Winston Churchill in 1944, provided extensive training. Over 32,000 Palestinian Jews fought in the British Army, providing many commanders for the 1948 war. Over 750 Palestinian Jews were killed in World War II. The 32,000 Jewish volunteers outnumbered the 9,000 Arabs in the British army. Almost no Jews deserted, while over 50 percent of the Arabs deserted or were discharged.[43] The Irgun military force (Etzel), under Menachem Begin, numbered 5,000 men and provided leadership and future officers.[44]

The Palmach, created in 1941 with two years' professional training for its soldiers, was a revolutionary volunteer force dedicated to socialist revolution. By 1948 it contained political commissars and sang Soviet marching songs, and soldiers were called "comrade." By 1949 80–90 percent of the 9,000 Palmachniks belonged to the Mapam Party. Its slogan was "We are always first."[45]

During the height of the German threat to Palestine (1940–42) the British created an informal, deniable and secret alliance with the Haganah. They sent Special Operations Executive (SOE) officers to Palestine, trained Jewish guerrillas and gave arms, radios and explosives to the Haganah. This stopped in the later stages of the war as the threat to Britain and Palestine receded.[46]

After World War II, the Jews faced a new task: before they took on the Arabs, they needed to expel the British. This seemed hopeless. Britain emerged from World War II as one of the three great powers that had defeated Nazi Germany and Imperial Japan. Britain had modern weapons, support from 40 million Arabs and a determination not to give up the empire. In Palestine the British deployed 100,000 troops and police (one for every six Jews in the country) and formed a naval blockade (to prevent new immigrants coming into the country). Its high commissioner had the power to declare martial law, impose collective punishment (Tel Aviv was closed down for four days), search without warrant and censor the press. The British hanged Irgun terrorists, created heavily defended security enclaves (Bevingrads) and sought to crush the resistance through numerous roadblocks, arrests, deportations, curfews and fenced-in areas.[47]

The poorly armed Jewish forces, divided among the Haganah, Irgun and Lehi, often worked together and inflicted 500 casualties on the British. This occurred despite their inability to organize and drill publicly. They repeatedly attacked British military and civil infrastructure, including the headquarters in the King David Hotel, and wreaked severe damage on the transportation and communications infrastructure of the country, pushing the British to yield the Mandate by 1947. The rise of the Soviet Union as a new enemy, the financial weakness of Great Britain, other colonial problems (especially India), a cold and difficult British winter, dependency on the United States and British malaise weakened determination to hold onto the empire and facilitated this process.[48]

By 1947 the Haganah had mobilized 45,000 troops from a Jewish population of 650,000 Jews. Many of the leading officers (Yitzhak Sadeh, Moshe Dayan, Yigal Allon) were kibbutzniks. There were 3,100 soldiers in the elite Palmach, 2,000–2,500 troops in the Irgun and several hundred members in the right-wing Stern Gang. The establishment of the state in May 1948 under a provisional government led in 1949 to the integration of the Haganah, Palmach, Irgun and Stern Gang into the Israel Defense Forces, in which the Haganah was the backbone. From the Haganah and Palmach they took revolutionary features such as democracy, civil control of the military, informality, flexibility, ideological currents, melting pot, ties to agricultural settlements and anti-militarism.[49]

The process of building an arms industry in the country was difficult. In the 1920s and 1930s small-scale arms production started in Palestine. By 1948 these workshops produced explosives, mortars, submarines, grenades and small arms ammunition. In the mid-1950s Israel began manufacturing small arms and ammunition and assembling weapons systems from scrap. Then, over the coming decade Israel began under French license to produce foreign weapons systems such as the Fuga Magister training jet. In the next stage it altered foreign systems and upgraded them. After that, it began to develop its own subsystems of foreign systems such as the Nesher version of the Mirage 5 jet or upgrading of the British Centurion. By the late 1960s Israel had reached a new level with the developing and production of major weapons systems. The great leap forward came from the late 1960s to the mid-1980s. In the 1970s it began producing fighters, tanks, missile boats and unmanned aerial vehicles. By the mid-1980s exports were ten times greater than only ten years before.[50]

By 2000 Israel was producing sophisticated weapons systems with the advantage of extensive practical military experience in using them. Israel built a first-rate military industry that by 2004 was the number three arms exporter in the world, only after the superpower United States and the former superpower Russia. By 2006 its arms exports were estimated at $4 billion, a large figure for such a small state (Table 12.1).[51]

Israel's record in fighting eight wars against the Arabs has been chronicled earlier in this book in Chapter 6. The impact of the revolutionary army was dramatically seen in so many victories against major Arab enemies.

Table 12.1 Level of Israeli military exports

Year	Level of military exports ($ million)
1965	12–15
1972	70
1975	170
1979	480
1982	800
1985	1,000
1989	1,500
2000	2,000
2004	4,000
2006	4,000

Sources: Y. Lifshitz, *The Economics of Producing Defense Illustrated by the Israeli Case*, Boston, MA: Kluwer Academic Press,
2003, p. 302; *Haaretz* articles.

Revolutionary secret police

Israel needed a strong revolutionary secret police to defend the beleaguered
state against its powerful enemies. Intelligence provided the time to mobilize
the reserves, which formed the bulk of the army. Israel with scant resources
has built world-class intelligence services. Israel has spent less than $2 billion
a year compared to $40 billion for the United States.[52] A 1976 CIA report,
later published by Iranian militants after the embassy takeover, praised the
capabilities of Israeli intelligence services, which synthesized elements from
American, Russian, French and British services and developed strong human
intelligence capabilities, for "Their expert personnel and sophisticated techniques have made them highly effective, and they have demonstrated strong
ability to organize, screen and evaluate information obtained from agents,
Jewish communities and other sources throughout the world."[53]

Why were the Jews able to build a successful revolutionary secret police
consisting of Mossad (external intelligence), Aman (military intelligence)
and Shin Beth (internal intelligence) with a small budget and with significant
disadvantages? Over 560 Israeli intelligence agents and operatives, including
over 70 Mossad agents, have been killed since 1948. Strong intelligence organizations, such as the Soviet KGB, Chinese, Eastern European and Arab intelligence organizations, ex-Nazis and Palestinian guerrilla groups, operated
against them. The immigration of millions of refugees opened up possibilities
to infiltrate their own enemy agents and informers into Israeli society.

Israel, after 1948, was short of money to deal with major immigration and
security needs. From 1950 to 1970 Shin Beth had only several hundred members. While other organizations might need 30 operatives to watch a person,
Israel could only afford ten people. Salaries and budgets were low and the risk
was high.[54] A significant number of agents had extensive foreign experience

and numerous foreign languages and could blend into the crowd creating excellent human intelligence. The agents had a shared background that promoted teamwork. The high cost of failure promoted intense allegiance to task and hard work. They focused largely on the Middle East and environs. The small size promoted daring, experimentation, teamwork and professionalism (three years of intense training) with only a small bureaucracy. There was strong élan, panache and *esprit de corps*, with dedication to the task.

Agents were treated as part of a small and intimate family, whose leaders often went abroad to scout out operations. The leaders, who were often ruthless with significant military experience, had personal experience of running resistance organizations and made extensive use of cutting-edge scientific and technical capabilities. After the Holocaust there were few Jewish traitors. There were a number of foreign intelligence friends (William Stephenson, James Jesus Angleton, Maurice Oldfield) and good relations with their organizations. Diaspora Jews contributed a number of helpers (sayanim).[55]

Leaders, such as Reuven Shiloah, Isser Harel, Yuval Neeman, Aharon Yariv, Meir Amit, Yehoshofat Harkabi, Yitzhak Hofi, Efraim Halevy and Chaim Herzog, provided outstanding leadership. Neeman, the 1969 winner of the Einstein Prize for theoretical physics, modernized the intelligence services and put it on the cutting edge of science and technology. Chaim Herzog went to Sandhurst, served as a major in the British Army after 1945 and district governor in Germany and ended up as the president of Israel.[56] Meir Amit went on to a distinguished career as the head of Koor.

The Israeli secret service began in the early 1930s. After the 1929 Arab riots, Chaim Arlosoroff, the head of the Jewish Agency's Political Department, sent Reuven Shiloah to Iraq to build ties with Jews, British and Arabs.[57] In 1937 Jewish Agency intelligence groups bugged the Peel Commission hearings.[58] In 1937 the Haganah founded the Mossad to promote illegal (*ha'apala*) immigration to Palestine. Eliahu Golomb and Shaul Avigor played a major role in the Mossad, which expanded to espionage, buying arms and counterespionage. By 1942 it was running secret courses at Mikveh Israel in map reading, cryptography, marksmanship and escape routes.

In 1940 the Haganah, after massive British raids, founded Shai (Sherut Yediot or Intelligence Service) for screening Haganah members, checking credentials, watching Arab agents, informing on the British police, checking on the Jewish Left and planting agents in customs, police, postal services and transport. While Shai accomplished a great deal, it was plagued by illegitimacy from the lack of a state, British repression, lack of personal and professional expertise, lack of state tradition, a strong sense of personal mission and often recklessness and dilettantism.[59]

In 1941 the Palmach created an Arab Section. By 1945 there were Jewish agents passing as Arabs in Haifa, Jaffa, Jerusalem and numerous towns and small villages. These deep-penetration agents were valuable intelligence assets for the future Jewish state. Palmach scouts served as guides, saboteurs and reconnaissance leaders on missions for the Allies in the Middle East in World War II.[60] During the war there was limited cooperation with the British against the Germans. In the winter of 1941 the British SOE ran a course on amphibious landings and salvage for 30 Jews in Tel Aviv. In 1942 the British ran a camp at Mishmar Haaemek on explosives and sharp shooting. In 1941 23 Haganah men left on a failed mission to Tripoli. In 1944, 7 of 26 Jews (including Hannah Senesh) sent into Nazi-occupied Europe to rescue downed air crews were killed.[61]

At the end of the war Shai gathered significant quantities of weapons left in arms depots in the Middle East, as well as buying surplus arms. By December 1947 the services had bought in Italy and France 1,500 rifles, 378 Bren machine guns, 193 Bren guns and a million rounds of ammunition.[62]

British General Barker, commander of British forces in Palestine, commented, "the Jews knew all government secrets and military plans within a day of our making a decision. Their intelligence system is uncanny."[63] The Haganah monitored and intercepted British telephone, telegraph and post messages. A. J. Sherman called the Jewish intelligence service "highly efficient."[64]

At the end of World War II the secret service created a secret organization to smuggle Jewish Holocaust survivors out of Europe and into Palestine. Operation Bricha (Escape) rescued concentration camp survivors and provided manpower for the future state. Shai brought 71,000 illegal immigrants from Europe to Palestine. It created a far-flung organization working with soldiers of the Jewish Brigade and part of the Allied occupation forces in Germany and Austria. The service established escape routes through Rotterdam, Antwerp, Marseilles, Genoa and Bari. In Greece the Jewish Agency created a training camp to prepare Jews in both self-defense and agriculture.[65] They faced, as Yigal Allon wrote, enormous problems and overcame them, for:

> The sheer weight of the details upon which the success of each single voyage depended would have discouraged any less committed group. Each party of refugees had to be moved, concealed under tarpaulin, in military vehicles, which stood a chance of getting past European frontier checkpoints, and taken to secret transit stations from which, in convoys, they were later driven to the ports of sailing; each voyage meant that documents, blankets, provisions had to be obtained in suitable amounts without attracting undue attention; each convoy had to be made self-sufficient in terms of spare parts and fuel; each ship had to be bought or chartered, repaired, disguised, turned into a floating dormitory and manned; and each ship had to find its way, past British radar, planes and eventually the might of the British navy, to Palestine, there to be met by the Haganah landing parties at exactly the right beach at exactly the specified time. All told in the thirty-odd months of the *ma'avak* [struggle], some seventy ships, bearing Jews, left Europe and arrived in Palestine.[66]

When the British in June 1946 carried out Operation Broadside (a massive roundup of Jewish Agency personnel), the majority of senior Haganah members escaped. The Haganah stole the black CID book (which reached hundreds of pages) which had dossiers on the thousands of Haganah members it wanted to arrest.[67]

Shai in 1941 created an Arab Department in two rooms. By 1943 the department was studying the Arab press and in 1944 Isser Harel organized its archives. In 1945 an expanded Arab department surveyed 600 of 800 Arab villages, including photographs and agent reports. The Palmach Arab Platoon, formed in 1943 under Yitzhak Sadeh, infiltrated many Arab villages and towns for reconnaissance.[68]

During the 1945–48 period the secret service built secret explosives factories in Palestine[69] and smuggled weapons and airplanes from Czechoslovakia to the American zone in Germany to Belgium to Palestine. It transferred captured German and Italian weapons from North Africa to Palestine in the mid-1940s. The Rekhesh operation stole arms from British and Allied bases, bought weapons on the black market, imported arms from legitimate sources in Europe and shunted Allied supply trains off to sidings. It learned to modify, dismantle, cannibalize and pack weapons, to enter Palestine without detection by the British, and to store them away from British and Arab eyes. Undercover, it learned to manufacture grenades, Sten guns, mortars, shells and bullets.[70]

By 1948, with 68 full staff members, 60 British and Jewish agents and 80 Arabs, Shai spent almost $700,000 a year. The Haganah ran courses for intelligence officers and prepared dossiers on every Arab village in Palestine. It began to operate in a number of Arab countries. Shai protected Ta'as (the arms industry) and Rekhesh (the search for arms). It created an underground radio station that the British were never able to find.[71]

During the war the small intelligence agencies did some important work. Shai wiretapped local calls through Jaffa, Ramle and Jerusalem, international calls to local Arabs, the lines of the British military and other headquarters and the British CID's own telephone-tapping headquarters in Jerusalem. Secretaries provided carbons of British documents.[72]

In 1948 the extensive Shai network, which included strong village files on the West Bank and Gaza Strip, collapsed when the borders were closed and the war ensued. While some intelligence came through, the Israelis were in the dark on such questions as British intentions in May 1948, Arab military movements and other key information.[73]

After the 1948 war, Ben Gurion built a unified intelligence service. He disbanded the Jewish Agency's Political Department, Shai and the Palmach in 1948 and the Political Department of the Foreign Ministry in 1951.[74] The core of the new intelligence services was the Mossad (foreign intelligence), Shin Beth (domestic intelligence) and Aman (military intelligence).[75] Minimal resources ($100,000 budget per year), lack of procedures, fights between various organizations and often poor leadership plagued the intelligence services.

Israel Beeri, Shin Beth's first director, was fired for involvement in the murder of a Jew (Captain Meir Toubianski) and Arab (Ali Kassem), as well as torture of Jules Amster, a friend of the mayor of Haifa, Abba Hushi.[76]

Reuven Shiloah, with intelligence experience from the 1930s, was the first director of the Mossad (1951–52), followed by Isser Harel and Meir Amit. Mossad started with three small rooms, 12 employees and an empty treasury in 1951.[77] Mossad built a good relationship with the CIA and European, Turkish and Iranian intelligence organizations.[78] In 1951 David Ben Gurion met in Washington with President Truman and General Walter Beddell Smith to cement the relationship. CIA official James Jesus Angleton, who worked as an OSS agent in Italy with Aliyah Beth agents after the war to uncover fascist spy rings, was the American liaison with Mossad.[79]

Israeli intelligence, as a revolutionary secret police, had to create itself without external help. In 1948 no intelligence organization provided technical aid to the Israeli secret service. As Isser Harel, the second head of the Mossad, put it:

> Contrary to the army and various ministries and other of the government departments, we have practically no chance of benefiting from the experience of others. By their very nature the methods of special services like ours are kept a closely guarded secret. Whatever and wherever those services may be, they are not going to open their headquarters, their files and their training schools to a young country that wants to learn from their experience. Moreover, why should they do so for Israel especially, since the appearance of our country on the map of the world has not exactly pleased several other nations?[80]

It also had unusual additional tasks, such as protecting Jews all over the world and bringing them to Israel and fighting Nazis abroad. Using diverse methods such as bribes and political deals, it mounted rescue operations to bring Jews in large numbers from Romania, Ethiopia, Iraq, Morocco and Algeria. In 1962 it spent enormous effort to find a ten-year-old boy, Yosef Schumacher, who had been abducted by ultra-Orthodox elements and taken to Brooklyn. In 1950 the Shin Beth was fruitlessly tasked to smash the black market.[81] Another unique responsibility was to punish Nazis (such as Adolph Eichmann) responsible for persecuting and killing Jews. An unusual role was to develop relations with countries with which Israel did not have diplomatic relations. It focused on relations with Middle East minorities (Iraqi Kurds, Lebanese Christians, Syrian Druze and Sudanese Christians) and developed secret ties with some non-Muslim countries (Iran, Turkey and Ethiopia) and Muslim countries (Jordan, Morocco and Indonesia).[82]

The three main intelligence organizations often cooperated with each other. For special operations they cooperated with the elite Sayeret Matkal (Israeli military's general staff reconnaissance team) trained for special missions.

The intelligence agencies drew agents from a wide range of backgrounds, including the former Haganah, Palmach, Stern Gang and Irgun. Its first undisputed leader, Isser Harel, like many of his predecessors, often went abroad on assignments with his agents.[83] Israeli intelligence has known some major triumphs.

At the time of the Czech arms sales to Israel in 1948, the Syrians ordered 6,000 rifles, 8 million rounds of ammunition and hand grenades from the Skoda Works. In Operation Thief, a Palmach underwater demolition team in April 1948 sank the SS *Lino* off the coast of Italy. The Syrians under Colonel Mardun raised the ship, salvaged most of the cargo, cleaned the weapons and ammunition and stored it in warehouses in Bari. They hired an old Italian corvette, the SS *Argiro*, to take the arms shipment to Syria. When the ship arrived in Bari in August 1948, two Italians working for the Mossad LeAliyah Bet (which organized the illegal immigration to British Mandated Palestine during and after World War II) were on board. After setting sail, they rendezvoused with another Israeli ship, whose agents took over the SS *Argiro*, sank it and transferred the arms to Israel in time for the Etzioni Brigade to use them in the war.[84]

The transition to self-rule in Morocco (1956) endangered 100,000 Jews who had not left for Israel from 1948 to 1956. Facing strong anti-Zionism and official hostility, the Mossad used extensive bribery, safe houses, organizations, Spanish and British help and visits by Isser Harel to move nearly all the remaining Jews to Israel by 1963.[85]

The intensification of fedayeen (guerrilla) raids in the middle 1950s threatened to disrupt the fabric of Israeli life. After the limited success of the retaliation missions led by Arik Sharon, in 1956 Israeli intelligence killed Colonel Mustafa Hafex, the chairman of Egyptian military intelligence in the Gaza Strip, who was in charge of the fedayeen. Next they killed Colonel Salah Mustapha, the Egyptian military attaché to Jordan. In both cases a book bomb was the chosen weapon and the impact reduced fedayeen raids.[86]

Nikita Khrushchev's secret speech in February 1956 was a blow to the Communist cause, as it denounced Stalinist errors. Israel, operating perhaps through an Eastern European diplomat, obtained the speech and provided it to the United States.[87]

Deceiving the Egyptians into believing that the 1956 Sinai Campaign would be fought against Jordan and not Egypt was a signal accomplishment for Aman. Aman gained good knowledge of the Egyptian, Jordanian and Syrian orders of battle down to the company level before the start of the war. Key members of the Egyptian army were Israeli agents. After the war, interrogation of thousands of Egyptian POWs revealed useful information on the functioning of the army. Aman broke the Egyptian codes and stole the officers' book of the Egyptian army.[88]

Mossad ran many spies in the Arab world in the 1950s. One of the most successful was Jacques Thomas, a charming Armenian businessman from Egypt who spoke perfect Arabic, English, French and German. Originally recruited to work against Nasser under a false flag operation (he thought he was working for NATO), Thomas continued to work for Israel. He posed as an exporter of upscale objets d'art. Having passed valuable information about the Egyptian military for three years, he was caught and hanged with two others in 1962. His frequent business trips to the Suez Canal Zone provided invaluable information on Katyusha rockets.[89]

The arrest in Argentina of Adolf Eichmann, the chief organizer of the Holocaust, was a major coup for Mossad. The problems were numerous: operating many thousands of miles away from home, heavy expenses ($250,000), government opposition, few photographs of Eichmann, his evasive moves and the Nazi network in Latin America. The help of Nazi hunters Simon Wiesenthal and Tuviah Friedman, the passive cooperation of the new Argentinian government and the reluctance of other governments to get involved paid off. Eichmann was seized in 12 seconds and transported to Israel in 1960 where, after an extensive trial, he was found guilty and became the only man executed in Israeli history in 1962.[90]

The use of hundreds of former Nazi scientists and technicians in Egypt in the early 1960s raised the specter of an Egyptian rocket program that could bring massive destruction to Israel. In 1962 Egypt launched four rockets 175–350 miles and displayed these rockets in an Egyptian military parade, where Egyptian President Nasser boasted that they could destroy any target "south of Beirut." A series of factories were built in Egypt with the help of German scientists and technicians. Mossad, using threats, letter bombs, kidnappings and killings, ended the Egyptian program. By 1964 Germany had quietly lured a number of these scientists home with the promise of higher salaries. Given the mediocre nature of the German scientists, the lack of a guidance system, the age of the rockets and the minimal amount of cobalt, the threat was probably exaggerated, but, less than 20 years after the Holocaust, the Israeli government had to deal with the threat.[91]

Given its precarious security situation, the Holocaust and the Arab invasion of 1948, Israel from the onset was interested in building an "equalizer" such as the atomic bomb. Israel had a strong scientific base with work at Weizmann Institute of Science, Technion and Hebrew University under the scientific direction of Ernst Bergmann and the political direction of Shimon Peres. Israel contributed to calculations about the atomic bomb, development of short-range ballistic missiles and the Mirage supersonic jet fighter.[92]

France, then an ally of Israel (1955–66), first aided Israel's nuclear program. Upset over their failure in the 1956 Sinai Campaign and fearful of Egyptian involvement in Algeria, in 1957 French Prime Minister Guy Mollet sold a 24-megawatt heavy water nuclear reactor to be built in Dimona in the Negev. Later a small second research reactor was built as well. The 5-megawatt American reactor, which came with a technical library, training in nuclear matters and provision of fuel and even sponsored research, was provided by the Eisenhower administration in 1955. It unwittingly advanced the Israeli quest for nuclear weapons. French–Israeli collaboration was further aided by a number of French scientists.[93]

While it could produce enough plutonium for one 20-kiloton bomb each year, Israel needed a reprocessing plant to extract the plutonium from the reactor's spent fuel rods. France in the early 1960s allowed a private company to sell its technology and plans to the Dimona reactor. Norway sold 21 tons of heavy water to Israel and South Africa evidently sold uranium. An American company seemingly was involved in the indirect export of almost 600 pounds of enriched uranium to Israel. South Africa, Argentina and Belgium evidently sold uranium to Israel, which had completed the Dimona basic plant in 1961 and put the reactor into operation in 1964.[94]

In 1967, after the French ended collaboration with Israel and American aid remained limited, Israel decided to go nuclear. In 1968 a Mossad and Lakam team spirited away 200 tons of uranium oxide needed as fuel for the reactors and shipped it to Israel.[95] By the mid-1970s Israel was estimated to have 10 nuclear weapons, by the mid-1980s 100 nuclear weapons, by 1990 200 nuclear weapons and today somewhere between 200 and 300 nuclear weapons. Some claimed that Israel had developed sophisticated varieties of nuclear weapons suited to the Middle East.[96]

The Israeli spy Wolfgang Lotz acquired significant information before being uncovered by the Egyptians. A German Jew who had come to Palestine in the 1930s, Lotz ran an equestrian academy whose clients included the head of security of the Suez Canal Zone and the deputy head of Egyptian military intelligence. For two years he learned details about Egypt's defenses and a full list of Nazi scientists working with Egypt on poison missiles. After he was uncovered, he was eventually released to Israel.[97]

Israeli spy Eli Cohen, after the rise of Hafez Al-Assad in 1963, frequently entertained ministers and leaders of Syria in his villa under the guise of being a rich export/importer. An Egyptian Jew expelled after the 1956 Sinai Campaign, Cohen obtained detailed information about the Syrian military and politics. An honorary major in the Syrian army, he visited closed military zones and was friendly with many generals and colonels. He traveled with the prime minister to Cairo. He was uncovered by accident when an old school friend turned him in after encountering him on the street. He was subsequently hanged in the main square of Damascus in 1965, but he had passed much information of value to Israel in the Six Day War.[98]

By the mid-1960s the arrival of the Soviet MIG 21 in Arab arsenals posed a threat to Israel, which needed to know vital information on the airplane. An Iraqi Jew (Joseph) had a girlfriend whose brother-in-law was a pilot for the Iraqi air force. The defecting pilot demanded in addition to $1 million that his large family be spirited to safety. The pilot, Munir, was moved to a base near Baghdad with fuel enough for the 600-mile flight complex operation that took several years to come to fruition. The pilot flew the plane to Israel, and his family, through Kurdistan, reached Iran.[99]

The intelligence services played a major role in the Six Day War. They wiretapped conversations, carried out aerial reconnaissance, interrogated POWs, used computers and broke secret ciphers. Mossad had informers and operatives in each Egyptian air base and military headquarters, including three staff officers at the general headquarters. Israeli intelligence broadcast false orders to Egyptian pilots and deceived the Egyptian army into thinking the assault was in the south. During the war Israel issued false orders to Egyptian army units. They made extensive use of humint (human intelligence), photint (photo intelligence) and sigint (signal intelligence).[100]

As Moshe Dayan observed, "All I can say is that the role of Intelligence had been all as important as that of the Air Force or the armored corps."[101] The IDF knew, when the planes were on the ramps for 9–15 minutes of service, which planes were real and which were dummies, what were the names of the Arab pilots and even to mimic Egyptian air force dispatches to tell them to bail out when hit. Israel broke Egyptian and Jordanian codes while protecting its own.

For 20 years Shin Beth, with help from the army, maintained relative quiet on the West Bank and Gaza Strip with over 1 million Palestinians in areas taken in 1967. After the war the Palestinians, emulating the Vietnamese and Algerian revolutions, tried to launch revolutionary warfare to liberate the territories from Israeli rule. How did the Shin Beth, which had only 500 members in 1967 and little experience in this area (save for a short time in the Gaza Strip after the 1956 Sinai Campaign), do this?

Many factors helped: the lack of ground cover (except around Hebron), the small size of the Gaza Strip (140 square miles), trading help in meeting the basic needs of the population for intelligence information and compliance with the authorities, the lenient occupation policy (seven new universities, free travel to Israel, 140,000 jobs in Israel), weakness of the PLO located outside the territories, and the positive attitude of Jordan. The extensive use of informers and secret agents speaking Arabic, demolition of houses, captured Jordanian documents on the West Bank, military deployment, significant repression, expert use of internal divisions among families and clans, computerization of records and recruitment of capable people prevented "no-go zones" and "liberated zones," and provided relative quiet until the outbreak of the first intifada in 1987. So too did the division of the West Bank and Gaza Strip into clusters of one or several villages, each under a single agent who knew many of the residents by name.

After the Six Day War, most Palestinians preferred peace and employment to revolution. The weakness of the PLO, which used simple codes, no compartmentalization, large groups, commanders knowing large numbers of cell members, and lack of escape routes, aided the arrest of 200 Palestinian guerrillas by December 1967. By 1968 on the West Bank and 1971 in Gaza (after tough action by Arik Sharon), the areas were relatively quiet. Good leadership, such as that of Avraham Avituv (1974–80), played a role. In 1980 Shin Beth solved 85 percent of its terrorist cases in the territories.[102]

In 1969 intelligence allowed an Israeli raiding party to blow up 13 planes in 29 minutes without casualties at Beirut International Airport.[103] After France cancelled the sale of 50 Mirage III planes in 1967, Israel feared it could take ten years to build its own version. Israeli intelligence found a collaborator in Alfred Frauenknecht, the senior development engineer for the Swiss Mirage. After he sent nearly two tons of blueprints to Israel, he was sentenced to four and a half years in jail but served only one and a half years.[104]

After several failures in the mid-1960s, Shin Beth reformed procedures to protect El Al airlines. El Al flew through dozens of foreign airports over which it had no control and was a visible and accessible target for Palestinian terrorism. Yet not a single successful hijacking or bombing of El Al has occurred since 1968, when an El Al flight from Rome to Tel Aviv was hijacked to Algeria. By spending close to $100 million a year, El Al has become the model for international airline security. Its luggage compartments are reinforced, the pilots have flown in the Israeli air force, there are special doors to prevent entry into the cockpit, and armed agents fly on board each plane. El Al offices at the airport hand-inspect luggage, screen passengers and screen again in the departure lounges. Penetration of Palestinian guerrilla organizations provided further security.[105] Israeli embassies are fortified with secure dead rooms for entrance, television cameras, sensors, Israeli and local guards, and use of intelligence sharing against threats.

During the 1969–70 War of Attrition along the Suez Canal, Israeli commandos, operating with strong intelligence, took over a radar site east of the Gulf of Suez, cut loose a seven-ton Soviet-built radar station and lifted it with the help of two helicopters back to Israel. The information was shared with the United States.[106]

After the French embargo, the Israelis wanted to obtain delivery of the five French gunboats for which they had paid. Working on Christmas Eve in 1969, the Israelis whisked the gun boats out of Cherbourg and to Haifa. For Operation Noah's Ark, the Israelis created a dummy company, brought 120 sailors to Cherbourg, arranged supplies for eight days at sea, secured 250,000 liters of fuel, braved winter weather and took the ships on a 1,000-mile journey. The five boats made their way to Israel at the end of 1969.

After Palestinian guerrillas killed 11 Israeli athletes at the 1972 Munich Olympics, the intelligence services sought to destroy Black September. In 1972 and 1973 Mossad agents killed five leaders in Europe. In April 1973 in Operation Springtime of Youth, Israeli commandos killed three leaders (Kamal Adwan, Kamal Nasser and Muhammed Najjar) in Beirut and airlifted their filing cabinets by helicopter to Israel. They used 6 Mossad agents on the ground, and 6 rubber Zodiacs to ferry 30 paratroopers and Aman agents arriving from the seas. Israel lost 2 men who were killed while killing over 100 Palestinian guerrillas. By June 1973, 14 top leaders had been eliminated, with Black September commander Ali Hassan Salameh killed in 1979.[107]

On the two-hundredth anniversary of American independence, Israeli forces in Operation Jonathan, flying over 2,500 miles from Israel, rescued over 100 Israeli hostages from a kidnapped airliner held at Entebbe Airport in Kampala, Uganda. With the loss of a single Israeli soldier (commander

Yonatan Netanyahu) and four hostages (including the hospitalized Dora Bloch), all the hostages were flown to Israel. Using intelligence gathered from released French passengers, the plans for the airport built by Solel Boneh, Mossad agents inside Uganda and Kenya, airplane photographs and aid from Kenya, the plan worked well. After a meticulous rehearsal, Israeli forces on four C–130 Hercules transports carrying elite paratroopers overcame 100 Ugandan troops and killed all but one of the terrorists and 35 Ugandan troops in 53 minutes. The airborne troops brought along armored cars, a medical team and a black Mercedes to deceive the Ugandans into thinking that Idi Amin had arrived.[108]

In 1981 eight F–16 fighter bombers and six F–15 fighter-interceptors as flying cover reduced the French-built Osirak nuclear reactor at Al Tuweithan near Baghdad to a pile of rubble. With the reactor set to go hot in the next several months, this set back the Iraqi nuclear program by decades. Both the French and the Americans had refused to help. The planes had to fly over Saudi Arabia and Jordan for one hour before reaching the reactor. But, afterwards, France refused to supply more weapons-grade uranium to Iraq.[109]

In October 1985 Israeli F–15s destroyed PLO headquarters in Tunis. The problems were many: a 2,500-mile round trip, alien territory, precise intelligence and penetrating the PLO. Israeli jets hit the targets and destroyed the buildings, killing 75 Palestinians.[110]

Although Israel had excellent relations with Ethiopia for decades, the ouster of Haile Selassie and the 1973 Yom Kippur War severed those ties and endangered the Ethiopian Jewish community. In 1980 in Operation Moses, Mossad began to run the Ethiopian emigration effort and by early 1985 had 20 agents in Sudan. There they bribed Sudanese officials to allow Jewish emigrants to transit Sudan. Mossad agents dealt with Sudanese officials, forged or bought travel documents, rented vehicles and safe houses and provided money to help the tide of Jewish refugees. Perhaps 8,000 Falashas, with help from the United States, reached Israel at the end of 1984 and beginning of 1985.[111]

In 1988 the Mossad killed Arafat's deputy, Abu Jihad, in Tunis in an operation that took 13 seconds. The Israelis used a Boeing 707 command ship, listening and jamming devices and silent plastic explosive. Extensive practice was required. Seven Mossad agents brought in three vehicles with teams of Sayeret Matkal (IDF general staff elite reconnaissance men), who launched rubber dinghies from an Israeli missile boat.[112]

From 2000 to 2005 the security service, mainly Shin Beth, faced a powerful challenge in the second Palestinian intifada, which took the lives of over 1,000 Israelis. Without a fence separating the Palestinians and Israelis and with significant Arab and Iranian money flowing to the Palestinians, the task was daunting. Only by 2003 and 2004 had the security services gained the upper hand and reduced the number of terrorist attacks by over 80 percent. They mixed old techniques (trading favors, detailed knowledge of villages and towns, 20,000 Arab collaborators, strong repression of terrorist cells, hundreds of roadblocks) with new techniques (building a sophisticated border fence, preemptive military strikes against guerrilla bases, raids aimed at decapitating the guerrilla leadership and their agents). Their actions led to a powerful downturn in the Palestinian economy, which helped bring the intifada to a halt. The isolation of Yasir Arafat in the Muqata in Ramallah until his death in November 2004 also played a role.

In September 2007 the Israeli air force, coordinating with special forces operating with extensive intelligence, evidently may have destroyed a budding Syrian nuclear facility in the northeast of the country with a precision air strike. Months earlier Israeli special forces evidently penetrated the base and brought back samples that allegedly showed that the facility was an integral part of a nuclear weapons program.

Israel also suffered many intelligence failures. Five of the first eight chiefs of Aman (military intelligence) – Isser Beeri, Benjamin Gibli, Yehoshofat Harkabi, Eli Zeira and Yehoshua Saguy – were fired.[113] From 1948 to 1951 Mossad, together with the local Shura self-defense organization and Mossad LeAliyah Bet under Shlomo Hillel, brought 104,000 Iraqi Jews to Israel. Near the end of the airlift, two Mossad agents and over 80 Jews were arrested. The Iraqis captured the Shura arms caches, printing presses, membership lists and typewriters. Two agents were killed and significant information about Israel's penetration of the Iraqi military may have been garnered.

Operation Suzanne, which in 1954 sought to carry out bombings in Cairo and Alexandria to undermine Anglo-American confidence in Nasser, failed disastrously. Poorly conceived and badly run, it was uncovered by Egyptian intelligence, who executed two agents while two committed suicide. Defense Minister Pinchas Lavon, refusing responsibility, caused a scandal that brought him down and harmed Ben Gurion.[114]

The arrest of Soviet spy Israel Beer, who was close to Israeli leaders, was a major intelligence failure. Beer, who came to Palestine in 1938 from Vienna, served in the 1948 war as head of Haganah operations in the Galilee and wrote an official history of the 1948 war. In the first three months of 1961 he met his Soviet controllers over 20 times and passed on diagrams, blueprints, classified military plans and detailed lists of Israeli military purchases to the Russians. He was given a ten-year sentence and died in jail.[115]

In 1973 the Israeli secret service killed an Arab waiter (Ahmed Bouchiki) in a remote Norwegian town instead of a leading Palestinian terrorist, Ali Hassan Salameh. Six operatives were captured in the aftermath of the botched operation. They were easily noticed in a small remote town and subjected to humiliating capture and interrogation.[116]

Aman, operating from fixed ideas about the Egyptians – a significant number of troops in Yemen, a weak economy, lack of Soviet support after the expulsion of advisers in 1972, lack of air cover and an anti-aircraft network, the greater power of Israel, Sadat as a buffoon – argued that there was a "low" likelihood of war before the Yom Kippur War. It failed to see, until the day before the attack, an elaborate Arab plan to deceive Israel and deny it the crucial 48 hours to mobilize its reserves before the war. The Agranat Commission found a lack of coordination between Mossad and Aman and that Aman provided misleading or erroneous information about Arab deployments, advances, intentions, Sagger missiles, SAM missiles and the movement of the Iraqi army. In the second phase of the war Aman did better in understanding enemy moves. The failure led to thousands of casualties and the firing of the chief of Aman (Meir Zeira) and his deputy (Aryeh Shalev) and others, including the chief of staff, David Elazar.[117]

Jonathan Pollard, a civilian intelligence agent working for the United States Naval Intelligence Anti-Terrorist Alert Center, in 1985 passed over 1,000 highly classified documents to Israel. Pollard, with a "courier card" that allowed him to borrow secret documents from top intelligence services, provided information on everything from Syrian chemical weapons to the Iraqi nuclear project and Arab weapons. He was arrested. His arrest outside the Israeli embassy and life sentence damaged Israeli–American relations. Inquiries led by Abba Eban and Zvi Zur led to the disbanding of Lakam, the Scientific Liaison Bureau running Pollard.[118]

In 1997 an Israeli Mossad effort to kill Khalid Meshal, the leader of Hamas in Amman, failed and led to the arrest of several Israeli agents in an embarrassing operation given Israeli–Jordanian friendship. In 1998 the Israelis failed to kill Abdullah Zein, the leading fundraiser for Hezbollah in Switzerland.[119]

The role of revolutionary factors has been strong in the military-security sector. Here, where the life or death of the people and nation was at stake, the revolutionary army and secret police and powerful will to fight manifested themselves clearly. Against armies with more men and equipment, only a revolutionary force could propel the Israeli army to repeated victories. There was no alternative to victory in such a tiny country. The will of the Jews to fight was, and remains (if diminishing some), strong, considerably stronger than that of its enemies. The Israel Defense Forces, drawing on revolutionary features, a strong will to fight and high technology, has won nearly every war or drawn at best (the summer of 2007 war in southern Lebanon). Mossad, Shin Beth and Aman, with their revolutionary features, have regularly drawn praise for their work.

13 Revolutionary factors
Aliyah, education, government and party

The building of key civilian institutions (especially party and government), massive immigration to Israel and education were also central to ultimate success.

Massive revolutionary immigration to Israel

Immigration and population flows have played a vital role in world history. Immigrants have often wrought a revolutionary transformation in a country through their contact with foreign and alien ideas and peoples. They are the ultimate marginal and alien people who can succeed only through hard work and utilizing their acquired ideas and skills.

Apart from Latin American countries, many immigrant societies have been highly successful. The four British settler colonies (the United States, Canada, Australia and New Zealand) and two Chinese immigrant destinations (Singapore and Hong Kong) have become First World areas against great odds.[1]

Leaving one's home, culture and language behind is a revolutionary act which the great majority of people have refused to do even under adverse circumstances. The persecuted Jews have been a disproportionate percentage of the world's immigrants. Most of the 5.4 million Israelis today reflect immigration to Israel within the last century. In 1900 less than 1 percent of the Jewish world lived in Israel; in 2007 40 percent do so.

In Israel's case they imported revolutionary socialism from Eastern Europe and Russia, and nationalism from Western Europe, fusing the two in a special way. Agriculture minister Pinchas Lavon asserted that for Israel immigration was a "bloodless revolution, proceeding at a much lower price than any other revolution in history. There could be no slackening in the Ingathering process."[2] Massive immigration before 1948 was critical to success. Over 500,000 Jews, despite restrictions, immigrated to Israel from 1900 to 1948. By 1929 there were 170,000 Jews in Palestine and, by 1948, 650,000 Jews. Without this immigration Israel could not have been created or flourished.[3] After 1948 over 2.5 million Jews immigrated to Israel. More than 1 million came from the former Soviet Union between 1989 and 2007.[4] The Jewish population of

Israel soared from 650,000 in 1948 to 5.4 million in 2007. Again, aliyah was central to success.

There was an important moral and psychological factor. The arrival of millions of persecuted Jews legitimated Israel as the homeland and protector of the Jews. The arrival of Jews from Ethiopia, Russia, Eastern Europe, European concentration camps, North Africa, South Africa, Western Europe, North America and the Middle East showed the centrality of Israel for world Jewry and the fulfillment of the Biblical prophecy of the return to the Promised Land from the four corners of the earth.

Revolutionary socialist party

For the First Zionist Socialist Revolution, a revolutionary party was required.[5] There would have been no October Revolution without the Bolsheviks, no Chinese Revolution without the Chinese Communist Party. Only a revolutionary mobilizing party could overcome major external and internal obstacles.[6] The Labor Party was the vanguard party creating a Zionist socialist society whose slogan was "from class to nation."[7] It would fulfill Maurice Duverger's image of a dominant party, for:

> Domination is a question of influence rather than strength [whose] . . . doctrines, ideas, methods [and] style came to be identified with an epoch . . . in every period some doctrine has provided the basic intellectual framework, the general organization of thought, with the result that even its adversaries have been able to criticize it or destroy it only by adopting its method of reasoning.[8]

The Labor Party was an elite party of 6,000 members in 1930, 24,000 members in 1941 and 41,000 members in 1948. With no state authority or bureaucracy and opposition from Jewish landowners and the ultra-Orthodox, the Labor party, representing those who opposed the old Yishuv dependent on foreign charity, small-scale capitalism, exploitation of Arab labor and a neo-colonial plantation economy, mobilized society in a democratic revolutionary manner.[9] The weak society and modest colonial authorities in the early twentieth century allowed the parties to shape the society, rather than the other way around. For the parties preceded the society, just as labor preceded capital and even created capital. This allowed the Labor Party to create authority to build common ideological goals, political mobilization and patterns of institutionalization.[10]

This movement created a socialist economy and innovative socialist organizations such as youth villages, youth aliyah, Nahal (pioneer youth villages), kibbutzim, moshavim, Histadrut trade unions and publicly run companies. This was rooted in a blend of Russian socialism and populism and Jewish nationalism. It created a viable and functioning rural socialist base which would provide leadership for the revolutionary movement. The new society was grounded in national revival, egalitarianism, supremacy of the community over the individual, education, sacrifice, universal military service and technology.

Revolutionary kibbutzniks dominated the party. In the 1930s, though less than 10 percent of the population, they made up over 60 percent of the members of the Labor Party in the 1930s and almost 40 percent in the 1940s. In a largely urban society, rural people made up two-thirds of the party. If Mapai was the pioneering Zionist socialist party, the kibbutz, with its economic equality, collective ideals, reclamation and settling of the land and military functions represented the values of labor pioneering and hard selfless work.[11]

The Zionist Left emerged from 1897 to 1906 in Palestine in a neo-feudal colony without significant bourgeoisie, proletariat or Jewish population. Its highly charged ideological goals were to redraw the political, psychological, economic and physical boundaries of the Jews. In 1905 the Poalei Zion under Berl Borokhov was founded in Jaffe to integrate Marxism and Zionism. The non-Marxist Ha Poel Ha Tsair, supporting A. D. Gordon's religion of labor, calling for pioneers to build a Jewish agricultural proletariat, was founded in the same year.[12] Most Second Aliyah veterans (1904–14) were politically affiliated, almost half were fluent in Hebrew and 55 percent were the children of merchants. Zionism thus became the only major migratory movement with ideology championing the working class that represented strongly downward social mobility.[13]

Tens of thousands of leftist Jews between 1904 and 1914 founded Kupat Holim health clinics, Hamashbir, labor exchanges, Ha Shomer and cooperatives. The nation was remade in the image of the universal working class. The lack of capitalism allowed socialism to become the dominant ethos. Although the gap between high class consciousness and low class reality was large, the pioneers became the vanguard for the new state. The Labor Party built a national consensus and led the democratic system with degrees of institutional and ideological separatism. In 1939 the non-Labor sector of the economy encompassed 55 percent of the population, but the Labor Party, "by its organization, dedication, dynamism and ideals," ruled over the religious and private sectors.[14]

In 1918 it founded the Achdut Haavodah Party and in 1920 the Histadrut (general confederation of Jewish labor), which became the predominant institution of the future socialist state. It ran health care, banks, newspapers, schools, labor exchanges, trade unions, education, public works and worker kitchens. By 1926, 70 percent of Jewish workers were enrolled in the Histadrut. By the middle 1930s, under David Ben Gurion the Histadrut ran banks, kibbutzim, a building company (Solel Boneh), schools, newspapers (*Davar*), culture and the defense forces.[15]

Ben Gurion rejected re-creation of Diaspora society and wanted a revolutionary socialist state. He wanted to replace the religious and political quiescence of Diaspora Jewry with a secular, democratic, socialist state. As he declaimed in "The Worker in Zionism":

In its essence, Zionism is a revolutionary movement. One can hardly imagine a more profound and fundamental revolution than that to which it aspires in the life of the Hebrew nation. It is not a question of a revolution against a political or economic regime but a revolution in the mode of life of our people.[16]

The modern Labor Party was born in 1930 as Mapai (Land of Israel's Workers Party), a union of Achdut Haavodah and Ha Poel Ha Tsair. In 1931 Mapai won 61 percent of the Palestinian Jewish vote for the Zionist Organization and obtained a majority of the Jewish Agency executive. In the New Yishuv, Mapai represented the hegemonic pillar with its own institutions in a segmented pluralism with four pillars (Labor, Religious, General Zionists, Sephardim). Mapai sought to carry out a socialist and political revolution. By 1930 the Labor Party had gained control of the Jewish Agency, which had departments for labor, finance, trade and industry, agricultural settlement, organizations, statistics and politics. By 1935 David Ben Gurion was the chairman of the Jewish Agency Executive.[17]

Its major competitor in the pre-war era was the Revisionists, formed in 1925 by Vladimir Jabotinsky. The Revisionists focused on nationalism rather than socialism, on the nation rather than class. As the founder of the Jewish Legion, Jabotinsky failed to build a mass base in Palestine. There were no settlements, institutions or economic enterprises associated with his movement. Instead of the worker, the Revisionists championed the cause of the shopkeeper, the middle class, the artisans and private settlers.[18]

By 1948, the role of the Labor Party was so powerful that Benjamin Akzin called Israel a party state.[19] The Labor Party ruled Israel for almost 30 years after the creation of the state (1948–77). It gained the greatest number of seats in every election, held all or most of the key Cabinet posts, provided the prime minister, dominated the Histadrut and ruled most local governments. As an integrative and aggregative party, it incorporated diverse forces, provided interest articulation and opened the door to rising forces in society.

The Labor Party eschewed ideological purity or pure radical socialism. In a politicized environment it conquered the middle ground with modest tilts to the left. Labor supported coalitions with the conservative religious parties and the General Zionists, a mixed economy, the use of private capital, not nationalizing industries and class cooperation.[20]

The demise of the domination of the Labor Party paralleled the demise of other one-party dominant parties, such as the Mexican PRI and Indian Congress Party. It showed the relevance of Duverger's dictum that the dominant party "wears itself out of office."[21] As Robert Michels has argued, such political dominance is doomed by the corruption and immobilism that develop within such a party.[22]

The changing nature of Israeli society (increasingly Sephardi, capitalist and religious) provided opportunity for other parties to represent the rising forces. Its failures (the run-up to the 1967 War and the 1973 Yom Kippur

War) damaged the party's image. So too did its internal struggles (the Lavon Affair, the retirement of Prime Minister Ben Gurion in 1953 and 1963) and failure to create an adaptive second generation. The arrival of television and commercial radio in the mid–1960s, combined with the advent of investigative journalism, undermined its control over the media. Gaining control over the territories in the Six Day War opened the door to ideological debates in which the Herut Party seemed to gain traction with its territorialism.

The creation of the state, while enhancing Mapai power, also drained it. The state stressed universalism, achievement and centralization, which ran counter to the Labor Party need for particularism, ascription and competing structures. It lost its selfless, creative idealism. While retaining some functions (such as the Kupat Holim health fund), it transferred such Labor-dominated institutions as the armed forces, labor exchanges, school system and partially civil service to the state. The new state did not require the high degree of politicization provided by the Labor Party for the Yishuv in defense, labor exchanges, education, literature and culture.[23]

The Labor Party changed over time. While in the early 1940s urbanites constituted barely one-third of the party, by the mid–1950s, after mass immigration, 70 percent of the party were urbanites. The kibbutzim and moshavim proved economically unviable. By 1959 government subsidies provided 35 percent of the net income of the established moshavim and 52 percent of the net income of the new moshavim. Engineers, scientists and lawyers rose in esteem, while workers and farmers lost status.[24]

The demise of Labor Party socialist dominance in retrospect seemed inevitable but for almost a century it played a powerful role in the creation of modern Israel.

Institutionalization of the revolution: government and the social system

Every revolution has thrown up a galaxy of talented leaders who have transformed the power of the state. The American Revolution, with leaders such as George Washington, Benjamin Franklin, John Adams, Thomas Jefferson, James Monroe, James Madison and Alexander Hamilton, had a brilliant core of revolutionary leaders.[25] The Russian Revolution produced such luminaries as Vladimir Lenin, Leon Trotsky, Yakov Sverdlov, Grigorii Zinoviev and Nikolai Bukharin. The Chinese Revolution was led by Mao Zedong, Zhou Enlai, Zhu De, Deng Xiaoping and Liu Shaoqi. Revolutions attract leaders who normally would not have gone into politics but were attracted by the revolution.

The Zionist Revolution produced leaders such as David Ben Gurion, Chaim Weizmann, Moshe Sharett, Golda Meir, Moshe Dayan, Abba Eban and Menachem Begin. The leaders were people of intellect, modernity and cosmopolitanism. Ben Gurion wrote over 30 books, kept a diary that covered 30 volumes and left behind an archive of 750,000 items. Like other leaders, he had lived in Russia, the United States, Palestine, Israel and Ottoman Turkey.[26] Chaim Weizmann was a scientist who developed a variant of acetone of importance to the British in World War I. David Ben Gurion retired to a two-room cottage in Kibbutz Sde Boker in the Negev, while Golda Meir had a two-bedroom apartment in Tel Aviv as well as her apartment in Kibbutz Revivim.

Its organizations – the Jewish Agency, Haganah, Palmach, kibbutzim, moshavim, Histadrut, the Labor Party, later the Likud Party, Youth Aliyah – were relatively modern, flexible organizations mobilizing and extracting resources from the society.

Revolutions also transform regimes lagging behind the world in political, economic, cultural and military power. The English, American, French, Russian and Chinese revolutions took lagging states and made them great powers over time. The Zionist Revolution transformed the power of the Jews as well. The Middle East and Palestine lagged far behind the level of the First World. Most Jews living in Eastern Europe, North Africa and the Middle East had their own autonomous communal organizations led by traditional secular (notables) and religious (rabbis) elites. The Jews were bound together by the rule of law, conservatism and tradition, consensual decision making, freedom from internal coercion and sanctions (deriving from law, public opinion, values and concern for continuity) against the ruling oligarchies. The leaders were answerable to public criticism in small traditional societies.[27] The revolution transformed these communities in Palestine and Israel and created much more powerful and capable institutions.

The flexibility, pragmatism and willingness to compromise of the leaders echoed that of the first Zionist leader, Theodor Herzl, who was prepared to meet any leader and try any program that might advance his goal. In *Alteneuland* Herzl envisaged good relations with the Arabs, a modern state, tolerance and a peace palace.[28] Only in 1942 did the Zionists define their task as creating a state.[29]

Chaim Weizmann carried out extensive negotiations with Prime Minister Lloyd George, Foreign Secretary Arthur Lord Balfour, Mark Sykes, South African Prime Minister Jan Smuts and Lord Cecil that produced the Balfour Declaration in October 1917. His biographer Jehuda Reinharz called his volume *The Making of a Statesman*.[30] In the United States, Zionist leaders such as Louis Brandeis and Stephen Wise, working with liberal and progressive Protestants, secured the active support of President Wilson, who expressed his "deep interest in Zionism."[31]

During World War I the flexible Zionists supported Arab nationalism. In 1917 Weizmann indicated his willingness to go to Palestine to negotiate with Arab leaders. In 1918 he met with Arab leaders and in 1919 with Emir Faisal, who stated that:

> Arabs and Jews are cousins . . . and have by happy coincidence been able to take first steps together towards the attainment of their national

> ideals. We Arabs . . . look on the Zionist movement with deepest sym-
> pathy . . . We will wish Jews a hearty welcome home and we will, so far as
> we are concerned, do our best to help them through.[32]

In 1917 the Jews accepted the Balfour Declaration even though it used the words "Jewish homeland" instead of "Jewish state." David Ben Gurion in 1918 declared that:

> Both the vision of social justice and the equality of all peoples that the
> Jewish people has cherished for three thousand years, and the vital inter-
> ests of the Jewish people in the Diaspora and even more so in Palestine,
> require absolutely and unconditionally that the rights and interests of
> the non-Jewish inhabitants of the country be guarded and honored
> punctiliously.[33]

From the beginning the Jews were willing to negotiate with the Arabs, pay a market price for the land, buy only British, waste and unoccupied land and respect holy sites.[34] From 1921 to 1947 the Haganah stressed the need for *havlagah* (restraint) with defensive actions against the Arabs. Organizations such as Brith Shalom and Ichud emphasized cooperation with the Arabs.[35]

In 1922 the Zionists reluctantly accepted the severing of 75 percent of the Palestinian Mandate, which was given to Transjordan.[36] In the early 1920s they bargained with Emir Faisal, supported Arab versus French claims to Syria, spoke of areas of Arab autonomy within Palestine, and discussed economic benefits for Arabs who would live in the Jewish homeland. During the 1920s the diaries of Colonel Kisch, the head of the Palestine Zionist Executive (1923–31), frequently discussed negotiations with the Arabs. The Jews reluctantly accepted the reduction of the size of Palestine at the hands of the French in southern Lebanon.[37] In the 1930s David Ben Gurion held extensive discussions with Arab leaders to find a compromise. During the 1936 Arab Revolt David Ben Gurion gave orders "not to touch innocent Arabs."[38]

In 1937 the Jewish leaders considered the truncated state of 1,554 square miles (20 percent of the land of West Palestine) offered by the Peel Commission. The Jews would not get Jerusalem, Bethlehem, the Negev, Aqaba, Tiberius, Safed, Nazareth, Acre and Haifa. The mini-Jewish state, with a 40 percent Arab minority, lacked defensible borders or access to the Jordan River or the Yarmuk River. Yet, the Twentieth Zionist Congress voted 300–158 to explore the British offer. The leading political pragmatists were Chaim Weizmann, David Ben Gurion and Yitzhak Ben-Zvi.[39]

In August 1939, a Zionist Congress meeting in Geneva sharply criticized the White Paper but refused to condemn Great Britain. Chaim Weizmann reassured the British that "their war is our war."[40] During World War II and the Holocaust, David Ben Gurion said that he would fight against the Nazis as though there were no White Paper and fight the White Paper as though there were no war against the Nazis.[41]

In 1942 the Zionist Biltmore Program "based itself on practical grounds rather than on an interpretation of the original intent of the Balfour Declaration, when it refrained from raising an issue concerning Transjordan." In 1947 the Zionists accepted a United Nations-backed state that lacked defensible borders, did not include Jerusalem, Jaffa, Nazareth or Beersheba and placed 100,000 Jews in an internationalized enclave in Jerusalem surrounded by the Arab state. The Jews accepted an Arab minority equal to 40 percent of the population of the Jewish state and gave up 30 Jewish settlements, western Galilee, western Negev and the coastal strip from Ashdod to Rafah.[42] As Ben Halpern wrote:

> In order to gain the most essential sovereign rights needed to solve the post-war problem of the Jews, the Zionists swallowed not only the substantive restrictions on their authority in other respects but the symbolic denial of their historic claim to restoration in Zion represented by the proposed internationalization of Jerusalem.[43]

The plan denied the Jewish state economic sovereignty by intertwining the Jewish and Arab state with a ten-year customs union, providing for Jewish subsidy of the Arab economy and setting of a common tariff by a Joint Economic Board. Between the November 1947 United Nations resolution supporting the creation of Israel (and a parallel Arab state) and the proclamation of the state of Israel in May 1948, the Israelis were the only entity to collaborate with the United Nations Palestine Commission.[44]

This pattern of compromise and pragmatic accommodation continued after independence. Since 1948 Israel has withdrawn from all or part of the Sinai desert three times (1949, 1956 and 1982), from parts of southern Lebanon four times (1949, 1978, 1985 and 2000), from the Gaza Strip four times (1948, 1957, 1994 and 2005) and part of the Golan Heights (late 1980s). It did not annex either the Gaza Strip or the West Bank.[45]

In 1949 Israel carried out armistice talks on the island of Rhodes with four states and offered to take in 100,000 Arab refugees to end the conflict. The Arabs refused to negotiate anything beyond a temporary armistice.[46] In 1957, under heavy American and international pressure and threats of international sanctions, Prime Minister David Ben Gurion withdrew Israeli forces back to the armistice lines in exchange only for promises.[47] After 1967 they were willing to return the bulk of the territories (especially Sinai and the Golan Heights) for peace.

In 1981 Likud Prime Minister Menachem Begin returned the Sinai peninsula (three times the state of Israel), with its oilfields, resorts, air bases and 11 upgraded settlements in return for a peace with Egypt. In 1994 Israel reached a peace agreement with Jordan. In 2000 Labor Prime Minister Ehud Barak withdrew entirely from the security zone in southern Lebanon. He offered, at Camp David in July 2000, 100 percent of the Gaza Strip, 94 percent of the West Bank, East Jerusalem Arab neighborhoods, sovereignty over the Temple Mount and 4 percent of Israel in return for keeping the main settlement blocs in the West Bank. In 2005 Israeli Prime Minister Arik Sharon withdrew from the Gaza Strip and four West Bank settlements. In 2007 Prime Minister Ehud Olmert spoke of a liberal peace plan with the Palestinians to resolve the conflict.

The leaders were willing to make compromises. After the 1948 war, Israeli leaders, hoping for support from Moscow and the Third World, refused to send troops to South Korea during the Korean War. In 1953 they were preparing to open an embassy in Beijing until American pressure prevented this move.[48] The close relationship with the great powers (today the United States) has been maintained ever since. Prime Minister Arik Sharon (2001–06) made 12 visits to Washington for frequent consultations.

Israeli leaders have made domestic concessions to the religious bloc ever since the beginning of the Zionist immigration. This was not easy given the frequent religious hostility towards Zionist socialism. The religious bloc (save for the National Religious Party) castigated mainstream Zionism as an evil and heretical secular nationalism, trying to create a Jewish state without waiting for the messiah and using the sacred language of Hebrew.

The largely secular Zionists understood that the religious dominated the Old Yishuv, enjoyed a moral stature in the Jewish community and were granted a special role by the British (rabbinical courts and the Chief Rabbinate). In 1897 at the First Zionist Congress the secular Theodor Herzl attended a synagogue in Basel and encouraged the growth of a religious Zionist movement (Mizrahi). In the 1920s Chaim Weizmann, president of the World Zionist Organization, integrated religious Jews into the movement by providing money, influence and a sense of participation and benefits for religious Zionists. In 1934 an agreement on power sharing with the religious Zionists formalized the relationship.

In 1949 David Ben Gurion and the National Religious Party made the status quo agreement accepting Shabbat as an official day of rest, providing army deferment for yeshiva students, maintaining the status quo on Shabbat, buses and restaurants, giving control of marriage and divorce to the religious, and keeping all official functions kosher. The Labor Party agreed to fund religious institutions and yeshivas and two tracks in the educational system, one secular and another religious. Proportional representation in the electoral system promoted a significant role for the religious parties (holding 10–20 percent of the seats) in any governing coalition. The anti-Zionist Agudath Yisrael Party, weakened by the Holocaust, signed the Declaration of Independence, sat in the provisional government and received a seat in the first Cabinet in 1949. For several decades the Labor Zionists ruled with the more conservative National Religious Party, which had two Cabinet seats in the first government in 1949.[49]

Before 1948 they put enormous efforts into national integration (absorbing 500,000 immigrants), economic and educational modernization and creating a modern society and economy.[50] The Zionist organizations were elected through a democratic parliament with a small bureaucracy. The Histadrut trade union created a strong economy with a major role for the workers. The Jewish Agency, a function of the World Zionist Organization, conducted relations with the Diaspora, represented the Yishuv abroad and coordinated immigration and settlement. Going back to 1920 its elected bodies levied taxes and supported institutions. The Jewish Agency, established by the League of Nations Mandate for Palestine, was the central political motor force. Dependent on public support, it was the peak of a network of inter-locking social, financial, educational, economic and military institutions. Political parties provided schools, banks, papers, loan funds, health care, youth movements, sports clubs, housing and welfare. Political parties, religious bod-ies, educational and cultural groups, burial societies, charity and social welfare groups, economic guilds, workers groups and private companies played sig-nificant roles. Efraim Karsh spoke of the extensive institution building and democratic mass mobilization of the Zionist movement from the beginning:

> The main source of strength of the Jewish national movement had been its ability to organize itself from an early stage as a "State in the making" based on democratic-parliamentary principles. It was all there, set up and running, within a year of two of the calling of the first Congress of Zionists in 1897: free elections on a constituency basis; universal suffrage ... a fully representative assembly; a political leadership responsible to that assembly; open debate on all major issues; and before long what might usefully be called a loyal opposition too ... [in the 1930s] the Jewish Agency Executive evolved into the foremost decision-making body of the Zionist movement and the "de facto" government of the Yishuv, managing its affairs, from the more mundane aspects of daily life to the critical political issues of the day.[51]

The Yishuv created a plethora of institutions before 1936:

- Mikveh Israel, 1870;
- Hebrew as a national language, 1889;
- the World Zionist Congress, 1897;
- the Jewish National Fund, 1901;
- Technion, 1914;
- Histadrut, 1920;
- the Jewish Agency, 1921;
- Hebrew University, 1925;
- Mapai, 1930;
- the *Palestine Post*, 1932;
- the Palestine Orchestra, 1936;
- the Maccabi Olympic Games, 1936.

The Jews created a strong social democratic economy. In the 1950s the state and public sector controlled nearly 50 percent of the economy. Even by 2007 the state budget accounted for over 50 percent of the economy.[52]

The Yishuv under the British Mandate created all the proto-government institutions for the state that emerged in 1948. Ever since the First Zionist Congress in 1897 the annual proceedings have followed the rules of parliamentary democracy with parties as the main actors. At that congress each delegate represented 100 Zionists. All the Jewish communities worldwide were represented with different and opposed views – tradition versus revolution, secular versus religious, political Zionism versus cultural Zionism, socialist versus non-socialist. Without any state power for the first 50 years, they learned to accommodate each other with "power-sharing, decentralization, mutual-veto, coalition-building, multidimensional politics."[53]

In 1948 the Jews created a state from scratch. The British left with no ceremonies, lowering of flags, marching bands, dignitaries or changing of the guard. The Jews drew on their own institutions and on centuries of experience in running their own affairs.[54] By early 1948 a Jewish inter-party committee had appointed a provisional Zionist Council of State under the leadership of David Ben Gurion. Its 13-member Council of Government collected taxes, while Jewish Agency and Va'ad Leumi officials assumed new ministerial responsibilities. A temporary capital was created in North Tel Aviv, offices were found for the new government with secretaries and clerks, and new postage stamps and paper currency were printed. The government in April 1948 expanded to include Sephardim, ultra-orthodox Jews (Agudath Yisrael) and the Revisionists (Herut) in the expanded 37-member People's Council.[55]

After 1948 Ben Gurion subordinated Labor Zionist institutions to the state, transferring many of their functions to the state. He nationalized many Labor party institutions (schools, army, education) and emptied them of socialist content. Ben Gurion chose not to expropriate the bourgeoisie or increase the socialist sector. He put nationalism and state power (*mamlakhtiut*) above socialism. He postponed socialism because of the urgent tasks of aliyah, defense and building the land. Even though Mapai and Mapam together had a majority of all seats in the Knesset after 1948 (65 out of 120 seats), he did not use this majority to press for socialism but rather for national goals.

After 1948 Ben Gurion sought to integrate the religious (status quo agreement), the Palmach (dissolved into the new army) and the Irgun (dissolved into the new army) in the new state. In the Irgun case there was the highly controversial bombing of the *Altalena* ship providing French arms to the Irgun. The goal was to create a unified nation state.[56]

Despite the socialist nature of the state, the private sector was alive and well. From 1881 to 1948 the main available capital was private capital from Diaspora Jews. During this period 85 percent of all capital was private capital, invested outside the framework of various Zionist organizations.[57] In the 1950s the private sector was not nationalized, and some private capitalism was allowed. To attract foreign investment and maintain full employment, capitalism was a necessity.[58] Ben Gurion said in 1957:

> The stories of our forefathers 4,000 years ago; the acts and life of Abraham; the wanderings of Israel in the desert after the Exodus from Egypt; the wars of Joshua and the judges that followed him; the lives and doings of Saul, David and Solomon; the deeds of Uziyahu, King of Judah, and Jeroboam II, King of Israel, all of these have more actuality, are closer, more edifying and meaningful for the younger generation maturing and living in the Land of Israel than all the speeches and debates of the Basle Congresses.[59]

In the 1950s the majority of the population worked in some form of socialist sector – the Histadrut cooperative sector, the national sector or the municipal sector. Numerous institutions were critical to the success of the Zionist Revolution – the Jewish Agency, the National Committee (Va'ad Leumi), the People's Council (Minhelet Ha'am), the Labor Party, Histadrut (trade unions), kibbutzim, moshavim, Kupat Holim (the medical fund) and leading universities (such as Hebrew University and Technion). All were brought up to the Western level with their capacity to train, mobilize and enact programs vital for national infrastructure development. The Hebrew language was revived, a vibrant press of dozens of newspapers arose and culture flourished, especially in Tel Aviv and Haifa.

By 1948 the Jewish national economy (£169 million) was bigger than the Arab national economy (£67.7 million). The Jewish economy on a per capita basis was almost five times larger than the Arab economy. In 1948 Jewish cities had budgets ten times the size of Arab cities. Jews owned 83 percent of bank deposits or ten times more per capita than the Arabs.[60]

The economic dynamism of the Yishuv was remarkable. From 1921 to 1939 the Jewish economy, despite the Great Depression, grew 13.2 percent a year, the sixth best performance in the world. The massive development of new enterprises and services and large-scale immigration had transformed Palestine by World War II. By 1941, despite the fact that Arabs outnumbered Jews more than two to one, Jewish income was 25 percent greater than Arab income.[61]

Building a modern education and technological system

The pre–1948 Jewish educational system had many tracks: yeshivas, the Zionist Organization, the Alliance Française, Hebrew and Baron de Hirsch schools. The new state integrated them into a two-track system, one secular and one religious. It derived from such early pioneers as the Evelyn Rothschild Girls School (founded in 1860) and the Mikveh Yisrael Agricultural School (founded in 1870), both run by the Alliance Israélite Universelle. By 1920 the majority of schools in Palestine educated in Hebrew.[62] The emerging state created Technion (1913), Hebrew University (1925) and Weizmann Institute (1932) long before independence.

Israel relentlessly promoted technological development to overcome its small physical size, population and resources. This great emphasis in the first socialist revolution would, together with a technical emphasis in the universities and army and massive immigration of technically skilled manpower from the former Soviet Union, play a powerful role in promoting the second partial capitalist revolution.

From 1948 on, Israeli Prime Minister David Ben Gurion venerated the role of science and technology as providing the qualitative edge to overcome its quantitative inferiority. Ben Gurion's "boys" (Moshe Dayan and Shimon Peres) were powerful supporters of technocratic developments in Israeli society.[63] By 2004, 70 percent of Israeli households already had computers and 57 percent were linked up to the Internet.[64]

The Zionists stressed education and technology as multiplier forces that could overcome inferiority in numbers and supplies. The idea for Hebrew University originated in the 1880s. In 1918 a university committee bought 25 acres on Mount Scopus from the estate of Sir Norman Hill. Chaim Weizmann spoke at a cornerstone-laying ceremony in 1918 to an enthusiastic crowd of 6,000 people. The university itself opened in 1925.[65]

In the critical areas of civilian institutions, building, immigration and education, the Jews created revolutionary forms that helped the state to come into existence and flourish. The immigration of 3 million Jews in the last century has made Israel a new society continually remaking itself. The record of building key voluntary, open, modern socialist institutions in a Third World colony before 1948 and sustaining themselves after 1948 as they transformed themselves under changing conditions also had a strong revolutionary tone. The Israeli Labor Party led the socialist revolution until the late 1970s and then was able to play a significant role in the new second semi-capitalist globalizing revolution still under way in Israel. Few countries have been able to manage both a socialist and a capitalist revolution – Israel has done far better than most of the socialist world in doing so.

14 International factors

Many of the explanatory factors of the Jewish victory and success derive from their position in the international arena: the role of the Jewish Diaspora, the role of non-Jews, alliances with the democratic West and temporary alliances with unlikely allies such as the Soviet Union and for a while the British Empire.

The role of the Diaspora

The Jewish Diaspora, initially cool to the idea of Zionism, became increasingly energized to support Zionism after the Holocaust, the creation of the state of Israel, the ingathering of millions of exiles, the 1948 and 1967 wars and the two intifadas that killed over a thousand Israelis. These traumas rallied the Diaspora, especially the Anglo-American Diaspora, to action on Israel's behalf. As early as 1950 David Ben Gurion called the Diaspora "a great political, economic and moral factor." The first director general of the Israeli foreign ministry observed that, unlike diplomats in other diplomatic services, the Israeli diplomat played a dual role: "He is Minister Extraordinary to the country to which he is accredited – and Envoy Extraordinary to its Jews."[1]

Many of the early leaders who created Israel from 1881 to 1948 were Diaspora leaders, from Theodor Herzl and Chaim Weizmann to Louis Brandeis, Rabbi Stephen Wise and Rabbi Abba Hillel Silver. "Hatikvah," the anthem of the state of Israel, was written by a Diaspora Jew (Naftali Herz Imber) to music by a Diaspora non-Jew (Bedrich Smetana). After 1948, the Diaspora role diminished considerably, although reviving in recent years during the second intifada. Abraham Ben-Zvi has written that American Jewry was a "highly significant factor in constraining successive administrations" and "frequently successful in promoting favorable policies and legislation."[2]

The role of the Diasporas has been important, especially for small communities like the Jews. The Diaspora "greatly helped in establishing the Jewish community in Israel and was the most important external partner in the creation of the Jewish state."[3] Gabriel Sheffer has concluded that, without the Jewish Diaspora work in the 1930s and 1940s in terms of money, manpower, weapons, political and diplomatic support and morale boosting, there probably would not have been a state of Israel. Its work thus was "essential" to creating Israel in May 1948. David Ben Gurion asserted that the Diaspora was "Israel's only absolutely reliable ally," while Michael Brecher found that the Diaspora was the "most important component" in Israel's global perception.[4]

Before 1948 the Israelis were heavily dependent on the Diaspora financially and politically. In the 1920s and 1930s wealthy British Jews, such as Albert and Frederick Stern (bankers), Waley Cohen (Shell Oil) and Alfred Mond (Imperial Chemical Industries) joined with wealthy American Jews (such as Felix Warburg and Herbert Lehman) to invest in Palestine. Leading Diaspora leaders, such as Abba Hillel Silver and Stephen Wise, were not offered Cabinet posts, while Chaim Weizmann found himself the president with little real power. The Western Jews gained ethnic, psychological and religious pride, while the Israelis received material, political and moral support. After 1948 the creation of Israel generated new energy into the Diaspora which saw Israel as arising from the ashes of the Holocaust, ending the shame and guilt of the past with new sabra heroes and victories and showing the vitality of the Jews.[5]

The Diaspora has been under siege from a variety of directions. Anti-Semitism, propagated by the Soviet Union, Nazi Germany and the Arab world, has been a threat to the community. Seven million Western Jews face significant assimilation, alienation from the community and low birth rates. In the 1990s the American Jewish community, despite Russian Jewish immigration, lost 300,000 Jews. In the last 20 years, the domestic needs of protecting the community in the West have conflicted with providing support for Israel. It also opens up the powerful question of whether Israel or the United States (the homes of the two strongest Jewish communities) is the center of the Jewish world.[6]

Mass aliyah (immigration) from the Diaspora has been decisive. Without it Israel would have 1 million Jews and be non-viable. The aliyah of over 3 million Jews (representing 60 percent of the non-North American Jews in the Diaspora) to Israel in the last 80 years has allowed the Jewish population to leap from 650,000 in 1948 to 5.4 million by 2007. It has brought enormous technical skills (50 percent of the employees in Silicon Wadi are from the former Soviet Union) and great entrepreneurial capabilities and provided a strong base for military victories and economic accomplishments.

Diaspora financial contributions, especially in the early years, were considerable. In 1948 Golda Meir in six weeks raised $50 million in the United States to buy arms for the fledgling state during the Israeli War of Independence. In the early years after independence Israel received 65 percent of the general funds raised by the American Jewish community. From 1948 to 1979 the United Jewish Appeal and the Joint Distribution Committee sent $3.7 billion to Israel. By the 1990s this had fallen to 30 percent of Diaspora money raised. In 1990 Diaspora donations to Israel totaled $300 million, investments $600 million and non-American donations $200 million, making a total of $1.1 billion. A similar pattern continued at the beginning of the twenty-first century. In 2006 the Israel Emergency Campaign raised $300 million during and after the war with Hezbollah.[7]

American Jewish political involvement, involving a complex maze of roles by the American Israel Public Affairs Committee (AIPAC), the Conference of Major American Jewish Organizations, other Jewish organizations (the Anti-Defamation League, the American Jewish Committee, the Zionist Organization of America, Hadassah, etc.), political action committees (PACs), interest groups and Jewish and non-Jewish friendly voters promoting American political, economic and military aid to Israel, has been considerable. AIPAC (the pro-Israel lobby) is often rated one of the top three most effective lobbies on Capitol Hill. Its detractors, such as Stephen Walt and John Mearsheimer, see it and its allies as almost all powerful, dictating American policy in this area.[8] The Jewish Diaspora has a 2,000-year history of caring for Jews in distress around the world. As Selwyn Ilan Troen has observed:

> The bonds that hold modern Jewry together have been severely tested to reach out over vast geographical distances and across diverse political systems. Even though Jews may speak a different language and participate in a different culture, they have continued to understand themselves as brethren and, as such, accept responsibility for one another. The commitment to act on behalf of fellow Jews has its roots in the centuries-old traditions that have always been part of the Diaspora experience.[9]

The rise of modern nationalism and capitalism brought the masses into politics and changed the ways that the Diaspora looked after other Jews. Before the 1850s the primary role was played by wealthy Jewish *shtadlanism* (notable intermediaries) such as Moses Montefiore and Adolphe Crémieux. By the latter nineteenth century, with the rise of modern anti-Semitism, the response became broader and new institutions were formed. These included the French Alliance Israélite Universelle (Paris, 1860), the Anglo-Jewish Association (London, 1870), the Joint Foreign Committee of the Board of Directors (London, 1878), the Hebrew Immigrant Aid Society (New York, 1884) and the Hilfsverein der Deutschen Juden (Berlin, 1901).[10]

The Western Diaspora, while providing few immigrants to Israel, has played an important political, economic and social role. Before 1920 Western Diaspora help was provided mainly by the British, French and German communities. In the interwar period, and after the Holocaust, the Diaspora came to mean the United States (and to some extent Canada). From a population of 600,000 Jews in 1870, the American Diaspora grew to 2.6 million Jews in 1914 and 5 million Jews by 1945. The rise of the United States to superpower status during World War II, as well as the destruction of the German Jewish community, partial destruction of the French Jewish community and decline in size and power of the British community after 1945 reinforced this trend.[11]

Initially, as we have seen earlier, the Diaspora was not very supportive of Zionism. The proclamation of the Balfour Doctrine in 1917 and the creation by future Justice Louis Brandeis of an American Zionism infused by progressive ideals transformed the situation. He attracted both Russian Jews and a small but influential German Jewish elite. The parallels between the Puritans, who knew Hebrew and saw themselves as the spiritual descendants of ancient Israelites, and the drive to create a new Zion in the wilderness had a natural appeal. American and Jewish values of democracy, justice, individuality and group responsiveness were very close. Zionism could be presented as a profoundly American movement on behalf of a persecuted minority, in this case the Jews. Too, Americans could sympathize with Jewish refugees fleeing oppression, especially if they wanted to go somewhere other than America. By 1919, after the proclamation of the Balfour Declaration, the number had rocketed to 175,000 members, only to fall precipitously to 17,000 in July 1921.[12]

Western leaders such as Stephen Wise, Louis Brandeis and Chaim Weizmann played a powerful role in the creation of Israel. By the end of World War I the American Diaspora, with 3.5 million Jews, provided the great majority of funds for the efforts in Palestine. Their efforts led to the support of President Woodrow Wilson.[13]

British Jewish leaders, such as Chaim Weizmann and Lord Rothschild, were key players in early Zionism. They were critical to the issuing of the 1917 Balfour Declaration to Lord Rothschild. Weizmann issued a communiqué with Emir Faisal in 1919 on Arab–Jewish cooperation in Palestine. At the Paris Peace Conference in Versailles in 1919, Chaim Weizmann, who met with President Wilson and Colonel House, led the Jewish delegation that gained American and British support for the Jewish state. Western Jews were essential to the 1922 wording of the British mandate for Palestine that incorporated the Balfour Declaration and called for recognition of the Zionist Organization.

In April 1920 the San Remo Conference approved the British Mandate for Palestine to carry out the Balfour Declaration. In 1921 the United States Congress passed a resolution, signed by President Wilson, supporting a Jewish homeland in Palestine.[14] In 1922 the League of Nations approved the British Mandate for Palestine.[15]

In 1926 Louis Brandeis and Louis Marshall founded the PEC Israel Economic Corporation to supplement Keren Hayesod to provide technical expertise and investment capital. In 1934 the Jewish Agency founded Rassco (Rural and Suburban Settlements Company) to develop settlements for middle-class immigrants. In 1942 Labor Zionists founded AMPAL (American Palestine Corporation) to guarantee loans for financial projects. After 1945 it financed construction of basic industries, utilities and housing.[16]

Many wealthy non-Zionists, such as Jacob Schiff, became attracted to the cause. Chaim Weizmann in 1920 became the leader of the new Zionist Organization at the London Conference which created Keren Hayesod to gain

Diaspora resources for Palestine. In 1929, after the Arab riots, the Diaspora raised $4 million to rebuild destroyed settlements and build patrol roads, fences, searchlights and shelters for the Yishuv.[17] By 1931 the World Jewish Congress was founded.[18]

The anti-Zionists and non-Zionists were still powerful and even a majority in the American Jewish community, the new center for Zionist activity after World War I. During the 1920s and 1930s the *New York Times*, led by publisher Adolph Ochs, was hostile to the Zionist cause. During the 1920s the American non-Zionists (the Jewish Distribution Committee, JDC) had far more money than the Zionists. In the 1920s several Jewish organizations spent $6 million to resettle over 200,000 Russian Jews on fertile soil in the Soviet Union, rather than Palestine.[19] The two sides argued intensely over European Jewish rehabilitation projects, which were supported by the JDC but opposed by the Zionists, who wanted the money to go to Palestine. They argued over the protection of Jewish rights in the Diaspora and the implications of work in Palestine. The anti-Zionists were divided into incompatible groups such as the religious Agudath Yisrael, the leftist Bundists, the radical Communists and wealthy American Jewish liberals.[20]

In the early 1930s, the Great Depression reduced the number of members of the Zionist Organization of America to only 8,800, even though dues were a mere $3 a year.[21] But the rise of Nazi Germany and mild economic recovery in the United States revived the fortunes of American Zionism. In May 1942 the proclamation of the Biltmore Program in New York supporting the creation of a Jewish state was an important step towards the creation of Israel. In November 1942, 58 senators and 194 congressmen voiced their support on the anniversary of the Balfour Declaration.[22]

In the late 1940s its financial and political support played a key role in Israel's ultimate success against great odds. In 1945 Ben Gurion met with 20 American Jewish businessmen, who provided millions of dollars each year (the Sonnenborn Fund) to buy arms, much of which was kept abroad until after independence was declared, and to fund the cost of immigration. In 1946 they bought boats, planes, jeeps, arms, radio stocks, tents, mobile kitchens and warehouses from American surplus stocks at cheap prices.[23]

From 1945 to 1948 American Jews raised $400 million ($4 billion in today's terms) to support Holocaust survivors and the future state of Israel. The American Zionist Emergency Council, under Rabbis Abba Hillel Silver and Stephen Wise, secured vital American support for the creation of the state of Israel. Most American Jews and many non-Jewish leaders, such as Charles Beard, Eleanor Roosevelt, Reinhardt Niebuhr, Paul Tillich, John Dewey, Mark von Doren and Carl Friedrich, and the American Federation of Labor (AFL) and the Congress of Industrial Organizations (CIO) joined the effort. After the war and the Holocaust, American Zionists, with strong public sympathy, showed an "unparalleled ability to galvanize American Jewish public opinion in times of crisis and its cultural viability and political diversity."[24] Canadian Jews in 1947 played a major role in successfully lobbying Lester

Pearson and Justice Ivan Rand, member of the United Nations Special Committee on Palestine.[25]

Facing strong opposition from the American State and Defense departments, British Foreign Office and Western anti-Zionist groups, who were influenced by pro-Arab sentiment, fears of Russia and desire for oil, from 1945 to 1948 American Jews launched "one of the most intense and successful lobbying efforts in American politics, that led to the de facto recognition of the Jewish state 11 minutes after its birth."[26] After the European Holocaust, American Jewry became the leading Diaspora to fight for a Jewish state. While in the 1930s American Jews had been divided and largely indifferent to Zionism, a flood of new recruits brought the number of American Jews joining Zionist organizations to over 500,000 members in the late 1940s.

After the 1942 Biltmore Conference, the American Zionist Emergency Council created 76 state and regional branches and over 400 committees. By 1945, 411 senators and congressmen had endorsed a Jewish commonwealth. Forty-one state legislators and hundreds of municipalities endorsed Zionism, while 67 senators, 143 congressmen and 22 governors were members of the American Palestine Committee.[27] Indeed:

> the American public overwhelmingly supported partition . . . The success of the Zionist effort in 1947 represented nearly five years of work, organization, publicity, education and the careful cultivation of key people in different fields. While the politicians may have reacted to the alleged existence of Jewish bloc-voting in major cities and states, the real power of the American Zionists resulted from their ceaseless and ultimately successful efforts first to win over the Jewish community and then the American public to its side, thus securing the help of influential men and women in the press, the Church, the arts and above all the government. In the process the plight of the displaced persons of Europe played an ever-present role.[28]

Eddie Jacobson, Truman's former business partner, played a key role in allowing Chaim Weizmann to meet with President Truman in March 1948. Both parties supported the creation of the state of Israel.

Since 1948 the Diaspora has provided major support for Israel. Politically, it has been a strong lobby for Israel. In 1954 a "Circle of Friends" of leading American Jews (including Philip Ehrlich, David Zellerbach and Eli Ginzberg) worked to reduce the hostile attitude of the Eisenhower administration towards Israel.[29] In late 1955 the efforts of the Eisenhower administration to divide the Jewish community failed, and Congressional leaders and public opinion leaders blunted the drive for sanctions.[30] In the 1967 Six Day War, American Jews raised $240 million for Israel. During the 1973 Yom Kippur War, American Jews pledged to raise $750 million, for food, medicines and goods.[31]

The American Diaspora played a major role in rallying American presidents. On the other side have stood oil companies, anti-Semites, the State Department and liberal Christian groups. But American Jews, who historically have voted overwhelmingly for the Democratic Party, have given their time, support and money. From Harry Truman and John Kennedy to Lyndon Johnson, the relations were often close.[32] Since the middle 1990s the Republicans have become increasingly sympathetic to Israel as well.

The Diaspora has rallied world and American opinion in favor of helping Jews to immigrate to Israel. Its battle on behalf of 2 million Soviet Jews was symbolized by the passing of the Jackson–Vannik Amendment (289–78) in 1974 tying most favored nation status for the Soviet Union to emigration of Soviet Jews. This helped push the Brezhnev and Gorbachev regimes to allow some and then many Soviet Jews to emigrate. Yeltsin and Putin have continued free emigration and allowed the Israeli government in Russia to operate freely to reach, educate and help Jews immigrate to Israel.

In the 1967 Six Day War Americans favored Israel over the Arabs by 55:4.[33] During the 1973 Yom Kippur War Americans favored Israel over the Arabs by 7:1, rather than blaming Israel for the Arab oil embargo or following the lead of oil companies and the Arab states. Only 1 percent of Americans blamed Israel for the 1973 Arab oil embargo after the war, while 75 percent saw Israel's survival as important to the United States. In the 94th Congress, 259 congressmen and 70 senators favored Israel.[34] In 2006 Americans by 54:5 favored Israel over the Palestinians.[35]

The first chairman of Israel Bonds, founded in 1950, was Henry Morgenthau, Jr., Roosevelt's Secretary of the Treasury. From 1951 to 1967, when Israel had trouble borrowing money in the international market place, Israel Bonds sold $1 billion worth of bonds, 85 percent of them in the United States. By 1963 Israel had shown its creditworthiness by redeeming $170 million in bonds. From 1948 to 2006 Israel Bonds sold $24 billion of bonds for Israel in the West. Jews, non-Jews, governmental organizations and trade unions have bought these low-interest bonds, which have gone to drain the Hula swamps, start the National Water Carrier, build oil pipelines to Eilat from Haifa, Ashdod and Ashkelon, explore for oil, develop solar and alternative means of energy and improve Ben Gurion Airport. Israel Bonds annually have raised more than $1.2 billion.[36]

Founded in 1901 by Theodor Herzl at the Fifth Zionist Congress, the Jewish National Fund by 1948 owned over 235,000 acres in Palestine, more than all Jewish-owned land. It prepared settlements and reforestation, especially in the Galilee, Samaria, Huleh Valley, Negev and Jezreel Valley.[37] It has built 150 water reservoirs, planted over 240 million trees, built over 40 recreation areas, as well as security roads in the north, and helped new immigrants settle in the Negev.

Founded in 1933 by Recha Freier, Youth Aliyah helped over 300,000 Jewish disadvantaged children to come to Palestine and Israel or to live more rewarding lives. Founded to bring children escaping the Holocaust (initially the cost was $180 a year), in its first 25 years (1933–58) it brought 50,000 youths to Israel, including 20,000 orphans after the war. From 1958 to 1970 it brought another 85,000 children from 80 countries.[38]

Named for its founder, Henrietta Szold, who settled in Palestine in the early 1920s, Hadassah, founded in 1912, is the Women's Zionist Organization, with over 300,000 members in the United States. In the 1920s it created welfare clinics, dispensaries, medical clinics and a nurses' training school and set the cornerstone for the Hadassah Hospital in Jerusalem. It is the largest Jewish women's membership organization in the United States. In the United States it promotes the American–Israel relationship and advocates for Israel. In 1947 Hadassah lobbied hard for international support of the creation of the state of Israel and in 1948 worked diligently to help the new state survive. Its Hadassah Medical Organization provides modern health care to 600,000 patients a year, both Jewish and non-Jewish, Israeli and foreign. Its annual budget for its two hospitals with 1,000 beds in Jerusalem and other facilities is over $400 million. It provides modern technical training at its Hadassah College of Technology and is a major supporter of both the Jewish National Fund and Youth Aliyah.[39]

Friends of Hebrew University, Technion, Tel Aviv University, University of Haifa and Ben Gurion University, Friends of Israel Museum, the Jerusalem Foundation and Friends of Sharei Tzedek Hospital have raised several billion dollars for their institutions since 1948.

Level of modernization of the Jews

The Jews historically have been a modern, even revolutionary, people. As Paul Johnson has observed:

> For the Jewish impact on humanity has been protean. In antiquity they were the great innovators in religion and morals. In the Dark Ages and early medieval Europe they were still an advanced people transmitting scarce knowledge and technology. Gradually they were pushed from the van and fell behind until, by the end of the eighteenth century they were seen as a bedraggled and obscurantist rearguard in the march of civilized humanity. Breaking out of their ghettos they once more transformed human thinking; this time in the secular sphere. Much of the mental furniture of the modern world too is of Jewish fabrication.[40]

The Soviet Commissar of Enlightenment, Anatol Lunacharsky, claimed that Jews had created six great religions, with Karl Marx representing "the last in the succession of the great Jewish prophets."[41] Thorsten Veblen in 1934 wrote an article entitled "The Intellectual Pre-eminence of the Jews in Modern Europe" in which he asserted that Jews "count particularly among the vanguard, pioneers, the uneasy guild of pathfinders and iconoclasts in science, scholarship and institutional change and growth."[42] The Western culture, called Judeo-Christian civilization, reflects the powerful role of the small Jewish minority, for as Thomas Cahill wrote in *The Gifts of the Jews*:

> The Jews started it all – and by "it" I mean so many of the things we care about, the underlying values that make all of us, Jew and gentile, believer and atheist, tick. Without the Jews, we would see the world through different eyes, hear with different ears, even feel with different feelings . . . the role of the Jews, the investors of Western culture, is also singular: there is simply no one else remotely like them: theirs is a unique vocation.[43]

Even their enemies have conceded this. Stalin, in 1952, called the Jews "rootless cosmopolitans." Malaysian Prime Minister Muhammad Muhatir, at the Organization of the Islamic Conference in October 2003, proclaimed with exaggeration that "We are up against a people [i.e. the Jews] who think. They survived 2000 years of pogroms not by hitting back but by thinking. They invented and successfully promoted socialism, communism, human rights and democracy . . . We must use our brains too."[44] These revolutionary ideas included monotheism, man made in God's image, social progress and justice, the perfectibility of mankind, free will to choose good over evil, human responsibility for one's own acts, a divine role in history as partner of mankind, messianism and the Sabbath day of rest and holiness.[45]

Once liberated from the ghettos of Europe in the first half of the nineteenth century, the Jews again became the symbol of modernity.[46] Jews made up 0.2 percent of the world's population and less than 2 percent of the population of the West, yet *Time* magazine's "Man of the Century" was Albert Einstein, a German Jewish physicist later asked to be the first president of Israel. Jews won 22 percent of Nobel prizes (160 prizes) in the twentieth century.[47] Constituting 1 percent of Germans in 1933, they won 33 percent of all Nobel prizes won by Germans. Forming 2 percent of Russians, they were over 30 percent of the leading physicists (Igor Kurchatov, Lev Landau) in the Soviet Union.

In Vienna, as early as the 1880s, Jews, who were 10 percent of the population, accounted for 75 percent of the lawyers, 69 percent of the leading literary figures and over 50 percent of the doctors.[48] In Hungary in 1920, Jews, who were 5 percent of the population, accounted for 51 percent of the lawyers, 46 percent of the physicians and 39 percent of the engineers.[49] In the United States today, Jews, who are 2 percent of the population, have been 83 percent of the founding fathers of the movie industry,[50] 61 percent of the songwriters and lyricists for the top ten movie songs of the first 100 years[51] and 58 percent of directors, writers and producers of the most highly rated television series and best-grossing motion pictures. Jews have been 60 percent of the leading 100 intellectuals,[52] 40 percent of American Nobel prize winners,[53] 40 percent of the ten donors of the largest philanthropic gifts,[54] 28 percent of the students in Ivy League schools and 20 percent of the members of the Forbes 400.[55]

Israel, the small Jewish nation, has achieved the cutting edge of modernity and pioneered in so many areas. In communal forms, they created kibbutzim, moshavim, youth aliyah villages and Nahal military settlements. In education, they have four elite universities (Hebrew University, Tel Aviv University, Weizmann Institute and Technion) and have created a new education form, the mechina program for advancement of underprivileged youth to the college level.[56] In technology they are in the world's elite in biotechnology (1,500 startups, number three in the world), high technology (4,000 high-tech companies with $10 billion in exports) and military technology (UAV, Arrow ABM system, Uzi machine guns, Tactical High Energy Laser program, Boost Phase Intercept). Israel's scientific papers are cited more often than those of India or China and at a higher rate per capita than any other country in the world.

Palestinian Jews early on embraced modernization and education. In 1930, 78 percent of Palestinian Jewish youth from 5 to 14 were in primary school, a level higher than in West Germany and Italy and equal to that of Austria. In 1950 the Israeli literacy rate of 97 percent exceeded that of Italy, equaled that of the First World and far exceeded that of neighboring countries such as Egypt (24 percent) and Lebanon (47 percent) and even Taiwan (47 percent).[57]

Non-Jewish support for Israel

Despite strong international support for the Arabs and Palestinians, there has been a significant amount of non-Jewish support for Israel. While this is weak in the Third World and modest but growing in Europe, it remains strong in the United States. Christian Zionists, motivated by a Restorationist ideology that sees the return of the Jews to Israel as fulfillment of Biblical prophecy presaging the End of Days, have been a powerful pro-Israel force in the United States. Christian Zionists represent 40–60 million evangelical and fundamentalist Christians. They see Israel as one of the keys to survival of Judeo-Christian civilization, are impressed by the Orthodox revival in Israel and overwhelmingly support Israel.[58] A 1999 poll found that 93 percent of Americans have a Bible at home, 79 percent of children get religious instruction, 66 percent believe that Jesus will return to earth and 46 percent believe that God promised the land of Israel to the Jews.[59]

The roots of the religiosity of Americans lie in the lack of a state Church, the separation of Church and state and the massive migration of religious minorities and dissidents to the United States. Early American history is suffused with the role of the Puritan dissidents, the two Great Awakenings and numerous revivals. The Puritans, through strict Sabbath laws, devotion to reading the Bible, stress on the Old Testament, interest in the Hebrew language and often seeing the Jews as the key to their hopes of a return to Palestine, saw themselves as the Children of Israel. The early British Protestant fascination with the restoration of the Jews to the Promised Land was brought to the New World.[60]

The first Great Awakening (1734) was followed in the next century by many clerics seeing the Jews as the forerunner of the Second Coming. American experiences of coming to a new land and conquering the wilderness gave rise to frequent parallels with the experience of the ancient Jews in the Promised Land. John Darby in the 1830s preached dispensational pre-millennialism in the apocalyptic tradition which would influence Cyrus Scofield, William Blackstone and Dwight Moody. The fundamentalist Darby stressed to the Plymouth Brethren that the ingathering of Jews to Israel was a necessary prelude to the End of Times. Darby asserted that human history is a succession of dispensations with the covenant, with the current one preceding the Second Coming. True Christians are prepared by God for the rapture of the true Church.[61]

Cyrus Scofield produced the fundamentalist Scofield Study Bible which since 1909 has been printed in 10 million copies as the primary tool of religious instruction in the United States. *Jesus Is Coming* (1878), written by William Blackstone, sold over 1 million copies. In 1891 he produced the first memorial for President Benjamin Harrison, signed by 413 prominent Americans, including John Rockefeller, Cyrus McCormick, J. Pierpont Morgan, the Chief Justice of the United States, the Speaker of the House and leading journalists, writers and editors. In reaction to the 1881 pogroms in Russia, the memorial asked:

> What shall be done for Russian Jews? Why not give Palestine back to them again? According to God's distribution of nations, it is their home, an inalienable possession, from which they have been expelled by force. Let us now restore them to the land of which they were so cruelly despoiled by our Roman ancestors.[62]

A second memorial was given to President Wilson in 1916.[63]

Two leading fundamentalist seminaries have played a key religious and political role. The Moody Bible Institute, founded by Dwight Moody in 1886 in Chicago, has 30,000 graduates, most of whom have gone on to careers ranging from pastors to missionaries. Many leading authors have attended this institute, which publishes 60 books and almost 3 million copies of the Bible every year. The Moody Institute stresses the inerrancy of the Scriptures, the Virgin Birth, the miracles, Jesus Christ atoning for sins and his bodily resurrection. The Dallas Theological Seminary, founded in 1924, which also believes in the inerrant Bible and dispensational pre-millennialism, has over 8,000 alumni and graduates such as Hal Lindsey, whose *The Late Great Planet Earth* (1970) was the bestselling novel of the decade.[64]

Several figures have played a notable role. First, there was Dr. Douglas Young, who founded in 1957 the Holy Land Institute that became the Jerusalem University College and in 1971 the International Christians for Israel Movement. His successor, Clarence Wagner, who also saw Israel as a Jewish state legitimized by Biblical, historical and moral mandate, founded the Bridges for Peace and issued Updates from Jerusalem. They distributed teaching videos, media material, aid for the hungry and support for Israel in offices in dozens of countries. Then there was Jan Willem van der Hoeven, who in 1980 in response to a United Nations Security Council resolution calling on all states to withdraw their embassies from Jerusalem, founded the International Christian Embassy Jerusalem. This embassy, representing Christian Zionists around the world, encouraged Christian visitors, Jewish aliyah and helping immigrants. In 1985 it staged the First Christian Zionist Congress in Basel, declaring its powerful support for Israel. Other significant groups include Christian Friends of Israel, National Christian Leadership Conference for Israel, Voices United for Israel, the Religious Roundtable, Christian Friends of Israeli Communities, Christian Israel Public Action Campaign and Evangelical Sisterhood of Mary (Germany).[65]

Politically, a number of fundamentalist Protestants have played an important role in mobilizing American support for Israel. They have included Pat Robertson, John Hagee (Christians United for Israel) and other leading forces in the Church.

The alliance with the democratic West and defeat of its enemies

Much of the Arab world has repeatedly chosen to ally itself with the enemies of the West – Ottoman Turkey, Nazi Germany, the Soviet Union, Nasser's Egypt, Saddam Hussein's Iraq and Islamic fundamentalism. The Jews, by nature modernizers and Westerners, have repeatedly allied with the democratic, revolutionary West – Great Britain (the Balfour Declaration), France (1955–67) and the United States (1962–2007). The Israelis, who had internal democratic elections even before statehood, agreed with their first prime minister, David Ben Gurion, who declared in 1941:

> There is an external precondition for Zionist policy – democracy. Zionist policy is inconceivable under dictatorship . . . In Russia, Germany and Italy . . . Jews ceased to be a factor and these countries ceased to be an address for Zionist policy . . . Wherever you do not have free speech, free thought, free press, free communications, free entrance and free exit . . . there is no possibility whatsoever for the implementation of Zionist policy . . . Zionist policy is based upon the action of the masses . . . Zionism is built upon the fact that part of the world is democratic.[66]

While in the 1930s Ben Gurion sought an alliance with the United States, Chaim Weizmann sought an alliance with Great Britain. From 1955 to 1966 Israel was aligned with France and then from 1967 until today with the United States. While in 1750 Europe and North America contributed 25 percent of world industrial production, by 1913 this figure had risen to 90 percent. As Michael Mann observes, "Industry could be converted into massive military superiority."[67] In the last 60 years the rise of the American Century has meant that Israeli alliance with the West and especially the United States has paid great dividends.

Equally important was the international arena. Had Ottoman Turkey survived World War I, had Nazi Germany won World War II or had the Soviet Union won the Cold War, there would have been no Israel. The Arabs, who mostly favored Ottoman Turkey in World War I, Nazi Germany in the 1930s and the Soviet Union in the Cold War, would have been the winners. If the United States had not ended open immigration after 1924, most migrating European Jews would have found their way to New York and not Tel Aviv.[68]

But Israel backed the democratic Western winners while the Arabs backed the losers. This gave Israel the space to survive and flourish. In the Cold War and post-Cold War era, a democratic, increasingly capitalist Israel could find its place in the sun. By backing losing authoritarian and repressive regimes, the Arabs lost a great deal.

The alliance with democratic France brought great benefits. In 1955 Israel broke the Western arms embargo by buying from France 24 Ouragon fighters and 30 modern AMX 13 tanks.[69] In a 1956 arms deal with France worth $80 million, Israel bought 300 Super Sherman tanks and 36 Mystere 4A jet fighters. Israel established the Dimona nuclear reactor and program with French help.[70] During the 1956 Sinai Campaign, 3,000 French soldiers arrived in Israel, two French battleships guarded the Israeli coast and two French air squadrons deterred attack on the Israeli homeland. Although the slow British–French advance started on the Egyptian mainland eight days after the first Israeli paratroop drop at the Mitla Pass, it helped Israel win the Sinai Campaign.[71] From 1962 to 1966 Israel imported $107 million worth of arms annually from France.[72]

In 1948 American recognition of Israel was of vital importance. While not directly providing economic or military aid in the first decade of Israel's existence, the American Import–Export Bank provided a $100 million loan in 1949, and in the first few years the majority of Israeli capital imports came from public and private sources in the United States.[73] John Kennedy in 1960 spoke for the first time of a "special relationship" with Israel. In 1962 President Kennedy, assuring Foreign Minister Golda Meir of aid if Israel were attacked by an aggressor, sold six batteries of Hawk anti-aircraft missiles to Israel. In 1965 President Lyndon Johnson sold 210 American Patton M48A tanks to Israel and, in 1966, 48 Skyhawk fighter-bombers.[74]

After the victory in the Six Day War in 1967 the alliance with the United States became a strong one. From 1967 to 1969 the United States exported $290 million worth of arms a year to Israel; from 1970 to 1972 the figure rose to $550 million a year.[75] After the 1973 Yom Kippur War the United States provided $1.8 billion in arms and $1.2 billion in economic assistance to its ally in the Cold War against the Soviet Union. This figure declined only in the late 1990s when Israeli Prime Minister Benjamin Netanyahu began a ten-year phase-out of economic aid. But in 2007 it may begin to increase, as President

Bush has proposed a ten-year program of providing $3 billion worth of military aid a year to Israel for ten years.

Unlikely alliances

The international political and security system frequently provides strange bedfellows. In World War I the democratic British and French allies (former enemies for 750 years) united with autocratic Tsarist Russia to form the Entente. In World War II the democratic British and American allies joined with the despotic Soviet Union to defeat Nazi Germany and Imperial Japan. When Lord Palmerston declared that Britain had no permanent allies, only permanent interests, he spoke for all nations, not just Britain.

One unlikely Israeli ally has been Jordan. Given that its Arab Legion, trained, armed and officered by the British, represented the greatest potential threat to Israel in 1948, its decision to reach a "secret political alliance" in 1948 was a gift of the first magnitude for the Jews. These "two seemingly unlikely partners," even more so because Jordan had a Palestinian majority, found much to push them together – fear of a Palestinian Arab state that would threaten their survival, distrust of the radical Palestinian leader Haj Amin Al-Husseini, fear of the intentions of other Arab states, the need to preserve their new states and worry of the consequence of total war. While Golda Meir did not prevent Transjordan from seizing the West Bank and East Jerusalem in 1948, King Abdullah refrained from attacking Israel within the borders set by the 1947 United Nations Resolution 181. In 1951, when he was assassinated, he had worked out a potential peace treaty with Israel. In 1967 King Hussein reluctantly attacked Israel and in 1973, at a critical juncture, refrained from attacking Israel. In turn, in 1970 Israel helped to prevent a Syrian victory when its forces invaded Jordan after Black September. From 1970 to 1994 the two sides met frequently in secret and in 1994 signed the Israel–Jordan Peace Treaty.[76]

In 1948 the Israelis found that the West would not sell them the arms needed to win the War of Independence. The increasingly anti-Semitic and Communist Soviet Union, which had destroyed Zionism and repressed 3 million Soviet Jews, seemed an unlikely source of help. But Stalin saw the British Empire as the greatest rival of the Soviet Union.[77] The creation of Israel would harm the empire and cause conflict in the region. The power of the Israeli Left (Mapam, Palmach and kibbutzim) suggested that Israel might become a Soviet satellite.

This was not the first time that the Soviet Union was objectively pro-Jewish. The major role of the Soviet Union in defeating Nazi Germany in World War II was a powerful contribution to the creation of the state of Israel. Without this victory, there could have been no Israel in 1948. The survival of 2.5 million Soviet Jews and 1.8 million European Jews was due significantly to the Red Army. During the height of Soviet support for the Arabs (1967–91), the Soviet Union urged the Arabs not to go to war (the War of Attrition and the Yom Kippur War, the Iraqi invasion of Kuwait) and seek a peaceful solution.[78]

The brief Soviet flirtation with Israel (1947–48) was important. Foreign Minister Andrei Gromyko in May 1947 supported the passage of Resolution 181 providing for the partition of Palestine. As he declared:

A large number [of survivors] are in camps . . . and are continuing to undergo great privations. The fact that no Western European state has been able to ensure the defense of the elementary rights of the Jewish people . . . explains the aspirations of the Jews to establish their own state. It would be unjust not to take this into consideration and to deny this right of the Jewish people.[79]

Gromyko's speech exploded "just like a bomb" with great influence not only on the Communist bloc but on the Americans as well. Superpower competition was unleashed with a dynamic that favored the Jews. At his first meeting with Jewish Agency representatives, Soviet delegate Tsarpkin toasted "the Jewish state that will come." Jewish Agency delegates shuttled daily between Soviet and American offices, leading Moshe Sharett to declare that "What happened to us with the Soviet Union was nothing but a miracle." On November 29, 1947 it was the Soviet Union that pressed for the vote that gave Israel the right to declare a state and pushed for UN troops to implement the resolution. After the vote, it opposed efforts by UN mediator Count Bernadotte to shrink the area allocated to a Jewish state.[80]

From 1945 to 1950 the Soviet Union allowed 280,000 Polish, Hungarian, Romanian and Czechoslovak Jews to board refugee ships to Palestine. In May 1948 the Soviet Union recognized Israel four days after its declaration of independence. Soviet and Eastern European votes for the creation of the state of Israel in November 1947 at the United Nations and the transfer of Czechoslovak weapons to Israel in 1948 were important to the creation of the state of Israel. In 1948 Israel bought $23 million worth of weapons from Czechoslovakia, compared to $2 million for Syria and a minimal amount for Egypt. This included 46,800 rifles, 6,100 machine guns, 80 million rounds of ammunition and 89 airplanes.[81] David Ben Gurion said, "They [Soviet weapons] saved the State. There is no doubt of it. Without these weapons, it's doubtful whether we could have won. The arms deal with the Czechs was the greatest assistance we received."[82]

However, the Soviet Union generally fought Zionism, tried to prevent the creation of Israel and, after a brief flirtation in 1948, by 1955 had begun arming Arab armies and training terrorist groups seeking to destroy the Jewish state. It was responsible for powerful anti-Semitic and anti-Israel campaigns over decades. As early as October 1948 it asked Czechoslovakia to stop selling military equipment to Israel.[83]

While the British Empire was in the late 1930s and 1940s hostile to the Jews, it also made a major contribution from 1917 to 1937. Initially, the

British Empire had been friendly towards the Jews and a Jewish state. This sentiment built on the support of such nineteenth-century Christian Zionists as George Eliot (author of *Daniel Deronda*), Lord Palmerston and Benjamin Disraeli (author of *Tancred*), who wanted to see a Jewish return to Palestine. The 1917 Balfour Declaration, the 1920 San Remo Conference support for a British Mandate in Palestine based on the Balfour Declaration, and the 1922 League of National Mandate for Palestine calling for establishing a Jewish national home in Palestine were very positive. In 1922 the House of Commons even approved the British government Mandatory policy by 292 to 35.[84]

Much of the British elite, for a mixture of religious Biblical sentiment, minimum cost and practical reasons (a pro-British Jewish buffer region in the Middle East and guarding the route to India, the desire for Russian and American Jews to support the Allied war effort, a desire to oust the French from Palestine, fear of a preemptive German recognition of Jewish rights in Palestine, gratitude for Weitzman's war and diplomatic efforts), was supportive of the Zionist endeavor in the critical 1917–22 period. This was true after the end of the hostile Asquith government and rise to power of the friendly government of Prime Minister Lloyd George (December 1916 until October 1922) and Foreign Secretary Arthur Lord Balfour. Their support for the Zionists coincided with the dissolution of the Ottoman Turkish Empire and British liberation of Jerusalem in December 1917. The issuance of the Balfour Declaration at the end of October 1917, a mere six weeks before General Edmund Allenby's army marched into Jerusalem, was a result of exquisite timing.[85]

The British conquest of Palestine in late 1917 and 1918 crushed the hostile Ottoman Turkish Empire and opened the door for the realization of the Zionist dream. The appointment as British high commissioner to Palestine of Viscount Herbert Samuel, a British Jew supportive of the Zionist enterprise (1920), seemed to symbolize the British embrace of Zionism. In the early 1920s the British envisioned a Jewish state with 3–6 million Jews, created through immigration of 50,000–80,000 immigrants per year.[86]

During the 1920s and 1930s, the British authorities allowed the immigration of 400,000 Jews, belatedly repressed the 1929 Arab riots and Arab Revolt (1936–39), built a port in Haifa, constructed roads, schools, hospitals, ports, railways and electric power and recognized Hebrew as an official language of the Mandate.[87] The British Mandatory government also created a legal system, solid bureaucracy and equitable treatment of all groups that benefited the Jewish community in Palestine. The British authorities allowed the Yishuv to create a democratic assembly (1920), legally recognized Knesset Israel (1926, with separate recognition for the Orthodox) and permitted the Yishuv and local councils to collect their own taxes (1930), build key institutions and gain 30 years of party experience by all segments of the Jewish world. During the 1930s and 1940s the Jewish community built a state within a state that ran its own economy, health care, education and, quietly, defense forces. During the Arab Revolt and World War II it tolerated some limited and semi-legal development of military units (Haganah, Palmach) for fear of the Arabs and the Germans.[88]

During World War II the British army and navy protected the Jews of Palestine from the Nazi panzer divisions of Erwin Rommel and smashed support for the forces of the Grand Mufti of Jerusalem. British victories in the Middle East in World War II and the crushing of pro-Axis forces in Syria (1940) and Iraq (1941) were central to the future creation of the Jewish state. The British military informally worked with the Haganah, even training Jewish guerrillas, handing over arms and explosives when the German threat to Palestine was palpable in 1942.[89] The Jews, as part of the British colony, enjoyed participation in the sterling bloc, manufacturing for the British war effort (Solel Boneh became the biggest such company in the region), an open market for Jaffa oranges and pounds from British tourists and military and civilian personnel. Even the form of government run by the British was superior to anything else in the region.[90]

The British played a significant role in the creation of the state. Unlike in most of their colonies where they supported traditional strong men, in Palestine even in the 1930s they supported or did not oppose strong Jewish institutions. For, as Migdal observed:

> Perhaps the single most important event in the formation of what would become Israeli society was the British hewing of Palestine out of the larger Ottoman Empire . . . Only with the beginning of British rule . . . did the local Jews begin to develop autonomous institutions . . . The array of new British and Zionist organizations in Palestine was critical in Jewish society formation, bridging some of the previous cleavages among Jews and thus preventing social fragmentation . . . British state organizations were entirely new, of course, and lent a whole new dimension to Jewish society . . . The new coherence to Jewish society created by the demarcation of a country called Palestine by the British allowed Zionist leaders to challenge domination by Jewish institutions from outside Palestine . . . British control, then, provided a framework for the establishment of a Jewish society whose outer social boundaries were those of the newly mandated territory. The critical elements that the colonial state provided, besides the boundaries themselves, were the rights of the Zionists to create countryside institutions for all Jews and of Jews worldwide to immigrate to Palestine.[91]

Even during the height of British hostility to the Jews from 1945 to 1949, a British Empire weakened by World War II and the Cold War did help the nascent state of Israel. It withdrew from Palestine, refused to provide significant arms supplies to the Arabs for 18 months after April 1948 and never implemented its October 1948 Plan A and Plan B to aid the Arab Legion and destroy the Israeli air force and armored units.[92]

Too, even the Holocaust did have one residual effect (if anything of this kind can be said of such an horrific event). For Diaspora Jewry, it:

> did shatter all hopes of remaining in the European or Middle Eastern Diasporas for those who remained. For North American Jews and Palestinian Jews, the Zionist ideology of the ineradicable hostility of the non-Jews seemed totally true and the only solution a Jewish state. For the few hundred thousands of Holocaust survivors there now was only one dream: to go to Palestine. After the war a United Nations Relief Agency survey in the camps found that 97 percent wanted to go to Palestine.[93]

British Biblical romanticism

An important religious ideological component in the success of Zionism has been provided by British Protestant Biblical romanticism in the last 400 years. With the invention of the printing press (1450s), the Protestant Reformation (1517) and relative freedom during and after the twin English revolutions (1640s, 1688–89), British Protestants focused on reading the Bible and applying it to their lives. Jews themselves were banned from Great Britain from 1290 to 1656, anti-Semitism among British Protestants remained quite strong for centuries, and current British Protestant thought is often markedly anti-Israel. Yet much of American fundamentalism and international sentiment in favor of the Jews returning to their ancient homeland is owed to British Protestant thought starting in the seventeenth century. As Gerhard Falk has observed, "The influence of English Protestantism on the restoration of the Jewish people to their ancient land cannot be exaggerated."[94]

English literature, while replete with harsh depictions of Jews (Shylock in Shakespeare, Fagin in Charles Dickens, Fernandez in Trollope), also has featured a number of positive portrayals of the Promised Land and calls for Jewish restoration to Palestine. John Milton and William Blake respectively wrote poems about the Promised Land and Jerusalem. In the nineteenth century Walter Scott in *Ivanhoe* called for Jewish restoration and George Eliot in *Daniel Deronda* wrote the first Christian Zionist novel.[95]

During the English Revolution, the Puritans, led by Oliver Cromwell (who approved the return of the Jews to Great Britain in 1656), were sympathetic to the Hebraic idealism of the Bible and Jewish suffering and hoped to fulfill the prophecy of the Jewish restoration to Palestine. Puritans, as we have seen earlier, often hoped for the Jewish return to Palestine as the key to their hopes of the End of Days. There could be no kingdom of Jesus without the Jewish return to Palestine. Reading the Bible in the vernacular led many Protestants to identify with the Jews of the Holy Scriptures. The emergence of a nation state in Great Britain led many to nationalize the New Israel as the elect nation. The end of universal Christendom led them to view themselves as the elect people, as the Children of Israel. Even many Anglicans and realists were philo-Semitic as well. John Locke and Isaac Newton learned Hebrew and favored Jewish restoration to Palestine.[96]

In the nineteenth century an evangelical revival propelled many Protestants in the Anglican Church towards the Jews and Zionism. John Darby and his Plymouth Brethren in 1831 provided the religious basis for later American fundamentalism and Armageddon theology. William Hechler, chaplain to the British embassy in Vienna, favored the Jewish return and was active in Zionist movements and a friend of Theodor Herzl in the 1890s. He thought a return would hasten the Last Days foretold in the Bible. The seventh Earl of Shaftesbury, who influenced Lord Palmerston, expected the End of Times after the Jews returned to Palestine. As late as 1906, 6 million children were studying in Sunday schools, half of them run by non-conformists.[97]

Prime Minister David Lloyd George, who had in his youth been tutored by a part-time Baptist preacher uncle, declared that "I was taught far more about the history of Israel than about the history of my own people." Foreign Secretary Arthur Balfour, who sent the declaration to Lord Rothschild, in a 1922 House of Lords debate declared that he supported the British Mandate in Palestine:

> in order that we may send a message to every land where the Jewish race has been scattered, a message that will tell them that the Christian dominions . . . [are] not unmindful of the service that they have rendered to the great religions of the world, and most of all to the religion that the majority of Your Lordships' house profess.[98]

This tradition also impacted some Labor leaders. In the 1920s a religious Labor prime minister, Ramsay MacDonald, wrote a book called *A Socialist in Palestine* (1921). Labor Foreign Secretary Arthur Henderson was an early Zionist.[99]

So many diverse international factors thus played a role in the survival and successes of Israel. Some were deliberate and logical, such as democratic Israel's support for the winning Western allies in the last 60 years, and the support of the Diaspora for Israel before and after statehood in all its ramifications. Others were fortuitous parallel relationships, in which Israel's needs wholly or partly coincided with those of its otherwise rivals and enemies, such as the Soviet Union after World War II or the British Empire during and after World War II. Some were totally fortuitous, such as the British Protestant romantic fascination in the nineteenth and early twentieth centuries with the Biblical return of the Jews to the Holy Land and the strong American Christian Zionist fundamentalist support for modern Israel. All played a role in helping revolutionary Israel overcome great obstacles to its existence, some of them ironically caused by some of these same forces – the Soviet Union, the British Empire after 1937 and British Protestantism after 1948.

15 Conclusions

Harry Truman once said that the only thing new in this world is the history that you don't know. About no country is this truer than for Israel.

For several decades before and after the creation of the state of Israel, there was recognition that something unusual had occurred in the international arena. The word "miracle" was used to describe how a people had arisen from the ashes of the Holocaust to create a state. A small, weak, persecuted and dispersed people, after almost 2,000 years of Exile, had returned to their homeland, fulfilling a Biblical prophecy, and overcome great powers to create a state. In the decades after 1948 they had created a strong First World country in the midst of the mostly Third World Middle East that largely shunned them and started numerous wars to destroy them.

This should have led to an outpouring of works about this remarkable feat. This would be even more likely since Third World success stories, until recently, have been few and far between. And yet, as we have seen, the story has been widely ignored.

The importance of the Israel story for the world

Political science, informed by theories from Marxism to structural functionalism, has tended to be rather deterministic. Many deep geographic, demographic, economic, political, military and cultural factors have structurally determined the world order of the last hundred years. The demise of multiethnic empires, the rise of the Third World, the transition to democracy and capitalism and the rise and fall of great powers reflected these deep trends. So too did the victory of the West over Communism in the Cold War and the Allied triumphs in both world wars reflect the correlation of forces.

Yet structural determinants, while favoring certain outcomes, have not totally determined them, especially in times of crises during and after World War I and World War II. Nor could they predict the future, because of the idiosyncrasies of human nature and the human ability to learn from the past. In the interstices created by the crises a number of voluntarist factors discussed in this book could play a key role. The structural factors – economic, political, military and ideological – did not favor the creation of Israel. But voluntaristic, human and individual factors – the will to power, the willingness to fight and die, the presence of capable leaders, pragmatic short-term decisions, ideas, consciousness and even accidents – could turn unlikely propositions into solid realities.

This was true of the outcomes of wars and revolutions often unpredicted by sage observers working within the structural and deterministic constraints. Wars and revolutions, seen by Hannah Arendt as the leading forces of the twentieth century, have often gone in unforeseen directions. In a postmodernist world that often deprecates wars and revolutions, their occurrence and outcomes have been decisive both in the world at large and in the creation and flourishing of Israel.

Major wars have often gone in unforeseen directions. Soviet victories in front of Moscow in 1941 and Stalingrad in 1942, the Chinese victory over the United States in Korea in 1950, the Vietnamese victory over the United States in 1975 and the Afghan victory over the Soviet Union in 1988 all shared one thing – they had been predicted by very few observers and were not totally explicable in terms of deep structural forces.

Revolutions also have gone in largely unexpected and unpredicted directions. Who in the 1640s expected the English Revolution or the decapitation of King Charles I? Who in 1777 thought the ill-armed and ill-financed American rabble could hold out against the redcoats of the world's strongest power? Who in 1848 thought that the verdicts would soon be reversed on the triumphant revolutions sweeping Europe? Who in February 1917 thought the 300-year-old Romanov dynasty would soon fall? Who in 1978 thought the Iranian Revolution was possible or worse inevitable?

The answers come not simply from political structuralism but from the historical voluntarism that gave rise to the creation and flourishing of Israel. For it was the strong will to power and the willingness of men to fight and die that brought all the radical movements to power over the opposition of stronger forces. This created what Trotsky called "the samurai" of the revolution in the Russian civil war. It was seen by the greater willingness of Chinese Red Army soldiers and Vietnamese soldiers to fight and die in their respective struggles against the Guomindang and the Americans. In the great revolutions it was the willingness of the English rebels to be the "saints" of the 1640s and of the American soldiers to survive at Valley Forge, and the will to fight of the Russian crowds in February 1917 that brought down the Romanovs.

Then there was the role of the individual. Could there have been an October Revolution without Lenin rallying the radicals in his "April Theses" and "Letters from Afar" against the cautious majority of party leaders? What would have happened to the Chinese Revolution after repeated defeats of urban insurrection in 1926 and 1927 without Mao's turning to peasant-based insurrection? Individuals and small groups can matter and especially in times of crises.

Organizational skills, with discipline, organization and unity, mattered as well. The strong organization of the Bolsheviks, the Chinese Communists and the Vietnamese Communists mattered in their ultimate victory. Look at all the revolutionary failures, from Russia in 1825 and 1905, China during the Taiping Rebellion, Europe in 1848 to France in 1871 to see how improbable victory was without such skills.

Ideas and consciousness played a strong role. The rallying of Communism and nationalism in Russia and China and the power of Islamic fundamentalism in Iran were important to victory. So too in World War II did the nationalism and patriotism of the Russian masses, reinforced by Nazi barbarism, help turn the tide in 1941 and 1942.

Even accidents mattered in history. Had Lenin died in August 1918 when he was shot by Fanya Kaplan, had Mao Zedong succumbed as so many others did during the Long March, had Oliver Cromwell not survived the three civil wars of the 1640s, the course of history might well have been altered.

In short, the Israeli story of success, in overcoming great odds through rallying the human and voluntarist element, showed the power of will, leadership, organization and consciousness to triumph over the seemingly inevitable big battalions of history. The Israeli story thus helps us to understand not only Israel but much that matters in world history. It also helps us to understand the Arab story, which was lacking in will to fight and die, good leadership, organizational skills and modernizing ideas.

Israel: the success story

Israel, despite being ridiculed by the left and despised by the anti-Semitic right, is one of the rare countries in the world that has been a success both from the socialist and the capitalist perspective. Israeli socialism was in many ways more successful than its more authoritarian socialist counterparts in the Communist world.

Unlike Russia, China, Vietnam and Yugoslavia, Israel, despite being surrounded by enemies, created a vibrant tolerant democracy that included even its Arab minority. In Israel, there were no Russian gulags, no Chinese re-education camps or great proletarian cultural revolutions, no Cambodian killing fields, no Eastern European show trials, no North Korean famines and no reigns of terror. Its socialist leaders (1949–77) did not have large villas, tolerate massive corruption, live sumptuously in private, hold lavish banquets or give costly gifts to their children as in Communist and many Third World states. Rather they, like David Ben Gurion, Golda Meir and Levi Eshkol, led lives of Spartan simplicity.

They created new socialist forms marked by egalitarianism, sacrifice, idealism and sacrifice for society. The kibbutz, moshav, youth aliyah village and nahal (military pioneering youth village) testified to the power of the socialist ideal in Israel for many decades. The great success of the kibbutz in Israeli society for decades stood in stark contrast to the miserable failure of the

Russian kolkhoz and sovkhoz and the Chinese commune, which had to be dismantled in the 1980s.

Despite the higher burdens of security and terrorism, Israeli socialist leaders were able to produce a considerably more successful economy than Russian (1917–91), Eastern European (1947–87) and Chinese (1949–78) Communists. By the end of the 1970s Israel was already poised to become a First World economy with a strong high-tech sector. In the agricultural area, ever an Achilles heel for the Communists, the Israelis were not only successful but frequently exported their produce and technically proficient manpower abroad. Israel made the transition from socialism to capitalism at a much lower cost and more successfully than the Russian and Chinese Communist regimes.

And yet, like the Communist states, Israel was able to win improbable victories in wars against superior enemies, create a powerful state out of a weak state and maintain a vast social welfare network to support the less fortunate in society. It also propagated socialist values on as wide a scale as, or a greater scale than, the Communist states.

Israel's second partial capitalist revolution (1977–2007) has been successful as well. Israel has vaulted into the First World with an $18,000 GNP per capita, exports of $34 billion and production of over $10 billion of high-tech goods. Its Silicon Wadi and military industry are in the top five in the world. Its intelligence services and military services, together with its Arrow ABM system (co-developed with the United States), are on the cutting edge of global technology. Its agriculture remains world-class, as do its four leading universities. In 2006 its FDI, thanks to large investments by Hewlett-Packard (Mercury) and Warren Buffett (Iscar Metals), reached $13.6 billion.[1] Israel has been a major success story, especially when the backwardness of the region and high burden of security and terrorism are taken into account.

Invisibility of the Israeli achievement

History, it is often said, is written by the winners. Clearly, this is the case for the history of the major powers and most Third World countries. But, as in so many other ways, the history of Israel is different. Its numerous accomplishments have rarely received significant attention in the world of academia or popular writing. And even the mainstream Israeli historians tend to focus on smaller issues than the bigger issues. Thus, Israeli successes in the face of great obstacles have often been ignored or even derided.

Especially after the Six Day War in 1967 and occupation of the West Bank and Gaza Strip, liberal, radical, Communist, neutralist and Third World opinion turned against Israel. One can search in vain for works that explain the success of the Jews in creating a state in 1948 and flourishing by the first decade of the twenty-first century.

There is great talk about other success stories – shining India, the Four Tigers of Asia, the Celtic Tiger (Ireland), the Chinese century. While these countries were remarkable success stories, none of them had to overcome what the far-flung Jews had to overcome to create their state or make it flourish. The great majority of Third World countries achieved their independence against largely nominal colonial resistance (save for Algeria, Vietnam and the like) in the territory where they had lived for centuries in large numbers with distinctive cultures, languages, religions and ethnic groups. The Israelis had none of these advantages and more dangerous enemies.

A seeming miracle

But, if the current global configuration was structurally determined, then how can we account for the rise and flourishing of Israel? For the correlation of forces in the world was strongly negative for the rise and flourishing of Israel. No other state succeeded against powerful and active resistance from key central states (Nazi Germany, Tsarist Russia, the Soviet Union, the British Empire 1937–49, the Ottoman Turkish Empire), regional powers (the Arab states), major religious movements (Islam, Roman Catholicism, much of mainline Protestantism) and most Third World states (the Muslim world, China, India).

Against these forces, the Jews, decimated by the Holocaust and scattered all over the world, constituted 0.2 percent of the world's population. Unlike the situation in all newly independent states, the great majority of the world's Jews did not live in the homeland. In 1900 less than 1 percent of the world's Jewish population (50,000 Jews) lived in Palestine and even in 1948 less than 7 percent (650,000 Jews) lived in Israel. Prosperous Jews in North America were not interested in going to Israel, while immigrants to Israel were largely poor and lacking education. It is no wonder that the Arab world has remained in a state of shock that the Jews created a state in the heart of the Arab Middle East and thrived.

Any objective marshalling of the evidence would suggest that most Israelis are right when they see their history as miraculous. How could Israel, with tiny numbers, minimal territory, no strategic depth, some Christian sympathizers, no great power allies until after 1967 (except for France from 1956 to 1967) and unprecedented obstacles create a state, win seven wars and flourish in the last six decades? How could a people so long oppressed, persecuted and stigmatized as weak, passive and effeminate suddenly rise up, return to Israel and create a modern powerful state in Zion after almost 2,000 years?

Given the correlation of force regionally and globally, Israel should never have come into existence and certainly never have flourished. Rather, the Holocaust in 1941–45 and the destruction of the nascent state of Israel in 1947–48 should have been seen as a process of the elimination of the Jews from history.

The lasting legacy

The powerful and active resistance of central and Third World states and religious movements damaged the position of Israel for decades. The Nazi Holocaust devastated the future Jewish state by killing 6 million Jews, or over 40 percent of all Jews in the world, the majority of those interested in immigrating to Israel.

With 5 million North American Jews unwilling to go to Israel, those killed in the Holocaust made up 60 percent of those interested in immigrating to Israel and 75 percent of all Jews west of the deepest German penetration into the Soviet Union. At least 2–3 million Eastern and Central European Jews, who probably would have immigrated to Israel from the historical centers of Zionism in Vilna, Kishinev, Odessa, Warsaw, Krakow and communities in Ukraine, Poland and the Baltics, were now dead. They represented the most Zionist stratum of world Jewry, those with the highest Jewish identification and the highest family size outside of Middle East Sephardim. And now they were gone. They left the new state with 650,000 Jews to fend off 27 million hostile Arabs in the region.

The Soviet Union, which after the October Revolution in 1917 had the strongest Zionist contingent in the world, seriously damaged the Jewish cause. In 1917, 300,000 Russian Jews, often fervent in their beliefs, belonged to the Zionist movement, which was quintessentially Russian and led predominantly by Russian Jews. In the 1920s the Soviet Union destroyed the Zionist movement and from 1917 to 1978 allowed barely 100,000 Russian Jews to go to Israel. But, although Stalin supported Israeli independence, sent arms through Czechoslovakia and allowed 280,000 Eastern European Jews ultimately to immigrate to Israel, he banned Russian Jewish immigration. In 1948 only one family of five people was allowed to go to Israel. Had 1–1.5 million Russian Jews been allowed to go to Israel, the impact would have been huge. Their ranks would have included as many as 100,000 Russian Jewish war veterans, including generals, colonels and majors, who had served in the Red Army in World War II. With their help, Israel would not have lost East Jerusalem, Gush Etzion, Latrun and the potash works in the Dead Sea. Israel would have been more powerful in the 1950s than its rather weakened state.

The third legacy was that left by the British Empire. While Great Britain did in the early years follow the Balfour Declaration and allow 400,000 Jews to immigrate to Palestine, in the late 1930s the British Empire slammed the door on Jewish immigration. At a time when over 70 percent of German and Austrian Jews fled abroad in the face of the oncoming Holocaust, the door was closed to 7 million European Jews living west of the Soviet Union. With almost all doors closed to Jewish immigration, perhaps 1–3 million European Jews would have been saved and gone to Palestine in the late 1930s. This would have transformed the situation of the Jews after World War II. Barely 10 percent of that number made their way to Israel, as most of the rest perished in the Holocaust. After the war the British tried hard to keep hundreds of thousands of European Jews from reaching Palestine and even interned tens of thousands in Cyprus and elsewhere. Their contribution to the war would also have been great.

The fourth legacy was left by the Ottoman Turkish Empire. It did reluctantly allow tens of thousands of Jews to enter Palestine from 1881 to 1917 as the number of Jews rose from 25,000 in 1881 to 85,000 in 1915. But, if the Turks had not repeatedly banned immigration and land sales and imposed other restrictions, at least tens of thousands of Jews and possibly 100,000–200,000 Jews might have chosen Palestine over North America. Their numbers, although small, could have been very important in the struggle for power after 1918. But it was not to be.

Finally, there was the legacy of the Arabs. Their unremitting hostility (save for Egypt and Jordan) and willingness to foment riots, revolts and intifadas and participate in eight wars against Israel inevitably drained the state of significant vitality and harmed its economy. Israel became a virtual garrison state, could barely trade with its neighbors and had to stand ready to ward off serious attack, on either its homeland or its offices abroad, at any time.

How many Jews decided to go to the United States rather than Israel because of the security situation and the economic situation? We know that their number had to be in the hundreds of thousands. When we add in the roughly 750,000 Israelis who emigrated abroad from 1948 to 2007, the total cost (there is always some emigration from every country) could easily have been in the 300,000–500,000 range, a huge burden for a state that started in 1948 with 650,000 Jews.

The power of revolution

Many factors help explain Israeli success against steep odds. The two revolutions, one socialist and one capitalist, played a powerful role in making Israel a success story. Yet these revolutions were carried out despite many obstacles that did not exist for central states in revolution. The central states did not have to contend with small size and vulnerability, powerful external threats to annihilate the state, the urgent need for foreign allies, the extreme heterogeneity of the population and massive immigration swamping the original Yishuv. These factors helped Israel limit the radical, violent, repressive nature seen in central state revolutions, like the Russian and Chinese revolutions, and eased the transition to the capitalist nature of the second revolution after 1977.

The revolutionary nature of the state produced a revolutionary party, state, government and aliyah which radically transformed Jewish history and changed a weak and dispersed, largely petty-bourgeois people into a strong First World state with significant capabilities. In this way the twin Israeli revolutions emulated the great societal impact of the English, French, American, Russian and Chinese revolutions. The revolution, with its radical ideas, organization, modernity and democracy, created a new Jewish world in Israel, one far removed from the Eastern Europe *shtetlakh* or North African and Middle East *mellahs*.

Second, there was the power of individuals, the power of human will, leadership and sacrifice for a cause. The Israelis were more willing to fight, sacrifice and die for their cause than the Arabs and Palestinians were for their cause. This powerful will to fight, reinforced by the Holocaust and the Arab proclaimed desire to throw the Jews into the sea, was seen in numerous Israeli victories, self-sacrifice, voluntarism, collectivism and dedication to such institutions as the army and the secret police. Israeli leaders such as David Ben Gurion, Golda Meir, Chaim Weizmann, Moshe Dayan and Yigal Allon were critical to ultimate victory.

There was the role of international alliances, historical accidents and strange bedfellows. The democratic nature of Israeli society proved vital to ultimate success. Time and again the Arabs sided with the authoritarian, repressive and ultimately losing powers, from Nazi Germany and the Soviet Union to Saddam Hussein's Iraq and at times Islamic fundamentalism. Israel allied itself with democratic Great Britain (1918–45), France (1956–67) and the United States (1962–2007), the winners in international politics. Israel, with its democracy, socialism and then capitalism, allied itself naturally with the democratic winners, who contributed greatly to both Israeli historical success and Israeli economic development, high technology and education.

There was the role of historical accidents. Imperial German intervention to save the Yishuv in Ottoman Turkey during World War I was important in preserving the remnant in Palestine. The 1924 Johnson Act ending mass immigration to the United States pushed many Jews towards Palestine rather than the more attractive choice of the United States. British victories in the Middle East in 1941 and 1942 preserved the Yishuv from Rommel's Panzer divisions ready to destroy the British colony of Palestine. Soviet and United Nations support during the short but vital period from 1947 to 1952 was improbable but vital to the Israeli declaration of statehood and victory in the 1948 War of Independence.

Finally, Israel flourished in large part because of the creativity, drive and determination of the Jews, who had survived for 4,000 years. The technological and scientific success of Israel also reflects the traditional Jewish values of education, learning and hard work. Today few echo the recent words of Emanuelle Ottolenghi that:

> Despite opposition, Zionism's astonishing success – the fulfillment of its goals within fifty-four years, its establishment achieved despite formidable challenges and tragedies faced by world Jewry in the twentieth century – bears witness to the potency of ideas and the strength of its appeal. . . Zionism revised the Jewish self-image, Jewish identity and the place of Jews in the world in unforeseen ways. . . a veritable success. . . it not only gave Jews a safe haven from persecution, it fostered the revival

of an original and modern national culture, and enabled Jews, in thinking and acting like a collective bestowed with national attributes, to be masters of their own identity and, for better or worse, to be a people like all other people.[2]

But this work has shown the power behind these rarely heard words. What does all this mean for the future? This is not to say that Israel did not suffer many failures. It has failed, in achieving real peace in the region, in treating its minorities (Sephardim in the 1950s and 1960s, Arabs from 1948 to 1965 and Russians in the 1990s) as well as it should have and in working out a modus vivendi with the Palestinians. The gap between rich and poor is huge and poverty is a major problem. Despite its accomplishments, Israel's small population and size, its long borders, the growing menace of a future nuclear-armed Iran and 3 million Palestinians in the territories leave it at risk in the future. The frantic nature of Israeli society, its ability to often overlook unpleasant truths, and its willingness to at times repress those not part of the debate also reflect the negative impact of revolution as well as the positive one.

Yet the factors that brought victory in the past – a strong will to fight, revolution, democracy, the support of major world powers, strong high-tech, biotech and nanotech capabilities, excellent Internet usage, and the first-rate Silicon Wadi, military and intelligence services and educational system – augur well in a world transiting to the New World Order. Sometimes a simple fact – that oil-poor Israelis, who form 2 percent of the oil-rich Middle East, account for 33 percent of the richest people in the region – shows the power of the second capitalist revolution.[3]

For how much longer can the Arab–Persian Middle East remain the black hole of the New World Order, virtually devoid of democracy, capitalism, civil society, entrepreneurism, gender equality and the Internet? In the 1970s no one imagined that, after a century of "shame and humiliation" and 25 years of Maoist radicalism, China would dramatically move towards a powerful capitalist economy. In the late 1980s no one saw authoritarian Eastern Europe or neutralist India on the verge of joining the New World Order. But that is what happened. Despite the surfeit of oil and lack of reform of Islam, this may yet occur in the Middle East, ridden as it yet is by Islamic fundamentalist regimes ruling in Iran and Gaza and threatening to take power throughout the region.

Israel, reviled in the region and around the world, through its numerous attributes of a successful First World country may yet be showing the face of the future to a region that has long scorned the Jewish state.

Notes

1 Introduction

1 See K. Phillips, *The Cousin's Wars: Religion, Politics and the Triumph of Anglo-America*, New York: Basic Books, 1999; J. Buchanan, *The Road to Valley Forge: How Washington Built the Army that Won the Revolution*, New York: John Wiley & Sons, 2004; E. Snow, *Red Star over China*, New York: Grove Press, 1968; and the *New York Times*, October 26, 1917.

2 Herzl wrote in his diary after the First Zionist Congress at Basel in September 1897, "At Basel I founded the Jewish State. If I said this out loud today, I would be answered by universal laughter. Perhaps in five years and certainly in fifty, everyone will know it." See M. Gilbert, *Israel: A History*, New York: William Morrow and Company, 1998, p. 15. Isaiah Berlin concurred that in 1900 "most sane, sensible reasonable people, both Jews and gentiles, who heard of this [Herzl's] plan, regarded it as quite insane." See I. Berlin, *Personal Impressions*, ed. H. Hardy, New York: Viking Press, 1980, p. 33.

3 This is a quote from a leading Islamic thinker, Rashid Rida, in 1898. See N. Mandel, *The Arabs and Zionism before World War I*, Berkeley: University of California Press, 1976, p. 45.

4 In 1882 Zeev Dubnov wrote to his brother (the historian Simon Dubnov) at the time of the Bilu (First Aliyah pioneers in Palestine) about a Jewish state, "Don't laugh, it is not a mirage . . . there will come that splendid day whose advent was prophesied by Isaiah in his fiery and poetic words of consolation . . . It does not matter if that splendid day will only come in fifty years' time or more." See D. Vital, *The Origins of Zionism*, Oxford: Oxford University Press, 1975, p. 85. As late as 1914 the Jews and the Zionists had no real international power. See D. Vital, *Zionism: The Crucial Phase*, Oxford: Oxford University Press, 1987, p. 190.

5 Even in 1908 religious Jews (Old Yishuv) outnumbered new socialist Jews (New Yishuv) by as much as 50 percent. See Mandel, *Arabs*, p. 28. A. Ruppin, the overseer of Jewish settlement development, in 1907 said that the majority of Jews were still dependent on halukah (foreign charity). See W. Laqueur, *A History of Zionism*, London: Weidenfeld & Nicolson, 1972, pp. 152–4.

6 Imagine what an analyst would have written in 1800 when there were only 5,000–10,000 Jews (mainly religious Sephardi Jews) in Palestine, constituting 3–7 percent of the local population and an even tinier 0.2 percent of the 3 million Jews in the world! See I. Troen, *Imagining Zion*, New Haven, CT: Yale University Press, 2003, p. 6, and Vital, *Origins*, p.16.

7 The reference is to population figures for 1900. See Mandel, *Arabs*, pp. 48, 90. Walter Laqueur referred to the Zionist movement in 1917 as being "of no political importance" and provided the data on agricultural workers belonging to the

socialist parties. See Laqueur, *History*, pp. 287, 590. For the ownership, see Vital, *Zionism*, p. 64.

8 Walter Laqueur spoke of the total isolation of the Zionists by 1939. See Laqueur, *History*, p. 523.

9 American military analysts (including Marshall) concurred that the Yishuv "could not withstand a concentrated military assault from an Arab world numbering over 50 million and in the early months of 1948 the Haganah seemingly fared poorly." See M. Urofsky, *We Are One! American Jewry and Israel*, New York: Doubleday, 1978, p. 170. For Montgomery, see Z. Schiff, *A History of the Israeli Army*, New York: Macmillan, 1985, p. 32; and for Yadin, see I. Black and B. Morris, *Israel's Secret Wars*, New York: Grove Weidenfeld, 1991, p. 39. For the CIA see *Haaretz*, October 22, 2004, and for British intelligence officers see Gunther Rothenberg, *Anatomy of the Israeli Army: The Israel Defense Forces, 1948–1978*, New York: Hippocrene Books, 1979, p. 36. Their American patron, seeing the prospects for success as "so dark," spoke of delaying partition and creating a United Nations trusteeship to replace the British Mandate. During the war, no fewer than 77,000 Jews were ousted from their homes, mainly in mixed cities like Jaffa, Jerusalem and Tiberias. See Troen, *Imagining Zion*, p. 210.

10 D. Raviv and Y. Melman, *Every Spy a Prince: The Complete History of the Israel Intelligence Community*, Boston, MA: Houghton Mifflin, 1990, p. 211.

11 Berlin, *Personal Impressions*, p. 37.

12 The calculation is that Jews, who formed 7–10 percent of the known world 1,700–2,000 years ago, should today be a similar percentage of 1.0–1.4 billion people in Europe, Russia, North Africa and European fragments (United States, Canada, Australia). This would yield a Jewish population today of roughly 100 million Jews. See H. Rubinstein, D. Cohn-Sherbok, A. Edelheit and W. Rubinstein, *The Jews in the Modern World: A History since 1750*, London: Arnold, 2002, pp. 413–14.

13 Laqueur, *History*, p. 72. Moses Hess, who wrote *Rome and Jerusalem*, in 1851 declared that the Jews were "a soul without a body, wandering like a ghost through the centuries" (Laqueur, *History*, p. 72).

14 Ibid., p. 57.

15 Vital, *Zionism*, pp. 1–2.

16 A. Oren, "Inside Track: A Disaster Waiting to Happen," *Haaretz*, October 22, 2004.

17 M. Gilbert, *The Routledge Atlas of the Arab–Israeli Conflict*, 8th edn., London: Routledge, 2005, p. 132.

18 S. Teveth, *Ben Gurion: The Burning Ground 1886–1948*, Boston, MA: Houghton Mifflin, 1987, p. 591. Winston Churchill that same year proclaimed that "A Jewish state is a mirage" (p. 597).

19 Ibid., p. 721.

20 Laqueur, *History*, p. 590.

21 Report of a 2004 conversation at the State Department at which Mossad was considered to be the best by experts.

22 *Business Week*, October 11, 2004, p. 102.

23 *Haaretz*, January 11, 2007, and Industrial Cooperation Agency, *High-Tech Leads Israel Strong Economic Performance*, Israel: Ministry of Trade, Industry and Labor, 2007.

24 A. Arian, *The Second Republic: Politics in Israel*, Chatham, NJ: Chatham House Publishers, 1998, p. 3.

25 Another Israeli study argues that the Four Tigers of Asia performed better than Israel, which in turn did better than the bulk of the Third World. See E. Helpman, "Israel's Economic Growth: An International Comparison," *Israel Economic Review*, 1, 2003: 1–10. For further data, see A. Maddison, *The World Economy: Historical Statistics*, Paris: OECD, 2003.

26 B. Halpern, *The Idea of the Jewish State*, Cambridge, MA: Harvard University Press, 1969, pp. 56–8, 90–2.

27 So deep was the Jewish aversion to authority that the hit musical about the Jewish *shtetl Fiddler on the Roof* featured a leading song entitled "God bless the Czar and keep him far away from us."

28 P. Medding, *The Founding of Israeli Democracy, 1948–1967*, New York: Oxford University Press, 1990, pp. 3–4. Other states, such as India and Costa Rica, had non-democratic interludes. See also G. Sartori, *Parties and Party Systems: A Framework for Analysis*, Cambridge: Cambridge University Press, 1976, pp. 151–5, where he argues for the uniqueness of Israeli democracy.

29 P. B. Kinross, *The Ottoman Centuries: The Rise and Fall of the Turkish Empire*, New York: William Morrow and Company, 1977. Two events famous in Jewish history, the 1492 statement by Ottoman Turkish Sultan Bayezid II welcoming Spanish Jewish exiles to emigrate to the Ottoman Turkish Empire and the trials and tribulations of the First Aliyah in Ottoman Turkish Palestine, rate not an entry. While they loom large in the Jewish imagination, they do not merit mention in a general history of the empire. Palestine does not rate an entry in the seven-page index.

30 E. Karsh (ed.), *Israel: The First Hundred Years*, London: Frank Cass, 2000. The chapters that each deal with this subject are: E. Karsh, "Introduction," *Israel's Transition from Community to State*, vol. 1, pp. 1–2; D. Tal, "The Forgotten War: Jewish–Palestinian Strife in Mandatory Palestine, December 1947–May 1948," vol. 2, pp. 3–4; M. Nisan, "Israel 1948–98: Purpose and Predicament in History," vol. 3, pp. 4–6; and S. Sofer, "Towards Distant Frontiers: The Course of Israeli Diplomacy," vol. 4, p. 2. See also E. Karsh, *Rethinking the Middle East*, London: Frank Cass, 2003, Preface, p. 191.

31 E. Said, *Orientalism*, New York: Pantheon Books, 1978.

32 E. Karsh, *Rethinking the Middle East*, Preface, pp. 196–8.

33 D. Wheeler, "Does Post-Zionism Have a Future?," in L. Z. Eisenberg, N. Caplan, N. Sokoloff and M. Abu-Nimer (eds.), *Traditions and Transitions in Israel Studies*, Albany: State University of New York Press, 2003, pp. 159–80.

34 For a critique see D. Hazony, Y. Hazony and M. Oren (eds.), *New Essays on Zionism*, Jerusalem: Shalem Press, 2006.

35 A. Eban, *My Country: The Story of Modern Israel*, New York: Random House, 1972; M. Gilbert, *Israel*; L. Stein, *The Hope Fulfilled: The Rise of Modern Israel*, Westport: Praeger, 2003; A. Bregman, *A History of Israel*, Houndsmill, Basingstoke: Palgrave Macmillan, 2003; and H. Sachar, *A History of Israel: From the Rise of Zionism to Our Time*, 3rd edn., New York: Alfred Knopf, 2007.

36 B. Halpern and J. Reinharz, *Zionism and the Creation of a New Society*, New York: Oxford University Press, 1998; Laqueur, *History*; M. Oren, *Six Days of War: June 1967 and the Making of the Modern Middle East*, Oxford: Oxford University Press, 2002; and Halpern, *Idea of the Jewish State*.

37 M. Barnett, "The Politics of Uniqueness: The Status of the Israeli Case," in *Israel in Comparative Perspective*, ed. M. Barnett, Albany: State University of New York Press, 1996, p. 4 and Ch. 1.

38 M. Barnett, "Israel in the World Economy: Israel as an East Asian State?," in *Israel in Comparative Perspective*, ed. M. Barnett, Albany: State University of New York Press, 1996, pp. 107–8.

39 R. Kook, "Between Uniqueness and Exclusion: The Politics of Identity in Israel," in *Israel in Comparative Perspective*, ed. M. Barnett, Albany: State University of New York Press, 1996, pp. 199–200.

40 M. Barnett (ed.), *Israel in Comparative Perspective*, Albany: State University of New York Press, 1996.

41 R. Hazan and M. Maor (eds.), *Parties, Elections and Cleavages: Israel in*

Comparative and Theoretical Perspective, London: Frank Cass, 2000. Gabriel Sheffer, for example, showed that many emerging features of the Israeli political system paralleled those emerging in Europe: a new social and political openness, decline of old grassroots politics, increasingly assertive individualism, weakened parties, decline in party mobilization, reliance on the state for finance, increasingly flexible campaigns, increased volatility of voting, the professionalization of politics and rising role of religion and the right wing (p. 167).

42 James Burk compared Israel and the United States in his chapter "From Wars of Independence to Democratic Peace: Comparing the Cases of Israel and the United States," in *Military, State, and Society in Israel*, ed. D. Maman, E. Ben-Ari and Z. Rosenhek, New Brunswick, NJ: Transaction Publishers, 2001, Ch. 2.

43 B. Kimmerling, *Zionism and Territory: The Socio-Territorial Dimensions of Zionist Politics*, Berkeley: University of California Press, 1983.

44 Troen, *Imagining Zion*.

45 S. Cohen (ed.), *Democratic Societies and their Armed Forces: Israel in Comparative Context*, London: Frank Cass, 2000.

46 A. Peled, *A Question of Loyalty: Military Manpower Policy in Multiethnic States*, New York: Cornell University Press, 1998.

47 D. Horowitz, "Dual Authority Politics," *Comparative Politics*, 14, 1982: 329–49.

48 D. Maman, E. Ben-Ari and Z. Rosenhek (eds.), *Military, State, and Society in Israel*, New Brunswick, NJ: Transaction Publishers, 2001.

49 J. Migdal, *Through the Lens of Israel*, Albany: State University of New York Press, 2001, p. 6; and M. Cohen, *Zion and State: Nation, Class and the Shaping of Modern Israel*, New York: Columbia University Press, 1992, p. xi.

50 The Taif Accords ended the Lebanese civil war in 1989 in which 150,000 people died.

51 Y. Dror, "Weaving the Future of Israel," in *Global Politics: Essays in Honor of David Vital*, ed. A. Ben-Zvi and A. Klieman, London: Frank Cass, 2001, p. 367.

52 Burk, "From Wars of Independence to Democratic Peace," p. 88.

53 S. Huntington, "Revolution and Political Order," in *Revolutions: Theoretical, Comparative, and Historical Studies*, 2nd edn., ed. J. Goldstone, Fort Worth, TX: Harcourt Brace, 1993, p. 38.

54 See for example C. Brinton, *The Anatomy of Revolution*, New York: Vintage, 1965; B. Moore, *Social Origins of Dictatorship and Democracy*, Boston, MA: Beacon Press, 1968; T. Skocpol, *States and Social Revolutions*, Cambridge: Cambridge University Press, 1979; T. Gurr, *Why Men Rebel*, Princeton, NJ: Princeton University Press, 1968; J. Goldstone, *Revolution and Rebellion in the Early Modern World*, Berkeley: University of California Press, 1991; C. Tilly (ed.), *The Formation of the Modern European State System*, Princeton, NJ: Princeton University Press, 1975; and N. Keddie (ed.), *Debating Revolution*, New York: New York University Press, 1995.

55 A. Roshwald, *Ethnic Nationalism and the Fall of Empires: Central Europe, Russia and the Middle East, 1914–1923*, London: Routledge, 2001.

56 Skocpol, *States and Social Revolutions*, Ch. 1.

57 J. Frankel, "The Crisis as a Factor in Modern Jewish Politics, 1840 and 1881–1882," in *Organizing Rescue: National Jewish Solidarity in the Modern Period*, ed. S. I. Troen and B. Pinkus, London: Frank Cass, 1992, p. 33.

58 J. Goldstone, "The Outcome of Revolutions," in *Revolutions: Theoretical, Comparative, and Historical Studies*, ed. J. Goldstone, Fort Worth, TX: Harcourt Brace, 1994, p. 194.

59 R. Khalidi, *The Iron Cage: The Story of the Palestinian Struggle for Statehood*, Boston, MA: Beacon Press, 2007, pp. xxvii–xxviii, xlvii, 203.

60 Interview with Saul Singer in the *Jerusalem Post*, February 16, 2004.

61 A. Shlaim, *The Iron Wall: Israel and the Arab World*, New York: W.W. Norton,

2000, p. 597; and Z. Maoz, *Defending the Holy Land: A Critical Analysis of Israel's Security and Foreign Policy*, Ann Arbor: University of Michigan Press, 2000.

2 Controversy over Israel

1 For an excellent work on failure in the Middle East, see Bernard Lewis, *What Went Wrong? Western Impact and Middle Eastern Response*, New York: Oxford University Press, 2002.

2 Unlike mainstream Western Jewish scholars (Bernard Lewis, Elie Kedourie, Efraim Karsh) who have written extensively on Middle Eastern history, few Arab scholars have written on the rise of Israel.

3 R. Khalidi, *The Iron Cage: The Story of the Palestinian Struggle for Statehood*, Boston, MA: Beacon Press, 2007, pp. 216–17; and J. Kovel, *Overcoming Zionism: Creating a Single Democratic State in Israel/Palestine*, London: Pluto Press, 2007, pp. 184, 233, 237.

4 J. Carter, *Palestine: Peace Not Apartheid*, New York: Simon & Schuster, 2006.

5 I. Troen, *Imagining Zion*, New Haven, CT: Yale University Press, 2003, p. xiv.

6 H. Gerber, "Foreign Occupiers and Stepchildren: Zionist Discourse and the Palestinians, 1882–1948," in *Arab–Jewish Relations: From Conflict to Resolution?*, ed. E. Podeh and A. Kaufman, Brighton: Sussex Academic Press, 2005, pp. 23–4, 93; and H. Cohen, "Why Do Collaborators Collaborate? The Case of Palestinians and Zionist Institutions, 1917–1936," in *Arab–Jewish Relations: From Conflict to Resolution?*, ed. E. Podeh and A. Kaufman, Brighton: Sussex Academic Press, 2005, pp. 40–5.

7 G. Shafir, "Zionism and Colonialism: A Comparative Approach," in *Israel in Comparative Perspective*, ed. M. Barnett, Albany: State University of New York Press, 1996, Ch. 9.

8 E. Karsh, "Introduction," in *Israel: The First Hundred Years: Israel's Transition from Community to State*, vol. 1, ed. E. Karsh, London: Frank Cass, 2000, p. 4.

9 For an excellent critique of the Arab and Israeli leftist version of Israel as a colonialist society, see A. Bareli, "Forgetting Europe: Perspectives on the Debate about Zionism and Colonialism," in *Israeli Historical Revisionism: From Left to Right*, ed. A. Shapira and D. Penslar, London: Frank Cass, 2003, pp. 99–120.

10 In 1939 Europe had 10 million Jews, 7 million of them outside the Soviet Union. In the one country (Germany) that allowed relatively open emigration from 1933 to 1939, 73 percent of all Jews emigrated abroad. Given the tight restrictions then in place for Jewish emigration (the failure of the 1938 Evian conference), several million would be a reasonable number.

11 D. K. Fieldhouse, *The Colonial Empires from the Eighteenth Century*, New York: Weidenfeld & Nicolson, 1966, pp. 11–22, 372; and G. Fredrickson, "Colonialism and Racism: The United States and South Africa in Comparative Perspective," in *The Arrogance of Race*, ed. G. Fredrickson, Middletown, CT: Wesleyan University Press, 1988, pp. 218–21.

12 The estimated 10 million native Americans in 1750 today have dwindled to 1–2 million people.

13 R. Kook, "Between Uniqueness and Exclusion: The Politics of Identity in Israel," in *Israel in Comparative Perspective*, ed. M. Barnett, Albany: State University of New York Press, 1996, pp. 212–13. Only after the end of the colonial period did the Jewish National Fund buy over 1,100 square miles of largely abandoned Arab land from 1948 to 1951 and by the late 1950s control over 90 percent of the land of Israel.

14 Shafir, "Zionism and Colonialism," pp. 232–3. In fairness to Shafir, the remainder of his argument points to considering Israeli settlement colonial (or neo-colonial) and accelerated after 1967. But many of the facts he cites can be used in the manner above.

15 Gerber, "Foreign Occupiers and Stepchildren," pp. 23–4.

16 Shafir, "Zionism and Colonialism," p. 232.

17 This does not include the 3.4 million Arabs in Jordan, which was originally part of historical Palestine and the mandate until severed from the original mandate by the British in 1922 to give a kingdom to the Hashemites in Transjordan.

18 D. Penslar, *Zionism and Technocracy: The Engineering of Jewish Settlement in Palestine, 1870–1918*, Bloomington: Indiana University Press, 1991, p. 7.

19 J. Mearsheimer and S. Walt, *The Israel Lobby and U.S. Foreign Policy*, New York: Farrar, Straus and Giroux, 2007.

20 Kovel, *Overcoming Zionism*.

21 M. Oren, *Power, Faith and Fantasy: America in the Middle East, 1776 to the Present*, New York: W.W. Norton, 2007, p. 488.

22 B. Reich, "The United States and Israel: The Nature of a Special Relationship," in *The Middle East and Israel: A Historical and Political Reassessment*, 3rd edn., ed. D. Lesch, Boulder, CO: Westview Press, 2003, Ch. 17.

23 B. Kimmerling and J. Migdal, *The Palestinian People: A History*, Cambridge, MA: Harvard University Press, 2003, p. 322.

24 S. Spiegel, *The Other Arab–Israeli Conflict: Making America's Middle East Policy, from Truman to Reagan*, Chicago: University of Chicago Press, 1985; and W. Quandt, *Peace Process: American Diplomacy and the Arab–Israeli Conflict since 1967*, Washington, D.C. and Berkeley: Brookings Institution Press and University of California Press, 1993.

25 M. Gazit, "The 1956 Sinai Campaign: David Ben Gurion's Policy on Gaza, the Armistice Agreement and French Mediation," in *Israel: The First Hundred Years: From War to Peace?*, vol. 2, ed. E. Karsh, London: Frank Cass, 2000, pp. 47–8. This embargo may have prevented a greater export of British arms to the Arab side, but this point remains inconclusive.

26 Reich, "United States and Israel," p. 251.

27 M. Nisan, "Israel 1948–98: Purpose and Predicament in History," in E. Karsh (ed.), *Israel: The First Hundred Years: Israeli Politics and Society since 1948: Problems of Collective Identity*, vol. 3, London: Frank Cass, 2000, p. 10; and Oren, *Power, Faith and Fantasy*, pp. 524–70. Kissinger said that "We could not make our policy hostage to the Israelis" (p. 533). But, later in the war, President Nixon said, "Whatever it takes, save Israel" (pp. 533–4).

28 W. Laqueur, *A History of Zionism*, London: Weidenfeld & Nicolson, 1972, p. 564.

29 H. Ben-Yehuda and S. Sandler, *The Arab–Israeli Conflict Transformed: Fifty Years of Interstate and Ethnic Crises*, Albany: State University of New York Press, 2002, p. 124.

30 *New York Times*, September 27, 2006.

31 E. Karsh, "Introduction," in E. Karsh (ed.), *Israel: The First Hundred Years: Israel's Transition from Community to State*, vol.1, London: Frank Cass, 2000. p. 2.

32 "Few Large Donations Go to Jewish Causes," *Forward*, April 4, 2003.

33 Kovel, *Overcoming Zionism*, p. 207.

34 A. Shlaim, *The Iron Wall: Israel and the Arab World*, New York: W.W. Norton, 2000, p. 598.

35 C. Tilly, *Coercion, Capital and European States, A.D. 990–1990*, Cambridge, MA: Blackwell, 1990.

36 For a strong case made for the neo-realist opposition to idealism and pacifism, see J. Mearsheimer, *The Tragedy of Great Power Politics*, New York: W.W. Norton, 2001.

37 This is not to deny the post-Zionist assertion that a significant number of Palestinians were driven out during the 1948 war. There is no question that this is true but for the majority of Palestinians, as in Haifa, this happened largely on their own accord.

38 A. Cordesman, *The Israeli–Palestinian War: Escalating to Nowhere*, Westport, CT: Greenwood Press, 2005, p. 18.
39 Although in 1967 the Israelis ultimately preempted the Arab attack, the Egyptian movement of 100,000 troops and 1,000 tanks into the Sinai and closing the Straits of Tiran precipitated the war.
40 Laqueur, *History*, p. 596.
41 Cordesman, *Israeli–Palestinian War*, pp. 3–8. Critics rightly point to the limitations of this offer – leaving in place the majority of settlement blocs, no right of return, no control over the Temple Mount, and a demilitarized state. See S. Telhami, *The Stakes: America and the Middle East*, Boulder, CO: Westview Press, 2002, p. 119. Yet, in the history of international negotiations (such as the Treaty of Brest-Litovsk in 1918 or Versailles in 1919), this was a remarkably generous starting offer to an oft defeated people, likely to be improved even further if Arafat had responded positively.
42 At Taba in the "non-paper" Israel offered to give the Palestinians 100 percent of Gaza and 94 percent of the West Bank, make Jerusalem an open city and divide the Old City, take in 40,000 refugees in five years and support family reunification. See Cordesman, *Israeli–Palestinian War*, pp. 78–91.
43 M. Gilbert, *The Routledge Atlas of the Arab–Israeli Conflict*, 8th edn., London: Routledge, 2005, p. 129; and Kimmerling and Migdal, *Palestinian People*, pp. 276–94. So bad was the economic crisis in the West Bank under Jordanian rule (1948–67) that 400,000 Palestinian left it before 1967 (p. 295).
44 A. G. Frank, "The Sociology of Development and the Underdevelopment of Sociology," *Catalyst*, 3, Summer, 1963: 20–73; I. Wallerstein, *The Capitalist World-Economy*, New York: Cambridge University Press, 1979; and L. S. Stavrianos, *Global Rift: The Third World Comes of Age*, New York: William Morrow and Company, 1981.
45 E. Chowder, "The Zionist Revolution in Time," in *New Essays in Zionism*, ed. D. Hazony, Y. Hazony and M. Oren, Jerusalem: Shalem Press, 2006, pp. 142, 151.
46 M. Barnett, "Israel in the World Economy: Israel as an East Asian State?," in *Israel in Comparative Perspective*, ed. M. Barnett, Albany: State University of New York Press, 1996, pp. 113–17.
47 Zeev Maoz, for instance, makes frequent reference to some of these factors in his work *Defending the Holy Land: A Critical Analysis of Israel's Security and Foreign Policy*, Ann Arbor: University of Michigan Press, 2000.
48 A. Shlaim, *Iron Wall*, pp. 21–2, 187, 229–30.
49 Ibid., pp. 40, 59, 221, 376.

3 The rise of Israel in comparative perspective

1 See J. Migdal, *Through the Lens of Israel*, Albany: State University of New York Press, 2001, Ch. 2.
2 For the classic work on European fragments and new societies, see L. Hartz (ed.), *The Founding of New Societies*, New York: Harcourt, Brace & World, 1964, with contributions by Kenneth McRae, Richard Morse, Richard Rosecrance and Leonard Thompson.
3 M. Ma'oz and G. Sheffer (eds.), *Middle Eastern Minorities and Diasporas*, Brighton: Sussex Academic Press, 2002, p. 31.
4 J. McCarthy, *The Ottoman Peoples and the End of Empire*, New York: Oxford University Press, 2001, pp. 82–3.
5 Ma'oz and Sheffer, *Middle Eastern Minorities and Diasporas*, pp. 32–7, 234–45; and A. Roshwald, *Ethnic Nationalism and the Fall of Empires: Central Europe, Russia and the Middle East, 1914–1923*, London: Routledge, 2001, pp. 192–3.

However, in 1943 Muslims, through the new regions added to the state, were already 40 percent of the state and Maronites made up only 32 percent.

6 A. Hourani, *Minorities in the Arab World*, London: Oxford University Press, 1947, p. 37.
7 D. Fromkin, *A Peace to End All Peace*, New York: Avon Books, 1989, p. 48.
8 M. Macmillan, *Paris 1919: Six Months that Changed the World*, New York: Random House, 2002, pp. 445, 449–50.
9 Ibid., pp. 453–4.
10 Central Intelligence Agency, *The World Factbook*, Washington, D.C.: CIA, 2003, chapter on Lebanon; Ma'oz and Sheffer, *Middle Eastern Minorities and Diasporas*, pp. 36–7; and R. D. McLaurin (ed.), *The Political Role of Minority Groups in the Middle East*, New York: Praeger, 1979, p. 276.
11 CIA, *World Factbook*, chapter on Armenia.
12 P. B. Kinross, *The Ottoman Centuries: The Rise and Fall of the Turkish Empire*, New York: William Morrow and Company, 1977, pp. 553–63.
13 Macmillan, *Paris 1919*, pp. 378–9.
14 M. Weber, "What Is the State?," in *Political Thought*, ed. M. Rosen and J. Wolff, Oxford: Oxford University Press, 1999.
15 As Mordechai Nisan depicted the Kurds, "Tribal life inhibited integral Kurdish national unity while augmenting Kurdish particularism in relation to other groups, the Kurds were unsuccessful in forging an adequately strong and coherent national community." See Nisan, *Minorities in the Middle East*, London: McFarland & Company, 2001, pp. 34, 53.
16 Macmillan, *Paris 1919*, p. 445.
17 B. Brentjes, *The Armenians, Assyrians and Kurds: Three Nations, One Fate?*, Campbell, CA: Rishi Publications, 1997, p. 130.
18 Nisan, *Minorities*, pp. 41–2.
19 Hourani, *Minorities*, p. 38.
20 McCarthy, *Ottoman Peoples*, p. 77.
21 Hourani, *Minorities*, pp. 96–7.
22 McLaurin, *Political Role of Minority Groups*, Ch. 7.
23 Fromkin, *Peace*, p. 400.
24 McLaurin, *Political Role of Minority Groups*, Ch. 7.
25 Hourani, *Minorities*, Ch. 9. The addition of Beirut and the coastal towns enhanced the economic viability of the new state. But it endangered the Christian, mainly Maronite, hold over Lebanon, a control which it lost in 1989 and 1991.
26 Ibid., pp. 95–6.
27 Ma'oz and Sheffer, *Middle Eastern Minorities and Diasporas*, p. 242.
28 Roshwald, *Ethnic Nationalism*, p. 186.
29 Hourani, *Minorities*, p. 63.
30 McCarthy, *Ottoman Peoples*, p. 123.
31 See E. Shils, "On the Comparative Study of the New States," and L. Fallers, "Equality, Modernity and Democracy in the New States," in *Old Societies and New States*, ed. C. Geertz, New York: Free Press, 1963, pp. 1–26, 158–219.
32 For the India–Israel reference, see J. Mendlikow, *Ideology, Party Change and Electoral Campaigns in Israel, 1965–2001*, Albany: State University of New York Press, 2003, Ch. 8.
33 For typical Third World societies, see C. Geertz (ed.), *Old Societies and New States*, New York: Free Press, 1963.
34 Hartz, *Founding of New Societies*.
35 Ibid., pp. 1–12, with quotes on pp. 4, 6.
36 W. Laqueur, *A History of Zionism*, London: Weidenfeld & Nicolson, 1972, p. 270.
37 Ibid., pp. 278–80, 309. In more recent post-socialist times, the 1 million immigrants from the former Soviet Union have brought a new wave of Russianness to Israel.

38 M. Mann, *The Sources of Social Power: The Rise and Classes of Nation-States, 1760–1914*, vol. 2, New York: Cambridge University Press, 1993, p. 660.
39 H. Rubinstein, D. Cohn-Sherbok, A. Edelheit and W. Rubinstein, *The Jews in the Modern World: A History since 1750*, London: Arnold, 2002, p. 417.
40 Louis Hartz, "United States History in a New Perspective," in *The Founding of New Societies*, ed. L. Hartz, New York: Harcourt, Brace & World, 1964, Ch. 4.
41 Mann, *Sources*, pp. 136–63.
42 R. Rosecrance, "The Radical Culture of Australia," in *The Founding of New Societies*, ed. L. Hartz, New York: Harcourt, Brace & World, 1964, Ch. 8.
43 C. Brinton, The *Anatomy of Revolution*, New York: Vintage Press, 1965, p. 29.
44 K. Marx and F. Engels, *The Communist Manifesto*, Harmondsworth: Penguin, 1967.
45 B. Moore, *Social Origins of Dictatorship and Democracy*, Boston, MA: Beacon Press, 1968.
46 T. Skocpol, *States and Social Revolutions*, Cambridge: Cambridge University Press, 1979.
47 J. Goldstone, *Revolution and Rebellion in the Early Modern World*, Berkeley: University of California Press, 1991, p. 33.
48 T. Gurr, *Why Men Rebel*, Princeton, NJ: Princeton University Press, 1968.
49 For the frontier and metropole concepts, see M. Barnett, "Israel in the World Economy: Israel as an East Asian State?," in *Israel in Comparative Perspective*, ed. M. Barnett, Albany: State University of New York Press, 1996, pp. 120–2.
50 Ibid., p. 122.
51 Ibid., Ch. 5.
52 S. Telhami, "Israeli Foreign Policy: A Realist Ideal-Type or a Breed of its Own?," in *Israel in Comparative Perspective*, ed. M. Barnett, Albany: State University of New York Press, 1996, Ch. 2.
53 M. Lissak, "Paradoxes of Israeli Civil–Military Relations: An Introduction," in *Israeli Society and its Defense Establishment*, ed. M. Lissak, London: Frank Cass, 1984.
54 M. Lissak, "Epilogue," in *Military, State, and Society in Israel*, ed. D. Maman, E. Ben-Ari and Z. Rosenhek, New Brunswick, NJ: Transaction Publishers, 2001, pp. 410–16.

4 Jewish issues

1 Amos Elon, *The Israelis: Founders and Sons*, New York: Holt, Rinehart and Winston, 1971.
2 This helps us to understand the irony, often noted in Israel, that, even with Likud or Kadima in power, their major ideas (such as withdrawal) were often Labor Party ideas. The Labor Party has often continued to promote and legitimize the second, semi-capitalist revolution, often without missing a step. It has thereby legitimated a powerful change in Israeli society, a change away from the socialist order that it ran for so many decades.
3 Many of the critics of Israel are often not wrong about some significant aspects of their criticism, but they fail to put their criticism into a comparative context and appreciate the achievements of the state. They ignore the context in which these failures have developed and often been overlooked by a leadership and population concerned with more pressing issues (such as survival). They also have failed to look at the revolutionary nature of the system and its resultant costs.
4 J. Talmon, *Israel among the Nations*, New York: Macmillan, 1970, pp. 130–2.
5 H. Rubinstein, D. Cohn-Sherbok, A. Edelheit and W. Rubinstein, *The Jews in the Modern World: A History since 1750*, London: Arnold, 2002, p. 428.

6   A. Arian, *The Second Republic: Politics in Israel*, Chatham, NJ: Chatham House Publishers, p. 31.
7   D. Vital, *The Origins of Zionism*, Oxford: Oxford University Press, 1975, pp. 72, 168.
8   D. Vital, *Zionism: The Crucial Phase*, Oxford: Oxford University Press, 1987, p. 3.
9   I. Howe, *The World of Our Fathers*, New York: Harcourt Brace Jovanovich, 1976.
10   W. Laqueur, *A History of Zionism*, London: Weidenfeld & Nicolson, 1972, p. 447.
11   S. M. Rubinstein, *The Communist Movement in Palestine and Israel, 1919–1984*, Boulder, CO: Westview Press, 1984, pp. 203, 211; and Z. Gitelman, *Jewish Nationality and Soviet Politics: The Jewish Sections of the CSPU, 1917–1930*, Princeton, NJ: Princeton University Press, 1972, pp. 434–5.
12   Laqueur, *History*, p. 389.
13   M. Gilbert, *From the Ends of the Earth: The Jews in the 20th Century*, London: Cassell, 2001, p. 30.
14   Laqueur, *History*, p. 274.
15   Ibid., pp. 407–13.
16   Ibid., pp. 9, 394.
17   B. Rubin, *Assimilation and its Discontents*, New York: Random House, 1995, p. xiv.
18   Rubin, *Assimilation*; Laqueur, *History*, pp. 25, 592. For the 2000 National Jewish Population Survey, see the North American Jewish Data Bank on the Internet.
19   Vital, *Zionism*, p. 36. The rate remained low even though only baptism in the Russian Orthodox Church could open the door to positions in the judiciary, officer corps, middle and high bureaucracy, secondary and university education and even seats in secondary and higher education.
20   Ibid., p. 75.
21   D. Hazony, "Zionism and Moral Vision," in *New Essays on Zionism*, ed. D. Hazony, Y. Hazony and M. Oren, Jerusalem: Shalem Press, 2006, p. 168.
22   A. J. Sherman, *Mandate Days: British Lives in Palestine, 1918–1948*, Baltimore, MD: Johns Hopkins University Press, 2001, p. 229.
23   Ibid., p. 40.
24   M. Urofsky, *American Zionism from Herzl to the Holocaust*, New York: Doubleday, 1975, p. 266.
25   B. Halpern and J. Reinharz, *Zionism and the Creation of a New Society*, New York: Oxford University Press, 1998, p. 47.
26   M. Levin, *It Takes a Dream: The Story of Hadassah*, Jerusalem: Gefen Publishing House, 2002, pp. 31, 70, 75, 106.
27   Sherman, *Mandate Days*, pp. 38, 51.
28   Ibid., pp. 43, 65; and B. Kimmerling, *Zionism and Economy*, Cambridge, MA: Schenkman Publishing, 1983, p. 56.
29   M. B. Zohar, *Spies in the Promised Land: Iser Harel and the Israeli Secret Service*, Boston, MA: Houghton Mifflin, 1972, pp. 11–12.
30   R. Kook, "Between Uniqueness and Exclusion: The Politics of Identity in Israel," in *Israel in Comparative Perspective*, ed. M. Barnett, Albany: State University of New York Press, 1996, p. 202.
31   B. Kimmerling, "Making Conflict a Routine," in *Israeli Society and its Defense Establishment*, ed. M. Lissak, London: Frank Cass, 1984, pp. 22–39.
32   A. Roshwald, *Ethnic Nationalism and the Fall of Empires: Central Europe, Russia and the Middle East, 1914–1923*, New York: Routledge, 2001, p. 141.
33   D. Fromkin, *A Peace to End All Peace*, New York: Henry Holt, 1989, p. 294; and Vital, *Zionism*, pp. 272–7.
34   M. Gilbert, *The Routledge Atlas of Jewish History*, New York: William Morrow and Company, 1993, p. 76.

35 Vital, *Origins*, p. 80.
36 Arian, *Second Republic*, p. 20.
37 Ibid., p. 24. Also see J. Parkes, *A History of Palestine from 135 A.D. to Modern Times*, New York: Oxford University Press, 1949, p. 307.
38 By 1967 250,000 Israelis, by 1990 600,000 Israelis and by 2007 over 750,000 Israelis had emigrated abroad. Given the higher standard of living in the West, easier life, greater cosmopolitanism, lack of terrorism or constant war and military service, and the tendency of Jews to live in the Diaspora, this was hardly surprising. The fact that over 22,000 Israelis had died since 1947 in war or terrorism was clearly a factor. For the earlier statistics, see H. Sachar, *A History of Israel: From the Rise of Zionism to Our Time*, 2nd edn., New York: Alfred Knopf, 2002, pp. 1005–8.
39 Vital, *Zionism*, p. 372.
40 Ibid., pp. 96–7.
41 2003 Pew Global Attitudes Poll.
42 Ibid., pp. 159–62.
43 Indeed, the very word for absorption (*klita*) indicates the depth of the problem. There is no comparable phrase that I am aware of in the United States or other countries for taking in new immigrants.
44 R. Kark and J. Glass, "The Jews in Eretz-Israel/Palestine: From Traditional Peripherality to Modern Centrality," in *Israel: The First Hundred Years: Israel's Transition from Community to State*, vol. 1, ed. E. Karsh, London: Frank Cass, 2000, p. 103.
45 S. Schecter, "Literature as a Response to Paradox," in *Traditions and Transitions in Israel Studies*, ed. L. Z. Eisenberg, N. Caplan, N. Sokoloff and M. Abu-Nimer, Albany: State University of New York Press, 2003, pp. 204–5.
46 Laqueur, *History*, p. 492.
47 Vital, *Origins*, pp. 326, 355.
48 S. Teveth, *Ben Gurion: The Burning Ground 1886–1948*, Boston, MA: Houghton Mifflin, 1987, p. xiii.
49 Z. Schiff, *A History of the Israeli Army*, New York: Macmillan, 1985, p. 59.
50 R. Mahler, *Politics and Government in Israel: The Maturation of a Modern State*, Lanham, MD: Rowman & Littlefield, 2004, p. 93.
51 J. Talmon, *Israel*, pp. 151–2.
52 D. Hacohen, "Mass Immigration and Demographic Revolution," in *Israel: The First Hundred Years: Israeli Politics and Society since 1948: Problems of Collective Identity*, vol. 3, ed. E. Karsh, London: Frank Cass, 2000, p. 179.
53 M. Bregmann and M. Jucovy (eds.), *Generations of the Holocaust*, New York: Columbia University Press, 1982, p. 57.
54 M. Urofsky, *We Are One! American Jewry and Israel*, New York: Doubleday, 1978.
55 This was one factor in their later strong support for the Likud Party starting in the 1970s.
56 D. Newman, "Controlling Territory: Spatial Dimensions of Social and Political Change in Israel," in *Traditions and Transitions in Israel Studies*, ed. L. Z. Eisenberg, N. Caplan, N. Sokoloff and M. Abu-Nimer, Albany: State University of New York Press, 2003, p. 71.
57 D. Raviv and Y. Melman, *Every Spy a Prince: The Complete History of Israel's Intelligence Community*, Boston, MA: Houghton Mifflin, 1990, p. 38.
58 For the Yemenites, see H. Lewis, *After the Eagles Landed*, Boulder, CO: Westview Press, 1989, pp. 57–60, 77, 144–9; Urofsky, *We Are One!*, pp. 195–6; and Rubinstein *et al., Jews in the Modern World*, p. 105.
59 Hacohen, "Mass Immigration," p. 184.
60 I. Zangwill, *Children of the Ghetto*, Philadelphia, PA: Jewish Publication Society, 1892.

61 Gilbert, *Routledge Atlas of Jewish History*, p. 89.
62 S. Avineri, *The Making of Modern Zionism: The Intellectual Origins of the Jewish State*, New York: Basic Books, 1981, p. 214.
63 For an excellent exegesis of this view, see J. Migdal, *Through the Lens of Israel*, Albany: State University of New York, 2001, Ch. 2.
64 Vital, *Origins*, p. 374.
65 Laqueur, *History*, p. 286.
66 Ibid., pp. 140, 159, 179.
67 Ibid., pp. 464, 503.
68 Ibid., p. 512.
69 Ibid., pp. 549, 594.

5 Hostility of the major powers

1 M. Oren, "Ben-Gurion and the Return to Jewish Power," in *New Essays on Zionism*, ed. D. Hazony, Y. Hazony and M. Oren, Jerusalem: Shalem Press, 2006, pp. 406, 408, 414.
2 J. Migdal, *Through the Lens of Israel*, Albany: State University of New York Press, 2001, p. 46.
3 B. Halpern, *The Idea of the Jewish State*, Cambridge, MA: Harvard University Press, 1969, pp. 105–8.
4 N. Mandel, *The Arabs and Zionism before World War I*, Berkeley: University of California Press, 1976, Chs. 1–2.
5 Ibid., pp. 1–90.
6 Ibid., pp. 19, 90.
7 D. Vital, *Zionism: The Crucial Phase*, Oxford: Oxford University Press, 1987, pp. 76, 126–7. In Jerusalem, for example, only 6,300 Jews out of 50,000 Jews had the right to vote.
8 M. Gilbert, *From the Ends of the Earth: The Jews in the 20th Century*, London: Cassell, 2001, pp. 84–5.
9 H. Sachar, *A History of Israel: From the Rise of Zionism to Our Time*, New York: Alfred Knopf, 2002, pp. 89–92.
10 Ibid., p. 113.
11 Ibid., p. 113.
12 D. Vital, *The Origins of Zionism*, Oxford: Oxford University Press, 1975, p. 30.
13 A. Vaksberg, *Stalin against the Jews*, New York: Alfred Knopf, 1994, p. 6. A similar statement was made by the liberal Count Sergei Witte to Theodor Herzl in 1903 in Saint Petersburg: "I used to say to the late Tsar Alexander III, 'Majesty, if it were possible to drown the six or seven million Jews in the Black Sea, I would be absolutely in favor of that. But if it is not possible, one must let them live.' " In another part of the conversation, Witte remarked that "One has to admit that the Jews provide enough reasons for hostility. There is a characteristic arrogance about them. Most Jews however are poor and because they are poor they are filthy and make a repulsive impression. They also engage in all sorts of ugly pursuits, like pimping and usury. So you see it is hard for friends of the Jews to come to their defense. And yet I am a friend of the Jews." See P. Johnson, *A History of the Jews*, New York: Harper & Row, 1987, p. 364.
14 Vital, *Origins*, pp. 37–50.
15 Ibid., pp. 109–11. Yet 400,000–500,000 Russian Jews served in the Tsarist army in World War I.
16 Halpern, *Idea of the Jewish State*, pp. 319–21; and Migdal, *Through the Lens of Israel*, p. 72.
17 A. J. Sherman, *Mandate Days: British Lives in Palestine, 1918–1948*, Baltimore, MD: Johns Hopkins University Press, 2001, pp. 16–27.

18 D. Fromkin, *A Peace to End All Peace*, New York: Henry Holt, 1989, p. 198. Many British officials were openly anti-Semitic.
19 Ibid., p. 322.
20 J. Parkes, *A History of Palestine from 135 A.D. to Modern Times*, New York: Oxford University Press, 1949, p. 318.
21 Fromkin, *Peace*, pp. 447, 515; and Sherman, *Mandate Days*, p. 53.
22 J. Reinharz, *Chaim Weizmann: The Making of a Statesman*, New York: Oxford University Press, 1993, p. 354; and Sherman, *Mandate Days*, p. 62.
23 Halpern, *Idea of the Jewish State*, pp. 294–6.
24 Ibid., pp. 319–20.
25 Fromkin, *Peace*, Ch. 6.
26 Halpern, *Idea of the Jewish State*, pp. 332–3.
27 W. Laqueur and B. Rubin (eds.), *The Israel–Arab Reader*, New York: Penguin, 2001, pp. 36–41.
28 M. Gilbert, *Israel: A History*, New York: William Morrow and Company, 1998, p. 92.
29 M. Kolinsky, *Britain's War in the Middle East: Strategy and Diplomacy 1936–43*, New York: St. Martin's Press, 1999, Ch. 7. The Axis threat to the Middle East and Palestine was real. By May 1943 the defeated Axis had lost 1 million men (70 percent Italian), 8,000 planes and 2,500 tanks in the region.
30 Ibid., p. 80. Colonial Secretary Ramsay Macdonald similarly observed the need to make concessions to the Arabs in order to placate them (p. 81).
31 M. Brown, *The Israeli–American Connection: Its Roots in the Yishuv, 1914–1945*, Detroit, MI: Wayne State University Press, 1996, p. 228.
32 Kolinsky, *Britain's War*, p. 85.
33 There is no way to know how many Jews might have come to Palestine. But, given a European Jewish population of over 7 million Jews outside the Soviet Union, a figure of 1–3 million would have been plausible at that time. In this way the British had a degree of complicity (together with other Western countries that closed their doors to Jewish immigrants) in the ultimate fate of European Jewry in the Holocaust.
34 S. Teveth, *Ben Gurion: The Burning Ground 1886–1948*, Boston, MA: Houghton Mifflin, 1987, pp. 531, 779.
35 Y. Allon, *Shield of David*, New York: Random House, 1970, p. 109.
36 Kolinsky, *Britain's War*, Ch. 10; H. Eshed, *Reuven Shiloah: The Man behind the Mossad*, trans. D. Zinder and L. Zinder, London: Frank Cass, 1997, pp. 44, 72; and Gilbert, *Israel*, p. 109.
37 Kolinsky, *Britain's War*, pp. 194–206, 189; and Parkes, *History*, p. 342.
38 S. I. Troen and B. Pinkus (eds.), *Organizing Rescue: National Jewish Solidarity in the Modern Period*, London: Frank Cass, 1992, Part 2 and especially p. 223.
39 Parkes, *History*, p. 346.
40 E. Karsh, *Fabricating Israeli History: The "New Historians,"* London: Frank Cass, 1997, p. 185.
41 W. Louis, *The British Empire in the Middle East 1945–1951*, Oxford: Oxford University Press, 1984, p. 534. This was hardly the worst. Sir John Trotbeck, the head of the Middle East Office in Cairo, in June 1948 characterized Israel as a gangster state (p. 532).
42 Sachar, *History*, Chs. 11–12.
43 Parkes, *History*, pp. 358–62.
44 E. Karsh, *Rethinking the Middle East*, London: Frank Cass, 2003, p. 181.
45 M. Urofsky, *We Are One! American Jewry and Israel*, New York: Doubleday, 1978, pp. 150, 154; and J. Burk, "From Wars of Independence to Democratic Peace: Comparing the Cases of Israel and the United States," in *Military, State, and Society in Israel*, ed. D. Maman, E. Ben-Ari and Z. Rosenhek, New Brunswick, NJ: Transaction Publishers, 2001, p. 97.

46 Z. Schiff, *A History of the Israeli Army*, New York: Macmillan, 1985, p. 32; and Allon, *Shield of David*, pp. 198–202.
47 M. Levin, *It Takes a Dream: The Story of Hadassah*, Jerusalem: Gefen Publishing House, 2002, pp. 219–43.
48 Sachar, *History*, Ch. 12; Halpern, *Idea of the Jewish State*, p. 390; Gilbert, *From the Ends of the Earth*, p. 256; and Schiff, *History*, p. 26.
49 Karsh, *Fabricating Israeli History*, Ch. 5.
50 Halpern, *Idea of the Jewish State*, pp. 382–3; and Urofsky, *We Are One!*, p. 186.
51 Halpern, *Idea of the Jewish State*, p. 427.
52 Eshed, *Reuven Shiloah*, p. 217; and M. Bar-On, *The Gates of Gaza: Israel's Road to Suez and Back, 1955–1957*, New York: St. Martin's Press, 1994, p. 208.
53 On the centrality of destroying the Jews to Hitler, see L. Davidowitz, *The War against the Jews*, New York: Holt, Rinehart and Winston, 1975; and D. Goldhagen, *Hitler's Willing Executioners*, New York: Alfred Knopf, 1996.
54 Teveth, *Ben Gurion*, p. 834.
55 B. Lewis, *What Went Wrong? Western Impact and Middle Eastern Response*, New York: Oxford University Press, 2002, p. 154.
56 M. Gilbert, *The Routledge Atlas of Jewish History*, New York: William Morrow and Company, 1993, pp. 98, 103.
57 Ibid., p. 135.
58 P. Celan, "Death Fugue," in *Voices within the Ark: The Modern Jewish Poets*, ed. H. Schwartz and A. Rudolf, New York: Avon Books, 1980, pp. 937–8.
59 M. Penkower, *The Holocaust and Israel Reborn*, Chicago: University of Illinois Press, 1994, p. 50.
60 Quoted from Tom Segev in J. Nitzan and S. Bichler, *The Global Political Economy of Israel*, London: Pluto Press, 2002, p. 101. In 1941 and 1942, before they knew about the Holocaust, David Ben Gurion and other Jewish leaders estimated that 2 million European Jews might reach Palestine. Now they were nearly all gone, save for the survivors. See B. Kimmerling, *Zionism and Territory: The Socio-Territorial Dimensions of Zionist Politics*, Berkeley: University of California Press, 1983, p. 56.
61 A post-war poll by the United Nations Relief Agency found that less than 1 percent of the camp survivors wanted to stay in Europe: fully 97 percent wanted to go to Palestine. See Urofsky, *We Are One!*, pp. 100–2.
62 A. Diskin, *The Last Days in Israel: Understanding the New Israeli Democracy*, London: Frank Cass, 2003, p. 1.
63 D. Vital, *The Survival of Small States: Studies in Small Power/Great Power Conflict*, London: Oxford University Press, 1971, pp. 4, 52–4, 78.
64 R. Wistrich, "Marxism and Jewish Nationalism: The Theoretical Roots of Confrontation," in *The Left Against Zion*, ed. R. Wistrich, London: Vallentine Mitchell, 1979, p. 1. Wistrich pointed out that many Eastern European Communist leaders opposed to Zionism were of Jewish origin.
65 Ibid., Ch. 1.
66 G. Goldman, *Zionism under Soviet Rule*, New York: Herzl Press, 1960, p. 15.
67 Vital, *Origins*, p. 298.
68 Z. Gitelman, *Jewish Nationality and Soviet Politics: The Jewish Sections of the CSPU, 1917–1930*, Princeton, NJ: Princeton University Press, 1972, pp. 75, 77.
69 Ibid, pp. 77–80.
70 Ibid., p. 78.
71 For an excellent discussion of the Evsektsiia, see Gitelman, *Jewish Nationality*.
72 Y. Gilboa, *The Black Years of Soviet Jewry*, trans. Y. Shacter and D. Ben Abba, Boston, MA: Little, Brown, 1971.
73 Gilbert, *Israel*, pp. 226–7.
74 Vaksberg, *Stalin against the Jews*, p. 197.

75 Bar-On, *Gates of Gaza*, p. 269.
76 J. Glassman, *Arms for the Arabs: The Soviet Union and the War in the Middle East*, Baltimore, MD: Johns Hopkins University Press, 1975.
77 Vaksberg, *Stalin against the Jews*, p. 112. A public opinion poll several years ago said that 64 percent of Russians would not vote for a Jewish president (compared to 5 percent in the United States).
78 Ibid., p. 120.
79 M. Oren, *Six Days of War: June 1967 and the Making of the Modern Middle East*, New York: Ballantine Books, 2003, pp. 27–9.
80 Ibid., pp. 115–19.
81 Glassman, *Arms for the Arabs*, Ch. 3; and Oren, *Six Days of War*, pp. 294–304.
82 Glassman, *Arms for the Arabs*, Ch. 4.
83 Ibid., Ch. 5.
84 Ibid., Ch. 6.
85 G. Golan, *Soviet Policies in the Middle East: From World War II to Gorbachev*, Cambridge: Cambridge University Press, 1990, Ch. 9.

6 Enmity of the Arab world and Iran

1 M. Oren, *Six Days of War: June 1967 and the Making of the Modern Middle East*, New York: Ballantine Books, 2003, p. 293.
2 Z. Maoz, *Defending the Holy Land: A Critical Analysis of Israel's Security and Foreign Policy*, Ann Arbor: University of Michigan Press, 2000, p. 5.
3 Robert Rotberg, *Israeli and Palestinian Narratives of Conflict: History's Double Helix*, Bloomington: Indiana University Press, 2006, pp. vii, 6, 180.
4 H. Ben-Yehuda and S. Sandler, *The Arab–Israeli Conflict Transformed: Fifty Years of Interstate and Ethnic Crises*, Albany: State University of New York Press, 2002, p. 93.
5 A. Kacowicz, Y. Ben-Siman-Tov, O. Elgstrom and M. Jerneck (eds.), *Stable Peace among Nations*, Lanham, MD: Rowman & Littlefield, 2000, pp. 220–30.
6 Ben-Yehuda and Sandler, *Arab–Israeli Conflict Transformed*, Ch. 1, pp. 181–95.
7 M. Bard, *Will Israel Survive?*, New York: Palgrave Macmillan, 2007.
8 Maoz, *Defending the Holy Land*, pp. 574–9.
9 B. Rubin, *The Long War for Freedom: The Arab Struggle for Democracy in the Middle East*, Hoboken, NJ: John Wiley & Sons, 2006, pp. 151–2.
10 A. Cordesman, *The Israeli–Palestinian War: Escalating to Nowhere*, Westport, CT: Greenwood Press, 2005, pp. 234–6.
11 M. Bar-On, *The Gates of Gaza: Israel's Road to Suez and Back, 1955–1957*, New York: St. Martin's Press, 1994, p. 210.
12 M. van Creveld, *The Sword and the Olive: A Critical History of the Israeli Defense Forces*, New York: Public Affairs Press, 1998, p. 66.
13 Ibid., p. 96; and Ben-Yehuda and Sandler, *Arab–Israeli Conflict Transformed*, p. 99.
14 Z. Schiff, *A History of the Israeli Army*, New York: Macmillan, 1985, Ch. 10; and M. Urofsky, *We Are One! American Jewry and Israel*, New York: Doubleday, 1978, pp. 159, 182.
15 Schiff, *History*, pp. 21–4; Y. Allon, *Shield of David*, New York: Random House, 1970, pp. 186–7; and van Creveld, *Sword and Olive*, p. 101.
16 E. Luttwak and D. Horowitz, *The Israeli Army 1948–1973*, Cambridge, MA: Abt Books, 1983, p. 124.
17 A. Ilan, *The Origins of the Arab–Israeli Arms Race: Arms, Embargo, Military Power and Decision in the 1948 Palestine War*, New York: New York University Press, 1996, Ch.2; and, for the broader issues, J. Adelman, *The Revolutionary Armies*, Westport, CT: Greenwood Press, 1980.

18 D. Tal, "The Forgotten War: Jewish–Palestinian Strife in Mandatory Palestine, December 1947-May 1948," in E. Karsh (ed.), *Israel: The First Hundred Years: From War to Peace?*, vol. 2, London: Frank Cass, 2000, pp. 9–17.

19 Luttwak and Horowitz, *Israeli Army*, Ch. 2.

20 Van Creveld, *Sword and Olive*, p. 78.

21 Schiff, *History*, pp. 24–6.

22 Ibid., pp. 26–31.

23 Ibid., pp. 39–45. The breakdown was as follows: 2,000 killed (November 1947 – May 1948), 1,200 killed (May 15, 1948 – June 10, 1948) and 2,500 killed (July 1948 – January 1949). No less than 4,500 of those killed were in the military and 1,200 were civilians. At Latrun 383 Israelis were killed. See van Creveld, *Sword and Olive*, pp. 98–9.

24 For the Russian and Chinese armies, see Adelman, *Revolutionary Armies*.

25 S. Helman, "Militarism and the Construction of the Life-World of Israeli Males," in *The Military and Militarism in Israeli Society*, ed. E. Lomsky-Feder and E. Ben-Ari, Albany: State University of New York Press, 1999, pp. 171–2.

26 Schiff, *History*, Ch. 5.

27 M. Golani, "The Limits of Interpretation and the Permissible in Historical Research Dealing with Israel's Security: A Reply to Bar-On and Morris," in *Traditions and Transitions in Israel Studies*, ed. L. Z. Eisenberg, N. Caplan, N. Sokoloff and M. Abu-Nimer, Albany: State University of New York Press, 2003, p. 28.

28 Ben-Yehuda and Sandler, *Arab–Israeli Conflict Transformed*, pp. 104–5.

29 Schiff, *History*, Ch. 6.

30 Ben-Yehuda and Sandler, *Arab–Israeli Conflict Transformed*, pp. 106–8.

31 Schiff, *History*, Ch. 9.

32 Allon, *Shield of David*, p. 258; and Oren, *Six Days of War*, pp. 304–5.

33 Schiff, *History*, Ch. 12.

34 Ben-Yehuda and Sandler, *Arab–Israeli Conflict Transformed*, p. 108.

35 Schiff, *History*, Ch. 14.

36 Ibid., Ch. 15.

37 R. Gal, "Organizational Complexity: Trust and Deceit in the Israeli Air Force," in *Military, State, and Society in Israel*, ed. D. Maman, E. Ben-Ari, and Z. Rosenhek, New Brunswick, NJ: Transaction Publishers, 2001, Ch. 13.

38 J. Lutz and B. Lutz, *Terrorism: Origins and Evolution*, New York: Palgrave Macmillan, 2005, p. 7.

39 Rubin, *Long War for Freedom*, p.181.

40 For an excellent overview of the history of the Palestinians and their current plight, see B. Kimmerling and J. Migdal, *The Palestinian People: A History*, Cambridge, MA: Harvard University Press, 2003.

41 Ibid., Ch. 4; and D. Divine, "The Imperialist Ties that Bind: Transjordan and the Yishuv," in *Israel, the Hashemites and the Palestinians: The Fateful Triangle*, ed. E. Karsh and P. R. Kumaraswamy, London: Frank Cass, 2003, p. 25.

42 I. Bickerton and C. Klausner, *A Concise History of the Arab–Israeli Conflict*, 4th edn., Upper Saddle River, NJ: Prentice Hall, 2002, pp. 55–6.

43 Kimmerling and Migdal, *Palestinian People*, pp. 154–65.

44 M. Gilbert, *The Routledge Atlas of the Arab–Israeli Conflict*, 8th edn., London: Routledge, 2005, p. 59.

45 Ibid., p. 276.

46 Gilbert, *Routledge Atlas of the Arab–Israeli Conflict*, pp. 72–9.

47 Kimmerling and Migdal, *Palestinian People*, p. 275.

48 Ibid., pp. 240–68.

49 Ibid., pp. 296–307.

50 A. Merari and S. Elad, *The International Dimensions of Palestinian Terrorism*,

Jerusalem: Jaffee Center for Strategic Studies Press, 1986; and Gilbert, *Routledge Atlas of the Arab–Israeli Conflict*, p. 99.

51 Of course in land the results were strikingly different. After Oslo II, the Palestinians had sole control of 3–4 percent of the territories, the Israelis still controlled 70 percent of the land with control of the Jordan Valley and settler areas and there was joint control of 27 percent of the territories. See Kimmerling and Migdal, *Palestinian People*, p. 332.

52 Ibid., pp. 332–54.

53 S. Shaq, *The Shahids: Islam and Suicide Attacks*, New Brunswick, NJ: Transaction Publishers, 2004, pp. xi–xv, Ch. 1, p. 54. Suicide attacks were not confined to Israel but occurred in Iraq, Syria, Sri Lanka, Chechnya, Tunisia, Kashmir, Afghanistan, Algeria and Egypt (Ch. 3).

54 Kimmerling and Migdal, *Palestinian People*, pp. 359–97.

55 A. Cordesman, *The Israeli–Palestinian War: Escalating to Nowhere*, Westport, CT: Greenwood Press, 2005, pp. 53–8.

56 S. Shaq, *Shahids*, pp. 12–22.

57 M. Levitt, *Hamas*, New Haven, CT: Yale University Press, 2006, pp. 20–2.

58 Ibid., pp. 53, 174–98.

59 Y. Alexander, *Palestinian Religious Terrorism: Hamas and Islamic Jihad*, Ardsley, NY: Transnational Publishers, 2002, pp. 1–34; and Levitt, *Hamas*, Ch. 1.

60 Levitt, *Hamas*, p. 6, Chs. 6–7.

61 Gilbert, *Routledge Atlas of the Arab–Israeli Conflict*, pp. 130, 165.

62 Ibid., p. 26.

63 A. Norton, *Hezbollah*, Princeton, NJ: Princeton University Press, 2007.

64 Cordesman, *Israeli–Palestinian War*, pp. 180–3.

65 A. Sarna, *Boycott and Blacklist: A History of Arab Economic Warfare against Israel*, Totowa, NJ: Rowman & Littlefield, 1986, p. 190.

66 Ibid., Ch. 12.

67 Ibid., pp. 4–69. Arab boycott activity against Palestinian Jews started in the 1890s and in places like Haifa was implemented as early as 1910. For this aspect and the numbers in 1970 in the Boycott Office, see G. Feiler, *From Boycott to Economic Cooperation: The Political Economy of the Arab Boycott of Israel*, London: Frank Cass, 1998, pp. x, 21.

68 Sarna, *Boycott and Blacklist*, pp. 46–51; and Feiler, *From Boycott to Economic Cooperation*, pp. 26–7.

69 Sarna, *Boycott and Blacklist*, Ch. 11.

70 Ibid., pp. 144–53; and Feiler, *From Boycott to Economic Cooperation*, pp. 209–19.

71 Sarna, *Boycott and Blacklist*, Ch. 10.

72 Ibid., pp. 51, 81–113.

73 Feiler, *From Boycott to Economic Cooperation*, pp. 49–60, 281–8.

74 Ibid., pp. 118–29.

75 Sarna, *Boycott and Blacklist*, pp. 58–72; Feiler, *From Boycott to Economic Cooperation*, p. 280. The Central Boycott Office estimated the cost to Israel at over $100 billion (Feiler, *From Boycott to Economic Cooperation*, p. 282).

76 Ben-Yehuda and Sandler, *Arab–Israeli Conflict Transformed*, p. 111.

77 A. Klieman, *Statecraft in the Dark: Israel's Practice of Quiet Diplomacy*, Boulder, CO: Westview Press, 1988, p. 6.

7 Major international and religious organizations

1 P. Merkley, *Christian Attitudes towards the State of Israel*, Montreal: McGill-Queen's University Press, 2001, p. 220.

2 The Church was indeed responsible for saving some Jews but there was no strong

Catholic stance against the Holocaust that might have saved millions of Jews in World War II.

3 A. Kenny, *Catholics, Jews and the State of Israel*, New York: Paulist Press, 1993, pp. 1–19.

4 G. Irani, "The Holy See and the Israeli–Palestinian Conflict," in *The Vatican, Islam and the Middle East*, ed. K. Ellis, Syracuse, NY: Syracuse University Press, 1987.

5 F. Khouri, "The Jerusalem Question and the Vatican," in *The Vatican, Islam and the Middle East*, ed. K. Ellis, Syracuse, NY: Syracuse University Press, 1987.

6 S. Minerbi, *The Vatican and Zionism: Conflict in the Holy Land 1895–1925*, trans. A. Schwarz, New York: Oxford University Press, 1990, p. 97.

7 Ibid., p. 97; and Merkley, *Christian Attitudes*, p. 138.

8 A. Kreutz, *Vatican Policy on the Palestinian–Israeli Conflict: The Struggle for the Holy Land*, Westport, CT: Greenwood Press, 1990, p. 33; and Minerbi, *Vatican and Zionism*, p. 100.

9 Kreutz, *Vatican Policy*, pp. 33–40; and Minerbi, *Vatican and Zionism*, p. 131.

10 Minerbi, *Vatican and Zionism*, pp. 158, 165; and Kreutz, *Vatican Policy*, pp. 40–1.

11 Minerbi, *Vatican and Zionism*, p. 181.

12 Kreutz, *Vatican Policy*, pp. 49, 60–1, 69.

13 Ibid., pp. 77–80; and Merkley, *Christian Attitudes*, p. 139.

14 Merkley, *Christian Attitudes*, pp. 149, 147.

15 A. Lopez, "Israel's Relations with the Vatican," in *Jerusalem Letter*, Jerusalem: Jerusalem Center for Public Affairs, March 1999.

16 Merkley, *Christian Attitudes*, pp. 147–8, 157.

17 Kreutz, *Vatican Policy*, Ch. 7, especially p. 138.

18 Ibid., Ch. 8.

19 Y. Manor, *To Right a Wrong: The Revocation of the UN General Assembly Resolution 3379 Defaming Zionism*, New York: Shengold Publishers, 1996, p. 273.

20 Merkley, *Christian Attitudes*, pp. 151–9.

21 M. Breger and G. Weigel, "Special Policy Forum Report: The Vatican and the Middle East – Pope John Paul II's Trip to the Holy Land," in *Peace Watch*, 250, Washington, D.C.: Washington Institute for Near East Policy, March 17, 2000.

22 H. Genizi, *The Holocaust, Israel and Canadian Protestant Churches*, Montreal: McGill-Queen's University Press, 2002, pp. 3–5.

23 Few Arabs actually converted to Christianity and specifically Protestantism. In 1954 only 4 percent of the Christians in Israel (or 1,700 people) were Protestants. See Uri Bialer, *Cross on the Star of David: The Christian World in Israel's Foreign Policy, 1948–1967*, Bloomington: Indiana University Press, 2005, p. 125.

24 H. Fishman, *American Protestantism and a Jewish State*, Detroit, MI: Wayne State University Press, 1973, p. 176.

25 Ibid., pp. 21–6.

26 Ibid., Ch. 1, especially p. 28.

27 Ibid., pp. 31–2, 37, 41, 43, 49.

28 Ibid., Ch. 6.

29 Ibid., Chs. 8, 9.

30 Ibid., Ch. 6, especially pp. 154–5.

31 Ibid., Ch. 11.

32 Ibid., pp. 172–5.

33 Genizi, *Holocaust, Israel and Canadian Protestant Churches*, pp. 8–11; and Merkley, *Christian Attitudes*, Ch. 8.

34 Genizi, *Holocaust, Israel and Canadian Protestant Churches*, pp. 10–15.

35 E. Nelson and A. Wisdom, *Human Rights Advocacy in Mainline Protestant Churches (2000–2003)*, Washington, D.C.: Institute on Religion and Democracy, 2004, p. 27.

36 Ibid. pp. 27–30.
37 G. Falk, *The Restoration of Israel: Christian Zionism in Religion, Literature and Politics*, New York: Peter Lang, 2006, p. 194.
38 R. Stockton, "Presbyterians, Jews and Divestment: The Church Steps Back," *Middle East Policy*, 13 (4), Winter 2006: 102–24.
39 Merkley, *Christian Attitudes*, pp. 126–32; and Pew Global Attitudes poll, 2006.
40 Merkley, *Christian Attitudes*, pp. 110–26.
41 R. Israeli, *Fundamentalist Islam and Israel*, Lanham, MD: University Press of America, 1993, Ch. 4.
42 A. Beker, *The United Nations and Israel: From Recognition to Reprehension*, Lexington, MA: Lexington Books, 1988, pp. 82–3.
43 Manor, *To Right a Wrong*, pp. 6–7, 16.
44 Ibid., pp. 1–3.
45 Ibid., pp. 236–61.

8 Western unwillingness to help Israel in crises

1 S. Spiegel, *The Other Arab–Israeli Conflict: Making America's Middle East Policy, from Truman to Reagan*, Chicago: University of Chicago Press, 1985, Ch. 1.
2 M. Urofsky, *American Zionism from Herzl to the Holocaust*, New York: Doubleday, 1975, pp. 216, 229.
3 A. Beker, *The United Nations and Israel: From Recognition to Reprehension*, Lexington, MA: Lexington Books, 1988, p. 27.
4 M. Penkower, *The Holocaust and Israel Reborn*, Chicago: University of Illinois Press, 1994, p. 227.
5 B. Halpern, *The Idea of the Jewish State*, Cambridge, MA: Harvard University Press, 1969, p. 377.
6 W. Louis, *The British Empire in the Middle East 1945–1951*, Oxford: Oxford University Press, 1984, p. 518.
7 Ibid., Chs. 6–8; and A. Oren, "Inside Track: A Disaster Waiting to Happen," *Haaretz*, October 22, 2004.
8 Halpern, *Idea of the Jewish State*, p. 377.
9 H. Eshed, *Reuven Shiloah: The Man behind the Mossad*, trans. D. Zinder and L. Zinder, London: Frank Cass, 1997, pp. 148–9.
10 Ibid., p. 103.
11 Halpern, *Idea of the Jewish State*, p. 425.
12 M. Oren, *Six Days of War: June 1967 and the Making of the Modern Middle East*, New York: Ballantine Books, 2003, pp. 8–10; Eshed, *Reuven Shiloah*, pp. 221–2; and M. Urofsky, *We Are One! American Jewry and Israel*, New York: Doubleday, 1978, p. 306.
13 H. Ben-Yehuda and S. Sandler, *The Arab–Israel Conflict Transformed: Fifty Years of Interstate and Ethnic Crises*, Albany: State University of New York Press, 2002, p. 102.
14 A. Ilan, *The Origins of the Arab–Israeli Arms Race: Arms, Embargo, Military Power and Decision in the 1948 Palestine War*, New York: New York University Press, 1996, p. 1.
15 M. Bar-On, "Seeking a War?," in *Traditions and Transitions in Israel Studies*, ed. L. Z. Eisenberg, N Caplan, N. Sokoloff and M. Abu-Nimer, Albany: State University of New York Press, 2003, p. 7.
16 M. Bar-On, *The Gates of Gaza: Israel's Road to Suez and Back, 1955–1957*, New York: St. Martin's Press, 1994, pp. 141, 152.
17 Ibid.
18 Halpern, *Idea of the Jewish State*, pp. 426–30; and Urofsky, *We Are One!*, pp. 313–17.

19 Eshed, *Reuven Shiloah*, p. 298.
20 Halpern, *Idea of the Jewish State*, pp. 431–9; and Oren, *Six Days of War*, p. 51.
21 Oren, *Six Days of War*, pp. 112–13, 138–9, 157.
22 J. Nitzan and S. Bichler, *The Global Political Economy of Israel*, London: Pluto Press, 2002, p. 247.
23 Spiegel, *Other Arab–Israeli Conflict*, p. 387.
24 S. Avineri, "Israel: A Normative Value of Jewish Existence," in *The Blackwell Reader in Judaism*, ed. J. Neusner and A. Avery-Peck, Oxford: Blackwell, 2001, p. 400.
25 C. Roth, *The Jewish Contribution to Civilization*, Cincinnati, OH: Union of American Hebrew Congregations, 1940, pp. 37–9.
26 M. Gilbert, *The Routledge Atlas of Jewish History*, New York: William Morrow and Company, 1993, p. 57.
27 Ibid., pp. 38, 43.
28 Ibid., pp. 46–8.
29 P. Johnson, *A History of the Jews*, New York: Harper & Row, 1987, p. 242.
30 Gilbert, *Routledge Atlas of Jewish History*, p. 58.
31 Ibid., p. 49.
32 Johnson, *History*, p. 309.
33 Gilbert, *Routledge Atlas of Jewish History*, p. 58.
34 K. Marx, *On the Jewish Question*, trans. H. Lederer, Cincinnati, OH: Hebrew Union College – Jewish Institute of Religion, 1958, pp. 39, 40, 42.
35 Johnson, *History*, p. 382.
36 Z. Gitelman, *Jewish Nationality and Soviet Politics: The Jewish Sections of the CSPU, 1917–1930*, Princeton, NJ: Princeton University Press, 1972, pp. 161–2.
37 See my new book, J. Adelman (ed.), *Hitler and His Allies in World War I*, London: Routledge, 2007, for more details.
38 H. Evans, *The American Century*, New York: Alfred Knopf, 1998, p. 289.
39 R. Atkinson, *An Army at Dawn: The War in North Africa, 1942–1943*, New York: Henry Holt, 2002, p. 288.
40 H. Sachar, *A History of Israel: From the Rise of Zionism to Our Time*, 2nd edn., New York: Alfred A. Knopf, 2002, Ch. 12.

9 Israeli issues

1 J. Parkes, *A History of Palestine from 135 A.D. to Modern Times*, New York: Oxford University Press, 1949, p. 363.
2 J. Migdal, *Through the Lens of Israel*, Albany: State University of New York Press, 2001, Ch. 6.
3 E. Luttwak and D. Horowitz, *The Israeli Army 1948–1973*, Cambridge, MA: Abt Books, 1983, p. 301. By the end of the war Israeli forces were only 25 miles from Amman, 31 miles from Damascus (occupying the high ground) and 250 miles from Cairo.
4 I. Black and B. Morris, *Israel's Secret Wars*, New York: Grove Weidenfeld, 1991, Ch. 4.
5 I. Galnoor, *The Partition of Palestine: Decision Crossroads in the Zionist Movement*, Albany: State University of New York Press, 1995, p. 27.
6 G. Biger, "The Boundaries of Mandatory Palestine: How the Past Influences the Future," in *Israel: The First Hundred Years: Israel's Transition from Community to State*, vol. 1, ed. E. Karsh, London: Frank Cass, 2000, p. 109; and D. Newman, "Controlling Territory: Spatial Dimensions of Social and Political Change in Israel," in *Traditions and Transitions in Israel Studies*, ed. L. Z. Eisenberg, N. Caplan, N. Sokoloff and M. Abu-Nimer, Albany: State University of New York Press, 2003, pp. 71–5.

7 C. Shindler, "Likud and the Search for Eretz Israel: From the Bible to the Twenty-First Century," in *Israel: The First Hundred Years: Israeli Politics and Society since 1948: Problems of Collective Identity*, vol. 3, ed. E. Karsh, London: Frank Cass, 2000, pp. 93–8.

8 B. Reich and G. Kieval (eds.), *Israeli National Security: Political Actors and Perspectives*, Westport, CT: Greenwood Press, 1988, pp. 1–2.

9 M. Levin, *It Takes a Dream: The Story of Hadassah*, Jerusalem: Gefen Publishing House, 2002, p. 263.

10 H. Sachar, *A History of Israel: From the Rise of Zionism to Our Time*, 2nd edn., New York: Alfred Knopf, 2002, p. 117.

11 A. Alesina and E. Spolaore, *The Size of Nations*, Cambridge, MA: MIT Press, 2003, pp. 3–4, 14, 81–2, 155.

12 Y. Lifshitz, *The Economics of Producing Defense Illustrated by the Israeli Case*, Boston, MA: Kluwer Academic Press, 2003, p. 59.

13 Ibid., p. 42.

14 J. Nitzan and S. Bichler, *The Global Political Economy of Israel*, London: Pluto Press, 2002, pp. 217, 259.

15 I. Troen, *Imagining Zion*, New Haven, CT: Yale University Press, 2003, p. 123.

16 B. Kimmerling, *Zionism and Economy*, Cambridge, MA: Schenkman Publishing, 1983, p. ix.

17 Ibid., p. 149.

18 B. Kimmerling, *Zionism and Territory: The Socio-Territorial Dimensions of Zionist Politics*, Berkeley: University of California Press, 1983, p. 12; and Parkes, *History*, p. 302.

19 Kimmerling, *Zionism and Territory*, p. 24. While in 1947 the Jews owned 14 percent of non-desert Palestine, by the early 1960s they owned 95 percent of the land (p. 100).

20 D. Horowitz, "Before the State: Communal Politics in Palestine under the Mandate," in *The Israeli State and Society: Boundaries and Frontiers*, ed. B. Kimmerling, Albany: State University of New York Press, 1989, p. 54.

21 M. Gilbert, *Israel: A History*, New York: William Morrow and Company, 1998, pp. 3, 9.

22 A. Arian, *The Second Republic: Politics in Israel*, Chatham, NJ: Chatham House Publishers, 1998, p. 3.

23 Parkes, *History*, p. 302.

24 S. Teveth, *Ben Gurion: The Burning Ground 1886–1948*, Boston, MA: Houghton Mifflin, 1987, p. 120.

25 Kimmerling, *Zionism and Territory*, p. 87.

26 Horowitz, "Before the State," p. 55; and Kimmerling, *Zionism and Territory*, p. 21.

27 M. Barnett, "Israel in the World Economy: Israel as an East Asian State?," in *Israel in Comparative Perspective*, ed. M. Barnett, Albany: State University of New York Press, 1996, p. 119.

28 M. Urofsky, *We Are One! American Jewry and Israel*, New York: Doubleday, 1978, p. 275.

29 Troen, *Imagining Zion*, p. 258.

30 Ibid., Ch. 1, p. 198.

31 Ibid., pp. 15–198.

32 Urofsky, *We Are One!*, pp. 195–8.

33 Ibid., p. 196.

34 Troen, *Imagining Zion*, Ch. 4.

35 Ibid., Ch. 2.

36 Ibid., p. 99.

37 Kimmerling, *Zionism and Territory*, p. 49.

38 Horowitz, "Before the State," p. 54.
39 Kimmerling, *Zionism and Economy*, p. 114.

10 Historical roots of the revolutions

1 A. Hertzberg (ed.), *The Zionist Idea: A Historical Analysis and Reader*, New York: Atheneum, 1959, p. 20.
2 N. de Lange and M. Freud-Kandel (eds.), *Modern Judaism: An Oxford Guide*, Oxford: Oxford University Press, 2005, pp. 55–6.
3 Indeed, until 1944, the majority of eminent rabbis fought Zionism while the ultra-Orthodox Haredim, condemning Zionism as "apostasy and heresy," saw David Ben Gurion as ominous and malevolent. See Y. Rabkin, *A Threat from Within: A Century of Jewish Opposition to Zionism*, Black Point, Nova Scotia: Fernwood Press, 2006, p. 152; A. Ravitzky, *Messianism, Zionism and Jewish Religious Radicalism*, Chicago, IL: University of Chicago Press, 1993, pp. 37–8, 182; and Y. Salmon, *Religion and Zion: First Encounters*, Jerusalem: Hebrew University Press, 2002.
4 J. Reinharz, "Zionism and Orthodoxy: A Marriage of Convenience," and especially S. Avineri, "Zionism and the Jewish Religious Tradition," in S. Almog, J. Reinharz and A. Shapira, *Zionism and Religion*, Hanover, NH: Brandeis University Press, 1998, pp. xi, 1–7.
5 E. Ottolenghi, "A National Home," in *Modern Judaism: An Oxford Guide*, ed. N. de Lange and M. Freud-Kandel, Oxford: Oxford University Press, 2005, p. 54. See also S. Almog, J. Reinharz and A. Shapira (eds.), *Zionism and Religion*, Hanover, NH: Brandeis University Press, 1998; and J. Neusner, *Judaism: The Basics*, London: Routledge, 2006.
6 D. Schwartz, *Faith at a Crossroads: A Theological Profile of Religious Zionism*, trans. B. Stein, Leiden: Brill, 2002.
7 B. Neuberger, "Zionism," www.mfa.gov.il.
8 R. Wisse, "Israel's Answer to the Zionist Dream," speech, Bar Ilan University, Ramat Gan, Israel, June 2003.
9 H. Sachar, *A History of Israel: From the Rise of Zionism to Our Time*, 2nd edn., New York: Alfred Knopf, 2002, p. 5. Sachar points out that the string of false messiahs had until the nineteenth century soured Eastern European Jewry on any immediate efforts to redeem the Holy Land.
10 See Neuberger, "Zionism," for much of the following material.
11 See www.jhom.com (Jewish Heritage Online Magazine).
12 Michael Walzer points out that this story "resumes in the modern period: from Bar Kokhba to Joseph Trumpeldor with not much in between" and that the survival of the Jews in the Diaspora is more than suffering and persecution, for "the real exilic story is not one of persecution and exile (though there was enough of that) but survival over many centuries, across many countries; and it is a remarkable story of political adaptability, innovation and collective stubbornness." See M. Walzer, "History and National Liberation," in *Israeli Historical Revisionism: From Left to Right*, ed. A. Shapira and D. Penslar, London: Frank Cass, 2003, pp. 2–3.
13 Sachar, *History*, Ch. 2.
14 S. Avineri, *The Making of Modern Zionism: The Intellectual Origins of the Jewish State*, New York: Basic Books, 1981, p. 34.
15 B. Halpern, *The Idea of the Jewish State*, Cambridge, MA: Harvard University Press, 1969, p. 5.
16 Hertzberg, *Zionist Idea*, pp. 33–40; and Halpern, *Idea of the Jewish State*, pp. 50–8.
17 H. Graetz, *History of the Jews*, Philadelphia, PA: Jewish Publications Society, 1967.
18 Avineri, *Making of Modern Zionism*, p.35.

19 Moses (Moshe) Hess, who co-edited the radical *Rheinische Zeitung* with Karl Marx, was called by Marx "my communist rabbi." See Avineri, *Making of Modern Zionism*, p. 37.

20 Neuberger, "Zionism."

21 Avineri, *Making of Modern Zionism*, Ch. 4.

22 Hertzberg, *Zionist Idea*, p. 114.

23 Ibid., Introduction.

24 S. M. Rubinstein, *The Communist Movement in Palestine and Israel, 1919–1984*, Boulder, CO: Westview Press, 1984, p. 33.

25 Avineri, *Making of Modern Zionism*, Chs. 5–6.

26 Ibid., Ch. 7, and especially p. 81.

27 D. Vital, *The Origins of Zionism*, Oxford: Oxford University Press, 1975, Ch. 6.

28 E. B. Yehuda, "A Letter to the Editor of Hashahar," in *The Zionist Idea: A Historical Analysis and Reader*, ed. A. Hertzberg, New York: Atheneum, 1959, p. 164.

29 Avineri, *Making of Modern Zionism*, Ch. 9; Hertzberg, *Zionist Idea*, pp. 72–3; and D. Penslar, *Zionism and Technocracy: The Engineering of Jewish Settlement in Palestine, 1870–1918*, Bloomington: Indiana University Press, 1991, p. 48.

30 Avineri, *Making of Modern Zionism*, p. 45 and Ch. 3.

31 Hertzberg, *Zionist Idea*, p. 73.

32 Avineri, *Making of Modern Zionism*, p. 108.

33 Ibid., p. 135.

34 Hertzberg, *Zionist Idea*, p. 78.

35 Ibid., p. 154.

36 Ibid., Ch. 16.

37 For a good overview of the subject, see A. Lindemann, *Esau's Tears: Modern Anti-Semitism and the Rise of the Jews*, Cambridge: Cambridge University Press, 1997, Ch. 13.

38 E. Mendelsohn, *Class Struggle in the Pale: The Formative Years of the Jewish Workers' Movement in Tsarist Russia*, Cambridge: Cambridge University Press, 1970, p. 156. Perhaps one reason for such high political consciousness among only 3 percent of the Russian population was that, while in 1897 60 percent of the Russian working class was illiterate, such illiteracy was quite rare among the Jewish workers (p. 157).

39 Z. Gitelman, *Jewish Nationality and Soviet Politics: The Jewish Sections of the CPSU, 1917–1930*, Princeton, NJ: Princeton University Press, 1972, p. 16. Lenin, personally free of anti-Semitism, had a number of Jewish deputies (Trotsky, Zinoviev, Kamenev).

40 R. Brym, *The Jewish Intelligentsia and Russian Marxism: A Sociological Study of Intellectual Radicalism and Ideological Diversity*, New York: Schocken Books, 1978.

41 Gitelman, *Jewish Nationality*, p. 106.

42 Laqueur, *A History of Zionism*, London: Weidenfeld & Nicolson, 1972, p. 420.

43 W. McCagg, Jr., "Jews in Revolutions: The Hungarian Experience," *Journal of Social History*, 6 (1), Fall 1972: 77–105; and R. Burks, *The Dynamics of Communism in Eastern Europe*, Princeton, NJ: Princeton University Press, 1961, p. 162. McCagg explains the prominence of Jews by their primary role as urban modernizers in a transitional society.

44 M. Gilbert, *From the Ends of the Earth: The Jews in the 20th Century*, London: Cassell, 2001, pp. 106–8.

45 Burks, *Dynamics of Communism*, pp. 158–70.

46 In addition, the majority of them were men who were not born in the Jewish Pale or lacked any real identity with the Jewish community. See Gitelman, *Jewish Nationality*, p. 109.

47 J. Talmon, *Israel among the Nations*, New York: Macmillan, 1970, p. 79. Isaac Deutscher depicted the fate of alienated Jewish radicals (both political radicals and others, such as Spinoza, Heine and Freud), vulnerable to religious fanaticism or extreme nationalism: "They were excommunicated by Jewish rabbis; they were persecuted by Christian priests; they were hunted down by the gendarmes of absolute rulers and by the soldateska; they were hated by pseudo-democratic philistines; and they were expelled by their own parties. Nearly all of them were exiled from their countries; and the writings of all were burned at the stake at one time or another." See I. Deutscher, *The Non-Jewish Jew and Other Essays*, London: Oxford University Press, 1968, p. 34.

48 V. Lenin, *What Is to Be Done? Burning Questions of Our Movement*, New York: International Publishers, 1929.

49 P. Johnson, *A History of the Jews*, New York: Harper & Row, 1987, p. 448.

50 Deutscher, *Non-Jewish Jew*, pp. 97–8.

51 B. Halpern and J. Reinharz, *Zionism and the Creation of a New Society*, New York: Oxford University Press, 1998, p. 44.

52 See L. Schapiro, "The Role of the Jews in the Russian Revolutionary Movement," *Slavonic and East European Review*, 40: 148–67, especially pp. 164–5.

11 Two modern Zionist revolutions

1 T. Skocpol, *States and Social Revolutions*, Cambridge: Cambridge University Press, 1979, pp. 161–2.

2 S. M. Lipset, *The First New Nation: The United States in Historical and Comparative Perspective*, New York: Basic Books, 1963.

3 J. Talmon, *Israel among the Nations*, New York: Macmillan, 1970, pp. 159–60.

4 N. Sharanksy, "The Political Legacy of Theodor Herzl," in *New Essays on Zionism*, ed. D. Hazony, Y. Hazony and M. Oren, Jerusalem: Shalem Press, 2006, pp. 105–12.

5 S. Avineri, *The Making of Modern Zionism: The Intellectual Origins of the Jewish State*, New York: Basic Books, 1981, pp. 13, 226.

6 D. Penslar, *Zionism and Technocracy: The Engineering of Jewish Settlement in Palestine, 1870–1918*, Bloomington: Indiana University Press, 1991, pp. 1, 7.

7 D. Vital, *The Origins of Zionism*, Oxford: Oxford University Press, 1975, p. 373.

8 J. Reinharz, "Zionism and Orthodoxy," in *Zionism and Religion*, ed. S. Almog, J. Reinharz and A. Shapira, Hanover: Brandeis University Press, 1998, p. 116. Only the rise of modern nationalism, early decay of the traditional community, modernizing tendencies and the blocking of Jewish integration into civil society opened the door for modern Zionism at the end of the nineteenth century.

9 D. Myers, *Re-inventing the Jewish Past*, New York: Oxford University Press, 1996, pp. 90, 102.

10 I. Troen, *Imagining Zion*, New Haven, CT: Yale University Press, 2003, p. 113. Tel Aviv, which was founded by 60 merchants and professionals in 1906 forming a private building society to build a Jewish suburb of Jaffa, was an amazing success. From no people in 1908, it rocketed to 3,000 people in 1920, 150,000 people in 1939 and 2.4 million people today in the metropolitan area, replete with modernity and sophistication.

11 Penslar, *Zionism and Technocracy*, p. 7.

12 A. Shapira, "The Religious Motifs of the Labor Movement," in *Zionism and Religion*, ed. S. Almog, J. Reinharz and A. Shapira, Hanover: Brandeis University Press, 1998, pp. 254–6.

13 A. Ravitzky, "Munkacs and Jerusalem: Ultra-Orthodox Opposition to Zionism and Aggudism," in *Zionism and Religion*, ed. S. Almog, J. Reinharz and A. Shapira, Hanover: Brandeis University Press, 1998, p. 81.

14 Myers, *Re-Inventing the Jewish Past*, p. 76.
15 Ibid.
16 A. Smith, "Sacred Territories and National Conflict," in *Israel: The First Hundred Years: Israel's Transition from Community to State*, vol. 1, ed. E. Karsh, London: Frank Cass, 2000, pp. 13–29.
17 A. Dowty, *The Jewish State: A Century Later*, Berkeley: University of California Press, 1998, pp. 50–60.
18 Ibid., p. 55.
19 J. Nitzan and S. Bichler, *The Global Political Economy of Israel*, London: Pluto Press, 2002, pp. 17–20, 92, 108.
20 R. Hazan and M. Maor (eds.), *Parties, Elections and Cleavages: Israel in Comparative and Theoretical Perspective*, London: Frank Cass, 2000, pp. 151–4, 174–8; and J. Migdal, *Through the Lens of Israel*, Albany: State University of New York Press, 2001, pp. 110–12.
21 Nitzan and Bichler, *Global Political Economy*, p. 137.
22 Ibid., pp. 96–7.
23 M. Barnett, "Israel in the World Economy: Israel as an East Asian State?," in *Israel in Comparative Perspective*, ed. M. Barnett, Albany: State University of New York Press, 1996, p. 122.
24 Nitzan and Bichler, *Global Political Economy*, pp. 98, 354.
25 Ibid., p. 351.
26 Barnett, "Israel in the World Economy," p. 120.
27 W. Laqueur, *A History of Zionism*, London: Weidenfeld & Nicolson, 1972, p. 325.
28 Nitzan and Bichler, *Global Political Economy*, pp. 134–5; and Barnett, "Israel in the World Economy," p. 130.
29 Dowty, *Jewish State*, pp. 67–75.
30 Barnett, "Israel in the World Economy," p. 120.
31 Nitzan and Bichler, *Global Political Economy*, p. 27.
32 Ibid., pp. 117–22.
33 Ibid., pp. 276–8.
34 Ibid., pp. 98–101, 122–9; and Barnett, "Israel in the World Economy," p. 131.
35 G. Sheffer, "Political Change and Party System Transformation," in *Parties, Elections and Cleavages: Israel in Comparative and Theoretical Perspective*, ed. R. Hazan and M. Maor, London: Frank Cass, 2000, pp. 156–61.
36 Barnett, "Israel in the World Economy," pp. 125–6.
37 Ibid.
38 M. Aronoff, "Wars as Catalysts of Political and Cultural Change," in *The Military and Militarism in Israeli Society*, ed. E. Lomsky-Feder and E. Ben-Ari, Albany: State University of New York Press, 1999, p. 41.
39 Dowty, *Jewish State*, pp. 124–6.
40 Ibid., p. 127.
41 B. Kimmerling, *Zionism and Economy*, Cambridge, MA: Schenkman Publishing, 1983, p. 133; and Nitzan and Bichler, *Global Political Economy*, Ch. 6, p. 133.
42 Sheffer, "Political Change," pp. 156–62; and Dowty, *Jewish State*, Ch. 6.
43 Dowty, *Jewish State*, p. 130.
44 A. Arian, *The Second Republic: Politics in Israel*, Chatham, NJ: Chatham House Publishers, 1998, pp. 15, 67.
45 Sheffer, "Political Change," pp. 162–5.
46 Nitzan and Bichler, *Global Political Economy*, p. 274.
47 Ibid., pp. 16–17, 354.
48 Ibid., p. 85.
49 Ibid., p. 88.
50 M. van Creveld, *The Sword and the Olive: A Critical History of the Israel Defense Forces*, New York: Public Affairs Press, 1998, p. 63. The Irgun was so small that in

December 1944 it had only 500 fighters with 60 pistols, 40 hand guns and 2,000 kilos of explosive (A. Perlmutter, *The Life and Times of Menachem Begin*, Garden City, NY: Doubleday, 1987, p. 157). Owing to its attacks that killed many civilians and its nationalist ideology, the Irgun remained controversial for decades. David Ben Gurion refused to sit in the Knesset with only two factions: Communists and Irgun. See Y. Ben-Ami, *Years of Wrath, Days of Glory: Memoirs of the Irgun*, New York: Robert Speller & Sons, 1982; G. Rothenberg, *Anatomy of the Israeli Army: The Israel Defense Forces 1948–1978*, New York: Hippocrene Books, 1979, p. 34; S. Sofer, *Begin: An Anatomy of Leadership*, Oxford: Blackwell, 1988, Ch. 4; and Perlmutter, *Life and Times of Menachem Begin*.

51 Van Creveld, *Sword and Olive*, p. 60.

12 Revolutionary military-security factors

1 N. Rotenstreich, "The Present-Day Relationship," in *The Blackwell Reader in Judaism*, ed. J. Neusner and A. Avery-Peck, Oxford: Blackwell, 2001, p. 400.

2 M. van Creveld, *The Sword and the Olive: A Critical History of the Israeli Defense Forces*, New York: Public Affairs, 1998, p. 125.

3 F. Nietzsche, *The Will to Power*, New York: Vintage Books, 1968.

4 A. Peled, *A Question of Loyalty: Military Manpower Policy in Multiethnic States*, New York: Cornell University Press, 1998, p. xvi.

5 D. Raviv and Y. Melman, *Every Spy a Prince: The Complete History of Israel's Intelligence Community*, Boston, MA: Houghton Mifflin, 1990, p. 1.

6 D. Vital, *The Survival of Small States: Studies in Small Power/Great Power Conflict*, London: Oxford University Press, 1971, Ch. 2.

7 Z. Schiff, *A History of the Israeli Army*, New York: Macmillan, 1985, p. 32.

8 M. Gilbert, *Israel: A History*, New York: William Morrow and Company, 1998, p. 249.

9 For a full account of the battle, see M. Larkin, *The Six Days of Yad-Mordechai*, Givatayim: Peli Printing, 1975.

10 Ibid.

11 Schiff, *History*, p. 34.

12 J. Burk, "From Wars of Independence to Democratic Peace: Comparing the Cases of Israel and the United States," in *Military, State, and Society in Israel*, ed. D. Maman, E. Ben-Ari and Z. Rosenhek, New Brunswick, NJ: Transaction Publishers, 2001, pp. 97–8.

13 J. Migdal, *Through the Lens of Israel*, Albany: State University of New York Press, 2001, p. 88.

14 C. Tilly, *Coercion, Capital and European States, A.D. 990–1990*, Cambridge, MA: Blackwell, 1990.

15 J. Mearsheimer, *The Tragedy of Great Power Politics*, New York: W.W. Norton, 2001, pp. 2–3.

16 M. Handel, *Israel's Political-Military Doctrine*, Occasional Paper 30, Cambridge, MA: Harvard University Center for International Affairs, July 1973.

17 A. Beker, *The United Nations and Israel: From Recognition to Reprehension*, Lexington, MA: Lexington Books, 1988, p. 37.

18 B. Rubin, *Assimilation and its Discontents*, New York: Random House, 1995, p. 115.

19 H. Kissinger, *White House Years*, Boston, MA: Little, Brown, 1979, p. 583.

20 A. Mintz, "The Military-Industrial Complex: The Israeli Case," in *Israeli Society and its Defense Establishment*, ed. M. Lissak, London: Frank Cass, 1984, pp. 115–24.

21 T. Skocpol, "Social Revolutions and Mass Military Mobilizations," *World Politics*, 60 (2), 1988.

22 See J. Adelman, *The Revolutionary Armies*, Westport, CT: Greenwood Press, 1980.

23 Y. Peri, "Party–Military Relations in a Pluralist System," in *Israeli Society and its Defense Establishment*, ed. M. Lissak, London: Frank Cass, 1984, pp. 46–7.

24 E. Luttwak and D. Horowitz, *The Israeli Army 1948–1973*, Cambridge: Abt Books, 1983, pp. vi–vii.

25 S. Helman, "Militarism and the Construction of the Life-World of Israeli Males," in *The Military and Militarism in Israeli Society*, ed. E. Lomsky-Feder and E. Ben-Ari, Albany: State University of New York Press, 1999, pp. 207, 213.

26 M. Cohen, *Zion and State: Nation, Class and the Shaping of Modern Israel*, New York: Columbia University Press, 1992, p. 183.

27 A. Bar-Or, "The Link between the Government and the IDF during Israel's First 50 Years: The Shifting Role of the Defense Minister," in *Military, State, and Society in Israel*, ed. D. Maman, E. Ben-Ari and Z. Rosenhek, New Brunswick, NJ: Transaction Publishers, 2001, p. 324.

28 Helman, "Militarism and the Construction of the Life-World of Israeli Males," p. 196.

29 Schiff, *History*, Chs. 7–8.

30 Gadna (youth battalions) involve most Israeli boys and girls from 14 to 18 in military drills, basic instruction in handling arms and map reading, touring Israel on camp excursions. Youth wear military uniforms but do not hold rank. Gadna was founded in 1940 as a part of Haganah. Tens of thousands of youth were enrolled in Gadna during the War of Independence and some fought in the battles for Jerusalem and Haifa. After 1948 it became part of the military and in 1954 was structured as a nationwide command with six special training camps. In the schools the Ministry of Education runs the units with IDF officers as advisers. During the 1967 and 1973 wars Gadna members served as orderlies in the hospitals, took the place of mobilized postal workers and aided in maintaining basic civilian services. Gadna also works to integrate juvenile delinquents into the army and society. See Schiff, *History*, pp. 100–4.

31 Luttwak and Horowitz, *Israeli Army*, p. 183.

32 For a good description of the mixed agricultural–military units formed formally in 1948, see Schiff, *History*, Ch. 4. The parallel with the Chinese Army's Production Corps is striking. See Adelman, *Revolutionary Armies*. Nahal created and maintain many fortified agricultural settlements in key border regions.

33 M. Lissak, "Epilogue," in *Military, State, and Society in Israel*, ed. D. Maman, E. Ben-Ari and Z. Rosenhek, New Brunswick, NJ: Transaction Publishers, 2001, pp. 410, 416.

34 Peri, "Party–Military Relations in a Pluralist System," p. 48; and Luttwak and Horowitz, *Israeli Army*, p. 6.

35 M. Gilbert, *From the Ends of the Earth: The Jews in the 20th Century*, London: Cassell, 2001, pp. 85–6.

36 J. Reinharz, *Chaim Weizmann: The Making of a Statesman*, New York: Oxford University Press, 1993, pp. 169, 283–4; and Schiff, *History*, p. 4.

37 Schiff, *History*, p. 5.

38 Ibid., pp. 10–11.

39 Van Creveld, *Sword and Olive*, pp. 20–30.

40 Luttwak and Horowitz, *Israeli Army*, p. 10.

41 Y. Allon, *Shield of David*, New York: Random House, 1970, Ch. 3; and van Creveld, *Sword and Olive*, pp. 38–41.

42 H. Sachar, *A History of Israel: From the Rise of Zionism to Our Time*, 2nd edn., New York: Alfred Knopf, 2002, pp. 215–16; Cohen, *Zion and State*, pp. 231–2; Schiff, *History*, pp. 11–12; and van Creveld, *Sword and Olive*, p. 43.

43 Allon, *Shield of David*, pp. 140–1; and Gilbert, *Israel*, pp. 119–20.

44 Schiff, *History*, pp. 15–19.

45 S. Stevens, *The Spymasters of Israel*, New York: Macmillan, 1980, pp. 51–3.

46　A. J. Sherman, *Mandate Days: British Lives in Palestine, 1918–1948*, Baltimore, MD: Johns Hopkins University Press, 2001, p. 154.

47　Van Creveld, *Sword and Olive*, p. 58.

48　Sherman, *Mandate Days*, pp. 185–228.

49　Y. Goldstein, "The Ideological and Political Background of the Israel Defense Forces," in *Israel: The First Hundred Years: Israel's Transition from Community to State*, vol. 1, ed. E. Karsh, London: Frank Cass, 2000, p. 179.

50　Y. Lifshitz, *The Economics of Producing Defense Illustrated by the Israeli Case*, Boston: Kluwer Academic Press, 2003, p. 229.

51　See Table 12.1.

52　I. Black and B. Morris, *Israel's Secret Wars*, New York: Grove Weidenfeld, 1991, pp. 321, 491.

53　Raviv and Melman, *Every Spy a Prince*, pp. 3, 12.

54　Ibid., Ch. 2.

55　Gordon Thomas estimates that there are 20,000 sayanim in the United States and Great Britain alone aiding Israeli intelligence agencies in a host of ways. See G. Thomas, *Gideon's Spies: The Secret History of the Mossad*, New York: St. Martin's Press, 1999, p. 68; and Luttwak and Horowitz, *Israeli Army*, p. 270.

56　R. Deacon, *The Israeli Secret Service*, New York: Taplinger, 1985, Ch. 14.

57　H. Eshed, *Reuven Shiloah: The Man behind the Mossad*, trans. D. Zinder and L. Zinder, London: Frank Cass, 1997, p. 324.

58　Black and Morris, *Israel's Secret Wars*, p. 12.

59　Eshed, *Reuven Shiloah*, pp. 110–11.

60　Stevens, *Spymasters*, pp. 51–3.

61　Eshed, *Reuven Shiloah*, Chs. 4, 7.

62　Deacon, *Israeli Secret Service*, pp. 38–40.

63　Cohen, *Zion and State*, p. 258.

64　Sherman, *Mandate Days*, pp. 29, 47.

65　Gilbert, *From the Ends of the Earth*, pp. 243–4.

66　Allon, *Shield of David*, p. 148. And this lengthy list did not include the earlier stages of finding, organizing and training the refugees for the harsh trip that lay before them!

67　Sherman, *Mandate Days*.

68　Black and Morris, *Israel's Secret Wars*, pp. 23–30.

69　Schiff, *History*, p. 191.

70　Allon, *Shield of David*, Ch. 5.

71　Ibid., p. 166; and Black and Morris, *Israel's Secret Wars*, pp. 46–8.

72　Black and Morris, *Israel's Secret Wars*, pp. 46–9.

73　Ibid., pp. 54–8, 98, 129.

74　Deacon, *Israeli Secret Service*, pp. 49–51.

75　By contrast, the United States has 16 major intelligence services.

76　M. B. Zohar, *Spies in the Promised Land: Iser Harel and the Israeli Secret Service*, Boston, MA: Houghton Mifflin, 1972, Chs. 6–7.

77　Stevens, *Spymasters*, Ch. 4.

78　Eshed, *Reuven Shiloah*, pp. 187–9, 328–33.

79　Raviv and Melman, *Every Spy a Prince*, pp. 78–9.

80　Zohar, *Spies*, p. 66.

81　Ibid., p. 70.

82　In particular, see Raviv and Melman, *Every Spy a Prince*.

83　Zohar, *Spies*, pp. 67–8, 106.

84　Black and Morris, *Israel's Secret Wars*, pp. 66–8.

85　Ibid., pp. 174–82.

86　Stevens, *Spymasters*, p. 87.

87　Ibid., p. 96.

88 Schiff, *History*, p. 194; and Black and Morris, *Israel's Secret Wars*, pp. 130–1.
89 Zohar, *Spies*, Ch. 22.
90 Deacon, *Israeli Secret Service*, Ch. 8.
91 Stevens, *Spymasters*, Ch. 13; Black and Morris, *Israel's Secret Wars*, pp. 192–201; and Zohar, *Spies*, Ch. 27.
92 E. Cochran, "Israel's Nuclear History," in *Israel: The First Hundred Years: From War to Peace?*, vol. 2, ed. E. Karsh, London: Frank Cass, 2000, pp. 129–34.
93 Ibid., pp. 129–56.
94 Ibid., p. 136.
95 Raviv and Melman, *Every Spy a Prince*, Chs. 4, 9.
96 Cochran, "Israel's Nuclear History," pp. 134–41.
97 W. Lotz, *The Champagne Spy: Israel's Master Spy Tells His Story*, New York: Valentine Mitchell, 1972.
98 Deacon, *Israeli Secret Service*, Ch. 5.
99 Stevens, *Spymasters*, pp. 122–3.
100 Schiff, *History*, Ch. 13; and Thomas, *Gideon's Spies*, Ch. 3.
101 Deacon, *Israeli Secret Service*, p. 167.
102 Black and Morris, *Israel's Secret Wars*, Chs. 8, 10; and Raviv and Melman, *Every Spy a Prince*, Ch. 8.
103 Van Creveld, *Sword and Olive*, p. 209.
104 Stevens, *Spymasters*, pp. 210–20.
105 Black and Morris, *Israel's Secret Wars*, pp. 263–4; and Raviv and Melman, *Every Spy a Prince*, Ch. 8.
106 Raviv and Melman, *Every Spy a Prince*, p. 181.
107 Deacon, *Israeli Secret Service*, Ch. 18; Stevens, *Spymasters*, Ch. 22; and Black and Morris, *Israel's Secret Wars*, pp. 269–75.
108 Deacon, *Israeli Secret Service*, Ch. 21.
109 Black and Morris, *Israel's Secret Wars*, pp. 332–7.
110 Ibid., pp. 453–5.
111 Ibid., pp. 448–50.
112 Thomas, *Gideon's Spies*, pp. 115–17; and Black and Morris, *Israel's Secret Wars*, pp. 469–72.
113 Schiff, *History*, Ch. 13; and Raviv and Melman, *Every Spy a Prince*, p. 118.
114 Stevens, *Spymasters*, Ch. 6.
115 Black and Morris, *Israel's Secret Wars*, pp. 168–72; and Zohar, *Spies*, Ch. 21.
116 Thomas, *Gideon's Spies*, Ch. 6.
117 Van Creveld, *Sword and Olive*, Ch. 14; Stevens, *Spymasters*, Ch. 25; and Black and Morris, *Israel's Secret Wars*, Ch. 9.
118 Thomas, *Gideon's Spies*, pp. 88–92; Black and Morris, *Israel's Secret Wars*, pp. 416–29; and Raviv and Melman, *Every Spy a Prince*, Ch. 14.
119 Thomas, *Gideon's Spies*, Ch. 17.

13 Revolutionary factors: aliyah, education, government and party

1 Jonathan Adelman, "Tolerance and Development," Washington, D.C.: Foundation for the Defense of Democracies, 2003.
2 M. Gilbert, *Israel: A History*, New York: William Morrow and Company, 1998, p. 275. Later as defense minister Pinchas Lavon was deeply involved and finally discredited by the Lavon Affair involving a failed intelligence effort in Egypt in 1954 to discredit the Nasser regime.
3 M. Cohen, *Zion and State: Nation, Class and the Shaping of Modern Israel*, New York: Columbia University Press, 1992, pp. 157, 177.
4 M. Gilbert, *The Routledge Atlas of Jewish History*, New York: William Morrow and Company, 1993, p. 133.

5 For a good study of the development of the Labor Party, see P. Medding, *Mapai in Israel: Political Organization and Government in a New Society*, Cambridge: Cambridge University Press, 1971.
6 At home the battle with the non-socialist General Zionist, the religious Zionist Mizrahi, the ultra-Orthodox non-Zionist Agudat Yisrael and other strands of socialism was itself a daunting battle.
7 Medding, *Mapai*, p. 17.
8 M. Duverger, *Political Parties*, London: Methuen, 1964, pp. 307–8.
9 Medding, *Mapai*, pp. 7–11.
10 P. Medding, *The Founding of Israeli Democracy, 1948–1967*, Oxford: Oxford University Press, 1990, Ch. 2. Even in the last two decades the main ideas of the Likud – unilateral disengagement from Gaza, the fence, concern over the occupation – came originally from the Labor movement.
11 Medding, *Mapai*, Ch. 2.
12 Cohen, *Zion and State*, pp. 95–101.
13 Ibid., Ch. 4.
14 Medding, *Mapai*, p. 10.
15 J. Migdal, *Through the Lens of Israel*, Albany: State University of New York Press, 2001, p. 62.
16 Cohen, *Zion and State*, p. 175.
17 Migdal, *Through the Lens of Israel*, pp. 60–7.
18 Cohen, *Zion and State*, pp. 120–9, Ch. 9.
19 B. Akzin, "The Role of Parties in Israeli Democracy," *Journal of Politics*, 17 (4), 1955.
20 Medding, *Founding of Israeli Democracy*, pp. 46–9, 220–1.
21 Y. Peri, "Party–Military Relations in a Pluralist System," in *Israeli Society and its Defense Establishment*, ed. M. Lissak, London: Frank Cass, 1984, p. 61.
22 R. Michels, *Political Parties*, New York: Free Press, 1968.
23 Medding, *Mapai*, Chs. 12–13.
24 Ibid., Chs. 1–2.
25 For the American Revolution, see J. Ellis, *Founding Brothers: The Revolutionary Generation*, New York: Alfred Knopf, 2000, as well as biographies of the founding fathers.
26 S. Teveth, *Ben Gurion: The Burning Ground 1886–1948*, Boston, MA: Houghton Mifflin, 1987, pp. xi–xiii.
27 D. Vital, "From 'State within a State' to State," in *Israel: The First Hundred Years: Israel's Transition from Community to State*, vol. 1, ed. E. Karsh, London: Frank Cass, 2000, pp. 35–6.
28 M. Gilbert, *From the Ends of the Earth: The Jews in the 20th Century*, London: Cassel, 2001, p. 24.
29 B. Halpern, *The Idea of the Jewish State*, Cambridge, MA: Harvard University Press, 1969, Chs. 9–10.
30 J. Reinharz, *Chaim Weizmann: The Making of a Statesman*, New York: Oxford University Press, 1993, pp. 137, 205.
31 Ibid. p. 170.
32 Ibid. p. 272–4.
33 Gilbert, *Israel*, p. 38.
34 Reinharz, *Chaim Weizmann*, p. 232.
35 M. Urofsky, *We Are One!: American Jewry and Israel*, New York: Doubleday, 1978, p. 204.
36 For a detailed discussion of this event, see I. Galnoor, *The Partition of Palestine: Decision Crossroads in the Zionist Movement*, Albany: State University of New York Press, 1995, Ch. 2. The loss of 7,000 square miles initially claimed by the Zionists in 1919 was a bitter pill for Chaim Weizmann (p. 41).

37 D. Fromkin, *A Peace to End All Peace*, New York: Avon Books, 1989, p. 521.

38 Teveth, *Ben Gurion*, p. 551.

39 For a detailed study of the Peel Commission and Jewish decision making, see Galnoor, *Partition*; and also M. Urofsky, *American Zionism from Herzl to the Holocaust*, New York: Doubleday, 1975, pp. 407–9.

40 A. J. Sherman, *Mandate Days: British Lives in Palestine, 1918–1948*, Baltimore, MD: Johns Hopkins University Press, 2001, p. 132.

41 Teveth, *Ben Gurion*, p. 718.

42 B. Kimmerling, *Zionism and Territory: The Socio-Territorial Dimensions of Zionist Politics*, Berkeley: University of California Press, 1983, p. 58.

43 Halpern, *Idea of the Jewish State*, p. 374.

44 Ibid., pp. 46–8, 372–7.

45 Galnoor, *Partition*, pp. 293–6.

46 Halpern, *Idea of the Jewish State*, p. 402.

47 M. Bar-On, *The Gates of Gaza: Israel's Road to Suez and Back, 1955–1957*, New York: St. Martin's Press, 1994, Afterword.

48 Conversations at the Chinese Foreign Ministry's think tank (China Institute of International Relations), summer, 2000.

49 A. Dowty, *The Jewish State: A Century Later*, Berkeley: University of California Press, 1998, Ch. 8; Migdal, *Through the Lens of Israel*, p. 43; and B. M. Friedman, "The State of Israel as a Theological Dilemma," in *The Israeli State and Society: Boundaries and Frontiers*, ed. B. Kimmerling, Albany: State University of New York Press, 1989, Ch. 7.

50 In this effort, they could draw on the traditions of the European Jewish *kehilla* (autonomous community) which, for 900 years, had largely governed itself. European Jews constituted a community of adult males in an alien environment where they had lawmaking authority, immigration control, receptiveness to grievances, elected leaders and rabbis, a welfare system, notables to deal with the outside world (*shtadlanism*), regulated wages and price and control of land acquisition. This traditional model could be modified for the Jewish community in Palestine under the Ottoman Turks and the British Mandatory Authority. See Dowty, *Jewish State*, p. 21.

51 E. Karsh, *Fabricating Israeli History: The "New Historians,"* London: Frank Cass, 1997, p. 78.

52 Cohen, *Zion and State*, p. 8.

53 Dowty, *Jewish State*, pp. 45–6.

54 Vital, "From 'State within a State' to State," pp. 32–4.

55 H. Sachar, *A History of Israel: From the Rise of Zionism to Our Time*, 3rd edn., New York: Alfred Knopf, 2007, pp. 308–9.

56 R. Deacon, *The Israeli Secret Service*, New York: Taplinger, 1985, pp. 48–51. Indeed, as early as 1944 the Jewish Agency had turned over the names and many of the addresses of 700 members of the Irgun to try to destroy any threat to Jewish unity through terrorism. See Gilbert, *From the Ends of the Earth*, p. 230.

57 I. Troen, *Imagining Zion*, New Haven, CT: Yale University Press, 2003, p. 101.

58 Cohen, *Zion and State*, Chs. 1, 11, 12. Cohen talks extensively about the triumph of statism over socialism under Ben Gurion. Of course, Mapai, with its dedication to European social democracy and the West, was considerably more moderate than the more radical Mapam that venerated the Soviet Union and such Communist leaders as Stalin and Tito.

59 Ibid., p. 215.

60 B. Kimmerling, *Zionism and Economy*, Cambridge, MA: Schenkman Publishing, 1983, p. 55; and M. van Creveld, *The Sword and the Olive: A Critical History of the Israeli Defense Forces*, New York: Public Affairs Press, 1998, p. 70.

61 Troen, *Imagining Zion*, pp. 51–2.

62　Halpern, *Idea of the Jewish State*, pp. 115–19.
63　Cohen, *Zion and State*, pp. 220–3.
64　*Haaretz*, September 14, 2004.
65　Reinharz, *Chaim Weizmann*, p. 258.

14　International factors

1　D. Vital, *The Survival of Small States: Studies in Small Power/Great Power Conflict*, London: Oxford University Press, 1971, p. 57; and D. Kimche, "The Traditional and the Transitional in Statecraft," in *Global Politics: Essays in Honor of David Vital*, ed. A. Ben-Zvi and A. Klieman, London: Frank Cass, 2001, p. 14.
 2　A. Ben-Zvi, "The US–Israel Special Relationship," in *Global Politics: Essays in Honor of David Vital*, ed. A. Ben-Zvi and A. Klieman, London: Frank Cass, 2001, p. 223.
 3　G. Sheffer, "Israeli–Diaspora Relations in Comparative Perspective," in *Israel in Comparative Perspective*, ed. M. Barnett, Albany: State University of New York Press, 1996, p. 67.
 4　M. Urofsky, *We Are One! American Jewry and Israel*, New York: Doubleday, 1978, p. 302.
 5　E. Glick, *The Triangular Connection: America, Israel and American Jews*, London: George Allen and Unwin, 1982, p. 125; I. Troen, *Imagining Zion*, New Haven, CT: Yale University Press, 2003, p. 122; and Urofsky, *We Are One!*, pp. 242–4.
 6　Sheffer, "Israeli–Diaspora Relations."
 7　Ibid., pp. 62–72; and Glick, *Triangular Connection*, pp. 108–10.
 8　S. Walt and J. Mearsheimer, "The Israel Lobby and U.S. Foreign Policy," Kennedy School of Government at Harvard University, Working Paper RWP06–011, March 2006.
 9　S. I. Troen, "Organizing the Rescue of Jews in the Modern Period," in S. I. Troen and B. Pinkus, *Organizing Rescue: Jewish National Solidarity in the Modern Period*, London: Frank Cass, 1992, p. 3 and Ch. 1.
10　Ibid., p. 7.
11　Ibid., Ch. 1.
12　D. Fromkin, *A Peace to End All Peace*, New York: Avon Books, 1989, p. 299; and M. Urofsky, *American Zionism from Herzl to the Holocaust*, New York: Doubleday, 1975, p. 78.
13　J. Reinharz, *Chaim Weizmann: The Making of a Statesman*, New York: Oxford University Press, 1993, pp. 367, 391; and Urofsky, *American Zionism*, p. 126.
14　Urofsky, *American Zionism*, p. 310.
15　M. Macmillan, *Paris 1919: Six Months that Changed the World*, New York: Random House, 2002, Ch. 28.
16　Urofsky, *We Are One!*, pp. 299–301.
17　M. van Creveld, *The Sword and the Olive: A Critical History of the Israeli Defense Forces*, New York: Public Affairs Press, 1988, p. 31. At a time when the average Arab peasant family was earning $135 a year, this was a serious Diaspora contribution.
18　W. Laqueur and B. Rubin, *The Israel-Arab Reader*, New York: Penguin, 2001.
19　Urofsky, *American Zionism*, pp. 316, 324.
20　B. Halpern, *The Idea of the Jewish State*, Cambridge, MA: Harvard University Press, 1969, p. 180.
21　Urofsky, *American Zionism*, p. 375.
22　W. Laqueur, *A History of Zionism*, London: Weidenfeld & Nicolson, 1972, p. 551.
23　Van Creveld, *Sword and Olive*, p. 62; H. Eshed, *Reuven Shiloah: The Man behind the Mossad*, trans. D. Zinder and L. Zinder, London: Frank Cass, 1997, p. 96; and Urofsky, *We Are One!*, pp. 155–6.

24 M. Raider, *The Emergence of American Zionism*, New York: New York University Press, 1998, pp. 3, 203; and Urofsky, *We Are One!*, p. 125. At the same time, the American Red Cross raised only $25 million a year.

25 E. Tauber, "The Jewish and Arab Lobbies in Canada and the UN Partition of Palestine," in *Israel: The First Hundred Years: Israel's Transition from Community to State*, vol. 1, ed. E. Karsh, London: Frank Cass, 2000, pp. 229–46.

26 Urofsky, *We Are One!*, p. 94.

27 Ibid., pp. 3–4, 31–49.

28 Ibid., p. 147.

29 Eshed, *Reuven Shiloah*, pp. 194–6.

30 Ibid., pp. 241–2; and M. Bar-On, *The Gates of Gaza: Israel's Road to Suez and Back, 1955–1957*, New York: St. Martin's Press, 1994, pp. 297–8.

31 Urofsky, *We Are One!*, pp. 356, 429–30.

32 Ibid., p. 385.

33 Ibid. p. 350.

34 Ibid. pp. 427, 437, 445.

35 See the study by the Israel Project, 2006.

36 Urofsky, *We Are One!*, pp. 202–3, 356.

37 Urofsky, *American Zionism*, p. 312.

38 Ibid. pp. 396–7.

39 M. Gilbert, *From the Ends of the Earth: The Jews in the 20th Century*, London: Cassell, 2001, p. 130.

40 P. Johnson, *A History of the Jews*, New York: Harper & Row, 1987, pp. 585–6.

41 A. Lunacharsky, *Religiya i sotsializm*, vol. 1, St. Petersburg, 1908, pp. 40, 188–90.

42 T. Veblen, "The Intellectual Pre-eminence of the Jews in Modern Europe," in *Essays in Our Changing Order*, ed. L. Ardzrooni, New York: Viking Press, 1934, pp. 219–31. Veblen asserted that "the Jewish people have contributed much more than an even share of the intellectual life of modern Europe. So also it is plain that the civilization of Christendom continued today to draw heavily on the Jews for men devoted to science and scholarly pursuits" (p. 221). Max Weber also looked at this phenomenon in his 1917 work *Ancient Judaism*, trans. H. Gerth and D. Martindale, New York, 1952.

43 T. Cahill, *The Gifts of the Jews*, New York: Doubleday, 1998, p. 3. As Paul Johnson has written, the Christians took the Torah, Prophets, Wisdom, liturgy, Sabbath, feast days, incense, burning lamps, psalms, hymns, prayers, priests, vestments, martyrs, sacred books and synagogue (church) from the Jews. See Johnson, *History*, p. 145.

44 Quoted in an Anti-Defamation League press release, New York, October 16, 2003.

45 A. Eban, *Heritage: Civilization and the Jews*, New York: Summit Books, 1984, Chs. 1–2; and Johnson, *History*, p. 15.

46 Of course, the success of Jews abroad as an emigrant minority does not necessarily have a direct reflection on what would happen to Jews as a majority culture. Chinese and Indians abroad traditionally did much better than Chinese and Indians at home.

47 B. Feldman, *The Nobel Prize: A History of Genius, Controversy and Prestige*, New York: Arcade Publishers, 2000, Appendix E.

48 B. Rubin, *Assimilation and its Discontents*, New York: Random House, 1995, p. 39.

49 H. Rubinstein, D. Cohn-Sherbok, A. Edelheit and W. Rubinstein, *The Jews in the Modern World: A History since 1750*, London: Arnold, 2002, p. 420.

50 These included Louis Mayer and Sam Goldwyn (Metro-Goldwyn-Mayer), Adolf Zukor (Paramount), Jack Warner (Warner Brothers), Harry Cohn (Columbia) and Irving Thalberg and William Fox (Fox Films). See N. Gable, *An Empire of their Own: How the Jews Invented Hollywood*, New York: Doubleday, 1989.

51 American Film Institute, *One Hundred Best Music Songs*, Los Angeles: American

Film Institute, 2004. The Jewish songwriters and lyricists helped compose "Over the Rainbow" (Yip Harburg, Harold Arlen), "As Time Goes By" (Jules Styne), "Singin' in the Rain" (Arthur Freed), "White Christmas" (Irving Berlin), "Mrs. Robinson' (Paul Simon and Art Garfunkel), "The Way We Were" (Barbra Streisand) and "The Sound of Music" (Richard Rodgers and Oscar Hammerstein).

52 R. Posner, *Public Intellectuals: A Study of Decline*, Cambridge, MA: Harvard University Press, 2001. Six of ten leading American public intellectuals were Jews: Henry Kissinger, Larry Summers, Robert Reich, Sidney Blumenthal, Arthur Miller and William Safire. The four non-Jews are Daniel Patrick Moynihan (now deceased), George Will, William Bennett and Salman Rushdie. See also C. Silberman, *A Certain People: American Jews and their Lives Today*, New York: Summit Books, 1985, pp. 143–56.

53 H. Zuckerman, *Scientific Elite: Novel Laureates in the United States*, New York: Free Press, 1977, p. 68. These numbers have not changed markedly since this study and the other two cited above.

54 *Chronicle of Philanthropy*, December 31, 2003.

55 Forbes 400 website.

56 Three of Israel's leading universities (Hebrew University, Tel Aviv University and Weizmann Institute of Science) are ranked in the top ten among Asia's top 100 universities. In addition, two other Israeli universities (Technion and Ben Gurion University) were listed as numbers 27 and 37 in Asia. See Shanghai JiaoTong University rankings of leading universities on the Internet at http:/ed.stju.edu.cn/rank-rank-Asia.

57 C. Geertz (ed.), *Old Societies and New States*, New York: Free Press, 1963, pp. 255, 268.

58 P. Merkley, *Christian Attitudes towards the State of Israel*, Montreal: McGill-Queen's University Press, 2001, pp. 200–7.

59 I. Anderson, *Biblical Interpretation and Middle East Policy: The Promised Land, America and Israel, 1917–2002*, Gainesville: University of Florida Press, 2005, p. 102.

60 Ibid., pp. 109–10.

61 Ibid., Ch. 7.

62 H. Fishman, *American Protestantism and a Jewish State*, Detroit, MI: Wayne State University Press, 1973, p. 20.

63 Anderson, *Biblical Interpretation*, p. 20.

64 Ibid., pp. 41–5.

65 Ibid., Ch. 7.

66 A. Gal, "David Ben-Gurion's Zionist Foreign Policy, 1938–48: The Democratic Factor," in *Israel: The First Hundred Years: Israel in the International Arena*, vol. 4, ed. E. Karsh, London: Frank Cass, 2000, pp. 16–17.

67 M. Mann, *The Sources of Social Power: The Rise of Classes and Nation-States, 1760–1914*, vol. 2, New York: Cambridge University Press, 1993, p. 14.

68 In the early 1920s, 70 percent of migrating world Jewry went through the open gates of New York while only 10 percent went to Palestine. But, from 1932 to 1938, fully 53 percent of all migrants went to Palestine while a small percentage were able to go to the United States. See B. Halpern and J. Reinharz, *Zionism and the Creation of a New Society*, New York: Oxford University Press, 1998, p. 230.

69 Bar-On, *Gates of Gaza*, p. 33.

70 Ibid., pp. 170–89.

71 Ibid., Ch. 15.

72 J. Nitzan and S. Bichler, *The Global Political Economy of Israel*, London: Pluto Press, 2002, p. 246.

73 Gal, "David Ben-Gurion's Zionist Foreign Policy," p. 26.

74 A. Ben-Zvi, "Influence and Arms: John F. Kennedy, Lyndon B. Johnson and the

Politics of Arms Sales to Israel, 1962–66," in *Israel: The First Hundred Years: Israel in the International Arena*, vol. 4, ed. E. Karsh, London: Frank Cass, 2000, pp. 29–59.

75 Nitzan and Bichler, *Global Political Economy*, pp. 242–6.

76 E. Karsh and P. R. Kumaraswamy (eds.), *Israel, the Hashemites and the Palestinians: The Fateful Triangle*, London: Frank Cass, 2003, pp. 24–8, 33.

77 M. Djilas, *Conversations with Stalin*, trans. M. Petrovich, New York: Harcourt, Brace & World, 1962.

78 E. Karsh, *Rethinking the Middle East*, London: Frank Cass, 2003, pp. 74–7; and Rubinstein *et al., Jews in the Modern World*, pp. 190–2.

79 Rubinstein *et al., Jews in the Modern World*, pp. 191–2.

80 A. Beker, *The United Nations and Israel: From Recognition to Reprehension*, Lexington, MA: Lexington Books, 1988, pp. 32–6.

81 A. Ilan, *The Origins of the Arab–Israeli Arms Race: Arms, Embargo, Military Power and Decision in the 1948 Palestine War*, New York: New York University Press, 1996, p. 180.

82 Z. Schiff, *A History of the Israeli Army*, New York: Macmillan, 1985, pp. 37–8; and Ilan, *Origins*, p. 160.

83 Ilan, *Origins*, p. 149.

84 H. Sachar, *A History of Israel: From the Rise of Zionism to Our Time*, 2nd edn., New York: Alfred Knopf, 2002, Ch. 5. Foreign Secretary Arthur Balfour in 1919 declared that "My personal hope is that the Jews will make good in Palestine and eventually found a Jewish State." Winston Churchill called in 1920 for "a Jewish State by the banks of the Jordan . . . which might comprise three to four million Jews" (p. 110). For the vote in the House of Commons (which differed from the vote in the House of Lords), see S. M. Rubinstein, *The Communist Movement in Palestine and Israel, 1919–1984*, Boulder, CO: Westview Press, 1984, p. 98. For the San Remo statement, see A. J. Sherman, *Mandate Days: British Lives in Palestine, 1918–1948*, Baltimore, MD: Johns Hopkins University Press, 2001, p. 53.

85 For an extensive treatment of this topic, see Reinharz, *Chaim Weizmann*, especially the concluding chapter, and D. Vital, *Zionism: The Crucial Phase*, Oxford: Oxford University Press, 1987, Ch. 6.

86 Halpern, *Idea of the Jewish State*, p. 352. Winston Churchill, then head of the Middle East Department of the Colonial Office, wrote an article before he took the post calling the idea of 3–4 million Jews in Palestine "beneficial" to Great Britain. See Gilbert, *From the Ends of the Earth*, p. 129.

87 David Ben Gurion's recognition of the positive role of the British mandatory authorities in the 1920s and 1930s is quoted in S. Avineri, *The Making of Modern Zionism*, New York: Basic Books, 1981, pp. 211–12.

88 J. Migdal, *Through the Lens of Israel*, Albany: State University of New York Press, 2001, p. 63.

89 Sherman, *Mandate Days*, p. 154.

90 Sachar, *History*, p. 313.

91 Migdal, *Through the Lens of Israel*, pp. 135–6.

92 Ilan, *Origins*, p. 141. The British enmity with Egypt after October 1946 and Iraq after January 1948, and its opposition to selling Syria 2,000–3,000 rifles and machine guns in November 1947, left only Transjordan as a friendly pro-British ally desirous of receiving British arms. The consequences of this British failure to consolidate its hold on Israel's neighbors and to supply them with modern weapons were clearly momentous for Israel (pp. 27, 54).

93 Urofsky, *We Are One!*, pp. 102–3.

94 G. Falk, *The Restoration of Israel: Christian Zionism in Religion, Literature and Politics*, New York: Peter Lang, 2006, p. 1 (see also p. 199).

95 Ibid., Ch. 3. William Blake wrote that "I will not cease from mental fight, Nor

shall my sword sleep in my hand, Till we have built Jerusalem, In England's green and pleasant land" (p. 160).

96 P. Merkley, *The Politics of Christian Zionism 1891–1948*, London: Frank Cass, 1998, Chs. 2, 4. Falk, *Restoration of Israel*, p. vii, Ch. 1; and R. Ruether and H. Ruether, *The Wrath of Jonah: The Crisis of Religious Nationalism in the Israeli–Palestinian Conflict*, 2nd edn., Minneapolis, MN: Fortress Press, 2002, pp. 69–81.

97 Merkley, *Politics of Christian Zionism*, Ch. 2; and Anderson, *Biblical Interpretation*, pp. 41, 47.

98 Anderson, *Biblical Interpretation*, p. 60.

99 Ibid., pp. 55–9.

15 Conclusions

1 *Haaretz*, January 11, 2007.

2 E. Ottolenghi, "A National Home," in *Modern Judaism: An Oxford Guide*, ed. N. de Lange and M. Freud-Kandel, Oxford, Oxford University Press, 2005, p. 64.

3 *Forbes*, October 1, 2007.

Bibliography

Adelman, J., *The Revolutionary Armies*, Westport, CT: Greenwood Press, 1980.
——, "Tolerance and Development," Washington, D.C.: Foundation for the Defense of Democracies, 2003.
—— (ed.), *Hitler and His Allies in World War I*, London: Routledge, 2007.
Akzin, B., "The Role of Parties in Israeli Democracy," *Journal of Politics*, 17 (4), 1955.
Alesina, A. and E. Spolaore, *The Size of Nations*, Cambridge, MA: MIT Press, 2003.
Alexander, Y., *Palestinian Religious Terrorism: Hamas and Islamic Jihad*, Ardsley, NY: Transnational Publishers, 2002.
Allon, Y., *Shield of David*, New York: Random House, 1970.
Almog, O., "Shifting the Centre from Nation to Individual and Universe: The New 'Democratic' Faith of Israel," in *Israel: The First Hundred Years: Israeli Politics and Society since 1948: Problems of Collective Identity*, vol. 3, ed. E. Karsh, London: Frank Cass, 2000.
Almog, S., J. Reinharz and A. Shapira (eds.), *Zionism and Religion*, Hanover, NH: Brandeis University Press, 1998.
American Film Institute, *One Hundred Best Music Songs*, Los Angeles: American Film Institute, 2004.
Anderson, I., *Biblical Interpretation and Middle East Policy: The Promised Land, America and Israel, 1917–2002*, Gainesville: University of Florida Press, 2005.
Arian, A., *The Second Republic: Politics in Israel*, Chatham, NJ: Chatham House Publishers, 1998.
Aronoff, M., "Wars as Catalysts of Political and Cultural Change," in *The Military and Militarism in Israeli Society*, ed. E. Lomsky-Feder and E. Ben-Ari, Albany: State University of New York Press, 1999.
Atkinson, R., *An Army at Dawn: The War in North Africa, 1942–1943*, New York: Henry Holt, 2002.
Avineri, S., *The Making of Modern Zionism: The Intellectual Origins of the Jewish State*, New York: Basic Books, 1981.
——, "Zionism and the Jewish Religious Tradition," in *Zionism and Religion*, ed. S. Almog, J. Reinharz and A. Shapira, Hanover, NH: Brandeis University Press, 1998.
——, "Israel: A Normative Value of Jewish Existence," in *The Blackwell Reader in Judaism*, ed. J. Neusner and A. Avery-Peck, Oxford: Blackwell, 2001.
Bachi, R., *The Population of Israel*, Jerusalem: Hebrew University Press, 1976.
Bard, M., *Will Israel Survive?*, New York: Palgrave Macmillan, 2007.

Bareli, A., "Forgetting Europe: Perspectives on the Debate about Zionism and Colonialism," in *Israeli Historical Revisionism: From Left to Right*, ed. A. Shapira and D. Penslar, London: Frank Cass, 2003.

Barnett, M., "Israel in the World Economy: Israel as an East Asian State?," in *Israel in Comparative Perspective*, ed. M. Barnett, Albany: State University of New York Press, 1996.

——, "The Politics of Uniqueness: The Status of the Israeli Case," in *Israel in Comparative Perspective*, ed. M. Barnett, Albany: State University of New York Press, 1996.

—— (ed.), *Israel in Comparative Perspective*, Albany: State University of New York Press, 1996.

Bar-On, M., "Seeking a War?," in *Traditions and Transitions in Israel Studies*, ed. L. Z. Eisenberg, N. Caplan, N. Sokoloff and M. Abu-Nimer, Albany: State University of New York Press, 2003.

——, *The Gates of Gaza: Israel's Road to Suez and Back, 1955–1957*, New York: St. Martin's Press, 1994.

Bar-Or, A., "The Link between the Government and the IDF during Israel's First 50 Years: The Shifting Role of the Defense Minister," in *Military, State, and Society in Israel*, ed. D. Maman, E. Ben-Ari and Z. Rosenhek, New Brunswick, NJ: Transaction Publishers, 2001.

Beker, A., *The United Nations and Israel: From Recognition to Reprehension*, Lexington, MA: Lexington Books, 1988.

Ben-Ami, Y., *Years of Wrath, Days of Glory: Memoirs of the Irgun*, New York: Robert Speller & Sons, 1982.

Ben-Yehuda, H. and S. Sandler, *The Arab–Israel Conflict Transformed: Fifty Years of Interstate and Ethnic Crises*, Albany: State University of New York Press, 2002.

Ben-Zvi, A., "Influence and Arms: John F. Kennedy, Lyndon B. Johnson and the Politics of Arms Sales to Israel, 1962–66," in *Israel: The First Hundred Years: Israel in the International Arena*, vol. 4, ed. E. Karsh, London: Frank Cass, 2000.

——, "The US–Israel Special Relationship," in *Global Politics: Essays in Honor of David Vital*, ed. A. Ben-Zvi and A. Klieman, London: Frank Cass, 2001.

Berlin, I., *Personal Impressions*, ed. H. Hardy, New York: Viking Press, 1980.

Bialer, U., *Cross on the Star of David: The Christian World in Israel's Foreign Policy, 1948–1967*, Bloomington: Indiana University Press, 2005.

Bickerton, I. and C. Klausner, *A Concise History of the Arab–Israeli Conflict*, 4th edn., Upper Saddle River, NJ: Prentice Hall, 2002.

Biger, G., "The Boundaries of Mandatory Palestine: How the Past Influences the Future," in *The First Hundred Years: Israel's Transition from Community to State*, vol. 1, ed. E. Karsh, London: Frank Cass, 2000.

Black, I., and B. Morris, *Israel's Secret Wars*, New York: Grove Weidenfeld, 1991.

Breger, M. and G. Weigel, "Special Policy Forum Report: The Vatican and the Middle East – Pope John Paul II's Trip to the Holy Land," in *Peace Watch*, 250, Washington, D.C.: Washington Institute for Near East Policy, March 17, 2000.

Bregman, A., *A History of Israel*, Houndsmill, Basingstoke: Palgrave Macmillan, 2003.

Bregmann, M. and M. Jucovy (eds.), *Generations of the Holocaust*, New York: Columbia University Press, 1982.

Brentjes, B., *The Armenians, Assyrians and Kurds: Three Nations, One Fate?*, Campbell, CA: Rishi Publications, 1997.

Brinton, C., *The Anatomy of Revolution*, New York: Vintage, 1965.

Brown, M., *The Israeli–American Connection: Its Roots in the Yishuv, 1914–1945*, Detroit, MI: Wayne State University Press, 1996.

Brym, R., *The Jewish Intelligentsia and Russian Marxism: A Sociological Study of Intellectual Radicalism and Ideological Diversity*, New York: Schocken Books, 1978.

Buchanan, J., *The Road to Valley Forge: How Washington Built the Army that Won the Revolution*, New York: John Wiley & Sons, 2004.

Burk, J., "From Wars of Independence to Democratic Peace: Comparing the Cases of Israel and the United States," in *Military, State, and Society in Israel*, ed. D. Maman, E. Ben-Ari and Z. Rosenhek, New Brunswick, NJ: Transaction Publishers, 2001.

Burks, R., *The Dynamics of Communism in Eastern Europe*, Princeton, NJ: Princeton University Press, 1961.

Cahill, T., *The Gifts of the Jews*, New York: Doubleday, 1998.

Carter, Jimmy, *Palestine: Peace Not Apartheid*, New York: Simon & Schuster, 2006.

Celan, P., "Death Fugue," in *Voices within the Ark: The Modern Jewish Poets*, ed. H. Schwartz and A. Rudolf, New York: Avon, 1980.

Central Intelligence Agency, *The World Factbook*, Washington, D.C.: CIA, 2003.

——, *The World Factbook*, Washington, D.C.: CIA, 2006.

Chill, D., *The Arab Boycott of Israel: Economic Aggression and World Reaction*, New York: Praeger, 1976.

Chowder, E., "The Zionist Revolution in Time," in *New Essays in Zionism*, ed. D. Hazony, Y. Hazony and M. Oren, Jerusalem: Shalem Press, 2006.

Cochran, E., "Israel's Nuclear History," in *Israel: The First Hundred Years: From War to Peace?*, vol. 2, ed. E. Karsh, London: Frank Cass, 2000.

Cohen, H., "Why Do Collaborators Collaborate? The Case of Palestinians and Zionist Institutions, 1917–1936," in *Arab–Jewish Relations: From Conflict to Resolution?*, ed. E. Podeh and A. Kaufman, Brighton: Sussex Academic Press, 2005.

Cohen, M., *Zion and State: Nation, Class and the Shaping of Modern Israel*, New York: Columbia University Press, 1992.

Cohen, S. (ed.), *Democratic Societies and their Armed Forces: Israel in Comparative Context*, London: Frank Cass, 2000.

Cordesman, A., *The Israeli–Palestine War: Escalating to Nowhere*, Westport, CT: Greenwood Press, 2005.

Davidowitz, L., *The War against the Jews*, New York: Holt, Rinehart and Winston, 1975.

Deacon, R., *The Israeli Secret Service*, New York: Taplinger, 1985.

Deutsch, K. and W. Foltz, *Nation-Building*, New York: Atherton Press, 1963.

Deutscher, I., *The Non-Jewish Jew and Other Essays*, London: Oxford University Press, 1968.

Diskin, A., *The Last Days in Israel: Understanding the New Israeli Democracy*, London: Frank Cass, 2003.

Divine, D., "The Imperialist Ties that Bind: Transjordan and the Yishuv," in *Israel, the Hashemites and the Palestinians: The Fateful Triangle*, ed. E. Karsh and P. R. Kumaraswamy, London: Frank Cass, 2003.

Djilas, M., *Conversations with Stalin*, trans. M. Petrovich, New York: Harcourt, Brace & World, 1962.

Dowty, A., *The Jewish State: A Century Later*, Berkeley: University of California Press, 1998.

Dror, Y., "Weaving the Future of Israel," in *Global Politics: Essays in Honor of David Vital*, ed. A. Ben-Zvi and A. Klieman, London: Frank Cass, 2001.

Druks, Herbert, *The U.S. and Israel from Roosevelt to Kennedy*, Westport, CT: Greenwood Press, 2001.

Duverger, M., *Political Parties*, London: Methuen, 1964.

Eban, A., *My Country: The Story of Modern Israel*, New York: Random House, 1972.

——, *Heritage: Civilization and the Jews*, New York: Summit Books, 1984.

Ellis, J., *Founding Brothers: The Revolutionary Generation*, New York: Alfred Knopf, 2000.

Elon, A., *The Israelis: Founders and Sons*, New York: Holt, Rinehart and Winston, 1971.

Eshed, H., *Reuven Shiloah: The Man behind the Mossad*, trans. D. Zinder and L. Zinder, London: Frank Cass, 1997.

Evans, H., *The American Century*, New York: Alfred Knopf, 1998.

Falk, G., *The Restoration of Israel: Christian Zionism in Religion, Literature and Politics*, New York: Peter Lang, 2006.

Fallers, L., "Equality, Modernity and Democracy in the New States," in *Old Societies and New States*, ed. C. Geertz, New York: Free Press, 1963.

Feiler, G., *From Boycott to Economic Cooperation: The Political Economy of the Arab Boycott of Israel*, London: Frank Cass, 1988.

Feldman, B., *The Nobel Prize: A History of Genius, Controversy and Prestige*, New York: Arcade Publishers, 2000.

Fieldhouse, D. K., *The Colonial Empires from the Eighteenth Century*, New York: Weidenfeld & Nicolson, 1966.

Fishman, Hertzel, *American Protestantism and a Jewish State*, Detroit, MI: Wayne State University Press, 1973.

Frank, A. G., "The Sociology of Development and the Underdevelopment of Sociology," *Catalyst*, 3, Summer, 1963: 20–73.

Frankel, J., "The Crisis as a Factor in Modern Jewish Politics, 1840 and 1881–1882," in *Organizing Rescue: National Jewish Solidarity in the Modern Period*, ed. S. I. Troen and B. Pinkus, London: Frank Cass, 1992.

Fredrickson, G., "Colonialism and Racism: The United States and South Africa in Comparative Perspective," in *The Arrogance of Race*, ed. G. Fredrickson, Middletown, CT: Wesleyan University Press, 1988.

Friedman, B. M., "The State of Israel as a Theological Dilemma," in *The Israeli State and Society: Boundaries and Frontiers*, ed. B. Kimmerling, Albany: State University of New York Press, 1989.

Fromkin, D., *A Peace to End All Peace*, New York: Henry Holt, 1989/New York: Avon Books, 1989.

Gable, N., *An Empire of their Own: How the Jews Invented Hollywood*, New York: Doubleday, 1989.

Gal, A., "David Ben-Gurion's Zionist Foreign Policy, 1938–48: The Democratic Factor," in *Israel: The First Hundred Years: Israel in the International Arena*, vol. 4, ed. E. Karsh, London: Frank Cass, 2000.

Gal, R., "Organizational Complexity: Trust and Deceit in the Israeli Air Force," in *Military, State, and Society in Israel*, ed. D. Maman, E. Ben-Ari and Z. Rosenhek, New Brunswick, NJ: Transaction Publishers, 2001.

Galnoor, I., *The Partition of Palestine: Decision Crossroads in the Zionist Movement*, Albany: State University of New York Press, 1995.

Gazit, M., "The 1956 Sinai Campaign: David Ben Gurion's Policy on Gaza, the Armistice Agreement and French Mediation," in *Israel: The First Hundred Years: From War to Peace?*, vol. 2, ed. E. Karsh, London: Frank Cass, 2000.

——, *Israeli Diplomacy and the Quest for Peace*, London: Frank Cass, 2002.

Geertz, C. (ed.), *Old Societies and New States*, New York: Free Press, 1963.

Gellner, E., *Nations and Nationalism*, Ithaca, NY: Cornell University Press, 1983.

Genizi, H., *The Holocaust, Israel and Canadian Protestant Churches*, Montreal: McGill-Queen's University Press, 2002.

Gerber, H., "Foreign Occupiers and Stepchildren: Zionist Discourse and the Palestinians, 1882–1948," in *Arab–Jewish Relations: From Conflict to Resolution?*, ed. E. Podeh and A. Kaufman, Brighton: Sussex Academic Press, 2005.

Gerschenkron, A., *Economic Backwardness in Historical Perspective*, Cambridge, MA: Harvard University Press, 1962.

Gilbert, M., *The Routledge Atlas of Jewish History*, New York: William Morrow and Company, 1993.

——, *Israel: A History*, New York: William Morrow and Company, 1998.

——, *From the Ends of the Earth: The Jews in the 20th Century*, London: Cassell, 2001.

——, *The Routledge Atlas of the Arab–Israeli Conflict*, 8th edn., London: Routledge, 2005.

Gilboa, Y., *The Black Years of Soviet Jewry*, trans. Y. Shacter and D. Ben Abba, Boston, MA: Little, Brown, 1971.

Gitelman, Z., *Jewish Nationality and Soviet Politics: The Jewish Sections of the CSPU, 1917–1930*, Princeton, NJ: Princeton University Press, 1972.

Glassman, J., *Arms for the Arabs: The Soviet Union and the War in the Middle East*, Baltimore, MD: Johns Hopkins University Press, 1975.

Glick, E., *The Triangular Connection: America, Israel and American Jews*, London: George Allen and Unwin, 1982.

Golan, G., *Soviet Policies in the Middle East: From World War II to Gorbachev*, Cambridge: Cambridge University Press, 1990.

Golani, M., "The Limits of Interpretation and the Permissible in Historical Research Dealing with Israel's Security: A Reply to Mar-on and Morris," in *Traditions and Transitions in Israeli Studies*, ed. L. Z. Eisenberg, N. Caplan, N. Sokoloff and M. Abu-Nimer, Albany: State University of New York Press, 2003.

Goldhagen, D., *Hitler's Willing Executioners*, New York: Alfred Knopf, 1996.

Goldman, G., *Zionism under Soviet Rule*, New York: Herzl Press, 1960.

Goldstein, Y., "The Ideological and Political Background of the Israel Defense Forces," in *Israel: The First Hundred Years: Israel's Transition from Community to State*, vol. 1, ed. E. Karsh, London: Frank Cass, 2000.

Goldstone, J., *Revolution and Rebellion in the Early Modern World*, Berkeley: University of California Press, 1991.

——, "The Outcome of Revolutions," in *Revolutions: Theoretical, Comparative, and Historical Studies*, ed. J. Goldstone, Fort Worth, TX: Harcourt Brace, 1994.

Graetz, H., *History of the Jews*, Philadelphia, PA: Jewish Publications Society, 1967.

Gurr, T., *Why Men Rebel*, Princeton, NJ: Princeton University Press, 1968.

Hacohen, D., "Mass Immigration and Demographic Revolution," in *Israel: The First Hundred Years: Israeli Politics and Society since 1948: Problems of Collective Identity*, vol. 3, ed. E. Karsh, London: Frank Cass, 2000.

Halpern, B., *The Idea of the Jewish State*, Cambridge, MA: Harvard University Press, 1969.

—— and J. Reinharz, *Zionism and the Creation of a New Society*, New York: Oxford University Press, 1998.

Handel, M., *Israel's Political-Military Doctrine*, Occasional Paper 30, Cambridge, MA: Harvard University Center for International Affairs, July 1973.

Hartz, L., "United States History in a New Perspective," in *The Founding of New Societies*, ed. L. Hartz, New York: Harcourt, Brace & World, 1964.

—— (ed.), *The Founding of New Societies*, New York: Harcourt, Brace & World, 1964.

Hazan, R. and M. Maor (eds.), *Parties, Elections and Cleavages: Israel in Comparative and Theoretical Perspective*, London: Frank Cass, 2000.

Hazony, D., "Zionism and Moral Vision," in *New Essays on Zionism*, ed. D. Hazony, Y. Hazony and M. Oren, Jerusalem: Shalem Press, 2006.

——, Y. Hazony and M. Oren (eds.), *New Essays on Zionism*, Jerusalem: Shalem Press, 2006.

Helman, S., "Militarism and the Construction of the Life-World of Israeli Males," in *The Military and Militarism in Israeli Society*, ed. E. Lomsky-Feder and E. Ben-Ari, Albany: State University of New York Press, 1999.

Helpman, E., "Israel's Economic Growth: An International Comparison," *Israel Economic Review*, 1, 2003: 1–10.

Hertzberg, A. (ed.), *The Zionist Idea: A Historical Analysis and Reader*, New York: Atheneum, 1959.

Horowitz, D., "Dual Authority Politics," *Comparative Politics*, 14, 1982: 329–49.

——, "Before the State: Communal Politics in Palestine under the Mandate," in *The Israeli State and Society: Boundaries and Frontiers*, ed. B. Kimmerling, Albany: State University of New York Press, 1989.

Hourani, A., *Minorities in the Arab World*, London: Oxford University Press, 1947.

Howe, I., *The World of Our Fathers*, New York: Harcourt Brace Jovanovich, 1976.

Hroub, K., *Hamas: A Beginner's Guide*, London: Pluto Press, 2006.

Huntington, S., "Revolution and Political Order," in *Revolutions: Theoretical, Comparative, and Historical Studies*, 2nd edn., ed. J. Goldstone, Fort Worth, TX: Harcourt Brace, 1993.

Ilan, A., *The Origins of the Arab–Israeli Arms Race: Arms, Embargo, Military Power and Decision in the 1948 Palestine War*, New York: New York University Press, 1996.

Industrial Cooperation Agency, *High-Tech Leads Israel Strong Economic Performance*, Israel: Ministry of Trade, Industry and Labor, 2007.

Irani, G., "The Holy See and the Israeli–Palestinian Conflict," in *The Vatican, Islam and the Middle East*, ed. K. Ellis, Syracuse, NY: Syracuse University Press, 1987.

Israeli, R., *Fundamentalist Islam and Israel*, Lanham, MD: University Press of America, 1993.

Johnson, P., *A History of the Jews*, New York: Harper & Row, 1987.

Kacowicz, A., Y. Bar-Siman-Tov, O. Elgstrom and M. Jerneck (eds.), *Stable Peace among Nations*, Lanham, MD: Rowman & Littlefield, 2000.

Kadushin, C., *The American Intellectual Elite*, Boston, MA: Little, Brown, 1974.

Kark, R. and J. Glass, "The Jews in Eretz-Israel/Palestine: From Traditional Peripherality to Modern Centrality," in *Israel: The First Hundred Years: Israel's Transition from Community to State*, vol. 1, ed. E. Karsh, London: Frank Cass, 2000.

Karsh, E., *Fabricating Israeli History: The "New Historians,"* London: Frank Cass, 1997.

——, *Empires in the Sand: Struggle for Mastery in the Middle East*, Cambridge, MA: Harvard University Press, 1999.

——, "Introduction," in *Israel: The First Hundred Years: Israel's Transition from Community to State*, vol. 1, ed. E. Karsh, London: Frank Cass, 2000.

—— (ed.), *Israel: The First Hundred Years*, London: Frank Cass, 2000.

——, *Rethinking the Middle East*, London: Frank Cass, 2003.

—— and P. R. Kumaraswamy (eds.), *Israel, the Hashemites and the Palestinians: The Fateful Triangle*, London: Frank Cass, 2003.

Keddie, N., *Debating Revolution*, New York: New York University Press, 1995.

Kedourie, E., *Politics in the Middle East*, Oxford: Oxford University Press, 1992.

——, *Democracy and Arab Political Culture*, London: Frank Cass, 1994.

Kenny, A., *Catholics, Jews and the State of Israel*, New York: Paulist Press, 1993.

Khalidi, W., *The Iron Cage: The Story of the Palestinian Struggle for Statehood*, Boston, MA: Beacon Press, 2007.

Khouri, F., "The Jerusalem Question and the Vatican," in *The Vatican, Islam and the Middle East*, ed. K. Ellis, Syracuse, NY: Syracuse University Press, 1987.

Kimche, D., "The Traditional and the Transitional in Statecraft," in *Global Politics: Essays in Honor of David Vital*, ed. A. Ben-Zvi and A. Klieman, London: Frank Cass, 2001.

Kimmerling, B., *Zionism and Economy*, Cambridge, MA: Schenkman Publishing, 1983.

——, *Zionism and Territory: The Socio-Territorial Dimensions of Zionist Politics*, Berkeley: University of California Press, 1983.

——, "Making Conflict a Routine," in *Israeli Society and its Defense Establishment*, ed. M. Lissak, London: Frank Cass, 1984.

—— and J. Migdal, *The Palestinian People: A History*, Cambridge, MA: Harvard University Press, 2003.

Kinross, P. B., *The Ottoman Centuries: The Rise and Fall of the Turkish Empire*, New York: William Morrow and Company, 1977.

Kissinger, H., *White House Years*, Boston, MA: Little, Brown, 1979.

Klieman, Aharon, *Statecraft in the Dark: Israel's Practice of Quiet Diplomacy*, Boulder, CO: Westview Press, 1988.

Kolinsky, M., *Britain's War in the Middle East: Strategy and Diplomacy 1936–43*, New York: St. Martin's Press, 1999.

Kook, R., "Between Uniqueness and Exclusion: The Politics of Identity in Israel," in *Israel in Comparative Perspective*, ed. M. Barnett, Albany: State University of New York Press, 1996.

Kovel, Joel, *Overcoming Zionism: Creating a Single Democratic State in Israel/ Palestine*, London: Pluto Press, 2007.

Kreutz, A., *Vatican Policy on the Palestinian–Israeli Conflict: The Struggle for the Holy Land*, Westport, CT: Greenwood Press, 1990.

Lange, N. de and M. Freud-Kandel (eds.), *Modern Judaism: An Oxford Guide*, Oxford: Oxford University Press, 2005.

Laqueur, W., *A History of Zionism*, London: Weidenfeld & Nicolson, 1972.

—— and B. Rubin (eds.), *The Israel–Arab Reader*, New York: Penguin, 2001.

Larkin, M., *The Six Days of Yad-Mordechai*, Givatayim: Peli Printing, 1975.

Lenin, V., *What Is to Be Done? Burning Questions of Our Movement*, New York: International Publishers, 1929.

Levin, M., *It Takes a Dream: The Story of Hadassah*, Jerusalem: Gefen Publishing House, 2002.

Levitt, Matthew, *Hamas*, New Haven, CT: Yale University Press, 2006.

Lewis, B., *What Went Wrong? Western Impact and Middle Eastern Response*, New York: Oxford University Press, 2002.

——, *Crisis of Islam: Holy War and Unholy Terror*, New York: Modern Library, 2003.

Lewis, H., *After the Eagles Landed: The Yemenites of Israel*, Boulder, CO: Westview Press, 1989.

Lifshitz, Y., *The Economics of Producing Defense Illustrated by the Israeli Case*, Boston, MA: Kluwer Academic Press, 2003.

Lindemann, A., *Esau's Tears: Modern Anti-Semitism and the Rise of the Jews*, Cambridge: Cambridge University Press, 1997.

Lipset, S. M., *The First New Nation: The United States in Historical and Comparative Perspective*, New York: Basic Books, 1963.

Lissak, M., "Paradoxes of Israeli Civil–Military Relations: An Introduction," in *Israeli Society and its Defense Establishment*, ed. M. Lissak, London: Frank Cass, 1984.

——, "Epilogue," in *Military, State, and Society in Israel*, ed. D. Maman, E. Ben-Ari and Z. Rosenhek, New Brunswick, NJ: Transaction Publishers, 2001.

Lopez, A., "Israel's Relations with the Vatican," in *Jerusalem Letter*, Jerusalem: Jerusalem Center for Public Affairs, March 1999.

Lotz, W., *The Champagne Spy: Israel's Master Spy Tells His Story*, New York: Vallentine Mitchell, 1972.

Louis, W., *The British Empire in the Middle East 1945–1951*, Oxford: Oxford University Press, 1984.

Lunacharsky, A., *Religiya i sotsializm*, vol. 1, St. Petersburg, 1908.

Luttwak, E. and D. Horowitz, *The Israeli Army 1948–1973*, Cambridge, MA: Abt Books, 1983.

Lutz, J. and B. Lutz, *Terrorism: Origins and Evolution*, New York: Palgrave Macmillan, 2005.

McCagg, Jr., W., "Jews in Revolutions: The Hungarian Experience," *Journal of Social History*, 6 (1), Fall 1972: 77–105.

McCarthy, J., *The Ottoman Peoples and the End of Empire*, New York: Oxford University Press, 2001.

McLaurin, R. D. (ed.), *The Political Role of Minority Groups in the Middle East*, New York: Praeger, 1979.

Macmillan, M., *Paris 1919: Six Months that Changed the World*, New York: Random House, 2002.

Maddison, A., *The World Economy: Historical Statistics*, Paris: OECD, 2003.

Mahler, R., *Politics and Government in Israel: The Maturation of a Modern State*, Lanham, MD: Rowman & Littlefield, 2004.

Maman, D., E. Ben-Ari and Z. Rosenhek (eds.), *Military, State, and Society in Israel*, New Brunswick, NJ: Transaction Publishers, 2001.

Mandel, N., *The Arabs and Zionism before World War I*, Berkeley: University of California Press, 1976.

Mann, M., *The Sources of Social Power: The Rise and Classes of Nation-States, 1760–1914*, vol. 2, New York: Cambridge University Press, 1993.

Manor, Y., *To Right a Wrong: The Revocation of the UN General Assembly Resolution 3379 Defaming Zionism*, New York: Shengold Publishers, 1996.

Ma'oz, M. and G. Sheffer (eds.), *Middle Eastern Minorities and Diasporas*, Brighton: Sussex Academic Group, 2002.

Maoz, Z., *Defending the Holy Land: A Critical Analysis of Israel's Security and Foreign Policy*, Ann Arbor: University of Michigan Press, 2000.

Marx, K., *On the Jewish Question*, trans. H. Lederer, Cincinnati, OH: Hebrew Union College – Jewish Institute of Religion, 1958.

—— and F. Engels, *The Communist Manifesto*, Harmondsworth: Penguin, 1967.

Masalha, Nur, *Imperial Israel and the Palestinians: The Politics of Expansion*, London: Pluto Press, 2000.

Mearsheimer, J., *The Tragedy of Great Power Politics*, New York: W.W. Norton, 2001.

—— and S. Walt, *The Israel Lobby and U.S. Foreign Policy*, New York: Farrar, Straus and Giroux, 2007.

Medding, P., *Mapai in Israel: Political Organization and Government in a New Society*, Cambridge: Cambridge University Press, 1971.

——, *The Founding of Israeli Democracy, 1948–1967*, New York: Oxford University Press, 1990.

Mendelsohn, E., *Class Struggle in the Pale: The Formative Years of the Jewish Workers' Movement in Tsarist Russia*, Cambridge: Cambridge University Press, 1970.

Mendlikow, J., *Ideology, Party Change and Electoral Campaigns in Israel, 1965–2001*, Albany: State University of New York Press, 2003.

Merari, A. and S. Elad, *The International Dimensions of Palestinian Terrorism*, Jerusalem: Jaffee Center for Strategic Studies Press, 1986.

Merkley, P., *The Politics of Christian Zionism 1891–1948*, London: Frank Cass, 1998.

——, *Christian Attitudes towards the State of Israel*, Montreal: McGill-Queen's University Press, 2001.

Michels, R., *Political Parties*, New York: Free Press, 1968.

Migdal, J., *Through the Lens of Israel*, Albany: State University of New York Press, 2001.

Miller, R., "The Other Side of the Coin: Arab Propaganda and the Battle against Zionism in London," in *Israel: The First Hundred Years: Israel's Transition from Community to State*, vol. 1, ed. E. Karsh, London: Frank Cass, 2000.

Minerbi, S., *The Vatican and Zionism: Conflict in the Holy Land 1895–1925*, trans. A. Schwarz, New York: Oxford University Press, 1990.

Mintz, A., "The Military-Industrial Complex: The Israeli Case," in *Israeli Society and its Defense Establishment*, ed. M. Lissak, London: Frank Cass, 1984.

Moore, B., *Social Origins of Dictatorship and Democracy*, Boston, MA: Beacon Press, 1968.

Morris, B., *The Birth of the Palestinian Refugee Problem, 1947–9*, Cambridge: Cambridge University Press, 1987.

Myers, D., *Re-inventing the Jewish Past*, New York: Oxford University Press, 1996.

Nebel, A., D. Filon, B. Brinkmann, P. Majordner, M. Faerman and A. Oppenheim, "The Y Chromosome Pool of Jews as Part of the Genetic Landscape of the Middle East," *American Journal of Human Genetics*, 69 (4): 1095–1112.

Nelson, E. and A. Wisdom, *Human Rights Advocacy in Mainline Protestant Churches (2000–2003)*, Washington, D.C.: Institute on Religion and Democracy, 2004.

Neuberger, B., "Zionism," available from www.mfa.gov.il.

Neusner, J., *Judaism: The Basics*, London: Routledge, 2006.

—— and A. J. Avery-Peck (eds.), *The Blackwell Reader in Judaism*, Oxford: Blackwell, 2001.

Newman, D., "Controlling Territory: Spatial Dimensions of Social and Political Change in Israel," in *Traditions and Transitions in Israel Studies*, ed. L. Z. Eisenberg, N. Caplan, N. Sokoloff and M. Abu-Nimer, Albany: State University of New York Press, 2003.

Nietzsche, F., *The Will to Power*, New York: Vintage Books, 1968.

Nisan, M., "Israel 1948–98: Purpose and Predicament in History," in *Israel: The First Hundred Years: Israeli Politics and Society since 1948: Problems of Collective Identity*, vol. 3, ed. E. Karsh, London: Frank Cass, 2000.

——, *Minorities in the Middle East*, London: McFarland & Company, 2001.

Nitzan, J. and S. Bichler, *The Global Political Economy of Israel*, London: Pluto Press, 2002.

Norton, Augustus, *Hezbollah*, Princeton, NJ: Princeton University Press, 2007.

Oren, A., "Inside Track: A Disaster Waiting to Happen," *Haaretz*, October 22, 2004.

Oren, M., *Six Days of War: June 1967 and the Making of the Modern Middle East*, Oxford: Oxford University Press, 2002/New York: Ballantine Books, 2003.

——, "Ben-Gurion and the Return to Jewish Power," in *New Essays on Zionism*, ed. D. Hazony, Y. Hazony and M. Oren, Jerusalem: Shalem Press, 2006.

——, *Power, Faith and Fantasy: America in the Middle East, 1776 to the Present*, New York: W.W. Norton, 2007.

Ottolenghi, E., "A National Home," in *Modern Judaism: An Oxford Guide*, ed. N. de Lange and M. Freud-Kandel, Oxford: Oxford University Press, 2005.

Parkes, J., *A History of Palestine from 135 A.D. to Modern Times*, New York: Oxford University Press, 1949.

Peled, A., *A Question of Loyalty: Military Manpower Policy in Multiethnic States*, New York: Cornell University Press, 1998.

Penkower, M., *The Holocaust and Israel Reborn*, Chicago: University of Illinois Press, 1994.

Penslar, D., *Zionism and Technocracy: The Engineering of Jewish Settlement in Palestine, 1870–1918*, Bloomington: Indiana University Press, 1991.

Peri, Y., "Party–Military Relations in a Pluralist System," in *Israeli Society and its Defense Establishment*, ed. M. Lissak, London: Frank Cass, 1984.

Perlmutter, A., *The Life and Times of Menachem Begin*, Garden City, NY: Doubleday, 1987.

Phillips, K., *The Cousin's Wars: Religion, Politics and the Triumph of Anglo-America*, New York: Basic Books, 1999.

Podeh, E. and A. Kaufman (eds.), *Arab–Jewish Relations: From Conflict to Resolution*, Brighton: Sussex Academic Press, 2005.

Posner, R., *Public Intellectuals: A Study of Decline*, Cambridge, MA: Harvard University Press, 2001.

Quandt, W., *Peace Process: American Diplomacy and the Arab–Israeli Conflict since 1967*, Washington, D.C. and Berkeley: Brookings Institution Press and University of California Press, 1993.

Rabil, R., *Embattled Neighbors: Syria, Israel and Lebanon*, Boulder, CO: Lynne Rienner Publishers, 2003.

Rabkin, Y., *A Threat from Within: A Century of Jewish Opposition to Zionism*, Black Point, Nova Scotia: Fernwood Press, 2006.

Raider, M., *The Emergence of American Zionism*, New York: New York University Press, 1998.

Ravitzky, A., *Messianism, Zionism and Jewish Religious Radicalism*, Chicago, IL: University of Chicago Press, 1993.

——, "Munkacs and Jerusalem: Ultra-Orthodox Opposition to Zionism and Aggudism," in *Zionism and Religion*, ed. S. Almog, J. Reinharz and A. Shapira, Hanover, NH: Brandeis University Press, 1998.

Raviv, D. and Y. Melman, *Every Spy a Prince: The Complete History of the Israel Intelligence Community*, Boston, MA: Houghton Mifflin, 1990.

Reich, B., "The United States and Israel: The Nature of a Special Relationship," in *The Middle East and Israel: A Historical and Political Reassessment*, 3rd edn., ed. D. Lesch, Boulder, CO: Westview Press, 2003.

—— and G. Kieval (eds.), *Israeli National Security: Political Actors and Perspectives*, Westport, CT: Greenwood Press, 1988.

Reinharz, J., *Chaim Weizmann: The Making of a Statesman*, New York: Oxford University Press, 1993.

——, "Zionism and Orthodoxy," in *Zionism and Religion*, ed. S. Almog, J. Reinharz and A. Shapira, Hanover, NH: Brandeis University Press, 1998.

Rosecrance, R., "The Radical Culture of Australia," in *The Founding of New Societies*, ed. L. Hartz, New York: Harcourt, Brace & World, 1964.

Roshwald, A., *Ethnic Nationalism and the Fall of Empires: Central Europe, Russia and the Middle East, 1914–1923*, London: Routledge, 2001.

Rotberg, R., *Israeli and Palestinian Narratives of Conflict: History's Double Helix*, Bloomington: Indiana University Press, 2006.

Rotenstreich, N., "The Present-Day Relationship," in *The Blackwell Reader in Judaism*, ed. J. Neusner and A. Avery-Peck, Oxford: Blackwell, 2001.

Roth, C., *The Jewish Contribution to Civilization*, Cincinnati, OH: Union of American Hebrew Congregations, 1940.

Rothenberg, G., *Anatomy of the Israeli Army: The Israel Defense Forces, 1948–1978*, New York: Hippocrene Books, 1979.

Rubin, B., *Assimilation and its Discontents*, New York: Random House, 1995.

——, *The Long War for Freedom: The Arab Struggle for Democracy in the Middle East*, Hoboken, NJ: John Wiley & Sons, 2006.

Rubinstein, H., D. Cohn-Sherbok, A. Edelheit and W. Rubinstein, *The Jews in the Modern World: A History since 1750*, London: Arnold, 2002.

Rubinstein, S. M., *The Communist Movement in Palestine and Israel, 1919–1984*, Boulder, CO: Westview Press, 1984.

Ruether, R. and H. Ruether, *The Wrath of Jonah: The Crisis of Religious Nationalism in the Israeli–Palestinian Conflict*, 2nd edn., Minneapolis, MN: Fortress Press, 2002.

Sachar, H., *A History of Israel: From the Rise of Zionism to Our Time*, 3rd edn., New York: Alfred Knopf, 2007 (2nd edn. 2002).

Said, E., *Orientalism*, New York: Pantheon Books, 1978.

Salmon, Y., *Religion and Zion: First Encounters*, Jerusalem: Hebrew University Press, 2002.

Sarna, A., *Boycott and Blacklist: A History of Arab Economic Warfare against Israel*, Totowa, NJ: Rowman & Littlefield, 1986.

Sartori, G., *Parties and Party Systems: A Framework for Analysis*, Cambridge: Cambridge University Press, 1976.

Schapiro, L., "The Role of the Jews in the Russian Revolutionary Movement," *Slavonic and East European Review*, 40: 148–67.

Schecter, S., "Literature as a Response to Paradox," in *Traditions and Transitions in Israel Studies*, ed. L. Z. Eisenberg, N. Caplan, N. Skoloff and M. Abu-Nimer, Albany: State University of New York Press, 2003.

Schiff, Z., *A History of the Israeli Army*, New York: Macmillan, 1985.

Schwartz, D., *Faith at a Crossroads: A Theological Profile of Religious Zionism*, trans. B. Stein, Leiden: Brill, 2002.

Segev, T., *One Palestine Complete: Jews and Arabs under the British Mandate*, trans. H. Watzman, New York: Metropolitan Books, 2000.

Sela, A. and Ma'oz, M., *The PLO and Israel: From Armed Conflict to Political Solution, 1964–1994*, New York: St. Martin's Press, 1997.

Shafir, G., "Zionism and Colonialism: A Comparative Approach," in *Israel in Comparative Perspective*, ed. M. Barnett, Albany: State University of New York Press, 1996.

Shapira, A., "The Religious Motifs of the Labor Movement," in *Zionism and Religion*, ed. S. Almog, J. Reinharz and A. Shapira, Hanover, NH: Brandeis University Press, 1998.

Shaq, S., *The Shahids: Islam and Suicide Attacks*, New Brunswick, NJ: Transaction Publishers, 2004.

Sharansky, N. "The Political Legacy of Theodor Herzl," in *New Essays on Zionism*, ed. D. Hazony, Y. Hazony and M. Oren, Jerusalem: Shalem Press, 2006.

Sheffer, G., "Israeli–Diaspora Relations in Comparative Perspective," in *Israel in Comparative Perspective*, ed. M. Barnett, Albany: State University of New York Press, 1996.

——, "Political Change and Party System Transformation," in *Parties, Elections and Cleavages: Israel in Comparative and Theoretical Perspective*, ed. R. Hazan and M. Maor, London: Frank Cass, 2000.

Sherman, A. J., *Mandate Days: British Lives in Palestine, 1918–1948*, Baltimore, MD: Johns Hopkins University Press, 2001.

Shils, E., "On the Comparative Study of the New States," in *Old Societies and New States*, ed. C. Gertz, New York: Free Press, 1963.

Shindler, C., "Likud and the Search for Eretz Israel: From the Bible to the Twenty-First Century," in *Israel: The First Hundred Years: Israeli Politics and Society since 1948: Problems of Collective Identity*, vol. 3, ed. E. Karsh, London: Frank Cass, 2000.

Shlaim, A., *The Iron Wall: Israel and the Arab World*, New York: W.W. Norton, 2000.

Silberman, C., *A Certain People: American Jews and their Lives Today*, New York: Summit Books, 1985.

Skocpol, T., *States and Social Revolutions*, Cambridge: Cambridge University Press, 1979.

——, "Social Revolutions and Mass Military Mobilizations," *World Politics*, 60 (2), 1988.

Smith, A., "Sacred Territories and National Conflict," in *Israel: The First Hundred Years: Israel's Transition from Community to State*, vol. 1, ed. E. Karsh, London: Frank Cass, 2000.

Snow, E., *Red Star over China*, New York: Grove Press, 1968.

Sofer, S., *Begin: An Anatomy of Leadership*, Oxford: Blackwell, 1988.

——, "Towards Distant Frontiers: The Course of Israeli Diplomacy," in *Israel: The*

First Hundred Years: Israel in the International Arena, vol. 4, ed. E. Karsh, London: Frank Cass, 2003.

Spiegel, Steven, *The Other Arab–Israeli Conflict: Making America's Middle East Policy, from Truman to Reagan*, Chicago: University of Chicago Press, 1985.

Stavrianos, L. S., *Global Rift: The Third World Comes of Age*, New York: William Morrow and Company, 1981.

Stein, L., *The Hope Fulfilled: The Rise of Modern Israel*, Westport: Praeger, 2003.

Stevens, S., *The Spymasters of Israel*, New York: Macmillan, 1980.

Stockton, R., "Presbyterians, Jews and Divestment: The Church Steps Back," *Middle East Policy*, 13 (4), Winter 2006.

Tabory, E., "A Nation that Dwells Alone: Judaism as an Integrating and Divisive Factor in Israeli Society," in *Traditions and Transitions in Israel Studies*, ed. L. Z. Eisenberg, N. Caplan, N. Sokoloff and M. Abu-Nimer, Albany: State University of New York Press, 2003.

Tal, D., "The Forgotten War: Jewish Palestinian Strife in Mandatory Palestine, December 1947–May 1948," in *Israel: The First Hundred Years: From War to Peace?*, vol. 2, ed. E. Karsh, London: Frank Cass, 2000.

Talmon, J., *Israel among the Nations*, New York: Macmillan, 1970.

Tauber, E., "The Jewish and Arab Lobbies in Canada and the UN Partition of Palestine," in *Israel: The First Hundred Years: Israel's Transition from Community to State*, vol. 1, ed. E. Karsh, London: Frank Cass, 2000.

Telhami, S., "Israeli Foreign Policy: A Realist Ideal-Type or a Breed of its Own?," in *Israel in Comparative Perspective*, ed. M. Barnett, Albany: State University of New York Press, 1996.

——, *The Stakes: America and the Middle East*, Boulder, CO: Westview Press, 2002.

Teveth, S., *Ben Gurion: The Burning Ground 1886–1948*, Boston, MA: Houghton Mifflin, 1987.

Thomas, G., *Gideon's Spies: The Secret History of the Mossad*, New York: St. Martin's Press, 1999.

Tilly, C. (ed.), *The Formation of the Modern European State System*, Princeton, NJ: Princeton University Press, 1975.

——, *Coercion, Capital and European States, A.D. 990–1990*, Cambridge, MA: Blackwell, 1990.

Troen, I., *Imagining Zion*, New Haven, CT: Yale University Press, 2003.

Troen, S. I., "Organizing the Rescue of Jews in the Modern Period," in *Organizing Rescue: National Jewish Solidarity in the Modern Period*, ed. S. I. Troen and B. Pinkus, London: Frank Cass, 1992.

—— and B. Pinkus (eds.), *Organizing Rescue: National Jewish Solidarity in the Modern Period*, London: Frank Cass, 1992.

Urofsky, M., *American Zionism from Herzl to the Holocaust*, New York: Doubleday, 1975.

——, *We Are One! American Jewry and Israel*, New York: Doubleday, 1978.

Vaksberg, A., *Stalin against the Jews*, New York: Alfred Knopf, 1994.

van Creveld, M., *The Sword and the Olive: A Critical History of the Israeli Defense Forces*, New York: Public Affairs Press, 1998.

Veblen, T., "The Intellectual Pre-eminence of the Jews in Modern Europe," in *Essays in Our Changing Order*, ed. L. Ardzrooni, New York: Viking Press, 1934.

Vital, D., *The Survival of Small States: Studies in Small Power/Great Power Conflict*, London: Oxford University Press, 1971.

——, *The Origins of Zionism*, Oxford: Oxford University Press, 1975.

——, *Zionism: The Crucial Phase*, Oxford: Oxford University Press, 1987.

——, "From 'State within a State' to State," in *Israel: The First Hundred Years: Israel's Transition from Community to State*, vol. 1, ed. E. Karsh, London: Frank Cass, 2000.

Wallerstein, I., *The Capitalist World-Economy*, New York: Cambridge University Press, 1979.

Walt, S. and J. Mearsheimer, "The Israel Lobby and U.S. Foreign Policy," Kennedy School of Government at Harvard University, Working Paper RWP06–011, March 2006.

Walzer, M., "History and National Liberation," in *Israeli Historical Revisionism: From Left to Right*, ed. A. Shapira and D. Penslar, London: Frank Cass, 2003.

Weber, M., *Ancient Judaism*, trans. H. Gerth and D. Martindale, New York, 1952 [1917].

——, *Economy and Society*, vol. 3, New York: Bedminster Press, 1968.

——, "What Is the State?," in *Political Thought*, ed. M. Rosen and J. Wolff, Oxford: Oxford University Press, 1999.

Wheeler, D., "Does Post-Zionism Have a Future?," in *Traditions and Transitions in Israel Studies*, ed. L. Z. Eisenberg, N. Caplan, N. Sokoloff and M. Abu-Nimer, Albany: State University of New York Press, 2003.

Wisse, R., "Israel's Answer to the Zionist Dream," speech, Bar Ilan University, Ramat Gan, Israel, June 2003.

Wistrich, R., "Marxism and Jewish Nationalism: The Theoretical Roots of Confrontation," in *The Left against Zion*, ed. R. Wistrich, London: Vallentine Mitchell, 1979.

Yehuda, E. B., "A Letter to the Editor of Hashahar," in *The Zionist Idea: A Historical Analysis and Reader*, ed. A. Hertzberg, New York: Atheneum, 1959.

Zangwill, I., *Children of the Ghetto*, Philadelphia, PA: Jewish Publication Society, 1892.

Zohar, M. B., *Spies in the Promised Land: Iser Harel and the Israeli Secret Service*, Boston, MA: Houghton Mifflin, 1972.

Zuckerman, H., *Scientific Elite: Novel Laureates in the United States*, New York: Free Press, 1977.

Index

Routledge
Taylor & Francis Group

Israel Affairs

EDITOR:

Efraim Karsh, *King's College, London*

Whether your major interest is Israeli history or politics, literature or art, strategic affairs or economics, the Arab-Israeli conflict or Israel-diaspora relations, you will find articles and reviews that are incisive and contain even-handed analysis of the country and its problems in every issue of *Israel Affairs*, an international multidisciplinary journal.

Scholarly and authoritative, yet straightforward and accessible, *Israel Affairs* aims to serve as a means of communication between the various communities interested in Israel: academics, policy-makers, practitioners, journalists and the informed public. It is essential reading for anyone anxious for a fresh analysis of a key country in one of the most confounding regions in today's world.

SUBSCRIPTION RATES
2008 - *Volume* 14 (*4 issues per year*)
Print ISSN 1353-7121
Online ISSN 1743-9086
Institutional rate (print and online): US$557; £338; €446
Institutional rate (online access only): US$529; £321; €423
Personal rate (print only): US$118; £84; €94

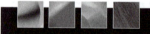

Israeli-Palestinian Peace Negotiations, 1999-2001

Gilead Sher

Written by Gilead Sher, the Israeli Chief of Staff during the tumultuous 1999-2000 peace negotiations, this book provides a fast paced description and analysis of the Israel-Palestine conflict.

January 2006: 234x156: 296pp
Hb: 978-0-7146-5653-3: **£90.00**
Pb: 978-0-7146-8542-7: **£28.99**

Navigating Perilous Waters
An Israeli Strategy for Peace and Security

Ephraim Sneh
Translated by **Haim Watzman**

2005: 198x129: 136pp
Hb: 978-0-7146-5633-5: **£90.00**
Pb: 978-0-7146-8518-2: **£23.99**

Between Capital and Land
The Jewish National Fund's Finances and Land-Purchase Priorities in Palestine, 1939-1945

Eric Engel Tuten

2005: 234x156: 256pp
Hb: 978-0-7146-5634-2: **£90.00**

Israel at the Polls 2003

Edited by **M. Ben Mollov, Jonathan Rynhold** and **Shmuel Sandler**

2005: 234x156: 304pp
Hb: 978-0-415-36019-7: **£80.00**

Israeli Democracy at the Crossroads

Edited by **Raphael Cohen-Almagor**

2005: 234x156: 296pp
Hb: 978-0-415-35023-5: **£75.00**

Israeli Institutions at the Crossroads

Edited by **Raphael Cohen-Almagor**

2005: 234x156: 216pp
Hb: 978-0-415-36360-0: **£75.00**

Lyndon B. Johnson and the Politics of Arms Sales to Israel
In the Shadow of the Hawk

Abraham Ben-Zvi

2004: 234x156: 152pp
Hb: 978-0-7146-5580-2: **£90.00**
Pb: 978-0-7146-8463-5: **£25.99**

H V Evatt and the Establishment of Israel
The Undercover Zionist

Daniel Mandel

2004: 234x156: 344pp
Hb: 978-0-7146-5578-9: **£90.00**
Pb: 978-0-7146-8461-1: **£29.99**

Israel's Quest for Recognition and Acceptance in Asia
Garrison State Diplomacy

Jacob Abadi

2004: 246x174: 324pp
Hb: 978-0-7146-5576-5: **£70.00**
Pb: 978-0-7146-8564-9: **£25.99**

Britain, Israel and Anglo-Jewry 1949-57

Natan Aridan

2004: 234x156: 336pp
Hb: 978-0-7146-5629-8: **£90.00**

War in Palestine, 1948
Israeli and Arab Strategy and Diplomacy

David Tal

2004: 234x156: 512pp
Hb: 978-0-7146-5275-7: **£75.00**

Israel, the Hashemites and the Palestinians
The Fateful Triangle

Edited by **Efraim Karsh** and **P.R. Kumaraswamy**

2003: 246x174: 222pp
Hb: 978-0-7146-5434-8: **£90.00**
Pb: 978-0-7146-8355-3: **£28.99**

The Israeli Palestinians
An Arab Minority in the Jewish State

Edited by **Alexander Bligh**

2003: 246x174: 324pp
Hb: 978-0-7146-5417-1: **£90.00**
Pb: 978-0-7146-8345-4: **£28.99**

The Last Days in Israel
Understanding the New Israeli Democracy

Abraham Diskin

2003: 246x174: 256pp
Hb: 978-0-7146-5421-8: **£90.00**
Pb: 978-0-7146-8383-6: **£27.99**

Rethinking the Middle East

Efraim Karsh

2003: 241x164: 208pp
Hb: 978-0-7146-5418-8: **£90.00**
Pb: 978-0-7146-8346-1: **£25.99**

The Conscience of Lebanon
A Political Biography of Etienne Sakr (Abu-Arz)

Mordechai Nisan

2003: 239x164: 208pp
Hb: 978-0-7146-5392-1: **£85.00**
Pb: 978-0-7146-8378-2: **£28.99**

ISRAELI HISTORY, POLITICS AND SOCIETY

Series Editor: **Efraim Karsh**, King's College London, University of London, UK

This series provides a multidisciplinary examination of all aspects of Israeli history, politics and society and serves as a means of communication between the various communities interested in Israel: academics, policy-makers, practitioners, journalists and the informed public.

Politics of Memory
Israeli Underground's Confrontations Over Boundaries of State Pantheon

Udi Lebel, Ben-Gurion University, Israel

Providing a new angle on state control and political legitimacy, this book addresses the efforts of successive Israeli governments to establish their political dominance and legitimacy through the selective production and collective assimilation of cultural practices associated with bereavement and commemoration of those who fell on their country's behalf.

January 2009: 234x156: 224pp
Hb: 978-0-415-41239-1: **£65.00**

Israel and the Family of Nations
The Jewish Nation-State and Human Rights

Alexander Yakobson, Hebrew University of Jerusalem, Israel and **Amnon Rubinstein**, Columbia University, USA

Amnon Rubinstein and Alexander Yakobson explore the nature of Israel's identity as a Jewish state, how that is compatible with liberal democratic norms and is comparable with a number of European states.

September 2008: 234x156: 256pp
Hb: 978-0-415-46441-3: **£70.00**

The Rise of Israel
A History of a Revolutionary State

Jonathan Adelman, University of Denver, USA

This book provides a general history of the rise of Israel since the early Zionist efforts at state building. In particular it seeks to show how unlikely Israel's creation was and that it should best be understood as a series of revolutions.

March 2008: 234x156: 280pp
Hb: 978-0-415-77509-0: **£80.00**
Pb: 978-0-415-77510-6: **£20.99**

Israel's National Security
Issues and Challenges Since the Yom Kippur War

Efraim Inbar, Bar-Ilan University, Israel

This book brings together a collection of essays that covers the main national security issues Israel has faced since 1973.

December 2007: 234x156: 304pp
Hb: 978-0-415-44955-7: **£70.00**

The Harp and the Shield of David
Ireland, Zionism and the State of Israel

Shulamit Eliash, Bar-Ilan University, Israel

Shedding light on Irish and Israeli foreign policy, Eliash examines the relationship between Ireland and the Zionist Movement and the state of Israel from the context of Palestine's partition and the delay in Ireland's recognition of the State of Israel until 1963.

April 2007: 234x156: 288pp
Hb: 978-0-415-35035-8: **£80.00**

The Origins of the American-Israeli Alliance
The Jordanian Factor

Abraham Ben-Zvi, Tel-Aviv University, Israel

This book demonstrates that the origins of the US-Israeli alliance lay in the former's concern over Egyptian influence in Jordan, contrasting with the widely-held view of the significance of the Six Day War.

February 2007: 234x156: 128pp
Hb: 978-0-415-41045-8: **£65.00**

Ben-Gurion, Zionism and American Jewry
1948 - 1963

Ariel Feldestein, Sapir Academic College, Israel

Based on archival material, this intriguing book examines David Ben-Gurion's influence on the relationship between the state of Israel, the Zionist Organization and American Jewry between 1948-1963 when he served as Prime Minister and Minister of Defence.

September 2006: 234x156: 240pp
Hb: 978-0-415-37240-4: **£70.00**

Trapped Fools
Thirty Years of Israeli Policy in the Territories

Shlomo Gazit

2003: 234x156: 256pp
Hb: 978-0-7146-5489-8: **£85.00**
Pb: 978-0-7146-8390-4: **£26.99**

Britain, the Hashemites and Arab Rule
The Sherifian Solution

Timothy J. Paris

2003: 241x164: 392pp
Hb: 978-0-7146-5451-5: **£90.00**

Decision on Palestine Deferred
America, Britain and Wartime Diplomacy, 1939-1945

Monty Noam Penkower

2002: 241x159: 392pp
Hb: 978-0-7146-5268-9: **£90.00**

A Dissenting Democracy
The Israeli Movement 'Peace Now'

Magnus Norell

2002: 238x167: 160pp
Hb: 978-0-7146-5350-1: **£90.00**

Israel: the First Hundred Years
Volume I: Israel's Transition from Community to State

Edited by **Efraim Karsh**

2000: 248x165: 264pp
Hb: 978-0-7146-4963-4: **£90.00**
Pb: 978-0-7146-8024-8: **£28.99**

Israel: the First Hundred Years
Volume II: From War to Peace?

Edited by **Efraim Karsh**

2000: 248x165: 288pp
Hb: 978-0-7146-4962-7: **£90.00**
Pb: 978-0-7146-8023-1: **£28.99**

Israel: The First Hundred Years
Volume III: Politics and Society since 1948

Edited by **Efraim Karsh**

2002: 241x165: 272pp
Hb: 978-0-7146-4961-0: **£90.00**
Pb: 978-0-7146-8022-4: **£28.99**

Israel: The First Hundred Years
Volume IV: Israel in the International Arena

Edited by **Efraim Karsh**

2004: 234x156: 288pp
Hb: 978-0-7146-4960-3: **£90.00**
Pb: 978-0-7146-8021-7: **£25.99**

To order any of these titles:

Call: +44 (0)1235 400400
Fax: +44 (0)207 017 6699
Email: info@routledge.co.uk (sales enquiries only, please do not include card details in your email)

For a full selection of titles, please visit
www.routledgemiddleeaststudies.com